BENGAL DISTRICT GAZETTEERS

FEUDATORY STATES OF ORISSA

BENGAL DISTRICT GAZETTEERS

Burdwan/ **J.C.K. Paterson**
Darjeeling/ **L.S.S. O'Malley**
Howrah/ **L.S.S. O'Malley**
Hooghly/ **L.S.S. O'Malley**
Santal Parganas/ **L.S.S. O'Malley**
Sambalpur/ **L.S.S. O'Malley**
Puri/ **L.S.S. O'Malley**
Gaya/ **L.S.S. O'Malley**
24 - Parganas/ **L.S.S. O'Malley**
Purnea/ **L.S.S. O'Malley**
Bhagalpur/ **J. BYRNE**
Feudatory States of Orissa/ **L.E.B. Cobden-Ramsay**
Sinhbhum, Saraikela and Kharsawan/ **L.S.S. O'Malley**

BIHAR AND ORISSA DISTRICT GAZETTEERS

Patna/ **L.S.S. O'Malley**
Shahabad/ **L.S.S. O'Malley**
Monghyr/ **L.S.S. O'Malley**
Saran/ **L.S.S. O'Malley**

EASTERN BENGAL DISTRICT GAZETTEERS

Dacca/ **B.C. Allen**

BENGAL DISTRICT GAZETTEERS

FEUDATORY STATES OF ORISSA

BY

L.E.B. COBDEN-RAMSAY

LOGOS PRESS

New Delhi-110 002

ISBN-13: 978-81-7268-216-3

First Published 1910

Reprinted 2011

Printed and Published by

LOGOS PRESS

Building No. 4788-90, Street No. 23, Ansari Road, Darya Ganj,
New Delhi-110 002 (India)

Phone : 23272187

Email : mail@logospressindia.com

Website : www.logospressindia.com

PREFACE

I have much pleasure in acknowledging the valuable assistance rendered by the Chiefs of the States of Mayur-bhanj and Dhenkānāl, and by the Superintendents of the Keonjhar and Nayāgarh States, in the preparation of the articles on their States. To Mr. F. D. Whiffin, Honorary Magistrate of the Gāngpur State, I am indebted for valuable information on the subject of the Fauna of the States. A considerable amount of the information concerning "The People" in the general portion of this volume is taken from notes prepared for the Ethnographic Survey of the Central Provinces. The description of the Gāngpur and Bonai states has been largely reproduced from Sir William Hunter's Statistical Account of those States.

L.C.R.

PLAN OF CONTENTS

TABLE OF CONTENTS

PART I
GENERAL ACCOUNT

CHAPTER I

PHYSICAL ASPECTS

CHAPTER II

HISTORY

CHAPTER III

THE PEOPLE

CHAPTER IV

PUBLIC HEALTH

CHAPTER V

AGRICULTURE

CHAPTER VI

NATURAL CALAMITIES

CHAPTER VII

RENTS AND WAGES

CHAPTER VIII

OCCUPATIONS, MANUFACTURES AND TRADE

CHAPTER IX

MEANS OF COMMUNICATIONS

CHAPTER X

LAND REVENUE ADMINISTRATION

CHAPTER XI

GENERAL ADMINISTRATION

CHAPTER XII

LOCAL SELF-GOVERNMENT

CHAPTER XIII

EDUCATION

PART II
STATES

CHAPTER I

ATHGARH STATE

CHAPTER II

ATHMALLIK STATE

CHAPTER III

BAMRA STATE

CHAPTER IV

BARAMBA STATE

CHAPTER V

BAUD STATE

CHAPTER VI

BONAI STATE

CHAPTER VII

DASPALLA STATE

CHAPTER VIII

DHENKANAL STATE

CHAPTER XII

KEONJHAR STATE

CHAPTER XIII

KHANDPARA STATE

CHAPTER XIV

MAYURBHANJ STATE

CHAPTER XV

NARSINGHPUR STATE

CHAPTER XVI

NAYAGARH STATE

CHAPTER XVII

NILGIRI STATE

CHAPTER XVIII

PAL LAHARA STATE

CHAPTER XIX

PATNA STATE

CHAPTER XX

RAIRAKHOL STATE

CHAPTER XXI

RANPUR STATE

CHAPTER XXII

SONPUR STATE

GAZETTEER

OF THE

ORISSA FEUDATORY STATES.

PART I.

GENERAL ACCOUNT.

CHAPTER I.

PHYSICAL ASPECTS.

General description. THE Feudatory States of Orissa consist of a group of 24 dependent territories attached to the Division of Orissa, and comprise the following States: Athgarh, Athmallik, Bāmra, Barāmbā, Baud, Bonai, Daspallā, Dhenkānāl, Gāngpur, Hindol, Kālāhandi, Keonjhar, Khandparā, Mayūrbhanj, Narsinghpur, Nayāgarh, Nīlgiri, Pāl Laharā, Patnā, Rairākhol, Ranpur, Sonpur, Tālcher and Tigiriā: of these the States of Bāmra, Kālāhandī, Patnā, Rairākhol and Sonpur were formerly attached to the Chhattisgarh Division of the Central Provinces; Bonai and Gāngpur were formerly attached to the Chotā Nāgpur Division and the remaining States formerly known as the Tributary Mahāls formed part of Orissa. They lie between 22° 34′ and 19° 2′ N., and 82° 32′ and 87° 11′ E., and have a population of 3,173,395 and an area of 28,125 square miles. **Boundaries.** They are bounded on the north by the State of Jashpur in the Central Provinces, the districts of Rānchī, Singhbhūm and Midnapore; on the east by the districts of Balasore, Cuttack and Purī; on the south by the districts of Ganjām and Vizagapatam in the Madras Presidency and Khondmāls (Angul); and on the west by the Raipur district and Raigarh State of the Central Provinces and the district of Sambalpur in the Bengal Presidency and Vizagapatam district in the Madras

Presidency. The district of Angul is situated practically in the centre of this block of country and was formerly one of the group of States known as the Tributary States of Orissa : on the southern border and conterminous with the border of the Ganjām district are the Khondmāls, a subdivision of the Angul district.

Configuration. The States form a succession of hill ranges rolling backwards towards Central India. They form three watersheds from south to north, with fine valleys between, down which pour the three great rivers of the inner tableland. The southernmost is the valley of the Mahānadī, spreading out into fertile plains watered by a thousand mountain streams. At the Barmūl pass, the river winds round magnificently wooded hills, from 1,500 to 2,500 feet high. From the north bank of the Mahānadī, the hill ranges tower into a fine watershed, from 2,000 to 2,500 feet high, forming the boundary of the States of Narsinghpur and Barāmbā. On the other side, they slope down upon the States of Hindol and Dhenkānāl, supplying countless little feeders to the Brāhmanī, which occupies the second of the three valleys. From the north bank of the Brāhmanī river, the hills again roll back in magnificent ranges, till they rise into the Keonjhar watershed, with peaks from 2,500 to 3,500 feet high, culminating in Malayagiri, 3,895 feet high, in the State of Pāl Laharā. This watershed, in turn, slopes down into the third valley, that of the Baitaranī, from whose eastern or left bank rise the mountains of Mayūrbhanj, heaped upon each other in noble masses of rock, from 3,000 to nearly 4,000 feet high, sending countless tributaries to the Baitarani on the south, and pouring down the waters of the Burābalang, with the feeders of the Subarnarekhā, on the north. The peaks are densely wooded to the summit, and, except at the regular passes, are inaccessible to beasts of burden. The intermediate valleys yield rich crops in return for negligent cultivation, and a vast quantity of land might be reclaimed on their outskirts and lower slopes. Cultivation is, however, rapidly extending in all the States, owing to improved means of communication and to the pressure of population in the adjoining British districts.

The natural beauties of the country are exceedingly fine: vast ranges of forest and tree-clad hills and mountain ranges alternate with well-watered valleys gleaming bright in the sun, with green waving crops of paddy, or in the winter season, with brilliant yellow crops of *surguja* contrasting brilliantly with the deep green foliage of the forest. In the open plains along the valleys of the large rivers miles of highly cultivated lands stretch out before the eye, shut in on the horizon by lofty peaks and forest-clad ranges. In the wild hill tracts of Mayūrbhanj, Keonjhar, Bonai, Kālāhandī and at Barmūl in Daspallā the soft beauty of the hill-clad ranges is relieved by wild precipitous bluffs scored and seamed by the storms of ages: in the rains raging torrents flashing for miles in the sunlight hurl themselves in fine waterfalls to the slopes below: the finest of these waterfalls drops over the sheer southern face of the Chheliātokā range (3,308 feet) in Bonai. In the highlands of Kālāhandī, Keonjhar, Mayūrbhanj and Bonai clear pellucid hill streams flow perennially, babbling over stones and rushing in tinkling waterfalls between grass-clad banks and sedgy shores, shaded by towering trees: many are the deep silent pools with the banks fringed with masses of white lilies, and the silence broken only by the gentle gurgle of the stream as it slowly trickles from the pools or by the splash of some rising fish: here the kingfisher darts to and fro in all his glory and birds of every hue imaginable brighten the scene: in the rains these streams become wild tearing torrents sweeping all before them. The hill area, or *dangarlā* as it is locally known in Kālāhandī, occupying 1,415 square miles, contains some of the finest scenery: the area is one vast mass of tangled hill ranges, the sides clad in the densest forest: this country is a plateau land averaging about 2,500 feet above sea level comprised of small valleys shut in on all sides by hills which rise as high as 4,000 feet and over: the tops of these ranges in several cases form fine plateau lands, averaging about 2 miles wide by 7 to 10 miles long: they are almost level, but generally run up to a small elevation at one end some 50 feet above the plateau which averages about 3,800 feet: these ranges are covered with long grass and are almost bare of trees and form the feeding grounds and sanctuary of all descriptions of game: the largest and finest of these ranges are the Karlāpāt range (3,981 feet) and Bafliāmālī, near the Kāshipur plateau: from Bafliāmālī (3,587 feet) a glorious view is obtained; as far as the eye or the glass can sweep vast billowing mountain ranges rise and fall and looking south are seen the peaks of Tikrigurā (3,683 feet) and Bankāsāmo (4,182 feet) in the Kālāhandī State and now the highest peak in Orissa: to the east on the horizon is seen the magnificent peak of Nimāigiri (4,972 feet) in the Ganjām district. In these hills of the *dangarlā* area the splendid stream of the Indrāvatī takes its rise near Thuāmūl: it quickly gathers volume and even in February roars and rushes down its hilly course in seething cataracts in its short wild rush to the plains and the State of Bastar to join the Godāvarī. It makes its way through the hill range which forms the southern boundary of Kālāhandī; not far from the place where the Indrāvātī flows south through this barrier the Hātī river rises on the northern slopes and flows due north in exactly the opposite direction.

HILL SYSTEM. The principal peaks are Bankāsāmo (4,182 feet), and the Karlāpāt plateau (3,981 feet), both in Kālāhandī; Malayagiri (3,895 feet) in the State of Pāl Laharā; Meghāsanī (the seat of the clouds, 3,824 feet) in Mayūrbhanj; Tikrigurā (3,683 feet) in Kālāhandī; Mānkarnācha (3,639 feet) in Bonai; Bafliāmālī (3,587 feet) in Kālāhandī; Bādāmgarh (3,525 feet), Kumritār (3,490 feet) both in Bonai; Gandhamardan (3,479 feet) in Keonjhar; Chheliātokā (3,308 feet) in Bonai; Thākurānī (3,003 feet) and Tomāk (2,577 feet) in Keonjhar; Pānchdhar (2,948 feet) in Athmallik; Goāldes (2,506 feet) in Daspallā; Suliyā (2,239 feet) in Nayāgarh and Kapilās (2,098 feet) in Dhenkānāl.

RIVER SYSTEM. The principal rivers are the Mahānadī, the Brāhmanī, the Baitaranī, the Burābalang, the Ang and the Tel.

Mahānadī. The Mahānadī enters the States of Orissa in the State of Sonpur, dividing that State into two portions; after a course of about 30 miles it enters the State of Baud forming the boundary between that State on the south, and Athmallik State on the north, it then divides the State of Daspallā which lies on either side of its banks: from Daspallā it forms the boundary of Khandparā on the south, and Narsinghpur, Barāmbā, Tigiriā and Athgarh on the north. In the State last named, it debouches through a narrow gorge at Narāj upon the Cuttack delta. It is everywhere navigable throughout the States and up to Sambalpur, by large flat-bottomed boats, and a considerable trade is carried on, though this has fallen off with the opening of the Bengal-Nāgpur Railway. The river would afford valuable facilities for navigation, but for the numerous rocks and sand-banks in its channel. The boatmen carry rakes and hoes, with which in the cold season they dredge a narrow passage just sufficient to let their crafts pass. When full, it is a magnificent river of great breadth and depth. Diamonds were occasionally found in the bed during its course through the Sonpur State, but of late years no stones have been found. It is liable to heavy floods, which from time to time cause serious damage to the river side villages in the Narsinghpur, Barāmbā, Tigiriā and Athgarh States. The most picturesque spot on the Mahānadī is the Barmūl gorge in the State of Daspallā. Its chief feeders in the States are—on its north or left bank, the Sāpuā in Athgarh, and the Dandātapā and Māno in Athmallik; on its south or right bank, the Kusumī, Kamāī, the Jorāmu, Hināmandā, Gānduni, Bolat, Sālki, Bāgh, Mārinī, Tel and Ang.

The Brāhmanī is formed by the confluence of the South Koel and Sankh at Pānposh, in the Nāgrā zamīndāri of the Gāngpur State: after a course which is unnavigable owing to extensive rock barriers and rapids of about 14 miles through the Gāngpur State, it enters the State of Bonai and after a course of some 38 miles in that State, flows for a short distance through the Bāmra State and then entering the State of Tālcher passes through it and Dhenkānāl into Cuttack district. Attempts have from time to time been made to float sleepers down the Brāhmanī, but unsuccessfully. It is navigable for a few months of the year as far as 4 miles below Tālcher, where there are some dangerous rocks. The confluence of the South Koel and Sankh is a spot of remarkable beauty and scantity: about half a mile below the junction of these two rivers a fine bridge on the Bengal-Nāgpur line spans the Brāhmanī. Common jasper is found in its bed and through Gāngpur and Bonai the local gold-washers (Jhorās) earn a small livelihood by washing gold from the bed. There are no feeder streams of any importance; hill streams all along its course force their waters into the Brāhmanī and probably the most important of these is the Kurādi stream in Bonai. Brāhmanī.

The Baitaranī rises among the hills in the south-west of Keonjhar State and forms during part of its course the boundary between that State and the State of Mayūrbhanj; its chief affluent is the Sālandi which rises in Mayūrbhanj. In the dry season the Baitaranī is navigable by small boats, but with difficulty, as far as Anandpur, a large trading village in Keonjhar on its north bank. Baitaranī.

The Burābalang rises in Mayūrbhanj and, after receiving two tributaries, the Gangāhar and the Sunāi, passes into Balasore. Burābalang.

The Tel enters the Kālāhandī State, from the north-west, and flowing north-east discharges itself into the Mahānadī, close to the town of Sonpur: it forms about half the length of the boundary between the States of Kālāhandī and Pātnā and then through the rest of its course, forms the boundary between the States of Sonpur and Baud: in the rains bamboos and timber are floated down from as far up the stream as where it forms the boundary between Kālāhandī and Patnā: its chief affluents are the Hātī, Sundar, Rāul and Suktel. Tel.

The Hātī river rises in the high hill ranges of the Mahulpātnā zamīndāri at the very southernmost extremity of the State of Kālāhandī and flows due north, draining the open country of the State, Hātī.

till it joins the Tel and the united streams flow down to the Mahānadī: the Hātī is liable to very sudden rises receiving as it does the water of countless streams from the highlands of the *dangarlā* area.

Ang. The Ang rises in the hills of the zamīndāri of Borāsambar in the Sambalpur district: for a short distance after its rise it flows in a northerly direction, but quickly swerves to the east and with a southerly tendency runs on to join the Mahānadī, between the village of Binkā and the town of Sonpur in the State of Sonpur: for a portion of its course it forms the northern boundary of the Patnā State with the State of Sonpur: though a river of considerable volume in the rains, it quickly dries up in the cold season.

GEOLOGY. The Orissa Division consists, geologically* as well as geographically, of two very distinct portions; the one, a belt of nearly flat country, from fifteen to fifty miles in breadth, extending along the coast; and the other, an undulating area, broken by ranges of hills, in the interior. The former is entirely of alluvial formations, the greater portion of its surface being probably composed of deposits from the great river Mahānadī, and the smaller streams, the Brāhmanī and Baitaranī. Near its western limit alone, a few hills of gneissose rock rise from the alluvial plain, especially between the Brāhmanī and Mahānadī. The inland hill tract, which forms the area covered by the Feudatory States, is chiefly composed of rocks of very ancient date, so completely altered and crystallized by metamorphic action, that all traces of their original structure are lost, and any organic remains obliterated which they may originally have contained. The same rocks cover an enormous area in Eastern and Southern India, and are usually spoken of, in works on Indian geology, as the crystalline or metamorphic series.

Further exploration in this area will doubtless show the existence of beds belonging to other formations; but hitherto the only instance in which any considerable area is known to be occupied by rocks of later date than the metamorphics, is in the tract known as the Tālcher coalfield, in the States of Tālcher, Athmallik, Dhenkānāl and Rairākhol. High up the Brāhmanī valley a series of very slightly altered or unaltered rocks, comprising slates with jasper, quartzites, and schistose beds, occur in the State of Bonai and are believed to occupy portions of Keonjhar.

The greater portion of the Feudatory States have never been explored geologically, and the information procurable

---

* This account is taken from Sir W. Hunter's article on the Geology of the Tributary States of Orissa with corrections to date.

as to their character is most imperfect. In Mayūrbhanj the Chief has had a geological survey conducted over the greater portion of the State: the vast area of the Simlāpāl range of hills has, however, not been investigated: the results of this geological survey are set forth in detail in the article on the Mayūrbhanj State. It is possible that other coalfields may exist, though not probable. Up to 1874-75 even the Tālcher coalfield had only received, for the most part, a very hurried examination. Excluding the formations of which no accurate information has been obtained, such as the slates, quartzites, and jasper, to be found in Keonjhar and Bonai, the following is a list, in descending order, of the rock systems hitherto described as existing in Orissa:—(8) *Blown sands.* (7) *Alluvium. b. River detta deposits. a. Older alluvium of coast plains.* (6) *Laterite.* (5) *Cuttack or Athgarh sandstone.* (4) *Mahādeva or Pānchet sandstone and grit.* (3) *Dāmodar sandstone, shale, and coal.* (2) *Tālcher sandstone, shale, silt and boulder bed.* (1) *Metamorphic or crystalline rocks.*

The following is a brief description of the characters of each of these formations, as found in Orissa:—

(1) METAMORPHIC OR CRYSTALLINE ROCKS.—These consist of various forms of gneiss, mica-schist, hornblende-schist, quartzite, etc. True granite is found in the form of veins traversing the gneiss, and is of various forms, the most common being a highly crystalline variety, with but little mica, and passing into pegmatite, of the kind known as graphic granite. This granite is apparently, for the most part at least, of cotemporaneous age with the metamorphism of the gneiss. But besides this, the gneiss itself frequently passes into a granitoid form, perfectly undistinguishable in blocks from granite; but which, when in place, is usually found to retain, every here and there, traces of its original lamination, and to pass by insensible degrees into a distinct laminated gneiss of the usual form.

Other prevalent forms are ordinary gneiss, composed of quartz, felspar, and mica; hornblendic gneiss in which the mica is replaced by hornblende, the latter mineral sometimes forming a very large proportion of the rock; the quartzose gneiss, in which the felspar and mica, or hornblende, are in very small proportion, and the quartz predominates. This gradually passes into quartzite, in which felspar and mica are either wanting, or occur only in very small quantities.

The above may be considered the prevailing forms of the crystalline rocks; but there are others of less frequent occurrence. Amongst these are diorite, amphibolite, syenite, and a magnesian rock—a kind of potstone. These may all very possibly be of later date than most of the metamorphics, though the serpentine-like potstone appears to be fairly intercalated.

(2) TALCHER GROUP.—The lowest beds associated with the coal-bearing strata are themselves destitute of useful fuel, and well distinguished mineralogically from the Dāmodar or coal-bearing rocks. They were first separated from the overlying beds in Orissa and named after the State in which they were found. They consist, in the case of the Tālcher coalfield, of blue nodular shale, fine buff or greenish sandstone, and extremely fine silt beds, often interstratified with sandstone more or less coarse in texture, in thin alternating laminæ. The sandstones frequently contain felspar grains, which are usually undecomposed. In the sandstone and fine silty shale, rounded pebbles, and boulders of granite, gneiss, and other crystalline rocks abound, some of them as much as four or five feet in diameter. This remarkable formation is known as the boulder bed. It is peculiar to the Tālcher group, and has been found in India wherever that group has been examined,—in the valleys of the Dāmodar, the Son, the Narbadā, and the Godāvarī, as well as in that of the Brāhmanī.

Of this singular association of large blocks of stone in a fine matrix, but few other instances are known, the most remarkable one being that of the "boulder clay" of Great Britain and other countries, which is now considered by most geologists to be of glacial origin. The boulder bed of the Tālcher group, however, differs entirely from the boulder clay. In the former the fine matrix is distinctly stratified, and the boulders are rounded, neither of which is the usual condition of the boulder clay.

(3) DAMODAR GROUP.—Above the Tālcher, or occasionally resting upon the metamorphic rocks, without the intervention of any other sedimentary beds, is found a series of sandstone and shale, with beds of coal. The sandstone is mostly a coarse grey and brown rock passing into grits. They are usually more or less felspathic, the felspar being decomposed and converted into clay, and are often ferruginous. Blue and carbonaceous shale, often more or less micaceous, and ferruginous shaly sandstone, are characteristic of this group. Fossil plants, chiefly consisting of ferns, such as *Glossopteris*, *Pecopteris Trizygœia*, *Equisetaceæ* and *Calamites* and above all, peculiar stems divided into segments (*Vertebraria*), believed to be roots of unknown affinities, are frequently found. Most of the fossil species found, perhaps all, are characteristic of the Dāmodar formation.

The peculiar interest attaching to this group of rocks is, however, derived from its being the only one in which workable coal has been found in the Peninsula of India. All the coals of Rānīganj and the other fields of the Dāmodar valley, as well as all those of the Narbadā valley, and of other parts of the Central Provinces, are in Dāmodar rocks. So far as they have hitherto been examined, the coals of Tālcher appear to be of inferior quality to those of Rānīganj, the Narbadā, and other localities. In the Himgīr zamīndāri of the Gāngpur State a coalfield has been located over an area of about 27 square miles and steps have been taken to work the coal. The coal-bearing strata of the Himgīr zamīndāri is equivalent to the Kāmthi group, which includes the Upper and Lower Dāmodars and should therefore be included in the Dāmodar and not in the Tālcher group.

(4) MAHADEVA GROUP.—Above the coal-bearing series in the eastern part of the Tālcher coalfield, a considerable thickness of coarse sandstone, grits, and conglomerates is found, quite different in character from the beds of the Tālcher and Dāmodar groups, and resting unconformably upon them. These rocks are usually coloured with various shades of brown, and are frequently very ferruginous. The separate beds composing them are massive, and not interrupted, as the Dāmodar sandstones frequently are, by partings of shale. They form hills of considerable size in the State of Rairākhol.

It is by no means clear that these beds are the representatives of the group in the Narbadā valley, to which the name Mahādeva was first applied; but there is a general subdivision of the rocks throughout the greater portion of the Indian coalfields into three principal groups. To the higher of these, the term Mahādeva has been given in the Narbadā valley, in Orissa, and Pānchet in Bengal.

(5) CUTTACK OR ATHGARH GROUP.—South-west of the town of Cuttack is a considerable area, reaching into the Athgarh State, occupied by grit, sandstone, and conglomerate, with one or more beds of white or pinkish clay. The beds are very similar in general character to those last described; but there is no evidence of any connection with them, and it appears at least as probable that the Cuttack rocks are of later date. No fossils have been found in these beds except some obscure impressions, apparently of vegetable origin, in the clays.

(6) LATERITE.—The laterite of Orissa is evidently of detrital origin and consists essentially of small pisolitic nodules, chiefly composed of hydrated oxide of iron (brown hæmatite) and coarse quartz sand, cemented together more or less perfectly into either a firm, though somewhat vesicular, rock, or into a less coherent mass, or at times remaining in a loose gravelly condition, and thus passing by various gradations into a sandy clay, with a few

pisolitic iron nodules. As a rule, the forms containing most iron are the most coherent, and *vice versa*. The more solid sorts are largely used as building stone, having the peculiar but important property of being softest when first cut, and of hardening greatly on exposure. Laterite is found all through the States of Orissa.

Beneath the detrital laterite, especially when a felspathic form of the metamorphic rocks occurs, the decomposed upper portion of the latter is frequently greatly impregnated with iron, and converted into a kind of lithomarge, which closely resembles the detrital laterite in appearance, and is employed for the same purposes. The massive form of laterite which caps many of the higher hills in Central India, and which is more compact than the detrital laterite, is not known to occur in Orissa.

Of the geology of the States of Pāl Laharā, Narsinghpur, Barāmbā and Tigiriā, lying north of the Mahānadī, and of all the States south of the Mahānadī river, viz., Baud, Daspallā, Khandparā, Nayāgarh, and Ranpur, nothing definite is known. It is pretty certain that a large proportion of their area consists of metamorphic rocks, and it is possible that no others may be found.

Of Keonjhar and Nīlgiri, only the edges bordering on Balasore district have been examined. Hindol has been traversed; portions of Dhenkānāl and Athmallik have been examined; whilst in Tālcher and Athgarh a more general survey has been made, but still far from a complete or detailed one.

NILGIRI AND KEONJHAR.—The hills bordering on Balasore consist entirely of metamorphic rocks of various kinds. In the northern part of the range, gneiss is found, so granitic that the direction of the foliation can scarcely be ascertained. It appears to be nearly parallel with the escarpment of the range. Granite veins are scarce; but greenstone dykes, or pseudo-dykes, many of them of great size, abound, and most of them, if not all, appear to run parallel with the gneissic foliation. These facts render it probable that the dykes in question are really beds, so altered as to be perfectly crystalline. A kind of black magnesian rock, intermediate in composition between potstone and serpentine, approaching the former in appearance, but less greasy in texture, is quarried to some extent, chiefly for the manufacture of stone dishes, plates, and bowls. The stones are roughly cut into shape in the quarry, and finished, partly with tools and partly on a lathe, in the villages. The rock employed is found interfoliated with the gneiss in several places, and is quarried at the villages of Sāntrāgoriā and Gujādihā, a few miles south of Nīlgiri, at a spot two or three miles from Jugjuri, and in scattered localities to the north-west. A few miles south-west of Jugjuri, near Pārkparā, the granitoid rocks are replaced by a tough, hard, indistinctly crystalline hornblendic rock, resembling diorite, but exhibiting more foliation than is seen in the hills near Nīlgiri. Still farther to the south-west, quartz schist appears in a well-foliated form, occasionally containing talc. A detached hill near Bākipur consists of this rock, and so does the whole south-west portion of the range as far as Ragadi, except in the immediate neighbourhood of the Sālandī river, where it leaves the hill. Here syenite occurs which forms a detached hill near Dārāpur. The southern portion of the range is free from the trap dykes which are so conspicuous to the north-east of Jugjuri. All the western portions of Keonjhar are unexplored, but the State is believed to contain good deposits of iron.

TALCHER AND ATHMALLIK.—*The Tālcher coalfield.*—The basin of sedimentary rocks known as the Tālcher coalfield is surrounded on all sides by metamorphics. This basin extends about seventy miles from west by north to east by south, with a general breadth of from fifteen to twenty miles, its eastern extremity at Khadakprasād on the Brāhmanī river being nearly fifty miles north-west of Cuttack town. Its western limit is not far from Rāmpur, in the State of Rairākhol, and it comprises nearly the whole of Tālcher, and a considerable portion of Rairākhol, with smaller parts of Athmallik, and Dhenkānāl. The western half of this field is chiefly occupied by the rocks already described as belonging to the Mahādeva group, conglomerate and coarse sandstone, which form hills of considerable height in a very wild, jungly, and thinly inhabited country. At the period when the Tālcher coalfield was first examined, nothing whatever was known of the classification of rocks which has since been adopted by the Geological Survey in the various coalfields of India. Indeed, one of the very first and most important distinctions, that of the Tālcher group, below the coal-bearing division, was made in this region, as already mentioned. The boundaries of the Mahādevas and Dāmodars, on the map in the *Memoirs of the Geological Survey of India*, are merely a rough approximation made from memory, and partly by guess, after quitting the field. The differences of the rocks have been noted in the field, but their area has not been mapped.

It is by no means improbable that the Dāmodar coal-bearing rocks will hereafter be found in portions of this area. Indeed, they have been observed at the village of Patraparā.

In the extreme west of the field, Tālcher beds occur in the upper part of the valley of a stream tributary to the Tikariā, near Dainchā, and also near Rāmpur, in Rairākhol. In both cases, Mahādeva rocks appear to rest directly on them, without the intermediary of any Dāmodars.

Besides occupying the western part of the field, the Mahādevas are found in two places along the northern boundary, which is formed by a fault of considerable dimensions. One of these places is near the villages of Borāharnā and Dereng, where the upper beds occur in a narrow belt, five or six miles from east to west, their presence being marked by low hills of hard conglomerate. Further to the west, they recur in another isolated patch, forming the rise called Khandagiri hill. This hill consists of sandstone, capped by conglomerate, the pebbles from which weather out and cover the sides of the hill, concealing the sandstone beneath.

The northern part of the field in which these outliers of the Mahādevas occur is much cut up by faults, or, to speak more correctly, by branches of one great fault. These faults are in some places marked by a quartzose breccia, containing fragments of sandstone and other rocks. The vein of breccia varies in breadth. At the village of Karganj it is so largely developed that it forms a hill of considerable height. Between the branches of the fault, Tālcher beds and metamorphics occur; north of all the faults, metamorphics only are found.

The eastern part of the field, from near Karganj on the Tikariā river, and Kānkurāi on the Tengrā, to the east of the Brāhmanī, is principally composed of Dāmodar rock. These may usually be recognised by the occasional occurrence of blue and black shale, the latter carbonaceous, and sometimes containing coal. The general section of the beds is as follows:—

Interstratifications of blue and black shale, often very micaceous, with ironstone and coarse felspathic sandstone. These are at least 1,500 feet thick.

Carbonaceous shale and coal, about 150 feet.

Shale and coarse sandstone, the latter prevailing towards the base; thickness doubtful, but not less than 100 feet.

If this be correct, the coal only occurs upon one horizon. It is by no means impossible, however, that other beds may be found. Coal is known to be exposed in three places. The most westwardly of these is at Patraparā, in Angul, a village on the Meduliā Jor, a tributary of the Aulī river. Here some six feet of carbonaceous shale and coal are seen on the banks of the stream, capped by clay, upon which rest the coarse grits of the Mahādeva group. The area occupied by the beds is small. The next place, which is far better known, is at Gopālprasād, in

Tālcher, on the Tengrā river. The rocks at this spot are nearly horizontal for a long distance, and the coal-bed extends for some miles along the banks of the stream, above the village. It also recurs lower down the stream. The thickness of the bed is considerable, but its quality is inferior, the greater portion being excessively shaly and impure. Selected specimens contain upwards of thirty per cent. of ash, but it by no means follows that better coal may not be found; and even the inferior fuel would be useful for many purposes, if any local demand existed; while from the horizontality of the beds, a large quantity might be procured with very little labour. The general dip in the neighbourhood is to the north; and any attempts at working the coal on a large scale, or further explorations by boring, should be made north of the Tengrā stream.

The third locality is in a small stream running into the Brāhmanī from the west, just north of the village of Tālcher. Beds lower than the coal are seen on the bank of the Brāhmanī, at the Chief's residence. The carbonaceous shale with coal is exposed about 400 yards from the river, in the small water-course. Only two or three feet are visible. The dip is north-west, and the coal is covered by micaceous, sandy, and shaly beds. A boring north-west of this spot would test the bed fairly.

There is another locality in which the section can be tested, at the village of Kankarāpāl, in Angul, about ten miles north-west of Gopālprasād. It is by no means certain that the Gopālprasād shale is close to the surface here; but the spot is the summit of an anticlinal, and some black shale seen in the stream resembles the uppermost portion of the rocks of Gopālprasād. It is highly probable that closer search will show other places where coal is exposed at the surface. The south-eastern part of the field consists of Tālcher beds, in which boulders are only occasionally found towards the base. They are micaceous near the village of Porongo. Above the silt-bed containing the boulders, there is a fine sandstone, frequently containing grains of undecomposed felspar. There is no chance of coal being found in this portion of the basin; that is, south of a line drawn from east by north to west by south, running about two miles south of Tālcher.

In several places in the Tālcher field, iron is worked. Sometimes the ironstones of the Dāmodar beds are used, but more frequently surface concretions, the supply of which is necessarily limited. Sometimes the little pisolitic nodules of the laterite are found washed from their matrix, and deposited in sufficient quantities in alluvial formations to be worth collecting. In one instance, the ore was derived from the metamorphic rocks, and brought from a distant locality. It resembled the mixture of peroxide of iron and quartz found at the outcrop of metallic lodes, and known as "gossan" in Cornwall. The method of smelting the iron in small furnaces is similar to that in use in other parts of India; but the bellows employed are worked with the foot, a peculiarity only found in the south-western dependencies of Bengal and Orissa.

The arenaceous ironstones of the Dāmodar group would, doubtless, yield a large supply of ore.

DHENKANAL AND HINDOL.—These regions require scarcely any notice. So far as is known, they consist of metamorphic rocks, except the western extremity of the first-named State, which comprises the eastern end of the Tālcher basin. The metamorphic rocks are of the usual descriptions.

ATHGARH.—The northern and western parts of this State consist of metamorphic rocks. Along the Mahānadī, from near Cuttack to the boundary of the State, within three or four miles of the village of Tigiriā, there is a belt four or five miles broad, of the same "Cuttack sandstones" as are seen south of the Mahānadī, in Purī district,—being, in fact, a portion of the same basin. The rocks are precisely similiar—coarse sandstone and conglomerate, with one or more bands of white clay.

GANGPUR.—Along the banks of the Koel river in the north-eastern portion of the State at a distance of about 8 miles from the railway station of Bisrā on the Bengal-Nāgpur Railway lime-stone quarries are worked: lime of excellent quality is obtained and exported to Calcutta. Deposits of manganese are found in several parts of this State and two thousand tons were raised in 1907-08. These deposits are probably superficial replacement deposits on the Dhārwār series.

KALAHANDI.—Graphite of good quality is found in this State and occurs in biotite gneiss. Bauxite (aluminium) is found in Kālāhandī occurring in laterite and is a superficial deposit.

ATHMALLIK AND PATNA.—Graphite is found in Athmallik and Patnā. Nothing is known about its mode of occurrence in these States, but in all cases it is probably associated with archæan rocks.

BOTANY.

The narrower valleys are often terraced for rice cultivation, and these rice-fields and their margins abound in marsh and water-plants. The surface of the plateau land between the valleys, where level, is often bare and rocky, but where undulating, is usually clothed with a dense scrub-jungle in which *Dendrocalamus strictus* is prominent. The steep slopes of the hills are covered with a dense forest mixed with many climbers. *Sâl* (*Shorea robusta*) is gregarious; and among the other noteworthy trees are species of *Buchanania*, *Semecarpus*, *Terminalia*, *Cedrela*, *Cassia*, *Butea*, *Bauhinia*, *Acacia*, and *Adina*, which are found aslo on the lower Himalayan slopes. Mixed with these, however, are a number of trees and shrubs, characteristic of Central India, such as *Cochlospermum*, *Soymida*, *Boswellia*, *Hardwickia* and *Bassia*, which do not cross the Gangetic plain.

The large area of the States of Orissa (28,125 square miles) is of one common physical aspect and the fauna are homogeneous. **FAUNA.**

The elephant (*Elephas Indicus*) however does not generally range south of the Mahānadī although fairly numerous in the central and north-eastern portion of the tract. A few stray occasionally across the Mahānadī into the State of Baud, but practically never move further south. In 1907 a few stray elephants appeared in the State of Kālāhandī for a few days and the occurrence was reported as most unusual and novel. The extensive and almost unpopulated tracts of the Simlāpāl in the State of Mayūrbhañj is a sanctuary for elephants and probably most of the elephants in Orissa frequent this magnificent elephant-forest at some time or other in the course of their existence.

Wild buffaloes (*Bos bubalis*) are now very rare. The wild buffalo was at one time quite plentiful in the Gāngpur State, along the valley of the Brāhmanī and at Kumārkelā some twelve miles west, but the advent of the railway proved his death-knell, and to-day there is not a single specimen left in Gāngpur or Bonai. In 1906 the sole survivor, a solitary bull, was killed by a villager in the north-east corner of Bonai. Occasionally a solitary buffalo crosses the border from Jashpur into Gāngpur.

Bison (*Gavaeus ganrus*) usually called *gayal* occur in the denser and remoter forests in every part of the States: they generally graze in close proximity to elephants often moving amongst a herd. They are numerous in the high hills of Kālāhandī.

The principal carnivora are the tiger, panther, hyæna, wild-dog, jackal and fox.

Tigers (*Felis tigris*) are found everywhere, and are very frequently destructive to human life. The great majority are game-killers. Some are cattle-killers and a few are man-eaters.

The native method for the destruction of man-eaters, which generally frequent a well defined tract, is to set traps in the form of a gigantic bow and arrow on the paths traversed by the man-eater. The arrow-heads are covered with a highly poisonous vegetable substance known as *mendhāsinghā :* tigers are also killed by smearing this vegetable poison into the kill tied up. In tracts where timber cutting is in progress the number of persons killed is naturally large from the nature of the work, and the opportunities afforded for man-killing. Rewards are given for their destruction.

Panthers (*Felis pardus*) are very plentiful throughout all these States. The largest shot in these States of which there is an authentic record was 7 feet 2 inches measured along the curve of the back from the tip of the nose to the tip of the tail, soon after he was killed ; as a rule they seldom exceed 6½ feet in length. They are mostly found in the small hills adjoining the cultivated area, where they levy toll from the flocks of goats and sheep. They are but rarely found in the largest and more extensive forests.

The *chitāh* (*Felis jubata*) or hunting leopard is not supposed to inhabit Bengal, but there are a few to be found in the west of the State of Gāngpur in the Himgīr zamīndāri. Two have been shot in the Garjan hill in the north-west of that zamīndāri and two more have been seen in south Himgīr on the border of Kodābagā. A *chitāh* was shot in Pālkot in the Gumlā sub-division of the Rānchī district, which proves that though rare, they do exist in Bengal.

The *Felis Chaus* and *Felis bengalensis* are the only other members of the cat tribe met with in these States. They are fairly common and it is chiefly to them that the scarcity of ground game is attributed.

The large civet cat (*Viverra zibetha*) occurs in these States, but is not common.

The palm civet (*Paradoxurus niger*) is fairly common, but is mostly found near villages where it is very destructive to poultry.

The common grey mungoose (*Herpestes pallidus*) is somewhat rare. It is seen occasionally in rocky hills in Gāngpur; it is larger than the common mungoose, rather more yellow in colour and has the tail tipped with black.

The jackal (*Conis aureus*) is found all over these States, but seems to avoid the heavy forests and chiefly inhabits the scrub-jungle near villages.

The common fox (*Valpas bengalensis*) is met with ; it is common in the more open States but rare in the heavily wooded areas.

The *Sciurdus maximus var—bengalensis* is a very handsome squirrel and is common in all the dense forest areas. The colour is chiefly of a chestnut red above with the rump and tail black, the lower parts are buff. They are easily tamed and make very amusing pets. Their flesh is much appreciated by the forest tribes.

The common Indian ground-squirrel (*Iciurrus pal marum*) is fairly plentiful.

Pteromys cineraceus.—Although this variety of the large flying squirrel is supposed to be peculiar to Burmah, Mr. F. D. Whiffin has obtained several specimens in Gāngpur and Bonai and in each case the colour has been the same, ash coloured above and white on the belly. A specimen was sent by Mr. Whiffin to the Calcutta Museum in 1892. They are entirely nocturnal in their habits, and feed on fruits, nuts and insects, and breed in the holes of trees. With the parachute extended they have been seen to cover a flight of quite 100 yards.

The common Indian porcupine (*Hystrix leucura*) is met with in all the rocky hills in these States but being entirely nocturnal in its habits is seldom seen. Its food consists chiefly of roots.

The *Lepus ruficavdatus* is the only hare found and owing to the hilly nature of the country and the abundance of vermin it is not at all common.

Manis Brachyura.—This quaint beast, the manis or pangolin, although seldom seen, is found in these States. It lives in deep burrows and feeds chiefly on insects, its favourite diet being the white ant. They grow from 2 to 2½ feet in length and are covered with scales of a light olive colour.

The hyæna (*Hyæna striata*) is very common and is to be found over any carcase.

Wild dogs (*Canis rutilans*) are very numerous and extremely destructive to game: very interesting stories are told of the intelligence with which packs work together in hunting down a quarry: it is said they will pull down a bison. The larger variety appears to be most common, but villagers state that a very small light coloured variety or species exists. The larger species stands higher than a jackal and in the cold season has a bright chestnut brown coat: the ears are erect, the tail very bushy with a dark tip. The smaller variety has been reported from both Keonjhar and the Simlāpāl range near the Meghāsanī hill in Mayūrbhanj. It is grey in colour. The larger variety is locally known as *kok* and the smaller as *baluā*: the smaller variety is said to be much the most destructive to game hunting in far larger packs than the *kok*.

The wolf exists but is very rare and found only in pairs: they may be seen occasionally in the Patnā State along the main road from Sambalpur to Bolāngir.

The common Indian sloth bear (*Ursus labiatus*) is found everywhere and is the only representative of the family. Although their favourite foods are the *mahuā* flowers (*Bassia latifolia*), berries and white ants, they do a great deal of mischief to sugarcane and maize, and now and again one develops carnivorous tendencies. They seldom attack people except when taken by surprise, yet as they are so numerous in the aggregate a great number of people are killed or injured by them. A she-bear with cubs is decidedly dangerous when taken by surprise or cowered.

The ratel or honey-badger (*Mellivora Indica*) seems to be closely allied to the above, so much so that in these parts it is generally called the *chhota bhālu*. It is a small beast measuring about 3 feet, the upper part of the body being of an ashy-gray and the rest of it coal-black. It is found throughout these States, but being entirely nocturnal in its habits is seldom seen. It lives chiefly in rocky caves in the hills and its diet consists of lizards, insects and honey.

The *sambar* (*Rusa aritotelis*) is a forest-loving animal and generally frequents the high and most inaccessible hills. It is the largest of the Indian deer, and occurs all through these States. It is nocturnal in its habits grazing chiefly at night and returning to the hill tops during the day, where it generally rests in some shady spot during the heat of the day. The horns of the *sambar* in these States do not attain to the same dimensions as elsewhere.

The spotted deer (*Axis maculatus*) or *chithal* is common all over the States and is generally found in small herds in low-lying lands near water. They are gregarious in their habits and less nocturnal than the *sambar*, and care little for the neighbourhood of man. They are seldom found in the more hilly tracts.

The Indian mouse deer (*Meminna Indica*), the smallest of its tribe, is found throughout the States, but owing to its diminutive size is seldom seen. It stands 10 to 12 inches at the withers and in colour is brown with white or buff spots and longitudinal stripes. It is locally known as *gurandi* and in Kālāhandī as *kebri*.

The *munitjac* (*Cervalus aurcus*) or rib faced deer (barking deer), although seldom seen, is often heard and is easily recognized by its dog-like bark and is common in the States.

The *nīlgāi* (*Portax pictus*) is found in all the less heavily wooded forest, where it feeds largely on wild berries, one of its favourites being the *aonlā* (*Phyllanthus emblica*) which it devours in great quantities

The occurrence of hog deer (*Cervus porcinus*) is doubtful.

The black buck antelope (*Antelope cervicapra*) only occurs in Kālāhandī and perhaps in Patnā in small numbers.

The four-horned antelope (*Tetracerus quadricornis*) is fairly common, the female and young male so resemble the barking deer that they are frequently mistaken for the latter animal. The horns of a good specimen shot in Bonai measured, anterior horns 1¾ inches, posterior horns 3¼ inches.

Pigs (*Sus Indicus*) are universal and destructive.

The monkeys (*Quadrumana*) in these States are restricted to two species only; the *langur* or *hanumān* (*Presbytes entellus*) and the small brow *bandar* (*Macacus rhesus*): of these, the former is most plentiful and is found distributed all over these States. Unlike his brother, in the more civilized and higher cultivated areas of India, he avoids the proximity of villages and keeps more to the hills and jungle, the reason for this probably being that he finds the forest tribes less sympathetic and hospitable in their treatment of him than their more civilized neighbours, the Hindus. Amongst their most deadly enemies are the Birhors, a wandering non-agricultural tribe who live chiefly on the animals they net, the chief amongst them being the unfortunate *hanumān* whose flesh they eat and whose skin is used for making the earthen drum called the *mandar*. The *bandar* is not so common as the *hanumān*, but is found scattered all over these States.

Pea-fowl are numerous and occasionally to a certain extent protected, not apparently from any religious feeling, but because they have been taken as the *santak* or emblem of some of the Chiefs. Birds.

Jungle-fowl and common spur-fowl are numerous. The painted spur-fowl occurs, but is uncommon. The partridge, black or grey, are comparatively rare. The great hornbill is often found in the forest tracts.

On the large and numerous irrigation dams to the south-west great flocks of geese, ducks and teal are found in the cold weather. The comb-duck (*Sarcidioruis melananotus*) breeds in the country and is found all along the Mahānadī river in suitable localities. The grey-duck (*Anas poceiloryuchus*) and pink-headed duck (*Rhodonessa caryophyllucea*) both breed in the States, but the latter is rare. The two whistling-teal and the little cotton-teal are common residents.

The following are the wild fowl most commonly recognised in Orissa:—(*a*) Geese—(1) the lag or grey, (2) the barred-headed. (*b*) Duck—(1) comb—also known as the black-backed spur-goose; the local term is *naktā*, (2) gadwall or grey, (3) pin-tail,

(4) pochard—red-crested, (5) pochard- red-headed, (6) sheldrake, (7) sheldrake—ruddy, (8) shoveller, (9) spot-bill, and (10) widgeon. (*c*) Teal—(1) blue-winged, (2) common, (3) cotton, and (4) whistling. (*d*) Plover—(1) golden, (2) ringed, and (3) turnstone. (*e*) Snipe—(1) fan-tail, (2) jack, (3) painted, and (4) pin-tail.

Some flocks of the demoiselle crane frequent the neighbourhood of the Mahānadī and Tel rivers. Snipe, and grey and golden plover occur where the ground is suitable. The black imperial pigeon is found in places, while the ordinary green fruit-eating pigeon sometimes assembles in enormous flocks.

Crocodiles. Both the snub-nosed crocodile and the long-nosed fish-eating *gharial* are found in the rivers.

Snakes. In addition to the usual snakes the hamadryad (*Oppiophagus elaps*) and some large pythons are occasionally found.

Fish. The principal fish are *rohi* (*Lobeo rohita*), *mirkāli* (*Cirrhuia mrigala*), *bhākur* (*Catla buchanani*), *sâl* (*Ophiocephalus marulius*), *seul* (*Ophiocephalus striatus*), *boāli* (*Wallago attee*), *hilsā* (*Clupea ilisha*), and numerous species of the carp and catfish families.

Mahsir occur occasionally in the upper waters of the Mahānadī and Brāhmanī and their affluents.

CLIMATE. The climate of the States is very similar to that prevailing in the rest of Orissa, except that it is probably hotter in summer and colder in winter. The climate of the States which border on the Purī, Cuttack and Balasore districts is naturally moister than that of the States further inland, and the temperature is no doubt somewhat lowered by the moist cool breezes from the sea. In the States in the neighbourhood of Sambalpur a shade temperature of 111 to 112 degrees in May and June is not uncommon and not infrequently rises three or four degrees higher. No record of temperature, however, has been kept. The high plateau lands in the south-eastern area of the State of Kālāhandī attain an elevation of 4,000 to 4,100 feet and the climate is very pleasant even during the hottest months: the surrounding country, however, right up to the very edge of the plateau, is extremely malarious. There are several other high ranges, the most suitable of which, for a change from the heated atmosphere of the plains, are the Meghāsanī range (3,824 feet) in Mayūrbhanj, Malayagiri (3,895 feet) in the State of Pāl Laharā and Gandhamardan (3,479 feet) in Keonjhar. In December and January the high grass is coated with thick rhyme in the plateau country of Kālāhandī and the western portion of the Patnā State and in the high lands of Bonai, Pāl Laharā and Keonjhar. A thermometer placed out on the open ground at Rampur, the

Temperature.

head-quarters of the Rāmpur-Thuāmūl zamīndāri, of the Kālāhandī State, in the early part of January, recorded temperatures of 33 and 34 degrees at 6 o'clock in the morning. Owing to the presence of low hills and forests, the climate of the greater part of the States is unhealthy, especially during the rainy-season and the beginning of the cold weather, when malaria prevails. The principal cause of fever and bowel complaints is the bad water: in the hill tracts there are streams of crystal clear water, but deadly to drink, charged with the poison of decaying vegetation deposited in the deep pools along their course. The average annual rainfall during the last five years is 56·68 inches: the average main distribution is January to May 5·64 inches and June to October 48·59. **Rainfall.**

CHAPTER II.

HISTORY.

PREHISTORIC PERIOD.

THE States have no connected or authentic history. Comprising, as they do, the western and hilly portion of the Province of Orissa, they were never brought under the central Government, but from the earliest times consisted of numerous petty principalities which were more or less independent of one another. They were first inhabited by aboriginal races, chiefly Bhuiyās, Savars, Gonds and Khonds, who were divided into innumerable communal or tribal groups each under its own Chief or headman. They carried on incessant warfare with their neighbours on the one hand and the denizens of the forests on the other. In course of time their hill retreats were penetrated by Aryan adventurers, who, by reason of their superior prowess and intelligence, gradually overthrew the tribal Chiefs and established themselves in their place. Tradition relates how these daring interlopers, most of whom were Rājputs from the north, came to Purī on pilgrimage and remained behind to found kingdoms and dynasties.

MEDIÆVAL PERIOD.

It was thus that the founder of the present Rāj family of the Patnā State 600 years ago set up his sway over a cluster of States known as the Athara Garhjāts or 18 forts: according to tradition this ancestor was a Chauhān Rājput Chief living near Mainpurī, and expelled from his territories by the Muhammadans: this family settled down in Patnā and quickly extended its power, till finally the whole of the country which is now the Sambalpur district and the adjoining States of Sonpur and Bāmra, the Chiefs of which were made tributaries, fell under its sway. The area under the sway of this family was divided up between two brothers: from this division originated the supremacy of the brother who received Sambalpur as his portion: Patnā rapidly became a dependency of the Chief of the Sambalpur State which had grown the most powerful of all the cluster of Garhjāt States. The State of Sambalpur fell before the Marāthās, and with it Pātnā. Jai Singh became ruler of Mayūrbhanj over 1,300 years ago, and was succeeded by his eldest son, while his second son seized Keonjhar. The Chiefs of Baud and Daspallā are said to be descended from the same stock, and a Rājput origin is also claimed by the Rājās of Athmallik, Narsinghpur, Pāl Laharā, Tālcher and Tigiriā. Nayāgarh, it is alleged, was founded by a Rājput from Rewah, and a scion of the same family was the ancestor of the present house of Khandparā. On the other hand, the Chiefs of a few States, such as Athgarh, Barāmbā and Dhenkānāl, owe their origin to distinguished servants of the ruling sovereigns of Orissa. The State of Ranpur is alleged to be the most ancient, the list of its Chiefs being said to cover a period of over 3,600 years. This family furnishes the only known instance in which, amidst many vicissitudes, the supremacy of the original settlers has remained intact. The States acknowledged the suzerainty of the paramount power and were under an implied obligation to render assistance in resisting invaders, but in other respects neither the ancient kings of Orissa nor their successors, the Mughals and Marāthās, ever interfered with their internal administration. All the States have annals of the dynasties that have ruled over them, but they are made up in most part of legend and fiction and long genealogical tables of doubtful accuracy, and contain very few features of general interest. The salient features in the particular history of each State have been mentioned in the separate articles on each of the States. Within its rugged barriers, each State was thus permitted to work out its own growth, its boundaries expanding or contracting according to the strength or weakness of its Chief, the jealousies of its neighbours and final appeal for help to the sovereign power preventing its total extinction at any time.

The valley of the Mahānadī formed the high road from the west, and it is thought that the Yavanas who were finally expelled from Orissa by Yayāti Kesarī, the first king of the Lion dynasty, in A. D. 474, and whom Sir William Hunter identifies with the Ionians, escaped to the Central India plateau through that route. Orissa under the Lion line (474-1132 A. D.) did not extend inland beyond Dhenkānāl and can hardly be said to include the group of States formerly known as the Tributary Mahāls of Orissa. The princes* of the Gangetic line pushed their territory inland to Baud which still continues the westernmost of the States formerly known as the Orissa Tributary Mahāls. It is said that the third monarch of the line, between 1175 and 1202, measured his kingdom from the Hooghly to the Godāvarī and from the sea to the frontier of Sonpur, the State, which adjoins Baud on the west.

---

* Hunter's *Orissa*, Vol. I, pp. 317 and 318.

BRITISH CONQUEST.

The British conquest of Orissa from the Marāthās took place in 1803, and was immediately followed by the submission of 10 of the States, the Chiefs of which were the first to enter into treaty engagements. Meanwhile, Major Forbes penetrated through the hilly and jungly country on the west and reached the famous Barmūl pass in Daspallā, the key to Berār and the Central Provinces. Here the Marāthās made a last stand, but on the 2nd November the pass was forced and the enemy fled in confusion. The Rājā of Baud and others hastened to tender their submission. Including Khurdā, the States were then 20 in number. In the following year the Chief of Khurdā rebelled, was vanquished and forfeited his State, which is now a Government estate and is administered as a subdivision of the Purī district. The Rājā of Bānki was deposed in 1840 for murder, and his State, which escheated to Government, has since been added to the district of Cuttack. In 1847 Angul was annexed on account of the misconduct of its Chief, who was found to be preparing to wage war against Government and to countenance those who opposed the officers of Government employed in suppressing Mariāh or human sacrifice among the Khonds in Baud. The large tract known as the Khondmāls with an area of 800 square miles, which professed a shadowy allegiance to the State of Baud came under British influence in 1855-56, when the Chief of that State made over the Khondmāls to British administration, being himself powerless to suppress the practice of Mariāh and to bring under subjection the refractory Khonds who had taken the side of the notorious Gumsur rebel Chakra Bisoi. Since then it has remained under British control, and in 1891 was formed into a subdivision of the scheduled district of Angul. Athmallik was a tributary of Baud and Pāl Laharā of Keonjhar, and they find no mention in the earlier treaty engagements. They were both recognised as separate States in the *sanads* of 1874, which at the same time conferred the hereditary title of Rājā on their Chiefs.

The 17 States named in the margin were variously known as the Tributary States, Tributary Mahāls or the Garhjāts of Orissa. Treaty engagements were exchanged with the first eleven States in 1803, immediately after the British occupation. After Major Forbes' success at Barmūl the Chiefs of Baud and Daspallā submitted and treaty engagements were entered into with them as well as with most of the remaining Chiefs in 1804.

1	Athgarh	9	Ranpur
2	Barāmbā	10	Tālcher
3	Dhenkānāl	11	Tigiriā
4	Hindol	12	Baud
5	Khandparā	13	Daspallā
6	Narsinghpur	14	Keonjhar
7	Nayāgarh	15	Mayūrbhanj
8	Nīlgiri	16	Athmallik
		17	Pāl Laharā

JURISDICTION. Cuttack States.

This group of 17 States or Tributary Mahāls of Orissa referred to above were ceded with the rest of Orissa by the Marāthās to the British Government on the conquest of Orissa in 1803-04, and it is with this year that the history of the dealings of the British Government with the States commences, but as they had never been regular districts, but rather Tributary States of the Native Governments, they were exempted from the operation of the general Regulation system prevailing in the British Provinces by sections 36, 13 and 11 respectively of Regulations XII, XIII and XIV of 1805. Engagements were entered into by all the Chiefs, binding themselves to maintain submission and loyalty to the East India Company's Government, and to pay an annual *peshkash* or tribute. All the Chiefs, except Keonjhar, are also bound under these engagements to depute a contingent force to assist Government against any opposition, the force to receive only rations from Government. In 1804 the Judge and Magistrate of Cuttack had certain jurisdiction in these States; but in 1814 he was superseded by a Superintendent, 'appointed and directed to endeavour to establish such a control over the conduct of the Rājās, as would prevent the commission of crimes and outrages.'

The Chiefs administered civil and criminal justice under the control of the Commissioner of the Orissa Division, as Superintendent of the States. Heinous offences which required more than two years' imprisonment, and all capital cases were sent to this officer, who also decided political causes and disputed successions. An appeal from his decision lay to the Government of Bengal. The Magistrates of Purī, Cuttack and Balasore were *ex-officio* Assistants to the Superintendent; but, with the exception of the Magistrate of Balasore, they did not ordinarily exercise criminal jurisdiction. The Superintendent had also an Assistant, who exercised the full powers of a Magistrate, and who tried such cases as the Superintendent made over to him. The States, during the minority of the Rājās or Chiefs, or when for political reasons they were placed under attachment, were managed by the Superintendent through a Government receiver (*Tahsīldār*). The jurisdiction of the Superintendent was defined by Regulation XI of 1816 and Act XXI of 1850.

In 1821 the Government ruled that the interference of the Superintendent should be chiefly confined to matters of a political nature: to the suppression of feuds and animosities prevailing between the Rājās of adjoining States, or between the Rājās and their subordinate feudatories; to the correction of systematic oppression and cruelty practised by any of the Rājās or by their officers towards the inhabitants; to the cognisance of any apparent gross violation by them of their duties of allegiance and subordination; and generally, to important points, which, if not attended to, might lead to violent and general outrage and confusion, or to contempt of the paramount authority of the British Government.

In 1839 suggestions were made for the introduction of a regular system of management, but the rules proposed were not approved. Instructions were, however, given to draw up some short, clear and well-defined regulations, making the Rājās responsible to the Superintendent in all cases of murder, homicide and heinous offences, without, however, interfering so far as to make them amenable to the Civil Court of the Superintendent in cases between the Rājās and their creditors. Rules were accordingly drawn up proposing that the Rājās should be prohibited from exercising the powers of life and death; from subjecting any offender to torture, mutilation, or other punishment opposed to the principles of British rule; and from allowing the practice of widow-burning and human sacrifices within their territories; that they should be made liable to punishment for murder, or other heinous offences committed by them, and should be held responsible for the amount of property robbed from travellers, if the commission of the crime and the non-recovery of the property were due to their imperfect police or want of care; that the Superintendent's power of interference should be increased, so as to take cognizance of offences committed by foreigners in the Tributary States, to hold preliminary inquiries in heinous offences committed by the Rājās, and to sentence all offenders except the Rājās to imprisonment for a term not exceeding seven years; that the punishment of the Rājās, and all punishments exceeding seven years, should be awarded by the Government of Bengal. The Bengal Government, however, thought it better not to pass any permanent or defined rules upon the subject; but directed that the spirit of the proposed rules should be acted up to in all future cases, with certain limitations, and that the Rājās should be informed that they are ordinarily amenable to the Superintendent's Court, subject to such instructions as may from time to time be furnished by the Government. These were the orders of 1840; and all sentences of more than seven years' imprisonment, although passed by the Superintendent, had then to be reported to Government for confirmation. In 1850 Act XX was enacted for settling the boundaries of these States. In 1858, the system of trying petty criminal cases *vivâ voce* was extended to the States.

The Penal Code was declared applicable to these States by an order of Government in December 1860, and in 1863. Under orders of Government the criminal authorities were directed to be guided in their proceedings as closely as possible by the spirit of the Criminal Procedure Code. Section 13 of Regulation XIII of 1805, and as regards the States under the Rājās, the proviso contained in Section 11, Regulation XIV of 1805, are still in force.

In 1862 adoption *sanads* were granted to the Chiefs by Lord Canning. The relations between the British Government and the Orissa Mahāls are defined in the treaties and engagements with the Chiefs as detailed in Aitchison's *Treaties*. Questions of inheritance and succession are decided by Regulation XI of 1816. In 1882 the Calcutta High Court ruled that the Tributary Mahāls of Orissa did not form part of British India. The decision was accepted as final by the Secretary of State, and a special Act, called the Tributary Mahāls of Orissa Act, XI of 1893, was passed to indemnify certain persons and to validate acts done by them in the Mahāls, and to admit of certain sentences passed there being carried into effect in British India. *Sanads* were granted to the Chiefs in 1894 defining their relations with the British Government and these *sanads* were revised in 1908.

The Chotā Nāgpur Mahāls, to which the States of Gāngpur and Bonai belong, were acquired by cession from the Marāthās; their position was only that of zamīndārs paying tribute, who were allowed certain powers of internal administration, liable to reduction or abolition at any time. The States of Chotā Nāgpur belong politically to two clusters of States known as the Sambalpur and Sirguja groups, each of which was once linked together by some sort of feudal tie. Chotā Nāgpur States.

The southern or Sambalpur group comprised Gāngpur, Bonai and other States now in the Central Provinces. In 1818 these States reverted to the British Government under a provisional agreement with Mādhujī Bhonslā (Appā Sāhib). They were finally ceded in 1826. On the cession of these States in 1818, the feudal supremacy of the Rājā of Sambalpur was annulled. In 1821 the tribute payable was fixed on a lower scale than had been levied by the Marāthās. Up to 1860 the Sambalpur States were administered from Rānchī by the Agent to the Governor-General on the South-West Frontier.

Under the rough military rule of the Bhonslā dynasty of Nāgpur the position of the Chiefs was of necessity uncertain and fluctuating. At one time they were held in some check by a strong local governor, and at another left in almost complete independence. The British Government adhered to the latter policy, and from the first declined to lay down any definite rules for the guidance of the Chiefs. Only the general line of policy was indicated. Separate engagements were taken from each Chief, binding him to the right administration of the judicial and police powers entrusted to him. In 1823 it was laid down that no sentence of death or of imprisonment extending beyond seven years, should be passed or executed without the previous sanction of the Agent. Precise rules for the guidance of the Chiefs in the administration of criminal justice and in the exercise of their police functions, were first promulgated in 1863.

There is a considerable difference between the position of the Chotā Nāgpur Mahāls and the Orissa Mahāls. With the former, treaties were entered into, but the latter only received engagements specifying the conditions on which their lands were settled with them. They were granted *sanads* in 1899, and in the case of Gāngpur and Bonai revised *sanads* were granted in 1905, bringing them within the Orissa Division.

Central Provinces States.

As regards the five States, Patnā, Kālāhandī, Sonpur, Bāmra, Rairākhol, transferred from the Central Provinces to Orissa in 1905, the position of the States and zamīndārs in the Central Provinces was the subject of enquiry in 1863. The States of Patnā, Sonpur, Bāmra, and Rairākhol formed a group known as the Sambalpur Garhjāts; Kālāhandī or Karond did not originally form one of the Garhjāts and was grouped with the tenures known as the Nāgpur zamīndāris. The exact origin of the tenure of the Sambalpur Garhjāt Chiefs is unknown, but is certainly very ancient; they were, as already stated, first independent, then held in subordination to the most powerful, the Mahārājā of Patnā, who afterwards had to yield supremacy to the Mahārājā of Sambalpur, till all fell under the Marāthās in A. D. 1755 as tributaries. When they came under British rule, this dependence was cancelled in 1821, and separate *sanads* were granted. The Nāgpur zamīndārs, in which group Kālāhandī was included, were, notwithstanding their official authority and administrative influence, dependent on, and subject to, the Government of the day, and this dependence was real under the Marāthā Government. Adoption *sanads* were granted to Karond or Kālāhandī in 1862, Bāmra, Patnā and Sonpur in 1865, and Rairākhol in 1866. In 1867 *sanads* were granted to these five States giving them powers of life and death subject to confirmation of an officer of the British Government. In 1905 revised *sanads* were granted to these Chiefs in accordance with the territorial change bringing them within the Province of Orissa.

It is the *sanads* which now define the status and position of all the States with reference to the British Government: and it has been accepted now that the States do not form part of British India. The Tributary Mahāls of Orissa received their *sanads* in 1894, the Tributary and Political States of Chotā Nāgpur in 1875-76 and which were reissued in 1899 and the five States noted above in the year 1867. In the *sanads* of 1894 and 1899 the Chiefs of the Orissa, and Chotā Nāgpur Mahāls are termed Feudatory Chiefs. In 1908 revised *sanads* were granted to the States formerly known as the Tributary Mahāls of Orissa. In the *sanads* granted in 1867 to the States transferred from the Central Provinces it is stated, with the exception of the Kālāhandī State, which did not originally form one of the Garhjāt States, that whereas these Chiefs were formerly Tributary Chiefs of a Garhjāt State they have been recognised as Feudatories. *Sanads.*

The tribute payable in the case of the States constituting the group formerly known as the Orissa Tributary Mahāls is fixed, but that payable by the five States transferred from the Central Provinces and by the States of Gāngpur and Bonai is liable to revision. Of the States comprising the group formerly known as the Orissa Tributary Mahāls only the States of Athmallik, Baud, Mayūrbhanj, Pāl Lahara are bound to pay *nazarāna* or succession fees: the five States transferred from the Central Provinces and the States of Gāngpur and Bonai are all bound to pay *nazarāna*. Tribute and *nazarāna*.

The States of Orissa as now constituted formerly consisted of three groups: the largest group is that formerly known as the Tributary Mahāls or Garhjāts, consisting of 17 States, which, since the conquest of Orissa, have been attached to the Orissa Division and whose dealings have always been with the Commissioner of Orissa at Cuttack: two of these States, Baud and Athmallik, however, for a time formed part of the South-West Frontier Agency with headquarters at Rānchī, but subsequently, on 11th April 1837, were handed over to Orissa. In October 1905, the five Oriyā-speaking States of Patnā, Kālāhandī, Sonpur, Bāmra and Rairākhol were transferred to the Orissa Division, from the Central Provinces and at the same time the two States of Gāngpur and Bonai from the Chotā Nāgpur Division. The States thus incorporated in the Division of Orissa now number twenty-four, and all the Oriyā-speaking States are now in one Division. Simultaneously with this amalgamation of the Oriyā States a Political Agent was appointed to assist the Chiefs. The amalgamated group of States are now known as the Feudatory States of Orissa. FORMATION OF THE STATES.

ARCHÆOLOGY. The States are by no means rich in archæological remains. The aboriginal tribes, who were the first occupants of the soil, and who are still found in considerable numbers, and the Aryan settlers who founded the various principalities, were too occupied in keeping order within and repelling the attacks of neighbours, to be able to devote much time to architecture. Owing to the precarious nature of their environments and the necessity of shifting their residences from place to place, no Chief ever thought of building a permanent dwelling-house, and till lately their palaces were mere wooden structures nestling invariably under a hill where refuge was sought when hard pressed below. There was a general absence also of stone temples upon which the Hindu sovereigns of Orissa lavished so much of their revenues. Fetichism was the earliest form of worship in the Garhjāts, and stones and trees dyed with vermilion constituted the main objects of adoration. They survive to this day as village gods and are propitiated by Aryans and non-Aryans alike, while in those tracts like the Bhuiyā *pīrs* in Keonjhar and the Khondmāls, where the aboriginal races preponderate, hardly any other objects of worship are ever met with. In Keonjhar, a Khond priest is still permitted as a relic of the past to perform rites to a rough hewn stone inside the Chief's house, although the ruling family has long since been converted to Vaishnavism. Very little trace of Buddhism has been found in the States. In Dhenkānāl and Barāmbā there are a few families of Saraks who are weavers by profession and who follow a religion which strongly resembles Buddhism. But tradition relates that the name of Baud, the most westerly State in the Mahānadī valley, was derived from some early settlers who professed the Buddhistic faith. It is possible that the Buddhist Javanas in their flight to Central India halted in Baud, as its open fertile country watered by the great river and its tributaries and separated from the coast by miles of rugged hills would naturally afford the first resting place to the fugitives. Several images of Buddha have also been found in different parts of this State.

Of Saivism, the next phase of religious belief in Orissa, there is ample evidence all throughout the Garhjāts. There is no village of any pretensions, no island rock, no site marked by natural beauty or having a commanding position, especially along the courses of the chief rivers, which does not boast of a shrine containing the mystic symbol of the all-destroyer.

Originally the temples like the houses of the Chiefs were mere mud huts, though some of them were subsequently replaced by more substantial buildings made of stone, and in a very few cases of burnt bricks. As in Bhubaneswar, the chief centre of Saivism in Orissa, the officiating priests are non-Brāhmans and belong to the Māli caste which is believed to be of non-Aryan origin. The priests of the village gods and deities are invariably of an aboriginal race: they carry on their worship to the sylvan gods side by side with the orthodox Hindu worship in the village. One of the most important functions of these priests is to know and guard the village boundaries and they are also supposed to possess the power of exorcism and by spell and hypnotism (*guni*) to throw their victims into a trance and elicit the desired information from them. From these facts and from the presence of Sāsani Brāhmans in all the States, who without exception still profess Saivism, it may be inferred that it was during the time of the Lion dynasty (474—1132 A.D) that the Aryan colonization of the Garhjāts occurred. The family annals of the Chiefs also point to the same conclusion. The oldest remains thus date back no earlier than the Saivic era.

The remains at Khiching are of considerable magnitude and consist of statues, pillars, mounds and ruins of several temples of stone and of bricks. The bricks measure 12 inches by 9 inches by 3 inches. The main group is thus described by Mr. Beglar:—

"But the great group near the village is one of the greatest interest and antiquity. One of the temples here faces south-east and is Saivic, enshrining his emblem, it is in the Barākar style, but the lower part of the tower is sculptured, while the upper part is quite plain, showing that at some period subsequent to its erection, it had been repaired. For reasons detailed in my report for season 1872-73, I ascribe the repairs to Rājā Mān Singh's time. Another of the temples is an unfinished one: it is roofed in the overlapping octagonal style, a style from which I infer the date of its erection to have been the 16th century, or Rājā Mān Singh's time, and I have no doubt the builder of this was also the repairer of the last one. Rājā Mān Singh is the only prominent figure in the local history of the district to whom I can reasonably attribute its erection. From an examination of the upper part of this unfinished temple, it is clear that each course of stone as laid down was then and there cut and smoothed *in situ*, that is, after being placed in the position it occupies; the stones for the outer facing of the various courses were left somewhat larger than needed to allow of the final cutting and trimming *in situ*."

Of the Baud temples, he says:—"Going now northwards through the unrivalled scenery of the Karmingiā Ghāt and the Khond country, we arrive at Baud, on the south bank of the Mahānadī, here are a number of small but exquisitely finished temples, the existing ones are all in one group within an inclosure. Contrary to the usual bigoted habits of the Oriyā Brāhmans, access to the courtyard of the temple is not denied. The principal shrine is a comparatively modern erection, well plastered over, consisting of a sanctum, a Mahāmandapa and a portico, in short it is a complete temple and possibly is only an ancient one repaired; it is dedicated to Rāmeswara, faces east, and is surrounded by no less than nine small shrines, all in decay and all of about the same age.

"Besides this great shrine, there are three smaller isolated temples, which have not been covered with plaster or repaired and which, therefore, now stand with all the beauty of their elaborate carving; so hard and durable is the stone, that the carvings appear nearly as sharp as the day they were executed, the colour too, a deep purplish red, adds in no small degree to the beauty. Each of these temples stands by itself on a raised platform, and each consists of a cell and its attached portico only. * * * * * but I cannot do justice to the elaborate carving which literally covers the temple from crown to base without the aid of the photographs of the temple. One faces west and two face east; they have all a group of the Nabagrahas over the entrance and as they are considered subordinate in sanctity to the great temple of Rāmeswara, I was allowed to approach and take a plan of one of them. These temples are planned on the principle of intersecting squares laid down by Fergusson as the most common type of the plan of mediæval temples in India. Really this form of intersecting squares is very rare, as may be seen on comparison of such plans as had yet been obtained, they are certainly extremely beautiful, and though small, they are gems of art in their own humble way. I cannot assign to them any great age, the ninth century is the earliest which may safely be assigned to them, and when we remember that most of the temples of Orissa (some of them inscribed and, therefore, not uncertain in date) are of this period and show a remarkable predilection for the Nabagraha, I think there will be no reasonable doubt in assigning this to that period also, an age not inconsistent with the elaborate and profuse minute ornamentation bestowed on them, or the general outline and disposition of the plan and facade."

Of later discoveries there was one of much importance made by Mr. K. G. Gupta (the then Commissioner of Orissa) in Narsinghpur in February 1902. There is a picturesque hillock named Bāneshwar-nāsī in the bed of the Mahānadī about 10 miles to the south-east of the headquarters of the State. Amidst the ruins of a brick temple on a ledge on the east face of the rock, several feet from the foot of the hill was found a sculpture half buried in the ground. It is carved on a slab of hard red sandstone 5′ 2″ long and 2′ 6″ broad, and consists of a central female figure, most exquisitely finished and one of the finest specimens of the kind to be met with in Orissa. But the point of most interest is, that while the main figure is obviously that of a Hindu deity, probably Lakshmī or goddess of fortune, it is surmounted by five small images of Buddha, symmetrically arranged, two above each shoulder and the fifth just over the head. Two small female figures, wearing what looks very much like boots, crown the top corners and are meant to represent the Buddhistic symbol of Swastika. The main figure has large meditative eyes so characteristic of Buddhistic images. The work evidently belongs to the transition period when Hinduism was regaining ascendancy, and Buddhism, though on the wane, had not altogether lost its influence. But judging by its perfect style, it must have been executed when stone sculpture had attained its greatest development in Orissa, which certainly was not the case earlier than the 9th century, if not later. The revival of Hinduism is contemporaneous with the establishment of the Lion line in 474 A.D. It is, therefore, certain that Buddhism lingered on in Orissa for several centuries after it had ceased to be the dominant religion. A little higher up on the same hill are the remains of a stone Saiva temple, the lower portions of the walls of which are still standing. There is a fine chlorite lingam inside, which is still worshipped, and another small lingam, also of chlorite, a little to the west. A figure in many respects similar to the one already described, also carved on a slab of red sandstone, rests against the broken north wall of the temple. There are, however, no figures of Buddha, nor any symbol of his faith. The villagers apparently worship it, and it is painted over with oil and vermilion.

In the adjoining State of Barāmbā, in a romantic islet in the bed of the Mahānadī, about three miles to the south-east of the headquarters of the State, there stands an old temple dedicated to Sinhanāth, a name of Siva. It has the four main divisions, viz., sanctuary, *jagamohana*, *nātmandir* and *bhogamandapa* and is surrounded by a cluster of smaller shrines. The sanctuary is elaborately carved outside, but being thickly plastered over at a later date, the figures are only visible where the plaster has fallen off. The stone used is the soft red sandstone which is so largely in evidence at Bhubaneswar and the carvings are gradually wearing off. Vaishnavism, which in its present form spread in Orissa with the advent of the Gangetic dynasty in the 12th century and is the prevailing religion to this day, cannot obviously boast of any remains of antiquarian interest. The principal village of each State has one or more stone temples dedicated to Vishnu in his popular form of Jagannāth and his two companions, Balabhadra and Subhadrā, but the buildings are all recent and the sculptures, wherever they exist, partake of the grosser degeneracy of later times.

Relics of an older civilisation are found in the site of the Sonpur town in the State of that name. Tradition is that about 1,000 years ago the town of Sonpur was a place of considerable size and importance, consisting of over 50,000 houses. The tradition is supported by the discovery, on the site of the present town, and within a distance of two or three miles, of relics of old masonry houses, temples, images, ornaments, gold coins and the old-fashioned wells, known as *nanda* and built by that sect of Brāhmans with big tiles: copperplate inscriptions of grants to Brāhmans (*tambā sāsan*) have also been found in this State; the inscriptions are in Sanskrit written in the Kutila character: these probably belong to the era of the Gupta Rājās of Orissa. In the State of Patnā five copperplate inscriptions of considerable interest have also been found: they are in the Kutila form of the Nāgari character and the language is Sanskrit. These were charters granted by the Somavansī Kings and with five other similar charters found near Cuttack are the only records possessed of this dynasty. The charters are land grants in the different districts of Kosala country, identifiable with the south-eastern parts of the Central Provinces. From the charters it would appear that this dynasty held sway on the banks of the Tel and Ang rivers and that the Patnā State formed part of their kingdom. A detailed account of these charters will be found in Volume I, 1905, of *The Journal of the Asiatic Society of Bengal.*

CHAPTER III.

THE PEOPLE.

In 1860-62 an estimate was prepared by the Topographical Survey of the number of villages in the States of Orissa and Chotā Nāgpur and a calculation of five and a half persons to each house was taken as representing the population: a similar calculation was made in 1863 for the five States recently transferred from the Central Provinces to the Orissa Division. The first enumeration of the population of the States was taken in 1872: this census disclosed a total population of 1,631,273 with an average density of 58 persons to the square mile: in 1881 the population had increased by 41 per cent. amounting to 2,302,422, the pressure of the population on the soil being 82 persons to the square mile. In 1891 the results of the census disclosed a population of 2,898,709 or 26 per cent. increase over the recorded population in 1881, and the average density had increased to 103 persons per square mile. In the last census of 1901 the total population was returned at 3,173,395 or an increase of 9·5 per cent. since 1891, and the average density was 113 persons to the square mile. According to these statistics the population has increased by 1,542,122 since 1872 or an increase of 94 per cent. The earlier enumerations were no doubt defective, and the large increases shown by each successive census are due in a great measure to improvements in the arrangements for counting the people. At the same time there has undoubtedly been a considerable growth in the population. There is ample room for expansion and the people are hardy and prolific. There has undoubtedly been a large extension of cultivation since 1901 due to the great improvements in communications, light rents and the large profits to be made by agriculturists who are now, owing to the advent of the Bengal-Nāgpur Railway through Gāngpur and Bāmra and the East Coast Section of the same railway, enabled to obtain a highly profitable market for their produce.

GROWTH OF POPULATION.

Census of 1881. The census of 1881 showed that the population of the State of Patnā had increased by 162 per cent. since 1872 and that of Kālāhandī, Bāmra, Nīlgiri, Athmallik, Mayūrbhanj and Gāngpur by 68·2, 51·6, 50·2, 49·8, 49·1 and 46·6 per cent. respectively: in the States of Bonai, Pāl Laharā and Tālcher there was a slight decrease.

Census of 1891. Of the total increase shown by this enumeration since 1881 the States of Gāngpur, Kālāhandī, Mayūrbhanj and Patnā accounted for more than half or 69 per cent.: the increase being Gāngpur 14 per cent., Kālāhandī 18 per cent., Mayūrbhanj 25 per cent. and Patnā 12 per cent. The State of Khandparā showed a slight decrease.

Census of 1901. In the year 1900 there occurred disastrous floods of the Mahānadī and Brāhmanī and famine in the States of Baud, Patnā and Sonpur. There was nevertheless a substantial increase in the population in spite of a loss of 1·4 per cent. in Baud, 16·4 per cent. in Patnā and 13 per cent. in Sonpur. Of the net increase the States of Dhenkānāl, Gāngpur, Kālāhandī, Keonjhar, Mayūrbhanj and Nayāgarh account for 89·5 per cent.: the respective increases were Dhenkānāl 12·89 per cent., Gāngpur 17·28 per cent., Kālāhandī 8·82 per cent., Keonjhar 13·10 per cent., Mayūrbhanj 28·45 per cent. and Nayāgarh 8·34 per cent. The greatest increase in the decade ending in 1901 took place in the sparsely inhabited States of Rairākhol and Athmallik, the latter of which gained by immigration from Baud and the Central Provinces: the gain in Gāngpur and Hindol was due to new settlers. The comparatively slow rate of increase in Tigiriā and Khandparā is explained by the fact that the population of these States is already denser than it is elsewhere. The only States which suffered a loss of population were Baud, Patnā and Sonpur as noted above: the State of Baud suffered much from epidemic disease and general unhealthiness, and many of the restless Khond inhabitants emigrated during the scarcity of 1900. In Patnā and Sonpur there was famine in the same year. As a general rule, the growth of the population has been greatest along the borders of the British districts of Cuttack, Balasore and Purī, where the country is comparatively level, and the proportion of arable land relatively high. The volume of immigration is very considerable, and the census of 1901 showed for the group of 17 States, formerly known as the Tributary Mahāls of Orissa, a net gain of 61,000 persons from contiguous territory in Bengal and 7,000 from the Central Provinces. The total population according to the census of 1901 was 3,173,395.

The table below illustrates the salient features of the census of 1901:—

Name of State.		Area in square miles.	Number of Towns.	Number of Villages.	Population.	Population per square mile.	Percentage of variation in population between 1891 and 1901.	Number of persons able to read and write.	Percentage of persons able to read and write on the total population of each State.
Athgarh	...	168	...	192	43,784	260	+19·6	2,100	4·8
Athmallik	...	730	...	460	40,753	56	+28·9	558	1·4
Bāmra	...	1,988	1	931	123,378	62	+18·2	5,011	4·06
Barāmbā	...	134	...	181	38,260	285	+17·6	1,675	4·4
Baud	...	1,264	...	1,070	88,250	70	— 1·4	1,474	1·7
Bonai	...	1,296	...	217	38,277	30	+19·1	373	0·97
Daspallā	...	568	...	485	51,987	92	+14·0	876	1·7
Dhenkānāl	...	1,463	2	968	273,662	187	+14·8	9,392	3·4
Gāngpur	...	2,492	...	806	238,896	96	+24·8	3,158	1·3
Hindol	...	312	...	234	47,180	151	+24·2	1,668	3·5
Kālāhandi	...	3,745	...	2,198	350,529	94	+ 7·4	6,129	1·7
Keonjhar	...	3,096	...	1,938	285,758	92	+15·2	7,348	2·6
Khandparā	...	244	...	325	69,450	284	+ 9·7	1,391	2·0
Mayūrbhanj	...	4,243	1	3,593	610,383	144	+14·7	13,115	2·1
Narsinghpur	...	199	...	198	39,613	199	+17·0	3,309	8·4
Nayāgarh	...	588	...	775	140,779	239	+19·4	12,013	8·5
Nīlgiri	...	278	...	466	66,460	239	+18·3	3,660	5·5
Pāl Laharā	...	452	...	265	22,351	49	+13·5	518	2·3
Pātnā	...	2,399	...	1,850	277,748	116	—16·4	5,142	1·9
Rairākhol	...	833	...	319	26,888	32	+32·2	281	1·05
Ranpur	...	203	...	261	46,075	227	+14·9	3,101	6·7
Sonpur	...	906	1	899	169,877	188	—13·0	1,758	1·03
Tālcher	...	399	...	293	60,432	151	+14·7	1,275	2·1
Tigiriā	...	46	...	102	22,625	492	+10·1	1,105	4·9
Total	...	28,046	5	19,026	3,173,395	113	+ 9·5	86,430	2·7

Population engaged in, and dependent upon, agriculture.

The population of the States is almost wholly agricultural. Out of a total of 3,173,395 (1901), no less than 2,216,498 or over two-thirds subsist on agriculture, viz.:—

Rent-receivers (including dependents)	...	77,848
Rent-payers	...	1,792,354
Agricultural labourers ...	...	346,296
Total	...	2,216,498

Of the remaining one-third, a very appreciable proportion, consisting of potters, barbers, washermen, blacksmiths and other village servants, who are usually paid in kind by their rural employers, also makes its living from the land.

General Characteristics. Density.

The average density of the population in 1901 was 113 persons to the square mile, the pressure of the population on the soil having nearly doubled since 1872, when there were only 58 persons to the square mile. The density per square mile is as high as 492 in Tigiriā, 285 in Barāmbā, 284 in Khandparā, 260 in Athgarh, 239 both in Nayāgarh and Nīlgiri and 227 in Ranpur. The high density in Tigiriā is due to the fact that the soil is very fertile, there is easy and cheap means of transport for surplus produce to Cuttack, the climate is healthy and rents are exceptionally low. In Khandparā there is the populous trading centre of Kantilo and the soil is fertile and communication with Cuttack is easy and cheap. In Nayāgarh, Nīlgiri and Ranpur there are large tracts of good lands, and these three States have ready communication with the railway line, and in consequence all these States are important exporting tracts. The density per square mile is as low as 30 in Bonai, 32 in Rairākhol, 44 in Pāl Laharā and 56 in Athmallik: the sparse population in these States is due to their isolated position and the vast hill ranges which occupy a large proportion of their areas.

Towns and villages. There are 5 towns in the States, namely, Sonpur (8,887), Bhuban (6,788), Deogarh (5,702), Bāripadā (5,613) and Dhenkānāl (5,609) with a population exceeding 5,000 each: besides these towns the population of Keonjhargarh, the headquarters of the Keonjhar State, amounts to 4,532 and that of Kantilo in the Khandparā State, 4,719: the population of Bhawānīpatnā, the headquarters of the Kālāhandī State, is 4,400 and that of Ranpur, the headquarters of the Ranpur State, 4,172: Bolāngir, the headquarters of the Patnā State, has a population of 3,706 and Binkā, in the Sonpur State, 3,843. Khandparā, the headquarters of the State of that name, has a population of 3,944 and Tālcher, the headquarters of the State of that name, 3,930. The total population of the 5 towns noted above is 32,599 or 1·03 per cent. of the total population of the States: the total population of the 5 towns and that of the eight large villages noted amounts to 65,845 or 2·7 per cent. of the total population of the States. The remainder of the population is clustered together in 19,018 villages. The people have developed no tendency to collect into cities: they appear to have an inherent aversion to town life. On the average there is one village per square mile and-a-half and the average population of each village is 165.

Races. The majority of the population of the States is Oriyā. There is a small sprinkling of Hindustānis who have settled down as traders or their agents: the majority of these are found in Gāngpur. There are a few Bengalis, but they only form 2·09 per cent. of the population. The States still form the refuge of large numbers of aboriginal and semi-aboriginal races, such as the Bhuiyās (91,581), Binjhāls (12,834), Bhumijes (68,118), Gonds (149,119), Hos (108,872), Juāngs (11,159), Khariās (38,478), Khonds (223,424), Korās (4,008), Oraons (51,185), Santāls (194,911), Savars (39,849) and Sudhas (27,324). In the five Sambalpur States there is a small number of Telugus, mostly in the Kālāhandī State, whither they have immigrated for trade from the districts of Madras. Some of the aboriginal tribes are impulsive and excitable, and there have been several instances of *melis* or risings, the most notable of which are the Bhuiyā rebellions of 1862 and 1892 in Keonjhar, and the Khond rebellions in Nayāgarh in 1894 and in Kālāhandī in 1878 and 1881-82. The news of an intended rising is circulated by means of a consecrated knot or *ganthi*, which is quickly passed on from village to village.

CHARACTER OF THE PEOPLE. The people are, on the whole, truthful, peaceable and law-abiding, the only exception being the Pāns, Doms and Gandās, who being for the most part landless and indolent, live from hand to mouth and furnish the larger proportion of the jail population. A not uncommon form of murder is that committed from dread of sorcerers: the belief in witchcraft is strong, especially amongst the Mundās in the Gāngpur and Bonai States, where murder of some unfortunate old woman, who is believed by the parents to have cast an evil eye on their child, is not an unknown occurrence. It is a common custom where affairs go persistently badly with a family or a village to call in a wizard or sorcerer, known as *guniā* or *rāudiyā*, usually one of the village priests, as an exorcist or to indicate the source of trouble in a family or village where affairs are not prospering, or to point out the person who has cast an evil spell: the wizard arrives and stays sometimes in the family or village and finally indicates the source of the trouble: this has been known to result in the person indicated as the source of the trouble taking the life of the head of the family or the headman of the village who called in the sorcerer and sometimes also his own life.

LANGUAGE. The language spoken throughout the States is Oriyā and is the mother tongue of 78·2 per cent. of the population. Mundāri dialects are spoken by 12·00 per cent., including Santāli (nearly 6·08 per cent.), Ho (3·25 per cent.), Bhumij (1·69 per cent.), and Juāng (0·34 per cent.); Khond 2·20 per cent., and Khariā 0·71 per cent. Mundāri and Ho are spoken chiefly in the country bordering on the Singhbhūm district, *i.e.*, in the Nāgrā zamīndāri of the State of Gāngpur and in the States of Bonai and Keonjhar. The Mundās and Hos, however, understand Oriyā and Hindī and in their dealings with the State officials generally prefer to speak in Hindī. The Santāls are mostly found in Mayūrbhanj, where they number 185,149. The great majority of the Khonds speak Oriyā and have forgotten to a very large degree their own tongue; these are the Khonds who have adopted Hindu customs, taken to regular cultivation in the more open country and become semi-Hinduised. The Khond language is practically only universal in the hill tracts of the Kālāhandī State and is spoken by about 45,000 Khonds or 20·1 per cent. of the total Khond population: the hill Khonds, however, all understand and can speak Oriyā and this is the language employed by them in their dealings with the State officials. Literature there is none.

Literature.

RELIGION. The vast majority of the population are Hindus who number 2,774,929 or 86·9 per cent. of the total population. Musalmāns number only 11,553 or 0·36 per cent. of the total population. Animists number 383,171 or 12·07 per cent. of the total population and Christians number 2,962 or 0·09 per cent. A few Buddhists are still found in the Barāmbā State and are apparently a survival of the days when Buddhism reigned in Orissa. Traces of Buddhism are also met with in the State of Baud, and at the village of Baud there are some very ancient temples apparently of Buddhist origin. The total number of Buddhists amounted in 1901 to 717. Though the Hindus apparently so largely predominate, it must be remembered that a very large number are really only semi-Hinduised aborigines: for example large numbers of the Khonds and Bhuiyās have adopted Hindu customs and worship Hindu gods, claiming to be orthodox Hindus, whilst at the same time they quietly worship their own tribal gods and sylvan deities. The Doms, Dumāls, Gandās, Ghāsiās and Pāns are scarcely genuine Hindus and the higher castes of Hindus in the States do not classify them as Hindus, despite their pretensions to be so. The table below illustrates the religious divisions of the people among the individual States:—

Serial No.	STATE.	RELIGION.				
		Hindus.	Animists.	Musalmāns.	Christians.	Others.
1	Athgarh	43,141	...	261	382	...
2	Athmallik	40,647	22	81	...	3
3	Bāmra	120,992	2,025	347	14	...
4	Barāmbā	37,441	...	116	...	703
5	Baud	87,988	83	176	3	...
6	Bonai	26,371	11,745	69	92	...
7	Daspallā	51,903	...	81	3	...
8	Dhenkānal	265,750	7,132	749	18	13
9	Gāngpur	146,549	88,949	1,640	1,758	...
10	Hindol	46,984	...	196	...	...
11	Kālāhandi	279,656	70,356	504	2	11
12	Keonjhar	246,585	38,567	699	3	4
13	Khandparā	69,429	...	21	...	...
14	Mayūrbhanj	507,738	98,485	3,785	368	7
15	Narsinghpur	39,455	...	155	3	...
16	Nayāgarh	133,995	6,190	585	9	...
17	Nīlgiri	58,895	7,302	101	161	...
18	Pāl Laharā	20,770	1,540	41	...	...
19	Patnā	229,095	47,967	513	142	32
20	Rairākhol	24,364	2,425	92	...	7
21	Ranpur	45,762	...	313	...	...
22	Sonpur	168,981	383	509	4	...
23	Tālcher	60,253	...	179	...	...
24	Tigiriā	22,184	...	441	...	...
	Total ...	2,774,920	383,171	11,553	2,962	780

Amongst the large body of semi-Hinduised races found in the States the worship of the Hindu gods proceeds side by side with that of the original gods of these races and the blending of Hinduism and Animism is clearly observable. In such villages there is almost invariably a village priest, in addition to the Hindu priest ; this village priest is a member of an indigenous or aboriginal race and is known by various terms such as *deori*, *kālu*, *jhānkar*, etc.: his duties are to appease the powers of evil and the sylvan deities of the tribe with sacrifices of goats and cocks and to guard the village boundaries. No expedition to the forest to hunt and drive for game is undertaken until the village priest has worshipped the village deities, which are represented by a log of wood or a stone smeared with vermilion and usually located in a dense grove or thicket. On the appearance of small-pox the village priest appeases the village deities; the earthen pots and pans of families who have been attacked by the disease are placed on the village boundary on the path leading to the next village and stacked there in broken heaps ; the belief being that thus the evil spirit of the disease is driven out ; these heaps of broken pots serve to warn travellers that there is small-pox in the village. Similarly it is not uncommon to find cairns of stones along the side of a road or path erected at places where the boundary of a village ends; the idea is that the traveller by placing the stone on the heap obtains absolution for any error or any omission he may have unwittingly committed within the boundaries of the village he has just left. Various are the customs observed. Amongst these may be noticed the custom observed in the Bāmra State by the growers of the tusser cocoon during the period of cultivation. They are on no account permitted to tell the truth : they may not eat during daylight nor may they set their eyes upon their wives : they also seek to propitiate heaven by putting in circulation injunctions to piety written on palm leaves. The circulation of these tracts is induced by the threat which they always wind up with that the village which fails to pass it on will be guilty of killing 10 Brāhmans and 50 cows.

Christians.

The census of 1901 returned 2,962 Christians in the States. The settlements are scattered throughout the States, the principal centres are in the States of Athgarh, Gāngpur, Mayūrbhanj, Nīlgiri and Patnā and accounts of these missions will be found in the separate articles on those States.

PRINCIPAL CASTES.

There are 30 castes and tribes in the States with a numerical strength exceeding 25,000 ; the total number of these castes and tribes amounts to 2,629,227 or 82·9 per cent. of the total population. The most prominent of these castes and tribes are Chasās

(240,439), Santāls (194,911), Pāns, Doms and Gandās (183,146, 73,920 and 85,241 respectively or 342,307 in all), Gauras (304,230), Hos (108,872), Khandaits (88,313), Brāhmans (102,976), Khonds (223,424), Bhumijes (68,118), Bāthudis (43,726), Bhuiyās (91,581), Kurmīs (57,473), Telis (78,733), Sahars (40,719), Gonds (149,119), Kewats (63,335), Kumhārs (44,518), Oraons (51,185) and Savars (39,849). The Hindus number 2,774,929 persons or 86·9 per cent. of the total population and Animists 383,171 or 12·07 per cent. The so-called Hindus include a large number of aboriginal and semi-aboriginal tribes. These are mostly met with in the mountainous jungle tracts of Baud, Bonai, Kālāhandī, Keonjhar, Mayūrbhanj and Pāl Laharā. The majority are of Dravidian stock and include the Bhuiyās, Bhumijes, Hos, Khonds, Pāns and Gandās, Santāls and Savars. The Bāthudis and Sahars are of uncertain origin. The Chasās, Gauras, Khandaits and Kurmīs are apparently derived from various elements and seem to be mainly non-Aryan. As regards these castes or tribes, an account of the Khandaits, Brāhmans, Gauras, Pāns, and Telis will be found in the Gazetteer of the Balasore district and the account there given applies equally to these castes in the States. The Bhuiyās and Khonds reside in more States than one and in addition to the account given of them in the articles on the Bonai and Kālāhandī States they are deserving of special mention from the position and influence they occupy and the large tract of country over which they spread.

Bānka. A small caste found principally in the Kālāhandī State and in 1901 numbering 4,261. The caste was formed from military service like the Khandaits, Paiks and Marāthās and some families bear the names of different castes, as Brāhman Bānka, Kumhār Bānka, and so on. They were formerly notorious free-booters but have now settled down to cultivation. Each man, however, still carries a sword or knife on his person and in Kālāhandī they are permitted to do this without taking out a license.

Bhuiyās.* The Bhuiyās rank fourth amongst the wild tribes of the States and numbered in the 24 States 91,581 according to the census of 1901. The members of this tribe are scattered over a large tract of country and are found in the following States:—Mayūrbhanj (31,753), Gāngpur (23,595), Keonjhar (20,465), Bonai (6,428), Bāmra (6,067), Pāl Laharā (1,869), Ranpur (420), Baud (282), Kālāhandī (256), Nīlgiri (201), Dhenkānāl (119), with a few

* This account of the Bhuiyās is taken from Colonel Dalton's Ethnology of Bengal and from the article on the Bhuiyās by Mr. D. A. Macmillan, Superintendent, Keonjhar State, and published in the *Calcutta Review*, Number CCV, July 1896.

families in the States of Tālcher, Khandparā, Rairākhol, Sonpur, Patnā, Athmallik and Nayāgarh. The home of the Bhuiyās is in the wild highlands of the inaccessible hill ranges of Bonai, Pāl Laharā and Keonjhar: this wild region the Bhuiyās have from time immemorial made their abode. The south-west border of Singhbhūm forms the northern boundary of this tract, the States of Pāl Laharā, Tālcher and Dhenkānāl the southern boundary, the States of Bonai and Bāmra the western boundary and the mountain area of Keonjhar the eastern boundary, the total area being about 1,600 square miles; of this area 250 square miles in the Keonjhar State represents the original seat of the Bhuiyās, but the pressure of population has caused the tribe to spread out its branches over a far wider tract. Keonjhar, however, has always been the stronghold of the Bhuiyās, and in this State they are undoubtedly the dominant race. They claim to be the children of the soil (*bhui*, earth) and to possess full proprietary rights over the soil in the same manner as other aboriginal tribes always term themselves zamīndārs. Though the Hindu population in Keonjhar far outnumbers that of the Bhuiyās, yet the claim of the hill (Pahāriā or Pauri) Bhuiyās to be the dominant race is admitted without question even by the Brāhmans and Rājputs. In Keonjhar they claim the indefeasible right to install the Chief on his *gadi* and in Bonai this right is similarly claimed by the Sāonts, a thoroughly Hinduized portion of the clan. There are two broad distinctions between the members of the clan, viz., the Bhuiyās of the hills and the Bhuiyās of the plains: the latter form the feudal militia of the State and hold their lands on service tenure and are supposed to be prepared to take up arms for their Chief whenever required, though they are equally prepared to turn their arms against an unpopular Chief. The true hill (Pahāriā or Pauri) Bhuiyās are not however bound to fight for their Chief, though they are perfectly prepared to take up arms against him: the duty of the hill Bhuiyās is to attend the Chief on his journeys and act as transport. In Keonjhar the hill Bhuiyās wield an extraordinary power and are capable at any moment of setting the country in a blaze of insurrection and revolt; the news that the hill Bhuiyās are up in arms spreading consternation throughout the country: on such an occasion the country is controlled by an oligarchy of the 60 chiefs of the hill Bhuiyās. Such outbreaks have not been uncommon and an account of them will be found in the article on the Keonjhar State.

Tribal divisions.

The Bhuiyās have divided themselves into different septs, with distinct customs varying in accordance with the degree in which they have come in contact with their Hindu neighbours. There are, however, four principal clans : the Māl or Desh Bhuiyās (*i.e.*, Bhuiyās of the country) who claim to be the superior clan and have preserved all the characteristics of a wild tribe : the Rājkuli Bhuiyās who are alleged to be the descendants of the Rāj family from a Bhuiyā concubine : the term *kuli*, *i.e.*, family, signifying royal birth or family : the next two clans are the Rāutāli and Pabana-ansha, who are smaller in number than the first two clans, having taken to regular cultivation and adopted many Hindu customs and are generally more enlightened and advanced than their wilder brethren of the hills. Amongst the Desh Bhuiyās the superior tribe is the true hill Bhuiyā (Pahāriā or Pauri) and their emblem is the *bāngi* (pole on which they carry goods); the emblem of the other clans is the *kānda*. The Desh Bhuiyās inhabit all the mountain tracts and the Rājkuli, Rāutāli and Pabana-ansha Bhuiyās are found on the slopes and foot of the hills. The Pahāriā Bhuiyās claim to have nurtured and established on the *gadi* of the Keonjhar State the young boy, who was stolen from the Mayūrbhanj family, when Keonjhar was separated from Mayūrbhanj and made into a separate State.

According to tradition it was the Bhuiyās who effected the separation of the two States. The perils and hardships of the journey from the remote hill fastnesses of their home to pay their homage and tribute to the ruling Chief of Mayūrbhanj led the Bhuiyās to the determination to install a Chief of their own. In accordance with this plan they stole one of the young sons of the Chief of the Mayūrbhanj State, being probably assisted in this design by intrigues within the Chief's family. They were successful in their attempt, and bringing the young boy to their mountain fastnesses, reared him with the greatest tenderness and care : Goālās (milkmen) and other necessary castes were imported into the hills to administer to him, his meals were specially prepared and no Bhuiyā was allowed to touch his cooked-food, lest it should thereby be defiled, and as a further precaution, the *chatti* or earthen vessel, in which the food was prepared, was broken daily by a leading Bhuiyā with an arrow. This custom of breaking the earthen-pot in which food has been prepared survives to this day amongst the Bhuiyās. In their selection of a site for the residence (*garh*) of their Chief the Bhuiyās were guided by the sight of a dog vanquished by a hare in fight. Similar traditions concerning the selection of the site of a *garh* are common in the States of Orissa. The site so selected for the *garh* was at the foot of the range of hills forming the boundary of the Bhuiyā *pīrs* (tracts): it had the advantage of keeping the Chief readily accessible to themselves and placed him in their power, if occasion arose, and facilitated ready escape to the hills from attack by the Marāthās or other foes. The Bhuiyās provided the young Chief with concubines from their own clan and from these unions are said to have sprung the Rājkuli Bhuiyās already mentioned. The site then chosen by the Bhuiyās as the *garh* for their Chief has remained unchanged ever since and it is here that the Bhuiyās install each successive Chief, claiming that until the Chief has been actually invested by them, the installation is not complete. The installation of a Chief is the occasion for a mustering of the Bhuiyā clans in their strength, headed by the hereditary master of the ceremonies. The Bhuiyās march into the courtyard of the residence of the Chief to the crash of drums and wild fantastic airs, their leader carrying a pumpkin, as a token of submission or allegiance. After the company is seated the Chief enters the apartment prepared for the ceremony and distributing *pān*, confections, spices and garlands to the company, retires. Then to the clash of the musical instruments of the wild Bhuiyās, the Chief re-enters mounted on the back of a Bhuiyā leader, who plunging, snorting and neighing, embodies the war-steed of the Chief. Dismounting from his human steed the Chief is seated on the lap of a Bhuiyā leader. The attendant Bhuiyās then receive from the servants of the Chief imitations of the insignia of royalty—banners, *pankhās*, *chāmars*, *chhatras* and canopies, and the hereditary office-bearers range themselves round the Chief. The principal Bhuiyā leader then goes through a religious ceremony by binding round the turban of the Chief a light flexible forest creeper as the *siropā* or honorary head dress conferred by the Bhuiyās: the bands strike up, bards chant odes of praise and the Brāhmans recite the Sāma Veda and finally the principal leader of the Bhuiyās marks the forehead of the young Chief with sandal wood, thereby conveying the *tikā* or emblem of investiture. The Brāhmans and the *Bawārta* or prime minister, then in their turn mark the seal of the *tikā* with sandal wood. A sword is then placed in the hands of the Chief and one of the Bhuiyā leaders coming forward kneels before the Chief, who touches him on the neck with the sword: this ceremony is symbolical of actual human sacrifice in earlier days: the Bhuiyā leader who has thus been touched with the sword at once disappears and does not return for three days when he presents himself to the Chief as miraculously cured. The Bhuiyās then make offerings to the Chief of rice, pulse, *ghī* (clarified butter), milk and honey and their leaders then solemnly address the new Chief, impressing on him that in accordance with the authority exercised by them from time immemorial they have invested him as Chief to rule the State with justice and mercy. The Chief then withdraws mounted on his human steed. Soon afterwards or on a subsequent date the Bhuiyās return, and prostrating themselves before the Chief ask for forgiveness of former misdeeds. Their leader then addressing the Chief inquires after his health, his establishment, horses and elephants. In return the State *karan* (writer) reads from a palm-leaf document prescribed inquiries touching the health of the Bhuiyās, their families, cattle, hill streams and fields. The leaders thereupon prostrating themselves raise the left-foot of the Chief and place it alternately first on one shoulder and then on the other, then touching the Chief's foot with their forehead retire. This ceremony is annually repeated in the month of May, but the installation portion of the ceremony is omitted. The Bhuiyās desire in their Chief a leader to whom they can appeal and obtain advice and have no desire for independence: they claim, however, a prescriptive right to approve of or resent the administrative acts of the Chief whom they have themselves created; the periodical rebellions which have taken place have been due to dislike of the individual ruler by the Bhuiyā clans. This attitude was manifest in the rebellion of 1890-1893 when the Chief fled to Cuttack leaving his family in the *garh* which could easily have been taken by the Bhuiyās. The Bhuiyās, however, made no attack on the *garh* as they had no animosity against the family of the Chief, but only against the Chief himself, who had fled. The Bhuiyā *pīrs* (tracts) have always been the property of the Rānī of the State, and the Bhuiyās hold her in high veneration, styling her "the mother." In one of their rebellions the Bhuiyās entered the *garh* seeking for the *Bawārta* (prime minister), they found him in the Rānī's apartments, where he had fled for sanctuary: horrified at the sacrilege that he should have seen the face of their revered mother they put him to death.

Character. The chief traits in the character of the Bhuiyās are fidelity and hospitality. Like other wild and unsophisticated races they are frank, honest and imbued with a passionate love of liberty. The hospitality of the Bhuiyās has passed into an Oriyā proverb: every stranger is an honoured guest, as amongst the Khonds. Every stranger entering a village is offered to partake of food and is a guest as long as he remains. In every village there is a *darbār* or town hall, which is used as a sleeping place for the young men of the village and for a rest-house for travellers. If the guest who comes to the village is a personage of importance he is met by all the women: on his entry the women meet him carrying small stools and vessels of water, in which is a little turmeric: the water is sprinkled with *sâl* (*Shorea robusta*) leaves on his feet, and the stools are carried as emblematic of offering rest to the traveller. After sprinkling the feet of the visitor the chief old lady kneels down placing the palms of the hands on the ground as a salutation and is followed in turn by the senior maiden and the guest is then led to the guest-house. Drunkenness is prevalent amongst the males and no ceremony is considered complete without intoxication: drunkenness amongst men is no disgrace, but women refrain from the cup. The women are the workers, finding the daily food and performing all the household duties: the men occupy themselves in a leisurely manner with their cultivation and hunting. They are a courteous race: their form of salutation consisting of bending the lower part of the body, joining and raising the hands to the forehead with palms uppermost and pronouncing in a loud tone the word *salām*. The boast of the Bhuiyā is that he reveres his parents, is a man of one word and of one race, not divided as their Hindu neighbours are.

The Bhuiyas are of Turanian type, the face is round, lips full, foreheads narrow, high cheek bones and the broad nose of the Gond and Kol, their eyes are well set and intelligent and usually brown in colour, though clear grey eyes are not uncommon amongst them. In colouring they are tawny to light, of stature short, about five feet two inches, but well proportioned, with fine chests and muscular limbs, hands and feet well shaped, and the free and easy gait of a hillman. The men shave their hair on the forehead, wearing it in long well greased and combed locks at the back: a small red comb is almost invariably carried over the ear and when not otherwise occupied the young Bhuiyā dandy sets his locks in order. The clothing of the hillmen is usually very scanty, consisting merely of a small strip of cloth, called the *kopni* between the legs, fastened front and back to a string round the waist: the use of the *dhoti* is however becoming more common. The young and old men generally wear, when at work, their strips of raw hide wound round the waist to afford support in lifting and carrying burdens: from the string round the waist they usually hang a small pair of pliers to remove thorns from the feet, and a receptacle to carry *gānja* or tobacco, both articles being made of metal. They wear a row or two of beads or berries round the neck and a few for show adopt the Brahmanical thread. The

Appearance.

women wear a short coarse cotton *sārī* (cloth), but never use it to veil their faces: they tattoo their arms and shoulders, and wear ear and nose rings, large bunches of beads and occasionally brass necklaces, covering the bosom and extending to the loins: on their arms, legs and toes they wear bracelets, anklets and rings, their hair they invariably adorn with scented flowers and orchids, interweaving them with coloured cotton.

Social status. The Bhuiyās are not considered a low caste: the Hindus take water from them and their touch is no defilement.

Language. It does not appear that the Bhuiyās ever possessed a language of their own: they speak a dialect of Oriyā, which they have strangely distorted; their vocabulary is very limited and their conversation usually consists of exclamations and questions.

Customs and habits. The Bhuiyā as a rule marries outside the village, as he is generally connected with the villagers: the greatest care is taken not to contract a marriage, which can in any way be considered to be incestuous: there is no restriction on marriage within the same sept or phatry, rather the marriage relationship should be formed within it. The essential conditions are that both parties should have reached maturity and the choice is entirely a free selection, though parents sometimes advise in the matter. According to village custom the boys and girls frequently dance together of a night, when a young man is at liberty to seize the hand of the girl he has selected and escape with her for two or three days: but the escape is no secret, the parents of the bride go to the bridegroom's relations and fix the dowry. A man will also place a white flower in the hair of the maid he selects and if it be accepted the engagement is held to be binding and no other man may lay claim to the girl. Another form of betrothal is for the lover to walk off with the girl, who has consented to become his wife, from a bevy of maidens in the forest. The maidens then return to the village and reporting that a tiger has carried off one of their number urge the villagers to go in pursuit. A search party is then organised which after going to the spot returns to the house of the parents of the lover: with shouts they demand the blood of the lad who has carried off one of the village maids the parents urge that though an offence has been committed the union must be allowed: they offer to pay blood money and to stand a village feast and the wedding is then celebrated with song and festival.

There is another form of obtaining a bride, but it is only resorted to as a last resource. If a young man has set his heart on a maid and is unable to obtain her owing either to her own unwillingness or that of her relatives, he organises a band of companions and when opportunity offers carries her off, his companions guarding the flight. This method of obtaining a bride often leads to sanguinary conflicts in the attempt of the friends to prevent the capture. If the young man is successful in the capture his task is not at an end until the girl has been induced to take food in her future husband's home.

The customs described above are only the preliminaries and the marriage is not consummated till the *desh* has been feasted. The actual marriage ceremony is conducted entirely by the women and the village priest. The ceremony consists in sprinkling the couple with water and turmeric, the bride and bridegroom being arrayed in new garments for the occasion. The essential right in the ceremony is however that the couple take their seat together on a yoke, when the nearest male relative offers the bride a coin intimating that he has given her all his wealth and that he trusts she will benefit by it and be true to her husband. Their future home is blessed by the priest who places an inverted earthen pot, under which are supposed to be the spirits of their ancestors, whom the couple must daily worship. Dowries are settled on the bride and often amount to a considerable head of cattle.

Incompatibility is sufficient to dissolve the marriage tie and adultery acts as a divorce. If the adultery occurs with a Bhuiyā, the matter ends with the man marrying the woman, but if the man belongs to another caste, the woman is outcasted. Chastity is not regarded as a virtue, but in such cases the matter is dealt with by the village elders making the girl over to the man and enforcing a marriage. The marriage tie is however faithfully observed and divorce or adultery is but rarely heard of.

Customs at birth.

Ten days after the birth of a child a festival is held and the mother purified. Those of the Bhuiyās who have come in contact with Hindus have their heads shaved by the barber and their clothes washed: amongst the wilder Bhuiyās, however, one of their own villagers shaves their heads with a razor, locally made, but the clothes are not washed. If a mother dies before delivery the embryo is removed from the corpse, both being burnt on opposite banks of a stream: this rite is performed to prevent the dead woman from becoming a witch; the idea is that no spirit can cross a stream and the mother is unable to become a witch without union with her child. The ceremony of naming is very similar to that practised by the Mundās and Hos. The name of the grandfather is given to the eldest son, that of the great-grandfather to the second son, and then the names of collateral relatives according to seniority. After the birth and naming ceremonies there are no ceremonies till marriage.

Another not unusual method of naming a child is to give a name in accordance with some event happening on the day of the child's birth. Thus if a European happens to pass through the village on the day of a child's birth, the child will be christened *Sāheb* or *Gorā* : so too, if a Musalmān, a dealer, a peon or a constable, pass through the village the child is christened *Pathān*, *Mahājan*, *Chaprāssi* and *Sipāhi*. The anniversary of a festival will also give an opportunity for a name, such as *Soniā* (the first day of the Hindu new year) or *Raja* and *Dasharā*.

Customs at death. On death the body is quickly buried in the forest and ten days later a feast is given. The dead are always buried in a deep well, dug grave, usually by the side of a hill stream, as all streams lead to the holy Baitaranī. After the death ceremony the relatives gather and perform the ceremony of reconciling the deceased with the family ancestral god. The assembled relatives seat themselves in rows in the house and the nearest relative sacrifices a he-goat, spilling the blood at the foot of the inverted earthen pot in which the spirits of the ancestors are supposed to dwell. The ancestors are then besought to receive the deceased and water is sprinkled over the company. In the case of a child dying a fowl is sacrificed. This ceremony is performed in all cases except on that of the death of a pregnant woman or of a leper. On the death of a leading Bhuiyā chief the inhabitants of all the neighbouring villages are summoned to the burial : during the nine days, which, in this case alone, are allowed to lapse before the burial, the women keep up the funeral dirge : the corpse is buried on the tenth day and after the death feast the *desh* assemble and nominate a successor.

Arms. The arms of the Bhuiyā consist of the bow and two-handed axe. No Bhuiyā ever enters the forest without these weapons. The bow is made of the male bamboo and the bow string of a thin strip from the outside of the bamboo. The arrow has an iron head with long curving fangs, which render it almost impossible to withdraw the head without causing a terrible wound : for birds and small game an arrow with a cylindrical wooden head is used. They also use a curved sword, a sling, and round disc of iron, but the bow and axe are their general weapons. The iron disc is not unlike a quoit : it is about an eighth of an inch thick and three inches in diameter, the outer edge is very sharp : the method of using it is to whirl the disc on the index finger and let the disc fly : an expert will sever a *sāl* sapling two inches thick at a distance of 40 yards. The Bhuiyā carries no shield, but guards with the handle of his axe.

The villages of the Bhuiyās are picturesquely placed at the foot of well-wooded hills by the side of a hill stream. The village nestles in a fine grove of jack trees, to the fruit of which the Bhuiyā is particularly partial. There is one broad street with the houses on either side. The house of the headman and the village elders is in the centre of the street: on the outskirts live the low castes of Pāns and Kols, who perform all the menial tasks of the Bhuiyās. In close proximity to the headman's house is the *darbār* or *mandap* (drum) house, where the bachelors of the village sleep and the place in front is used as the village dancing ground. The *darbār* house is also the village guest-house, here are stored the provisions contributed by the villagers and made up into bundles ready for the immediate use of the guest. Every Bhuiyā tills his own land. During sowing and harvest time he rises before dawn and works till dusk without cessation, but when clearing forest he rests at midday and takes a meal: after his work he bathes, returns to a substantial meal and then goes to the dancing ground. The Bhuiyās construct no tank, holding it contrary to religion to excavate. The men and women always bathe at separate places and great care is exercised never to surprise a female bathing. In the larger villages schools have been established by the State, but the Bhuiyās look on them as useless encumbrances: if a parent be taken to task for the irregular attendance of his children he will, in perfect good faith, offer, in order to give satisfaction, to attend on their behalf. There is a village priest—the *deori*, and a *gharmangi* who is the representative of the maidens and settles love affairs and regulates the dancing. The village.

Amongst the Bhuiyās the family is supreme, and the social bond is not that of the village but of the household. Each sept consists of a number of families claiming a common ancestor. Sons have no property during the lifetime of their father and they and their wives share the father's meals, cooked by the common mother assisted by her daughters-in-law. The tribes form federal groups, with a chief in authority over each: succession to the chiefship depends on personal fitness; if the chief's eldest son be suitable he succeeds his father, otherwise he is tacitly ignored and the nearest suitable male relative is selected. The chiefship only carries with it the respect of the community—the leader is a first among equals—the seat of honour at public meetings, an occasional harvest offering of good-will and the best share of the chase. He cannot transact public affairs of importance without calling the assembly of elders. As regards theft the principle is restitution, but only for the first offence : for a second offence the culprit is outcasted. In cases of hurt caused in a squabble, the village council admonishes both parties, who then take a brand from a heap of lighted faggots, and as a sign of conciliation extinguish it by spitting on it. On the rare occasions when the State Courts punish an offender, the elders also deal with him, holding that the punishment by the State was for its own satisfaction only.

Revenue. Before the settlement made by Colonel (then Captain) Sir James Johnstone, Government Agent, after the rebellion in 1868 there appears to have been no fixed revenue levied from the Bhuiyās: a house-tax of four annas per house and eight annas per plough was then imposed. A school-fee of one anna per house was also imposed and the old duty of thatching certain State buildings and supplying transport for the Chief, when on tour, was also regulated and duly enforced. The next settlement was made by Mr. H. P. Wylly, Government Agent, after the rebellion of 1893 : the rates were fixed at thirteen annas per plough, six and a half annas per house and the school-tax was doubled : on those villages, which objected to the thatching duties, a further tax of three annas was levied : printed *pattās* or leases were given to the headmen. The village sites are changed about once in twenty years or sometimes less. The Bhuiyā cultivates by felling and burning the forest and on the clearings he grows cereals the first year, rice in the next and vegetables in the third year : the plot is then exhausted and a new area is cleared. When all the culturable area accessible is exhausted the village site is removed. In a few villages there are patches of wet cultivation carried on in a primitive method, but there are signs of a gradual increase in wet cultivation. No complicated land tenures exist : the right to the soil depends on priority of occupation by the village and within the village upon priority of occupation by the individual. No Bhuiyā will cultivate fallow land until he has ascertained from the council of the village that it is unappropriated. Land and agricultural stock always descend in the male line, daughters receiving the moveable property : the idea is that no one should possess land who cannot work it. This is the land revenue system amongst the Pahāriā (hill) Desh Bhuiyās, but the Desh Bhuiyās who have settled elsewhere in the State are amenable to the ordinary land revenue system of the State. All Bhuiyās, however, have to supply once every two years logs for the car festival and ropes made of forest creepers. The collections are made by giving an individual demand statement to the headman of each village: this demand the headman can check with his *pattā* and he then collects the dues paying them to the head of the *pīr* or tract, who in turn pays in his collections to the treasury. The appointments of headman (*sardār*) of the *pīr* and village headman (*pradhān*) are made by the State, due regard being paid to hereditary claims and the wishes of the people. The *sardār* and *pradhān* receive a strip of silk to wind round the head as a badge of office: they also receive a small commission, but to this they attach little importance. Rice is by no means their staple food, and is only eaten as a relish or at feasts: fruits, bulbs, forest produce and the spoil of the chase are their principal foods.

Religion. The religion of the Bhuiyās is virtually one of blood. There are good and bad spirits, but attention is only paid to the latter, as the good spirits require no appeasement. Their gods comprise deities undoubtedly of aboriginal origin and others derived from Hindu theology. The aboriginal deities are (1) Badām, (2) Gāinsarī, (3) Bārāhīpīt, (4) Jāunlipāt, (5) Baitaranīpāt, (6) Lakshmīpāt, (7) Mandalpāt, (8) Mahāthākurānī, (9) Pariālbāgiā and (10) Pitrupāt. The principal deity is the earth god and his son, the tiger god: next come the village mother god, the water god, and the deities of the forest, air and rain. The symbols of these gods are rough stones or logs placed under a lofty *sâl* tree. The Bhuiyā pantheon is a mixed one, but the priests are invariably Bhuiyās. The form of oath consists of swearing on a tiger's skin, holding a little earth from an ant's heap in the hands: an oath is regarded as final.

Trial by ordeal. Trial by ordeal is a favourite form of decision. The tests are various: a piece of copper, generally a coin (considered the emblem of justice) is placed in a mixture of boiling cow dung and has to be extracted by dipping in the hand without scalding: another form is for an accused to take his stand on the top of a swaying ladder of twelve rungs, 18 inches apart, and pour a mixture of milk and rice into a circle below, which has been previously sanctified: the severest ordeal is to carry in the palms of the hand a piece of molten iron about a pound in weight, with seven green *pīpal* leaves between each, a fibre of a creeper (*Bauhinia triandra Rox.*) being placed on the hands as a slight protection: the molten mass to be carried seven paces. Failure to perform the test involves expulsion from the village.

The gathering of the clans for war or any other purpose resembles in its rapidity the "fiery cross" of the Scottish clans. A meeting of the tribal chiefs is held, the priest blesses the meeting: a thin rope is then made of the *Bauhinia* creeper and three knots are tied in it, the first in the name of their god, the second in that of their Rājā and the third in the name of the Mahādesh.* Below the three knots a number of small knots are tied indicating the number of days within which the gathering is to take place. The sacred emblem is then despatched by a runner to the nearest village, which at once forwards it to the next village.

Festivals.

The Bhuiyās attend the car festival at the headquarters of the State, but this is in connection with the duties they have to perform in supplying timber for the axles and to pull the car with the creeper ropes supplied by them. The Bhuiyās observe with full religious zeal two festivals. The first occurs in February and is known as the *Māgh Porāi.* Each village in turn observes the festival, so that there is no one fixed date for its performance. The festival is an occasion of much debauchery and intoxication and the celebrants paint and cover themselves with filth ; foul songs and jests are indulged in : the women join in the ribaldry but not in the drinking. The festival lasts for three days.

The next important Bhuiyā festival takes place after the harvest and is known as the *Karamā*, the object of the festival is the joining in matrimony of two branches of the *karamā* tree, as king and queen; the two branches are placed in the ground together, snakes and birds are netted, the former with their lips sewn together being loosed amongst the women. The union of the two branches is looked upon as essential for a year of plenty. There is a third festival called the *Gamhā Punāi* taken from the Hindus. Both festivals are the occasion of much feasting and ribaldry. To the Bhuiyā festivals there is no fixed date, though there is usually a definite limit for their duration.

The hunting festival *akhin pārdhi* lasts two days and all the males take part in it. Each village organises large beats : the spoil is taken to the *pradhān*, headman of the village, who rewards the successful shots with strips of cloth, six yards being given to the slayer of a tiger : the headman receives the lion's share of the spoil.

The Bhuiyās hold the cow sacred; its slaughter or consumption is punished by outcasting. The Bhuiyās use cows in their ploughs, but do not drink their milk and will not milk them.

Future of the race.

The Bhuiyās are not a decaying race and their numbers are on the increase, in 1891 they numbered 87,327 and in 1901, 91,581. The pressure of growing population has driven them to migrate in considerable numbers to the open country abandoning very

---

* Mahāthākurānī, Mahārājā, Mahādesh.

largely the primitive customs prevalent in their hill fastnesses. Assimilation with other castes is countenanced and regular marriages between Bhuiyās and Goālās take place.

All villages have their *darbār* hall where the bachelors (*dhāngars*) of the village sleep, and in some villages there is also a *dhāngarin basā* where the maidens reside. The space between the two houses is the dancing ground. Whenever the young men of the village go to the *darbār* and beat the drums, the young girls join them there, and they spend the evenings, dancing and enjoying themselves without any interference on the part of the elders. The Bhuiyā dances have their peculiar features, but, compared with the lively and graceful movements of the Kols, they are tame performances. The men have each a rude kind of tambourine; they march round in a circle, beating these, and singing a very simple melody in a minor key on four notes. The women dance opposite to them, with their heads covered, and bodies much inclined, touching each other like soldiers in line, but not holding hands or wreathing arms like the Kols. The dances, when confined to the people of the village, are regarded as mere rehearsals. The more exciting and exhilarating occasions are when the young men of one village proceed to visit the maidens of another village, or when the maidens return the call. The young men provide themselves with presents for the girls, generally consisting of combs for the hair and sweetmeats, and going straight to the *darbār* of the village they visit, they proclaim their arrival loudly by beating their drums or tambourines. The girls of that village immediately join them. Their male relations and neighbours must keep entirely out of view leaving the field clear for the guests. The offerings of the visitors are now gallantly presented and graciously accepted, and the girls at once set to work to prepare dinner for their beaux. After the meal they dance and sing and flirt all night together, and the morning dawns on more than one pair of pledged lovers. Then the girls, if the young men have conducted themselves to their satisfaction, make ready the morning meal for themselves and their guests; after which the latter rise to depart, and, still dancing and playing on the drums, move out of the village followed by the girls, who escort them to the boundary. This is generally a rock-broken stream with wooded banks; here they halt, the girls on one side, the lads on the other, and to the accompaniment of the babbling brook, sing to each other in true bucolic style. The song ended, the girls go down on their knees, and bowing to the ground respectfully salute the young men, who gravely and formally return the compliment, and they part. The visit is soon returned by the

Dances.

girls. They are received by the young men in their *darbār*, and entertained, and the girls of the receiving village must not be seen.

Bhuliā. The Bhuliā is a weaver caste and is also known by the name of Bholiā, Bhoriyā, Bholwā, Mihir and Meher. A curious fact about this caste is that, though solely domiciled in the Oriyā territories, many families belonging to it, talk Hindī in their own houses. According to tradition they immigrated to this part of the country with the first Chauhân Rājā of the Patnā State. Various local derivations of the name are current, generally connecting it with Bhūḷuā, to forget. The Bhuliās occupy a higher rank than ordinary weavers and assume the honorific title of Meher. The caste has no sub-castes, except that in Kālāhandī a degraded section is recognised who are called Sânparā Bhuliās and with whom the others refuse to intermarry. The caste are remarkable as having no regular *barāt* or wedding procession. They employ Brāhmans for ceremonial purposes.

Chasās. The Chasās or Tasās number 240,439 in the States and are the chief cultivating class of Orissa. In the Sonpur and Pātnā States they are also termed Haliyā. They are often confused with the Kaltuyās or Koltās and the latter are not infrequently termed as Koltā Chasās. The Chasās are for the most part of non-Aryan descent. Each family has a sept and family name and marriages are arranged by families, union of members of the same family alone being forbidden. The sept names are totemistic such as *nāga* (cobra), *hastī* (elephant), *dīpa* (lamp), etc., and the family names are territorial or titular, *e.g.*, Pitāmundiā and similar names, all names of villages in Angul, and Padhān (leader, chief), Nāyak (headman), Kandrā (bamboo worker), etc. As is usual the various septs worship their totem, drawing figures of them on their houses and will not in any way injure them. The Chasās do not marry within the same family but a man may take a wife from his mother's family. A girl must be wedded before adolescence: if no husband be available, she may be married to an arrow or flower or through the form of marriage with any man in the caste and when a suitable partner is subsequently found, is united with him by the form of widow marriage: divorce is allowed. The dead are usually buried if unmarried and burnt if married.

Dumals. The Dumâls number 29,610 and are mostly found in the State of Sonpur (20,139). They are a sub-caste of Gauras or Ahīrs. The Dumāls admit that they were formerly a branch of Gauras, but now have no connection with them. They are said to derive their name from a village Dumlā Hadap in the Athmallik State. The Dumāls have no sub-castes, but they have a complicated system of exogamy. This includes three kinds of divisions or sections, the *gotra* or sept, the *barga* or family title, and the *māti* or earth from which they sprang. Marriage is prohibited only between persons who have the same *gotra*, *barga* and *māti*, if any one of these is different, it is allowed. The names of the *mātis* or villages show that their original home was in the States, formerly known as the Orissa Tributary Mahāls, while the totemistic names of the *gotra* indicate their Dravidian origin. The marriage of first cousins is prohibited and girls must marry before adolescence, otherwise a heavy penalty is imposed, the girl being taken to the forest and tied to a tree with a thread, this signifying her exclusion from the caste. In practice, this penalty is avoided by marrying her to an old man, who then divorces her and she can then be married as a widow. Widow marriage is allowed and the widow may marry the younger brother of her late husband or not as she pleases. The women are tattooed on the hands, feet and breast.

The Gandās are a servile and impure caste numbering in 1901, 85,241: they remove dead bodies, both of human beings and animals. The majority are met with in the Patnā and Sonpur States where they number 45,774 and 22,203 respectively. They are a servile caste of village drudges acting as watchmen, weavers of coarse cloth and musicians. In some of the States they are still looked upon as a primitive tribe being generally known as Pān, Pāb or Chik. Under the title of Pān they are largely found in the States of Dhenkānāl, Keonjhar, Mayūrbhanj and Nayāgarh where they number 45,825, 31,295, 24,762 and 12,543 respectively and in the Kālāhāndī State they are found under the name of Doms numbering in 1901, 62,462. The total number of Gandās, Pāns and Doms taken together in the States is 342,307 or 10·8 per cent. of the total population. The Pankās are probably a sub-caste of Gandās: but Gandās and Pankās are generally held to be the same, the real term being Pankā: those who have taken to agriculture should be termed Gandās and those who live by weaving Pāns or Pankās. The Gandās have exogamous septs of the usual low-caste type named after plants, animals or other inanimate objects. Marriage is prohibited within the sept and between the children of two sisters, though the children of brothers and sisters may marry. The remarriage of widows is permitted and the younger brother of the deceased husband takes the widow if he wishes to do so. The Gandās and Pāns have strong criminal tendencies. They

Gandās, Pāns and Doms.

are considered as impure and though not compelled actually to live apart from the village, have usually a separate quarter and are not permitted to draw water from the village well or to enter Hindu temples.

Gauras. These are the great pastoral caste of Orissa and in the States number 304,230. They possess large and valuable herds of cows and buffaloes and in the States their special avocation is making *ghī* or clarified butter: the pasturage is good and the *ghī* exported from the States commands an exceptional demand. In many of the States it is usual for them to pay in addition to the ordinary pasturage fees, a payment in kind known as *lawardhām ghī*, that is to say, a contribution in *ghī* for the right to erect cattle pens in the forest and take timber for the purpose. They also take charge of cattle from the people of the plains for pasturage in the hot weather and often receive into their custody the bullocks of those engaged in the sleeper carrying trade or the pack-bullocks of traders who in the hot weather and rains return to their homes up-country and return after the rains to ply their trades again. There are several sub-castes of which the Mathurāpurī ranks highest because its members do not carry the *pālki* (palanquin). The Gopapurī sub-caste is noticeable for the fact that the women are almost the only ones in Orissa who do not wear nose ornaments, a circumstance, which they pretend, connects them with Krishna's mythical milkmaids. The young women of both sub-castes prepare the butter and *ghī* which the elder ones take round for sale with their milk. Field labour of all kinds is eschewed by the Gaura women. The sub-caste known as Magadhā ranks last and is probably a recent accretion from some aboriginal tribe.

Ghāsis. The Ghāsis number 15,542 in the States. They are a very low caste. The Ghāsis are said to come from Mayūrbhanj, but are commonly met with in Gāngpur: they serve as sweepers and grass-cutters to horses. They apparently belong to the Karuā sub-caste of the Hāris. They eat the flesh of swine and cattle. They call themselves Hindus, but their priests are of their own caste.

Hāris. The Hāris number 20,642 and are mostly found in the States of Dhenkānāl, Mayūrbhanj and Nayāgarh. According to their own tradition Brahmā, after creating the four main castes of Manu, found that he had not created any one to keep the world clean. He accordingly rubbed some dust from his arm and with it made the first Hāri. The name is said to be derived from *hār*, a bone. There are various sub-castes, but the Mehtar Hāri alone act as sweepers removing night-soil, but being averse to touching bodies of dead animals: the sweeper sub-castes eat pork and leavings.

The Juāngs are the wildest tribe met with in the States and are probably the most primitive people in existence on the east side of India. They number 11,159 of whom 5,412 are found in Keonjhar, 5,346 in Dhenkānāl, 401 in Pāl Laharā. The tribe is thus confined to a clearly defined tract of country, consisting of the continuous highlands of the large mountain ranges which comprise the northern portion of the Keonjhar and Pāl Laharā States with outlying spurs in Dhenkānāl. The tribe has shown but very slight signs of increase: in 1891 they numbered 9,173 souls and only showed a further gain of 1,986 in 1901. They are exceedingly timid and shy, living as far away as possible from others and their garments in former times consisted of nothing but *āsan* leaf aprons. Captain Johnstone, Political Agent in Keonjhar in 1869, was the first to introduce the Juāng women to wearing clothes and distributed cloth amongst them: but even to this day their raiment is of the scarcest, and though when they visit the marts they now wear some scanty clothing, in their own homes and at work on their *jhūms* in the recesses of the forest they are found clad in their aprons of *āsan* leaves. Practically no change has taken place in the development of the tribe since Colonel Dalton described them in his Ethnology of Bengal (pages 152-158), and from which the following account, as given in Sir W. Hunter's Statistical Account of the Orissa Tributary States, is almost entirely extracted:— **Juāngs.**

"The tract of country held by the Juāngs is not occupied by them alone but hill Bhuiyā villages and many colonies of Goālās occupy the larger portion of it. It is probable that they have been ousted by the Bhuiyā from the fertile valleys, and are thus compelled to restrict their cultivation to the steep hill-sides. The Juāngs have no traditions which affiliate them with any other race; and notwithstanding a similarity in their languages they repudiate all connections with Hos or Santāls. They aver positively that they are autochthones, the direct descendants of the first human beings that appeared in the world. They assert a claim to be the first produced of the human race, though they make no pretensions to be the fathers of mankind. The headquarters of the tribe, or cradle of the race, they consider to have been at Gonāsikā in Keonjhar in 21° 30′ N. and 85° 37′ E., where issues from two holes in a rock, supposed to bear a resemblance to the nostrils of a cow, a stream which is the source of the Baitaranī. They assert that the Baitaranī is older than the Ganges; and that the present Juāng inhabitants of the village of Gonāsikā, and other villages in the vicinity, occupy the very soil from which the parents of their race were produced. They have no traditions to record.

Habits and customs.

"In habits and customs, the Juāngs are most primitive. They occupy a hill country in which stone implements are occasionally found; and though they have now abandoned the use of such implements, and have lost the art of making them, it is not improbable that they are the direct descendants of these ancient stone-cutters. Until foreigners came amongst them, they must have used such weapons, for they had no knowledge whatever of metals. They have no ironsmiths nor smelters of iron. They have no word in their own language for iron or other metals. They neither spin nor weave, nor have they ever attained to the simplest knowledge of pottery. They are still semi-nomadic in their habits, living together in hamlets during a portion of the year, but often changing the sites, and occupying isolated huts in the midst of their patches of cultivation whilst the crops are on the ground.

"The huts are amongst the smallest that human beings ever deliberately constructed as dwellings. They measure about six feet by eight, and are very low, with doors so small as to preclude the idea of a corpulent householder. Scanty as are the above dimensions for a family dwelling, the interior is divided into two compartments, one of which is the storeroom, the other being used for all domestic arrangements. The head of the family and all his belongings of the female sex huddle together in this one stall, not much larger than a dog-kennel. For the boys there is a separate dormitory situated at the entrance of the village with two apartments. One of these is an inner and closed one, in which the musical instruments of the village are kept, and in which most of the boys sleep; the other is open on three sides,—that is, it has no walls,—but the eaves spread far beyond the plinth, and the inmates are effectually protected. This is where all guests are lodged. The Juāngs cultivate by girdling the forest trees, burning them and spreading the ashes over the land. They thus raise a little early rice, Indian-corn, pulses, pumpkins, sweet potatoes, ginger, and red pepper, the seed being all thrown into the ground at once, to come up as it can.

"They pay and render personal service to the Chief by repairing his house and carrying his burdens when required; they are addicted to ardent spirits and buy what they consume, as they have not acquired the art of distilling, or even of brewing rice beer. In regard to food, they are not in the least particular, eating all kinds of flesh, including mice, rats, monkeys, tigers, bears, snakes, frogs, and even offal. The jungles abound in spontaneously produced vegetables. In the quest of such food they possess all the instinct of the animal, discerning at a glance what is nutritive, and never mistaking a noxious for an edible fungus or root.

"The Juāngs are not a warlike people; but when urged by the Bhuiyās, whose lead they invariably follow, they are sometimes troublesome. They use the bow and arrow, but their favourite weapon is the primitive sling, made entirely of cord. For missiles, they take pebbles or stones as they find them; they have no idea of fashioning them so as to produce more efficient projectiles.

"The Juāngs take young shoots of the *āsan* (*Terminalia tomentosa*), or any tree with long soft leaves, and arrange them so as to form a flat and scale-like surface of the required size; the sprigs are simply stuck in the girdle composed of several strings of beads, from which these small curtains of leaves depend before and behind and the costume is complete. The beads that form the girdle are small tubes of burnt earthenware made by the wearers. Their dances resemble very closely those of the Bhuiyās and are monotonous and lacking in execution. Colonel Dalton,* however, saw several animal dances executed by them: the animal dances given being the bear dance, a strutting pigeon, pig and tortoise dance, the quail dance and vulture dance.

"When Colonel Dalton first met the Juāngs in 1866 the males of the community had abandoned the leaves, and used in lieu the smallest quantity of cotton cloth possible for decency. The women were long deterred by superstition from following their example. Several traditions exist to account for this, apparently of Brahmanical concoction. The simplest and prettiest of these, is connected with the origin of the Baitaranī. The river goddess, emerging for the first time from the Gonāsikā rock, came suddenly on a rollicking party of Juāngs dancing naked; and, ordering them to adopt leaves on the moment as a covering, laid on them the curse that they must adhere to that costume for ever or die. It was Captain Johnstone in 1869 who induced the Juāng women to wear cotton cloth, but even at the present day they only wear these when they visit the public marts.

"The Juāng women tattoo their faces with the same marks that are used by the Mundās, Khariās, and Oraons: namely, three strokes on the forehead just over the nose, and three on each

---

* See Colonel Dalton's *Ethnology of Bengal*, 1872, pp. 152-158, and Sir W. Hunter's *Statistical Account of the Orissa Tributary States*, p. 245.

of the temples. They attach no meaning to the marks, have no ceremony in adopting them, and are ignorant of their origin.

"The Juāngs are a small race, like the Oraons, the males averaging less than five feet in height, the women not more than four feet eight inches.

"The Juāngs appear to be free from the belief in witchcraft, which is the bane of the Kols, and perniciously influences nearly all other classes in the States. They have not, like the Khariās, the reputation of being deeply skilled in sorcery. Their language has no words for "god," for "heaven" or "hell"; they have no idea of a future state. They offer fowls to the sun when in distress, and to the earth to give them its fruits in due season. On these occasions an old man officiates as priest, called Nagām.

"Marriage is recognised, but is brought about in the simplest manner. If a young man fancies a girl, he sends a party of his friends to propose for her; and if the offer is accepted a day is fixed, and a load of rice in husk is presented on his behalf. The bridegroom does not go himself to the bride's house; his friends go, and return with her and her friends. Then they make merry, eating and dancing, and all stay and make a night of it. In the morning, the bridegroom dismisses the bride's friends with a present of three measures of husked and three of unhusked rice; and this is a full and sufficient solemnization. A man may have more wives than one if he can afford it. They are divided into tribes, and are exogamous.

"The Juāngs burn their dead, and throw the ashes into any running stream; their mourning is an abstinence for three days from flesh and salt. They erect no monuments, and have no notion of the worship of ancestors. The dead are burned with their heads to the south; in this respect they agree with the Hos and Sāonts."

Kaltuyā or Kolthā. An important agricultural caste numbering in 1901, 30,161: they are mostly met with in the States of Patnā (12,190), Sonpur (8,996) and Kālāhandī (3,330). According to tradition they immigrated from the State of Baud, where they had settled during their wanderings with Rāma in the Oriyā country. According to another legend Rāma, when wandering in the forests of Sambalpur, met three brothers and asked them for water: the first brought water in a clean brass pot and was called Sudha (good-mannered): the second made a cup of leaves and drew water from a well with a rope; he was called Dumāl from *dorī-māl*, a coil of rope: the third brought water only in a hollow gourd and he was named Kolthā from *Ku-rītā*, bad-mannered. The Kolthās, Sudhas and Dumāls thus acknowledge some connection and will take food together at festivals. The Kaltuyās are, however, probably an offshoot of the great Chasā caste: several of their family names are identical with those of the Chasās and there is actually a sub-caste of Kaltuyā-Chasā. The Kaltuyās will not, however, intermarry with other groups of the Chasā caste. The Kaltuyās have exogamous groups and a girl must be married before maturity and if no suitable husband be forthcoming a nominal marriage is arranged. Widow marriage and divorce are allowed. The caste worship the goddess Rāmchandī, whose principal shrine is at Sarsarā in the State of Baud. Brāhmans take water from them. The Kaltuyās are excellent cultivators, very industrious and prepared to resort to any degree of litigation where land is involved. They are very skilful in irrigation but are not popular, chiefly because of their greater prosperity. The rising of the Khonds in Kālāhandī in 1882 was due to their discontent at being ousted from their lands by Kaltuyās, a large number of whom had been imported by the Chief of Kālāhandī. These Kaltuyā cultivators speedily got the Khond headmen and their tenants into their debt and possessed themselves of all the best lands in the Khond villages. In May 1882 the Khonds rose and slaughtered more than 80 Kaltuyās, while 300 more were besieged in the village of Norlā.

The Karan, Karnam, Mahānti is the indigenous writer caste of Orissa. In 1901 a total of 21,740 Karans were enumerated in the States. The caste fulfils the same functions in Orissa as the Kāyasthas elsewhere, and it is said that their original ancestors were brought from Northern India by Yayāti Kesarī, King of Orissa (447-526 A.D.) to supply the demand for writers and clerks. The word Karan is said to be derived from Sanskrit *karan*, a doer. The derivation of Mahānti is obscure, unless it be from *mahat*, great. The caste prefer the name of Karan, because that of Mahānti is often appropriated by affluent Chasās and others who wish to get a rise in rank. Marriage is regulated according to the table of prohibited degrees in vogue among higher castes. Girls are commonly married before they are ten years old, but no penalty attaches to the postponement of the ceremony to a later age. **Karan.**

The Khandaits are the military caste of Orissa, the name being derived from the Oriyā word *khandā*, a sword. In 1901 they numbered 88,313 in the Orissa States and are found in greatest strength in the State of Keonjhar (29,279). The Khandaits **Khandaits.**

are like the Marāthās and the Paiks, a caste formed from military service, and though recruited for the most part originally from the Dravidian tribes, they have obtained a considerable rise in status owing to their occupation and the opportunity offered to many of them to become landholders. The best Khandaits now aspire to Rājput rank, while the bulk of them hold the position of cultivators, from whom Brāhmans will take water. Early marriage is usual, polygamy is permitted, but looked down upon and the person resorting to it is nicknamed *māipakhiā* or wife-eater. Widow marriage and divorce are permitted.

Khariās. The Khariās are a tribe closely allied linguistically to the Juāngs. In 1901 the census returns showed the total number of Khariās in the 24 States at 38,478, of whom 25,838 reside in Gāngpur. This shows a very marked increase in the tribe since the census of 1872, when there were 3,942 Khariās in the States formerly known as the Tributary Mahāls of Orissa and 1,613 in the Tributary States of Chotā Nāgpur, or a total of 5,555. The increase has been most marked in Gāngpur, and the census reports of 1901 attribute this to more careful classification. Tradition has it that the Khariās, with another tribe called Purāns, are aborigines of Mayūrbhanj; and they aver that they and the family of the Rājā (Bhanj) were all produced from a pea-fowl's egg, the Bhanj or family of the Rājā from the yolk, the Purāns from the white, and the Khariās from the shell.

The primitive and wildest members of this tribe reside in the Tarai country round the Simlāpāl and Meghāsanī hill ranges in the Mayūrbhanj State. They are the only persons to wander forth over this wild tract of country, spend days and weeks wandering through the dense and tractless forests and vast hill ranges, in search of jungle products, such as honey and horns: they are experts at catching young birds, especially the hill talking *mayanā* and the large brown tree squirrel, which they sell to the people of the plains.

Khonds. The Khonds are the most important and most numerous of the aboriginal tribes in the States. According to the census of 1901, the Khonds numbered 223,424, of whom 103,086 were found in the State of Kālāhandī, 33,400 in the Patnā State, 14,914 in the State of Baud and 6,399 in the Bāmra State. The Khond population in the 17 Tributary States of Orissa in 1901 totalled 71,484 and members of this tribe are found in all the States. So far as the States are concerned the Khonds are most prominent in the Kālāhandī State, where are found the wildest and most uncivilised members of the tribe: a detailed account of the

Khonds of this tract will be found in the separate article on the Kālāhandī State. The practice of human sacrifices was in former years universal amongst the Khonds and special measures had to be enforced to put down this infamous custom. Lieutenant (afterwards Major) Macpherson, one of the officers engaged in these operations, drew up in 1841 a full report on the habits and customs of the Khonds. With the spread of civilisation and the improvement in communications, the Khonds have gradually more and more adopted Hindu customs and large numbers have abandoned their ancestral hills and forests for regular cultivation in the plains : a large proportion, however, of the tribe still cling to their mountain fastnesses and preserve intact their ancestral traditions. With the advent, however, of settled rule of the British Government, the dispensation of criminal justice by the Khonds according to their tribal principles has ceased and only petty assaults or trifling thefts, when the parties concerned agree, are dealt with by the tribal headmen. An exhaustive and detailed account of the history, and social and religious customs of the Khonds, will be found in the Gazetteer of the district of Angul.

Paiks. The Paiks form the bulk of the old feudal militia of Orissa, being as the name indicates "foot-soldiers." They are especially predominant in the State of Kālāhandī (13,598) and Patnā (2,353). The Paiks are classified as a subdivision of Chasās. Sterling gives the following account of the Paiks:—

"The Paiks or landed militia of the Rājwārā, combined with the most profound barbarism and the blindest devotion to the will of their Chiefs, a ferocity and unquietness of disposition, which have rendered them an important and formidable class of the population of the Province. They comprehend all castes and classes, chiefly perhaps the Chasā or cultivating tribe; occasionally individuals of the lowest castes are found amongst them, as Kandrās, Pāns and Bauris ; and the fashion has often prevailed of adopting into their order some of the more savage inhabitants of the remote hills called Khonds, as also even Musalmāns and Telingas. They are paid by service lands, which they cultivate with their own hands in time of peace, subject to the performance of military and rude police duties whenever called upon by their Chiefs."

With the establishment of settled rule, there is no longer any necessity for the large bodies of Paiks. Their service lands have in most cases been gradually resumed, and they have laid aside the sword for the plough. But the assessment of their *jāgīrs* has not been accomplished without difficulty. Mr. Commissioner Ravenshaw writing about 1873 says: "It has been always found to be a most difficult matter to bring the Paik under a system of revenue payment and repeated instances have occurred in the Tributary States where insurrection has resulted from rash attempts to assess service tenures. The process, however, has been gradually carried out; and most of the Paiks now pay a nominal rent for their *jāgīrs* generally in kind." The Paiks are still exempt from *bethī* or the liability to carry loads and render other menial service.

In Kālāhandī the Paiks, however, still hold a very prominent position and are men of substance cultivating each six *putis* of land rent-free. In this State they are known as *Naliā sipāhis* being armed with match locks. The Khandaits appear to have been the leaders and officers of the militia and the Paik, the rank and file, mainly recruited from the forest tribes and they are counted as a comparatively low caste.

Sahars. The Sahars are numerous in Orissa and in the States number 40,719. They are found chiefly in the States of Dhenkānāl, Athgarh, Keonjhar, Mayūrbhanj, Ranpur, Tālcher, Khandparā, Tigiriā, and Pāl Laharā. They are said to be different from the Savars. Many are day-labourers. They subsist largely on jungle products and are skilful hunters and fowlers. They employ no Brāhmans, and their chief object of worship is the Grām Devati. There are three endogamous sub-castes, Basu, Palia and Paika. Nothing is known about their origin. They allow divorce and the remarriage of widows. They drink wine and eat all kinds of animals.

Sansiā Oriyā. A caste of masons and navvies of Orissa. The caste are really a branch of the great migratory Ud or Odde caste of earth-workers, whose name has been corrupted in various forms. The term Oriyā is here a corruption of Odde, and it is the one by which the caste generally prefer to be known, but they are generally called Sansiā by outsiders. The caste sometimes class the Sansiās as a sub-caste of Oriyās. In 1901 the Sansiās numbered 7,285 in the States. They enjoy a fairly high position, and Brāhmans will take water from them. They have totemistic exogamous septs, usually derived from the names of sacred objects as *kach-hap* (tortoise), etc. The caste are usually stone-workers, making cups, mortars, images of idols, and other articles. They also dig tanks and wander from place to place for this purpose in large numbers.

Sudhas. The Sudhas or Suds numbering 27,324 are most numerous in the States of Baud, Athmallik, Sonpur, Narsinghpur, Rairākhol and Ranpur, and also occur in the States of Hindol, Bāmra, Tālcher, Daspallā, Nayāgarh, Dhenkānāl, Patnā, Khandparā,

Pāl Laharā, Keonjhar, Kālāhandī, Athgarh and Mayūrbhanj. According to tradition they were the dominant power in Baud, with whose Chief they still claim relationship. Though now cultivators they believe that they were formerly soldiers and adore guns in consequence. They adore the *bakul* tree and on no account will fell it. They are divided into four sub-castes, (1) the Bara or high Sudhas, (2) the Dehrī or worshippers, (3) the Kabāt-koniā or those holding the corners of the gates, and (4) the Butkā. The latter are the most primitive and think that Rairakhol is their first home. They relate they were born of the Pāndava hero Bhīm Sen and the female demon Hidimbī and were originally occupied in supplying leaves for the *srāddha* ceremonies of the Pāndava brothers, hence their name Butkā or "one who brings leaves." The Butkās are practically a forest tribe carrying on shifting cultivation like the Khonds. They claim to have once ruled Rairākhol: during the constant wars between Bāmra and Rairākhol the whole of the Rāj family of Rairākhol were killed except one boy who was hidden in a cradle on uprights by a Butkā woman, and when the Bāmra soldiers came to seek for him the Sudhas swore, "If we have kept him either in heaven or earth may our God destroy us." The Bāmra people were satisfied and the child was saved: he received the name of Jenāmani or "Jewel among men" which the family still bear. In consequence of this incident, the Butkā Sudhas are considered by the Rairākhol house as a relation on their mother's side: they have several villages allotted to them and perform sacrifices for the family. In some of their villages nobody may sleep on a cot or sit on a high chair, so as to be between heaven and earth in the position in which the child was saved.

The Sudhas have totemistic *gotras* such as *bhaluka* (bear) and *bargas* or family names such as Thākur, and Dānaik. The *bargas* are more numerous than the totemistic septs and marriage either within the *barga* or within the sept is forbidden. There are no intermarriages between the Sudhas of Baud and Athmallik and those residing in the other States. They practise infant marriage. When a girl reaches adolescence, she is, if no suitable bridegroom be forthcoming, married to an old man who divorces her immediately afterwards or is married to an arrow. She can then remain single without blame until a suitor appears whom she marries by the form of widow remarriage. In this respect the Sudhas resemble the Chasās. A betrothal is sealed by tying an areca nut in a knot made from the clothes of a relative of each party and pounding it seven times with a pestle.

Taonlās. A small non-Aryan caste. They reside principally in Dhenkānāl, Hindol, Barāmbā, Tālcher and Narsinghpur and numbered about 17,295 persons in 1901. The name is said to be derived from Tālumūl, a village in the Angul district; and they came to Bāmra and Sonpur during the Orissa famine in 1866. The Taonlās appear to be a low occupational caste of mixed origin, but derived principally from the Khond tribe. Formerly their profession was military service, and it is probable that like the Khandaits and Paiks they formed the levies of some of the Oriyā Rājās and gradually became a caste. The Taonlās are said to be allied to the Savars and to admit a member of any caste from whose hands they can take water into the community. In Sonpur the Taonlās admit a close connection with Chasās and say that some of their families are descended from the union of Chasā men and Taonlā women. The Taonlās have no exogamous divisions: their marriages are therefore regulated by relationship in the ordinary manner. Divorce and widow remarriage are permitted.

CHAPTER IV.

PUBLIC HEALTH.

MEDICAL INSTITUTIONS.

THE number of dispensaries maintained by the States was 39 in 1907-08 and two more are in course of construction. In all the States, with the exception of Tigiriā, where there is only an Ayūrvedic Hall, dispensaries are maintained at the headquarters and in the larger States of Bāmra, Dhenkānāl, Gāngpur, Kālāhandī, Keonjhar, Mayūrbhanj and Sonpur, and also in the States of Bonai and Nayāgarh there are dispensaries in the interior, mostly situated at the headquarters of subdivisions and important zamīndāris. All the dispensaries are in charge of qualified Civil Hospital Assistants, and in the States of Bāmra, Dhenkānāl, Gāngpur, Keonjhar, Mayūrbhanj, Nīlgiri, Patnā and Sonpur there are Medical Officers in charge with qualifications equivalent to those of Assistant Surgeons. All the dispensaries are well supplied with medicines and surgical instruments and have accommodation for male and female in-door patients: the dispensaries and their equipments at Bāmra, Dhenkānāl, Gāngpur, Kālāhandī, Mayūrbhanj, Patnā and Sonpur are excellent. Medical attendance for females has of late years begun to receive attention, and there are female Civil Hospital Assistants attached to the dispensaries of Dhenkānāl, Kālāhandī, Keonjhar, Mayūrbhanj, Nīlgiri and Patnā. A great change has come over the people of the Garhjāts in their attitude towards the use of European medicine and submission to surgical operations. The figures below of patients treated during the last five years show the great increase in the popularity of the State dispensaries during that period:—

1903-04	273,167
1904-05	275,624
1905-06	293,719
1906-07	305,617
1907-08	333,566

At any important centre there is now a great anxiety evinced by the people of all classes and races for the location of a dispensary, and any Civil Hospital Assistant who is capable and sympathetic quickly gains a large attendance. The change is a remarkable one, but perhaps only to be expected with the general advancement that is now rapidly taking place.

PRINCIPAL DISEASES. The principal complaints are fever and bowel complaints, and these two, especially fever, account for the majority of the number of deaths: severe outbreaks of cholera not infrequently visit the States: these outbreaks are generally due to imported infection, the Garhjāts forming a highway for vast numbers of pilgrims on their way to and from Purī: the greater number of these pilgrims are of the poorer classes travelling on foot, who readily succumb to the attacks of any epidemic. Small-pox visitations are often severe, especially in the 17 States formerly known as the Orissa Tributary Mahāls, but with the spread of vaccination are becoming less virulent and less common. In the Sambalpur States small-pox but rarely occurs. Syphilis is exceedingly common in the Garhjāts and is of a very virulent type: leprosy is not uncommon and elephantiasis is bad in the States bordering on the Purī district.

VACCINATION. One of the most marked features of recent years is the rapid strides made in vaccination work in the States. In some of the States, principally the 17 States formerly known as the Tributary Mahāls of Orissa, vaccination is paid for by the people: in the Sambalpur States, (except in Bāmra) and in Gāngpur and Bonai, vaccination is free: in all cases the work is carried on by properly trained vaccinators, who in many instances are local men trained in the vaccination class maintained by the States for this purpose, at the Medical School, Cuttack, though in some cases with the employment of fully qualified Medical Officers, these vaccinators are now locally trained in the States. The vaccinators in all instances are supervised by Inspectors who are generally Civil Hospital Assistants and, in addition to their duties of supervision of vaccination, are peripatetic doctors rendering medical assistance to the villagers, being deputed to attend on occasions of outbreaks of cholera, small-pox and cattle diseases in the interior: these peripatetic Civil Hospital Assistants also attend to village sanitation. Vaccination is mostly from lymph, but in the Sambalpur States, vaccination direct from the calf, is available for those who prefer it. All the Chiefs are now entirely responsible for the vaccination work in their States: till recently in the 17 States, formerly known as the Tributary Mahāls of Orissa, and the States of Gāngpur and Bonai the Sanitary Department used to conduct and supervise the work. Vaccination generally has received much greater attention for some years in the five States transferred from the Central Provinces than in the other States of this Agency: this has no doubt been due to the personal influence of the Chiefs and probably to a large degree to the fact that vaccination is free: this is supported by the fact that in Gāngpur and Bonai where free vaccination has been introduced for the last two years there has been a most marked increase in the operations. Revaccination in the 17 States, formerly known as the Tributary Mahāls of Orissa, and the States of Gāngpur and Bonai was up to within the last three years very little practised and previously was practically unknown: it has, however, now made a beginning as the figures below show. In Patnā and Kālāhandī revaccination has always received the greatest attention and a case of small-pox, except an occasional imported case, is now almost unknown. The extensive operations, especially of revaccination, in Patnā and Kālāhandī, are worthy of note in view of the very large Khond population (136,486) in these two States. The statement below illustrates the progress of vaccination and re-vaccination of recent years.

YEARS.	17 STATES FORMERLY KNOWN AS THE TRIBUTARY STATES OF ORISSA.		STATES OF GANGPUR AND BONAI.		5 SAMBALPUR STATES.	
	Primary vaccination.	Revaccination.	Primary vaccination.	Revaccination.	Primary vaccination.	Revaccination.*
1904-05	56,857	117	10,941	925	37,906	27,390
1905-06	59,426	2,383	10,796	1,138	51,012	20,752
1906-07	70,637	5,063	9,777	4,676	44,186	34,030
1907-08	66,807	17,314	10,568	13,370	39,910	40,050
TOTAL ...	253,727	24,877	42,082	20,109	173,014	122,222

* Of these the figures for revaccination were—

	Patnā.	Kālāhandī.
1904-05	13,985	8,453
1905-06	16,035	2,094
1906-07	18,563	9,081
1907-08	21,045	12,525
Total ...	69,628	32,753

CHAPTER V.

AGRICULTURE.

GENERAL DESCRIPTION. THE States of Orissa present very varying conditions of soil and conformation of surface, from the bare rock of the mountain peaks, the loamy but rocky soil on the hill slopes, the rich deposits of the valleys in the hills to the wide open plains along the course of the large rivers of the country. In all cases, however, the system of agriculture is the same and is entirely dependent on the rainfall: canals and embankments on any large scale are unknown, though in Bāmra, Mayūrbhanj and Dhenkānāl a commencement has been made in this direction.

SYSTEM OF CULTIVATION. In nearly all the States the most primitive system of cultivation, *dāhi* or *jhūm*, is pursued alongside regular systematic cultivation: the degree to which this primitive system is followed in each State depends on the amount of forest or open country available. When preparing a *jhūm* the large trees are ringed, and the smaller ones are cleared by the hatchet and fire. The soil is then scratched with primitive hand-ploughs, and a fairly good miscellaneous crop, consisting of early rice, maize, millets, oil-seeds, turmeric, etc., is raised for two or three seasons: the site is abandoned for a fresh one and is allowed to rest until again covered with jungle when the same process is repeated. In the States of Athmallik, Bāmra, Bonai, Kālāhandī, Keonjhar, Pāl Lahạrā and Rairākhol, where the country consists for the most part of vast tracts of lofty hills and dense forests, the system of *dāhi* cultivation is followed to a very large extent, whilst in more open country, such as is found in parts of Baud, Dhenkānāl, Mayūrbhanj, Patnā and Sonpur, regular plough cultivation of a high order is universal: in all the States, however, both systems exist side by side: the Kaltūyās of Kālāhandī and the Sambalpur States, and the Agariās of Gāngpur and along the valley of the Brāhmanī in the Bonai State are first class cultivators and past experts in skilful terracing, and the construction of tanks and *bandhs* to irrigate their lands. It is extraordinary to find side by side with cultivation of this nature the reckless and wasteful system of *dāhi* cultivation. With the interest now being taken by the States in the proper conservation of their forests this system of *dāhi* cultivation has received a check. In a few instances the members of the indigenous tribes have been removed from their *jhūms* within the reserved forest areas and assigned prescribed areas within which to practise this form of cultivation or settled on the open country being provided with land, bullocks and seeds: endeavours are also being gradually made to induce others to give up this destructive form of cultivation by offering lands and advances for seed and plough bullocks. The practice of *dāhi* cultivation by regular cultivators in addition to their plough cultivation has now been stopped. The system is, however, on the wane; let alone the fact that the area has been restricted by the formation of forest reserves, the pressure of population has compelled the indigenous races to burn their *padās* or *jhuming* tracts every third or fourth year, whereas formerly it was possible to allow a *padā* eight to ten years' rest: this is naturally rapidly deteriorating the productiveness of the system and it is rarely now-a-days that a really good crop can be reaped off the *padās*. This no doubt accounts for the fact that so many of the two principal wild tribes of these States, the Bhuiyās and Khonds, are becoming Hinduised and settling in villages and working lands alongside regular cultivating classes: at the same time, however, they generally hanker after a small piece of *dāhi* cultivation on a hill-side neighbouring on their plough cultivation. No more pitiable sight can be seen than that presented by the Bhuiyā *pīrs* (tracts) of Bonai, Keonjhar, and Pāl Laharā and the *padās* of the Khonds in the extensive expanse of hills on the eastern side of the Kālāhandī State: hill-sides which formerly carried magnificent timber are now either bare or covered with small poles and scantlings, which are immediately felled so soon as they will yield enough ash to raise even a scanty crop.

IRRIGATION.

The valleys and open plains are fine undulating country, which readily lends itself to the construction of tanks and small embankments for irrigation: the villages along the banks of the Mahānadī and Brāhmanī, especially in the Sonpur, Baud and Tālcher States, are exceptionally equipped with fine tanks. In the Sambalpur States and in some of the other States it has for several years been a fixed policy to encourage the village lessees or *gaontiās* to improve their villages in this way by granting those, who do so, a protected status, which prevents their being ousted at the time of re-settlement, if they are prepared to enter into a new agreement on fair and reasonable terms and have not been guilty of regular default, or failure to comply with their prescribed duties.

PRINCIPAL CROPS.

The system of cultivation has been described in the articles on each individual State and requires no detailed mention. It may be briefly stated that there are the following forms of cultivation:

(1) Regular (*jami*) rice cultivation; (2) Upland (*āt*, *gorā*, *tānr*) cultivation of rice entirely dependent on the rainfall; (3) cultivation of oil-seeds, millets, and cotton on high clearings in forest land, where the low scrub-jungle is burnt, or boughs are cut, dragged to the spot and burnt, the ashes being ploughed into the ground as a fertiliser; this form of cultivation is locally known as *beurā*; and (4) lastly, the regular *dāhi* or *jhūming*.

Rice. The staple crop is rice, of which generally speaking two varieties are grown, viz., *āus* or *biāli* reaped in September, and *āman* or *sārad*, the late winter rice, and the chief crop of the country. In a few places, but to quite an insignificant extent, spring rice or *dālua* is cultivated along the edges of basins which remain wet throughout the year: this early spring rice is a feature of the southern tracts of Kālāhandī. The methods of cultivation are identical with those prevailing elsewhere in Orissa.

Other cereals and pulses. Rice is, of course, the principal food crop but is supplemented by millets, such as *chīna*, *māndiā* or *maruā*, etc., and maize and pulses form a large part of the dietary of the people, including *bīrhi*, *mūga*, *kulthī*, *rahar* and gram. The chief oil-

Oil-seeds. seeds grown are mustard, sesamum and castor-oil-seeds, castor-oil being sometimes used by the poorer classes for cooking.

Sugar-cane. Sugarcane is extensively cultivated and a considerable export trade is carried on in the sugar manufactured.

Wheat. Wheat grows luxuriantly in the hill area of the Kālāhandī State, but is not regularly grown by the Khonds, who prefer the rough and ready system of *dāhi* or *jhūm* cultivation and the raising of turmeric for export. Wheat is cultivated by the zamīndārs of these tracts in their home-farms and by members of their families, holding villages as maintenance grants. The wheat is readily irrigated from the perennial springs which cover this country in every direction. There is nothing to prevent wheat being cultivated here on a large scale, and with the advent of the Raipur-Vizianagram railway should prove a very profitable undertaking to the cultivators: some water-power mills from Dehrī on the Son have recently been introduced.

Cotton. Cotton is largely grown, but is mostly of a very inferior quality: a good deal of it is locally manufactured for home use, but a certain quantity is exported.

Tobacco. Tobacco is raised on the rich silt deposits of rivers and near

Turmeric. homesteads, where cattle manure is plentiful. Turmeric is extensively grown, especially by the Khonds, for export, and all the

Vegetables. ordinary vegetables are cultivated, the commonest being the brinjal or egg-plant and pumpkin.

Edible roots. The forests produce various edible roots, such as the *kandā* (large yam) and *tikhuri* (arrow-root): the latter is prepared by placing the root in earthen jars with water and then boiling: the aborigines largely subsist on these products. As a result of the growth of population within the States, of immigration from outside and of improved communications, cultivation is steadily on the increase; extensive clearances are being made on all sides, and the problem in every State is how to devise measures for the proper conservation of the forests without unduly restricting the reclamation of waste lands.

In most of the States little has been done to introduce new varieties of crops or improved seeds. In the State of Mayurbhanj, however, an experimental farm is maintained and useful work done: experiments with jute, potatoes, the Central Provinces drought-resisting *āus* paddy, and various other kinds of paddy and ground-nuts have been carried out: Messrs. Shaw, Wallace & Co. have undertaken in this State experiments in cotton cultivation; on their farm various kinds of cotton have been tried including the Sambalpur tree cotton; the cultivation is, however, still in the experimental stage. At Nayāgarh an experimental farm has been opened for three years, experiments being conducted in jute-growing which have been fairly successful and several of the well-to-do tenants are taking up its cultivation: experiments have also been tried with fair success in drought-resisting paddy and the seeds distributed to the tenants. In Bāmra the Chief has a large farm near Balam, some ten miles from the headquarters, and here superior crops and vegetables of various kinds are grown on an extensive scale. In Athgarh the Chief takes an interest in agricultural experiments and has started an experimental farm where superior varieties of paddy are experimented with. EXPERIMENTAL FARMS.

Sericulture is also being carefully and scientifically carried on in the States of Mayūrbhanj, Dhenkānāl and Keonjhar: progress has so far been greater in the former State and tenants of certain Christian villages as well as other tenants of the State have taken up the industry: both shrub and tree mulberry are grown; in Keonjhar the work has made less progress: in all these States the sericultural operations are in charge of experts and scholarships are given by the Dhenkānāl State to students to proceed to Rājshāhi to study. The Dhenkānāl State has sent a student to Japan to study sugar-making. In the five States transferred from the Central Provinces, the cultivation of *jowār* is encouraged by awarding prizes to schoolmasters for the best crop raised during the year: to all the schools small gardens are attached and the children taught to grow English vegetables; there are similar gardens attached to the police stations and good vegetable seed thus finds its way amongst the people generally. It is by no means uncommon SERICULTURE.

in the cold season when touring in these States to receive a present of a good cabbage or cauliflower grown in the garden of the headman of the village.

PLOUGH. The plough in use is very similar in all the States. The tribes who practise *dāhi* cultivation use a small hand plough; it is little more than a curved bough. The plough in use varies slightly in different places to suit the variety of soil met with. The ploughs in use for regular cultivation are of two kinds, the distinguishing feature being in the one case the use of two wooden pegs on the yoke within which to confine the neck of the bullock, and in the other only a single peg on the inner side is used to which is fastened by a hook or through a hole at its lower end a cord passing round the neck of the bullock and attached to a small knob on the outer extremity of the yoke. The former type is found in the wilder parts of the country, such as Bonai, where the cattle are allowed to graze in herds in the large forests, and are very wild and unmanageable when yoked in the plough: the two wooden pegs make it easier to steady the bullocks, but have the disadvantage that it is very difficult to turn and direct them and the ploughing is naturally inferior: the latter type is found in the more open and cultivated tracts. In Bonai the Bhuiyā cultivator uses a plough of *bandhan* wood: the wood is not kept to season as it perishes unless made up at once: this plough only lasts for about a year and the cost of the plough including the iron share is ten annas: a plough without the yoke (*juāli* or *juādi*) costs four annas and the yoke, if bought separately, costs two annas. The plough-stock (*nangal*) is made in one piece with a slot for the share (*phāl* or *kasanā*): there is no iron band or ring to keep the share firm in the stock. The share is a long narrow piece of iron. The plough is fashioned by means of a chisel known as *bindhani* and a wooden mallet (*katā*). The plough has two wooden pegs on the yoke for harnessing the bullocks. The other type of plough is usually made of *sâl* and has a longer life and costs in the States round Sambalpur about eleven and-a-half annas. The yoke has only *parchali* or inner pegs and no outer pegs (*kānkhilā*); the place of the latter are taken by two small knobs on the top of the yoke, from which a piece of cord is attached; this cord passes under the neck of the oxen and is fastened to the lower end of the *parchāli* by an iron hook or through a hole made therein.

DOMESTIC ANIMALS. The ordinary value of each kind of domestic animal is—cow, Rs. 5 to 15, bullock, Rs. 5 to 20, she-buffalo, Rs. 10 to 20, he-buffalo, Rs. 10 to 30, goat, Rs. 1 to 3, pony, Rs. 10 to 50.

Ponies are not much used except for riding by the few well-to-do people, such as the headmen of the villages; these ponies are very small and only up to very light weights, but are extremely hardy. The better class of ponies have all to be imported: Bhutiā ponies do well and are a favourite type with those who can afford them.

Buffaloes and bullocks are employed in ploughing, the former being specially useful in tilling hard soil. Cow and she-buffaloes are prized for their milk, which besides being drunk is largely utilized for making *ghī* (clarified butter) both for local consumption and export. Pasture lands are generally plentiful on account of the existence of extensive waste lands and forest areas and no difficulty is experienced in feeding cattle. In fact, herds are annually brought in large numbers from the plains to graze in the States. The local breeds of cattle, however, are exceedingly poor and of small stature. The quantity of milk which a cow gives is very small: it is difficult to find an animal which will give a seer a day: the sale price of a milch cow is one rupee per chittack ($\frac{1}{16}$th of a seer) of milk given daily. CATTLE.

CHAPTER VI.

NATURAL CALAMITIES.

FAMINE. THE States of Orissa are not subject to the ravages of severe famine. The great famine of Orissa in 1866 did not affect the Garhjāts. In recent years, however, in 1897, 1900 and 1908 some of the States have suffered from considerable scarcity. In 1900 the distress from scarcity was severe in the Patnā and Sonpur States, relief works were undertaken and kitchens played a prominent part in the relief given, but so far disastrous and wide-spread famine has been unknown. The distress of 1908 was due to two causes, viz., early cessation of the rains and devastating floods of the Mahānadī and Brāhmanī rivers along the riparian villages on the lower portion of their courses. This immunity to real famine is due to the conformation of the country, which renders it little subject to flood except in certain limited areas, and which, owing to forest-clad hills, is better able to retain moisture than the country of the plains. The population is sparse, but its annual expansion and the consequent disappearance of the forests is apparently rendering the country more liable to sudden floods. The country lends itself to easy irrigation by the construction of tanks and embankments at no great cost. The villages and forests abound with mango, jack, *mahuā*, *chār* and ebony trees, which yield favourite articles of food with the people: the jungles produce many kinds of edible roots and tubers. The population is very largely composed of indigenous races, who regularly subsist, when short of rice or *māndiā*, on the jungle products and the spoils of the chase. During the season when the *sāl* is in flower the Kols practically eat nothing else, and this they do from choice. The Kol, Bhuiyā and Khond will frequently not take the trouble to cultivate, even though he can readily do so, enough rice or *māndiā* to supply the needs of himself and his family throughout the year.

CHAPTER VII.

RENTS AND WAGES.

REGULAR surveys and settlements were till lately rare in the States. The measurement was usually done roughly by bamboo poles, rents being supposed to bear some relation to outturn, but the mode of calculation was often very crude. There is seldom any rack-renting. In the States which have come under the administration of Government, the lands have been regularly classified and rents assessed according to the classification. In the State of Mayūrbhanj the Chief has undertaken regular settlements on scientific principles and a regular settlement staff is maintained to keep these settlements up-to-date. In the five States transferred from the Central Provinces, regular settlements based on the soil factor, and soil unit system in vogue in the Central Provinces have been made for some years past, but in the wilder tracts of these States large areas populated by the Khonds, Binjhāls and other wild tribes have only been summarily settled, the rents being merely nominal and based on the supposed seed capacity of the soil. In Gāngpur a regular settlement is now in progress, but hitherto the only system known has been an estimation by a body of umpires, who, after examining a village, assess approximately in their opinion the quantity of first, second and third class rice lands in the village: the system is known as the *nazarpaimās* or eye-measurement; villages so settled are known as *kut* villages and opposed to *akut* villages where no such settlement has been made. In the Pābari *pargana* of Bonai the rents are assessed on the plough and the Bhuiyās of Bonai, Pāl Laharā and Keonjhar pay only a house-tax. The Chiefs have large *khamārs* or farms which they either cultivate themselves or let to under-tenants from whom they receive half the produce as their share. Rent-free grants to Brāhmans, temples and others cover large areas and are seldom violated. It is also usual to grant service tenures or *jāgīrs* to *paiks* (feudal militia), servants and dependants and *khanjā* or maintenance grants to relatives, which are, however, resumable at the option of the Chief. A few tenures are held at a quit-rent. The rest of the land is the RENTS.

property of the State and is known as the *khālsa* area: it is held by tenants who pay rent direct, intermediate rights or tenures being practically unknown. Formerly the whole or a part of the rent used to be realised in kind, but cash payments have now to a large extent become the rule. The right of occupancy is firmly established by custom, and so long as the tenant pays rent his possession is undisturbed, but alienation by sale, gift or mortgage is subject entirely to the permission of the Chief, and is usually carefully guarded against and in several States is strictly forbidden.

WAGES.

There is little of skilled labour in the Garhjāts, except carpenters, blacksmiths and masons who are paid 2 annas 3 pies to 1 rupee 4 annas per diem. Unskilled labour does not cost more than two to three annas per diem while agricultural labour is generally paid in kind. The custom of paying the village artisans and menials and *chaukidārs* (watchmen) in kind at harvest time is common. For a detailed account of the various classes of land labourers in the States a reference may be made to the articles on the States of Kālāhandī, Nayāgarh, Patnā, Rairākhol and Sonpur.

Bethī begāri.

It is a generally recognised custom for the Chiefs to demand and obtain *begāri* or free labour from certain castes and classes for carrying their luggage or that of any official, and performing various other domestic services, such as thatching houses, etc. But the persons while so employed are always given full daily food, and in some cases they also have small rent-free grants. The privilege extends to certain favoured persons such as the relations or principal officers of the Chiefs.

The headmen or *gaontiās* of the villages and also the Chiefs for their *khamārs* or private lands receive *bethī* labour: this consists of free assistance from each house of cultivating tenants of one plough for preparing the lands for sowing, one plough at time of re-ploughing (*bihurā*) and two sickles at harvest.

CHAPTER VIII.

OCCUPATIONS, MANUFACTURES AND TRADE.

OCCUPATIONS.

THE great majority of the population, 70·4 per cent., of the States follow agriculture as their means of livelihood: the proportion of the population following industries and profession is only 13·9 and 0·27 per cent. engage in trade.

MANUFACTURES.

The States are not remarkable for any very special manufactures; at Kantilo in the Khandparā State and in the Narsinghpur State a considerable manufacture of brass utensils is carried on: these find their way throughout the States, but are entirely of the ordinary pattern and in nowise remarkable either for design or workmanship: the next most important industry is the weaving of tusser cloth at Sonpur and Binkā in the Sonpur State; an account of this industry will be found in the article on that State. At Māniābandha in the Barāmbā State a small settlement of Buddhists manufacture silk and cotton cloth of excellent quality and artistic patterns. In the States of Rairākhol and Athmallik a considerable number of Lohārs (smiths) earn a livelihood in smelting iron, which is of excellent quality and highly valued. In Baud, Daspallā, Dhenkānāl, Khandparā, Mayūrbhanj and Tālcher blacksmiths make, for local use, iron implements, such as axes, bill-hooks, crow-bars, shovels, spades, sickles and knives, some of which are very well turned out. In Dhenkānāl and Nayāgarh ivory work of good quality is still made by one or two families, and in Baud there are skilful silversmiths. In Bonai the Bhumij fashions utensils from the soap stone found there, and similar vessels are manufactured in the Nīlgiri State.

In almost all the villages of the States are found the local cotton weavers, who are Pankās or Pāns, Chiks and Mehers. The cloth woven is very coarse; it is however very much more durable than the mill-made article. The weavers eke out a precarious existence from the proceeds of their toil. In certain parts the sands of the Brāhmanī, Ib and Mahānadī are washed by a tribe known as Jhorās, and an account of this industry will be found in the article on the Bonai State. It will thus be seen that there are virtually no manufactures in the States and such industries as these are petty. The villages are self-contained with their own blacksmith, potter, carpenter, etc.; their wants are few and the few articles of luxury are obtained by barter.

Mines and deposits. There are no mines in the States: at Bisrā in the Gāngpur State there are extensive limestone quarries worked by a European firm and the manufactured lime has obtained a ready sale and high reputation in the Calcutta market: dolomite deposits in the same State on the banks of the Brāhmanī have also been worked. Manganese in fair quantity is found in the Gāngpur State and in 1908 nearly 2,000 tons were raised: in the Himgīr zamīndāri of the same State a coalfield of good quality exists and a company has been formed to work it. The enormous resources of iron ore in the Gurumasaiāni hill in the State of Mayūrbhanj are well known and the ore is about to be exploited by the large Steel Works to be started by Tātā and Sons. The granite quarries in the Nīlgiri State are now being exploited by a company which has built a tramway from Balasore to Nīlgiri. As regards other minerals which exist in the States, but have so far not been worked, an account is given under the head of Geology.

TRADE. Traders in the States are represented by itinerant dealers from the British districts; there are but very few local traders. Trade **Imports and exports.** is carried on principally in rice, pulses, oil-seeds, etc., and timber and other forest produce in return for salt, dried fish, European cotton piece-goods, cotton twist and kerosene oil; tusser cocoons are also exported. There is a considerable export trade in hides and horns. Most of the export and the import trade is carried on with Cuttack and to a smaller extent also with Balasore, Purī and Sambalpur. Regular weekly or bi-weekly markets are held **Trade centres.** in all the States at convenient centres where the ordinary necessaries of a rural population, such as salt, cloth, dried-fish, etc., are bartered for grain. There are, however, no central markets of great importance, but Kantilo in Khandparā, Anandpur in Keonjhar, Bhuban and Dhenkānāl in Dhenkānāl and Tarbhā in Sonpur are important marts. The system is for traders to push on into the hill tracts, inaccessible for cart traffic, early in the year: they settle down with their pack-bullocks or ponies and scour the country side, bringing in head-loads of grain by means of cooly transport: in due course these supplies are transferred to the pack-bullocks and ponies, which either carry them to the places where the carts are waiting for them, or transport them direct to their destination. Here, as elsewhere, the wandering race of Banjārās are found engaged in their traditional pursuit of transport carriers and sutlers.

There are some fairs, the most noted of which are Kapilās in Dhenkānāl, Deogāon in Keonjhar and Dhabaleswar in Athgarh. Large numbers of pilgrims including visitors from outside congregate on the Sivarātri day (February-March) at Kapilās and Deogāon and at Dhabaleswar on the Kārttik Pūrnimā day (October-November), but these places do not attract much trade, being resorted to chiefly for purposes of devotion and for the cure of diseases and infirmities. **Fairs.**

Want of communications forms the chief obstacle to the growth of trade. The larger rivers are open to country boats for about eight months in the year, during which they are also largely used along their lower reaches for floating down rafts of timber and bamboos. But the bulk of the trade is carried on from November to May in country carts, where there are fair-weather roads, and elsewhere on pack-bullocks which still form the chief means of carriage. Solid block-wheeled carts (*sagars*) are used for bringing down timbers and stones from the forests and for carrying other goods in places where nothing better than tracks are to be found. **Transport.**

CHAPTER IX.

MEANS OF COMMUNICATION.

General feature.

Roads.

One of the greatest signs of advancement noticeable in the States of Orissa during recent years has been the very marked improvement effected in communications. All the twenty-four States have good and, in some cases, excellent roads to their headquarters and there are many good surface feeder roads. The principal and most important roads are, the Cuttack-Angul-Sambalpur (171 miles), Cuttack-Sonpur-Sambalpur (205 miles), and Sambalpur-Patnā-Kālāhandī (140 miles). The former lies to the north of the Mahānadī and runs through the States of Athgarh and Dhenkānāl, the Angul district, the States of Athmallik and Rairākhol and the Sambalpur district: this road, except in the Dhenkānāl and Rairākhol States, is maintained by Government and there are rest-houses at convenient distances of about 10 miles apart up to the border of the Rairākhol State: bungalows are now in course of erection in this State and the Sambalpur district.

Cuttack-Angul-Sambalpur road.

The Cuttack-Sonpur-Sambalpur road runs on the south side of the Mahānadī, following closely the bank of the river: it runs through Domparā and Bānki in the Cuttack district, the States of Khandparā, Daspallā, Baud and Sonpur and the Sambalpur district. It is maintained throughout its length as far as the Sonpur border by Government, except in the short length situated in the Pancharā zamīndāri of the Sonpur State, which lies in the State of Baud near the river Tel: this section is maintained by the Sonpur State: the road throughout its length in the Sonpur State is maintained by the Chief: after leaving the Sonpur State the road runs through the Sambalpur district crossing the Mahānadī at Dhamā, about 15 miles below Sambalpur. The northern section of the road is not an easy one for traffic, as after entering the State of Baud many large streams and rivers have to be crossed: the worst of these are the Sālkī, Bāgh, and Mārinī in Baud, the Tel and Ang in the Sonpur State. The road, except the portion in the Sonpur State and the portion between Dhamā and Sambalpur which are good gravelled sections, is a surface road, and running as it does in

Cuttack-Sonpur-Sambalpur road.

close proximity to the river is in many parts poor owing to the sandy nature of the soil and to the fact that in many places, especially near Harbhangā in the Baud State, it is overtopped by high floods: there are bungalows at regular intervals all the way from Cuttack to Sonpur, and there is also a bungalow at Binkā in the Sonpur State and one at Dhamā. The crossing at Dhamā is an exceedingly difficult one, and accordingly a diversion is under construction from Dhamā along the north bank of the river to the Sonpur border, whence the road will be carried on by the State and the crossing made at Binkā, an important village in the Sonpur State on the south bank of the river.

Sambalpur-Patnā-Kālāhandi road.

The Sambalpur-Patnā-Kālāhandī road crosses the Mahānadī at Sambalpur, where, except in the rainy season, an excellent pontoon bridge is maintained by the Bengal-Nāgpur Railway and travels *viâ* Attābīrā, Bargarh and Barpāli to the Sonpur border, a distance of about 48 miles: as far as Bargarh the road is a metalled one, and from there to the Sonpur border a good gravelled road has been constructed. The road runs for a distance of 8 miles through the Sonpur State and then crosses the Ang river, which forms the border between the States of Sonpur and Patnā, crosses the Suktel and runs on to Bolāngir, the headquarters of the Patnā State: the road as far as Bolāngir from the Sambalpur-Sonpur border is an excellent gravelled road and the smaller streams are bridged. The distance from Sambalpur to Bolāngir is 76 miles. From Bolāngir, a good surface road runs on to Bhawānīpatnā, the headquarters of the Kālāhandī State, 64 miles from Bolāngir: the section of the road from Bolāngir to the Tel, a distance of 32 miles, and the boundary of the Patnā and Kālāhandī States is of heavy gradients running in a series of switchbacks and the surface is only moderate: from the border of the Kālāhandī State the country greatly improves, the gradients are comparatively easy and the surface is in fair order: the last five miles of the road before entering Bhawānīpatnā is in excellent order and bridged throughout: the whole length of the road is possible for a motor. There are bungalows at Attābīrā (17th mile), Bargarh (30th mile), Barpāli (40th mile) and Chārmundā (46th mile), all in the Sambalpur district: there are also bungalows at Dungrīpāli in the Sonpur State (53rd mile), at Sālebhattā (57th mile), just across the Tel river, at Bolāngir (76th mile) and Deogāon (88th mile) in the Patnā State and in the State of Kālāhandī at Kasurparā (116th mile), Utkelā (126th mile) and Bhawānīpatnā (140th mile). This route is a very important one for trade and commerce.

Raipur-Bhawānīpatnā road.

Another important road, but which, with the transfer of the five Sambalpur States from the Central Provinces to Orissa, has naturally become of somewhat less importance than before, is the Raipur-Bhawānīpatnā road which enters the Patnā State on the border of the Khariār zamīndāri in the Raipur district, and after running for about 12 miles through the south-western extremity of the Patnā State through Sindhekelā, it crosses the boundary of the Patnā and Kālāhandī States six miles further meeting the Tel river: from here the road runs due south for a distance of 7 miles to Mādingpadar, then turns south-east across the Kālāhandī State entering the Ganjām district of the Madras Presidency at Sikarkupā: the road is a gravelled one and maintained in excellent order: throughout its course in the Patnā and Kālāhandī States there is only one bungalow and that at Mādingpadar in the Kālāhandī State 12 miles from Bhawānīpatnā, with which it is connected by a good road. A considerable amount of traffic goes by this road to Ganjām and there is a traffic-registering station at Sikarkupā. The road passes Bhawānīpatnā, the headquarters of the Kālāhandī State, at a distance of 9 miles to the north.

These are the principal roads for traffic in the States. The States of Mayūrbhanj, Kālāhandi, Bāmra and Sonpur are well provided with good roads: and there are also good village roads in the States of Patnā, Dhenkānāl, Tālcher and Nayāgarh: internal communications are defective in the States of Baud, Bonai, Daspallā, Gāngpur, Khandparā and Tigiriā; but there are good roads in all cases to the headquarters of the States with bungalows at the headquarters. In the Mayūrbhanj State communications are excellent and the roads are well provided with travellers' bungalows: there is a good road from the headquarters, Bāripadā, to Karanjiā and thence to the Keonjhar border: in this State there are 149·50 miles of metalled road and 350 miles of surface road. In Kālāhandī there are 53½ miles of gravelled road and 116½ miles of good surface road: in this State a fine piece of engineering has recently been completed in the Ampānighāt road, which now gives through communication between the fertile plains of the State and the zamīndāri of Jaypur in Madras: the road is available for cart traffic and winds its way across the lofty barrier of the hills on the southern border, reaching at its summit a height of nearly 2,000 feet. In Bāmra, there is a good gravelled road from the railway station, Bāmra Road, on the Bengal-Nāgpur Railway to Deogarh, the headquarters of the State, a distance of 58 miles, with bungalows at Bāmra, Kuchindā and Sirid. In the State of Keonjhar a first class

Bāripadā-Karanjiā road.

Bāmra-Deogarh road.

gravelled road, 114 miles in length, is under rapid construction from Champuā on the Baitaranī river, opposite to Jaint in the Singhbhūm district, to the border of the State with the Cuttack district, passing through the headquarters and the subdivision of Anandpur: bungalows have been built along the entire length at easy stages: this road will give direct access from the Chakradharpur station on the Bengal-Nāgpur line in the Singhbhūm district to the Vyās Sarovar station on the East Coast section of the Bengal-Nāgpur Railway in the Cuttack district. A good road is under construction from the railway station of Pānposh on the Bengal-Nāgpur Railway in the Gāngpur State to Bonaigarh, the headquarters of the Bonai State. **Champuā-Vyās Sarovar road.** **Pānposh-Bonaigarh road.**

POSTAL AND TELEGRAPH COMMUNICATIONS. The Imperial post now plies in all the States, with sub-post offices or branch post offices at all the headquarters, except at Tigiriā. The five States transferred from the Central Provinces are well served in their postal communications, there being letter-boxes at the school houses in most of the important villages: the dealings of the post offices in these States are considerable, especially in the State of Kālāhandī. The Imperial post travels by the Sambalpur-Patnā-Kālāhandī road from Sambalpur and there is a telegraph office at Bargarh: at Bolāngir and Bhawānīpatnā there are sub-post offices and letter-boxes at all the places where there are bungalows and also at other important villages *en route*: from Bhawānīpatnā the mail runs on to Madras, *viâ* Ampānighāt in the southern extremity of the Kālāhandī State. Telegraph lines connect Sundargarh, the headquarters of the Gāngpur State, with Jharsagurā in the Sambalpur district, Nīlgiri with Balasore, Dhenkānāl with Cuttack, Bāripadā with Rūpsā station on the East Coast section of the Bengal-Nāgpur Railway, and there is a telegraph line from Cuttack to Bānki which gives ready means of communication with the States of Khandparā, Tigiriā, Barāmbā and Daspallā. Besides there are combined sub-post and telegraph offices at Pānposh and Kumārkelā in the Gāngpur State and at Bāmra. A telephone line runs from Bāmra to Deogarh and from Deogarh to Bārkut and to Sagrā. **Telephone line.**

WATER COMMUNICATIONS. The Mahānadī and Brāhmanī form broad waterways during half the year, but there is no steamer or regular boat service on either of them.

RAILWAYS. The Bengal-Nāgpur Railway runs through the States of Gāngpur and Bāmra for 45 miles in the former, and 22 miles in the latter: the East Coast section of the same line passes in proximity to the States of Ranpur, Nīlgiri and Mayūrbhanj. The only State railway in the States is the narrow gauge line, 33 miles long, from Rūpsā station on the East Coast section of the Bengal-Nāgpur line to Bāripadā, the headquarters of the Mayūrbhanj State. A broad gauge line is about to be constructed from Kālimàti station on the Bengal-Nāgpur Railway to the foot of the Gurumāsaiāni hill in the Mayūrbhanj State to transport the iron ore for the Steel Works to be erected at the former place: an extension of the railway system in the Mayūrbhanj State is also under contemplation.

TRAMWAYS.

There are light tramways for the transport of minerals only in the Gāngpur State: these light tramways run from the Bisrā railway station on the Bengal-Nāgpur line to Ursu, a distance of five miles, and from Rourkelā to the Brāhmanī, a distance of 3 miles, to transport limestone and dolomite: a light tramway has also been constructed from the railway station of Dharuādiha on the Bengal-Nāgpur Railway to Gariājor, a distance of 9 miles, to transport the manganese ore worked at the latter place. The granite quarries at Nilgiri are connected by a tramway with the Balasore railway station.

CHAPTER X.

LAND REVENUE ADMINISTRATION.

LAND REVENUE SYSTEM.

THE land revenue system is a very simple one and is practically homogeneous throughout the States. Ownership in the land rests with the State, but the right of occupancy rests with the actual cultivator who, so long as he pays his rents, is left in undisturbed possession. There is little or no subinfeudation but there are a few large estates. Alienation by sale, gift or mortgage by a tenant of his holding is illegal, and subjects both the transferer and transferee to unconditional ejectment. The influence of the Mughalbandi districts is, however, observable in the States neighbouring on the Cuttack, Balasore and Purī districts. Such alienation is strictly prohibited and disallowed in the five States transferred from the Central Provinces, the States of Bonai and Gāngpur and those States, such as Baud, Pāl Laharā and Athmallik which are more in touch with Sambalpur than Cuttack; in some of the States such transfers are allowed with the permission of the State authorities, but even in such cases the permission is sparingly given and only after close scrutiny. The Khonds, Binjhāls, Juāngs and Bhuiyās claim to be the real owners of the soil and when questioned "Who are you?" the answer invariably given, however humble in origin and position the member of these races may be, is "I am a zamīndār," or owner of the soil. The wild non-Hinduised Khond has never consented to pay a regular land revenue: this class of Khond is mostly found in Kālāhandī, where a nominal fee is paid for the *padā* or *jhūming* area, and it is paid more as an act of concession than as a rental: of late years the Khonds have been induced in Kālāhandī to pay an increased revenue, but this has been chiefly an amicable arrangement. The Bhuiyās similarly pay a house-tax. There are practically no intermediate rights in the soil, except in the case of service tenures and other beneficiary grants.

SETTLEMENTS.

In those States which have come from time to time under the administration of Government, regular settlements have been made: in the States formerly known as the Tributary Mahāls of Orissa, settlements are made by means of a local standard pole known as the *dusti padikā* and a rough classification of the soil, or on an approximate estimate of the produce of the land. In these States the tenants are more advanced and are now accustomed to the methods of enumeration by *māns* (two-thirds of an acre), *gunths* and *biswās* of their land. In the five States transferred from the Central Provinces regular settlements have been made for many years past and the measurements recorded in acres : the tenants of these parts, however, and also of Gāngpur and Bonai, always denominate the area of their lands by the seed capacity. This system, too, is the common one even in the 17 States formerly known as the Tributary States of Orissa, and in those States the denomination in *māns*, etc., though well known and understood, is practically only used before the State officials or in presenting petitions. The periods of these settlements are generally for 10 to 15 years.

REVENUE-PAYING LANDS.

Revenue.

The rents are now mostly paid in cash and additional contributions at fixed rates, usually of rice, grain, *ghī* (clarified butter) and goats, are levied on the occasions of certain festivals : these payments in kind have in certain States been commuted to cash payments and the tenants have the option of paying the value in cash if they so desire. In the case of villages held by *lākhirājdārs* the tenants usually cultivate on the *bhāg* principle, or half division of produce, but this custom is rapidly disappearing. In most of the States supplies (*rasad*) are given free to the Chief and his officials on tour, and this supply is to be regarded as part of the revenue: the system of providing *begāri* or free labour, in return for daily feeding, is also really a revenue asset.

Rates of assessment.

The revenue paid is supposed to bear some relation to outturn, but the mode of calculation is often crude. The rate per acre for rice lands ranges from Re. 0-9-8 to Rs. 3-14-6 and for miscellaneous crops grown on uplands from Re. 0-2-6 to Re. 1-12-7. The assessments are light and pressure is rarely exercised in collection and the tenants readily obtain suspensions. In all the States the village headmen hold leases or *pattās* in which all payments due are noted and also the lands assigned in the village for village servants, who generally consist of the *chaukidār* (village policeman), water-bearer to supply water to visitors and the *jhānkar*, who is a village factotum, being the priest of the village sylvan gods, watcher and identifier of the boundaries and an assistant *chaukidār*, and a helper to the village headman in rent collection. The land revenue is collected by means of farmers termed variously *gaontiās*, *gānjhus*, *sarbarāhkārs*, *pradhāns* and *thikādārs*. The villages are leased to these men for the period of settlement and in the case of villages which have not been regularly settled, the lease is usually for 5 years. These rent

Village administration.

collectors receive either commission varying from 5 to 15 per cent., or in several of the States have certain service or *jāgir* lands known as *bhogrā* which go with the office : these lands are nowhere supposed to exceed 20 to 25 per cent. of the total lands of the village and are generally not more than 20 per cent. and usually less. The total *jamā* of the village is taken and the lands held by the farmer are taken as lands paying a rental equivalent to one-fourth of the total *jamā* if the *jāgir* is allowed at 25 per cent. and so on, in proportion. In large villages these *jāgir* lands are a great attraction and well-to-do cultivators are eager to take up the *gaontiāhi* of such villages: these lands are known as *bhogrā* and in all the States except Gāngpur are assessed and the *gaontiā* pays for them, but is only too glad to do so, as they are naturally about the best lands in the village. A *salāmi* or bonus is sometimes levied when renewing leases; there is no fixed rule as to the amount, but it usually does not exceed one year's rental or the arrears due on the village. In some of the States, however, these *bhogrā* lands have disappeared and the *gaontiā* only gets his commission: in such cases it is difficult to obtain good men and collections suffer.

Gaontiās. The right of a *gaontiā* is in no wise hereditary; it emanates entirely from the State and a *gaontiā* cannot transfer by sale, gift or mortgage, his village or his *bhogrā* lands; if he does so he *ipso facto* loses his village: he may privately partition the *bhogrā* lands amongst members of his family or allow tenants to cultivate them, but all such encumbrances are immediately voided when he ceases to be the *gaontiā*. *Gaontiās* who have held their office for twenty years or have executed substantial improvements in their villages obtain a protected status: that is, they are not ousted if they properly conduct the affairs of the villages, duly collect the rents and perform the other duties they are bound to and do not alienate their *bhogrā* lands or their villages. In cases where the *gaontiā* is *bona-fide* unable to collect rents he receives assistance from the State, but he must first pay in the total demand and then the State takes action on his behalf. The land revenue is a first charge on the land.

Ganjhus. In some instances these headmen are the original clearers of the soil, and this class is common in Gāngpur and Bonai, where they are specially identified by the name of *ganjhus*: they generally hold their leases for longer periods than the ordinary *gaontiā* and their villages generally have not been regularly settled and in consequence rentals are lighter.

ZAMINDARIS. The only States in which there are zamīndāris are Bāmra, Gāngpur, Kālāhandī, Keonjhar, Patnā and Sonpur. In Kālāhandī the zamīndārs are members of the Rāj family and obtained their grants originally as maintenance grants. In Patnā and Sonpur the zamīndārs are members of the aboriginal races such as Gonds and Binjhāls: the incidences of their tenures are dealt with in the articles on these States.

REVENUE-FREE LANDS. **Rāj family grants.** **Other grants.**

Besides the zamīndāris, there are in all States grants to members of the Rāj families known as *khanjā*, *bābuānā* and *khorposhdāri* grants: all such grants are liable to resumption and in some States regular rules exist whereby the grants gradually become absorbed and assessed to full rates: the other grants are the usual gifts to Brāhmans in the shape of *lākhirāj* grants, *debottar* grants (religious), *brahmottar* and *māfi* (free) grants for various reasons: in some States these grants have been freely made to *paiks* (militia) who in former days were wounded or killed fighting for their Chief: such grants usually consist of isolated plots known as *phutkar* and the grants are styled *rakta-phutkar* (blood plots): *paiks* and others hold service lands (*jāgīrs*) for various reasons.

CHAPTER XI.

GENERAL ADMINISTRATION.

ADMINISTRATIVE CHARGES, POWERS AND STAFF.

THE Chiefs administer their States in accordance with the provisions of their *sanads* which define their status, position and powers. The five Sambalpur States transferred from the Central Provinces in 1905 received their *sanads* in the year 1867. The States formerly known as the Tributary Mahāls of Orissa received their *sanads* in 1894 and the States of Gāngpur and Bonai in 1899, and in 1908 revised *sanads* were issued to the former States. All the 24 States are now known as the Feudatory States of Orissa.

The actual powers exercised by the Chiefs vary; in some States the power of imprisonment extends to two years, and all cases of heinous crime are committed to British officers for trial: in other States the Chiefs exercise full criminal powers, except that in the case of capital sentences the records of the case are submitted for confirmation by the Commissioner of the Orissa Division. The Chiefs, however, are not entitled to try offences in which Europeans are concerned.

The Chiefs usually invest their chief executive officer, the *Dīwān*, with these powers or somewhat smaller powers and confine themselves to dealing with appellate cases. In the case of the States which from any cause come from time to time under the administration of Government, the Superintendents appointed by Government to be in direct charge of the States exercise the powers enjoyed by the Chief of the State.

As regards cases tried by British officers, the warrants of these officers are executable in a British jail. Those States which do not exercise full criminal powers, commit all cases which they are not entitled to try to a British officer: for the disposal of these cases the District Officers of Purī, Cuttack, Balasore, Midnapore, Sambalpur, and Angul and the Political Agent exercise the powers of Sessions Judges, over whom is the Commissioner of Orissa, exercising the function of a High Court. In the exercise of their residuary jurisdiction British officers are guided by the law of British India, relating to offences and criminal procedure, in so far as it is applicable, and in cases where the Chiefs and their subjects are concerned in so far as it is not inconsistent with any local law or custom.

The *sanads* provide that the Chiefs shall follow the advice of the officer duly appointed for that purpose by Government and lay down the general principles of administration. The management of excise is specially provided for in all the *sanads* and a prohibition is made against the levying of transit duties on merchandise. All the States are bound to deliver over offenders from British or other territory who take refuge in the States and to assist British officers who may pursue offenders within the States.

REVENUE. The total income of the States in 1892-93 was reported at Rs. 16,12,443 and in 1901-02 at Rs. 27,09,559. In 1907-08 it amounted to Rs. 41,43,385. The budget system is supposed to be followed and in many instances is carefully adhered to, but in some cases the actual system of accounts is not always as correct or systematic as they might be: the figures given above are, however, approximately reliable, as the States have from time to time come under Government administration and their finances conducted under regular account rules. On the whole, however, finances are well managed and a distinct improvement is taking place, and many of the States have annually a very fair balance set aside to meet unexpected emergencies and others have invested funds to meet necessity in the shape of famine or other misfortunes. The State of Mayūrbhanj has nearly 12 lakhs so invested in Government securities, the States of Dhenkānāl, Bonai, Kālāhandī and Nayāgarh similarly have fair sums invested: in the State of Bāmra there is a special invested famine fund and the Patnā State has commenced to invest money for a similar fund. These invested funds are in addition to the annual closing balance for which a minimum equivalent to three months' average working expenses is sought to be aimed at. **Land revenue.** The land revenue of the States amounted in 1892-93 to Rs. 10,72,868, in 1901-02 to Rs. 15,26,646 and in 1907-08 to Rs. 19,77,684. The principal source of income is in most States the land revenue, which is supplemented by excise, stamps, judicial fines and license fees from various minor monopolies. In some of the States the **Forest revenue.** forests yield a handsome profit. **Excise revenue.** The excise revenue consists of the license fees from the outstills, and from *gānja* and opium shops. **Stamps.** Some of the States have introduced the stamp and court-fee rules; the fees charged are generally below the rates prevailing in British territory. In all the States stamp fees are charged by the Chiefs, but in many cases the stamp merely consists of placing an impression of the State emblem on plain paper by a rubber seal and writing in the value. The miscellaneous revenue of the States is derived from several minor sources, such as fines and fees, *salāmis* or *nazarānas* and license fees for the sale of various forest products. According to a time-honoured custom, certain sums are subscribed as *māgan*, or voluntary contributions, on the occasion of the marriage, birth or death of a Chief. **Miscellaneous revenue.**

FORESTS. General description.

A large proportion of the total area of the States consists of forests, but a great proportion of this area is scrub. The character of the forests is the same throughout the States, except that the teak is found indigenous alone in the Kālāhandī State. The forests of the States were at one time extensive timber-producing tracts; reckless clearings, the wasteful system of *dāhi* cultivation, or felling and burning forests on the hill sides to raise catch-crops in the ashes, and in former days the felling and removing of any tree for the manufacture of railway sleepers without regard to any suitable girth limit, and the former indiscriminate ringing, a practice which has now been made a punishable offence, of *sâl* (*Shorea robusta*) for resin or *dhūp* by the forest tribes have very largely depleted them of good and valuable timber. Even where good tracts of forest still remain they have been spoilt and rendered very difficult of reservation by the indiscriminate location of villages and hamlets within their limits. The Chiefs do not now lease their forests without first obtaining advice and assistance from Government: suitable leases are now thus obtained for the States.

Forest administration.

Till recent years there was no idea of conservancy, and it is only during the last few years that the Chiefs have begun to realize the necessity of enforcing a regular forest administration, if any permanent and continued source of revenue is to be enjoyed from their forests. This has been forced upon their attention by the rapid disappearance of their forests before the spread of cultivation and the continued demands of villages for fresh forests from which to draw their supplies for domestic and agricultural purposes. The States formerly exercised no control over the forest areas allowed to the villagers, with the result that these areas quickly disappeared before the rapacity of the axes of the Kol and indigenous races, and the States are now having to find fresh areas for the villagers out of tracts, which have always been regarded as set apart as State forests. From the absence formerly of all conservation and protection against fire, reproduction has greatly diminished. Many of the States have awakened to the necessity of a forest policy and are taking vigorous action to re-establish their forests as far as possible. The advent of the railway and the great improvements which have taken place of late years in communications have added a greatly increased value to the forests. There is now very little really good timber left in the vicinity of the Mahānadī and Brāhmanī rivers, which furnish the best waterways, but elsewhere and further inland the forests owe their partial preservation to the absence of good roads and difficulty of transport. In the States of Daspallā, Kālāhandī, especially in the zamīndāri areas, Khandparā, Mayūrbhanj, Nayāgarh, Pāl Laharā, and the western portion of Patnā, fine and valuable forests still remain. But for the Khonds in Kālāhandī and the Juāngs in Pāl Laharā the forests in these two States would stand unrivalled. In the Rāmpur-Madanpur zamīndāri of the Kālāhandī State the *sâl* attains to great dimensions.

It is, however, only comparatively recently that any system of forest conservancy has been introduced into the States: whenever States have come under the administration of Government, steps have been taken to separate and properly demarcate the State forests from the village forests, to constitute properly reserved areas and to exercise some degree of control over the village or protected forests to prevent their sheer wanton destruction. The States which have led the way in forestry are Mayūrbhanj and Dhenkānāl. In the former State there is one tract of forest which deserves especial mention: this is the range known as the Simlāpāl, in which there are large quantities of magnificent *sâl*. In this State there is a fully organized Forest Department, with a trained Forest Officer in charge and properly qualified assistants under him. In the State of Dhenkānāl a survey of the forests was made by a Government Forest Officer during the period it was under administration: the work of demarcation, surveying and preparation of working-plans was taken in hand and is being carried on by the present Chief: a trained officer is in charge of the department with Dehra Dun students under him. The State of Nayāgarh is under the administration of Government, and the demarcation and survey of the very valuable forests on the southern border have been nearly completed. The same policy has been undertaken in Pāl Laharā during the period of its administration and a capable Forest Officer is in charge. In Patnā and Kālāhandī the demarcation of the State forests from the village jungles is in progress. In Bāmra the Chief has commenced a regular system of forestry and has a Dehra Dun student in charge, and two local men are being trained for the State in the British Forest Division of Singhbhūm. In Gāngpur the Chief has recently appointed a Dehra Dun student to organize the Forest Department. In Narsinghpur and Barāmbā there are small but valuable forests, and rules have been drawn up for their working

In all the States where there are forests of any value, forest rules now exist for their management. The Chiefs now evince genuine interest in the preservation of their forests. From all the States where there are forests, of any value, local men are being regularly sent to Singhbhūm for a course of training in forestry. The present time marks an era in the history of forestry in the States of Orissa.

Village forests. As regards the administration of the forests themselves, it is a recognised custom and one based on immemorial usage that the villagers have a right to the forests round the village site: in former times this no doubt was taken as giving a right to the forest for such a distance as the villagers were able to proceed and remove the timber and produce to their homes: the growth of neighbouring villages, however, with similar rights led to difficulties, and it was necessary for the State to assume some control over these forests. **Fees.** The result is that now-a-days the people pay commutation fees for the right to cut and remove what are classified as third class timber from these village forests for domestic purposes and also a certain amount of *sāl* for their agricultural implements: if timber of any other class is required or there be a demand for a larger supply of *sāl*, these are obtained from the State forests on payment of license fees at reduced rates, if they are genuine residents of the State. These commutation fees are, in the more advanced States and where it is desired to obtain a more precise and scientific assessment, levied on the cultivation at the rate of one anna per *mān* (or two-thirds of an acre) of rice lands and half an anna per *mān* on uplands and culturable waste. In the case of non-cultivators a special rate is provided for according to the class of calling followed, a blacksmith naturally having to pay more than a weaver. In the more backward States the fee is charged on the number of ploughs possessed by a cultivator and on the industrial classes a special fee per house is levied, but in these cases the fee is generally known as a *pātki*, literally a cess paid by a weaver of the Pān class, but generally used to express the fee charged for wood taken for domestic and professional purposes by the industrial classes: thus there is the *dālkāti* or fee paid by the rearers of tusser cocoons, *lohāri*, fee paid by the blacksmith, *kumhāri*, fee paid by the potter, etc. It is usual for the commutation fee to cover the price of *sāl* required for carts and cart-wheels, but this is not universally so: the solid-wheeled carts (*sagars*) necessitate a very extravagant use of timber, two large-sized planks being required from which to cut out the half circles required to make the wheel. In some parts a *tangāhi* is also levied; this is, however, really an item of land revenue receipt, being a charge of so much on each family using an axe for cultivation, in other words, the rent paid by those races who live by the method of *dāhi* cultivation described above.

Edible fruit-trees.

Both in the State and the village forests all edible fruit-trees are strictly preserved: these are the *kendu* or ebony (*Diospyros melanoxylon*), *mahuā* (*Bassia latifolia*), mango (*Mangifera indica*), tamarind (*Tamarindus indica*), *jām* (*Eugenia jambolana*), jack (*Artocarpus integrifolia*), *āmrā* or hog-plum (*Spondias mangifera*), and *chār* (*Buchanania latifolia*).

Timber trees.

The principal timber trees are *sāl* (*Shorea robusta*), *piāsāl* (*Pterocarpus marsupium*), *sissū* (*Dalbergia Sissoo*), *karam* (*Adina cordifolia*), *bandhan* (*Ougeinia dalbergioides*), *gamhāri* (*Gmelina arborea*), *kendu* or ebony (*Diospyros melanoxylon*), *mahuā* (*Bassia latifolia*) and *āsan* or *sahāj* (*Terminalia tomentosa*). A certain amount of teak (*Tectova grandis*) of good quality and fair size is met with in Kālāhandī especially on the south-western side in the hills bordering on the Khariār zamīndāri.

Other common trees.

Among other common trees are the mango (*Mangifera indica*), tamarind (*Tamarindus indica*), *jām* (*Eugenia jambolana*), jack (*Artocarpus integrifolia*), *āmrā* or hog-plum (*Spondias mangifera*), *chār* (*Buchanania latifolia*), *dhaurā* (*Lagarstæmia parvi flora*), *haritakī* (*Terminalia chebula*), *kuchilā* (*Strychnos Nux-vomica*), *khair* (*Acacia catechu*), *gundi* (*Mallotus philippinensis*), *bādārā* (*Terminalia belerica*), *semul* or cotton tree (*Bombax malabaricum*), *tūn* (*Cedrela toona*), *karanj* (*Galedupa indica*), *kusum* (*Schleichera trijuga*), banyan (*Ficus indica*) and *pīpal* (*Ficus religiosa*).

Minor forest products.

The minor forest products are honey, bees-wax, tusser, lac, a dye called *gundi* and various medicinal drugs. *Sabai* grass (*Ischæmum angustifolium*) grows largely in Dhenkānāl, Keonjhar, Mayūrbhanj, Nīlgiri, Pāl Laharā, Tālcher and other States, and is used locally for the manufacture of ropes; there are *sabai* grass pressing machines at Bānki in the Bonai State, and at Bisrā in the Gāngpur State, the pressed bales being exported to Calcutta.

Forest revenue.

The revenue from forests for the 24 States of Orissa amounted in 1907-08 to Rs. 7,38,850.

EXCISE ADMINISTRATION.

Opium.

In the case of opium all the States draw their supplies from a Government treasury and make their own arrangements for sale within the States; the States formerly classified as the Tributary Mahāls of Orissa obtain their supplies at the price prevailing in the British districts of Cuttack, Balasore and Purī. The States of Gāngpur and Bonai, which were formerly comprised in the Chotā Nāgpur Division draw their supplies from the Government treasury at Puruliā. The five Sambalpur States transferred from the Central Provinces obtain their supplies from the Sambalpur district. The States follow the system in force in British India and annually auction out the right to sell opium to licensed vendors.

In the case of *gānja* the States formerly known as the Tributary Mahāls of Orissa obtain their supply under what is known as the Cooch Behār system, the States obtaining Rājshāhi *gānja* at cost price on the condition of not selling the drug at a lower rate of duty than that levied in the neighbouring British districts of Orissa; the system was introduced in 1895 in order to prevent the smuggling into British India of Garhjāt *gānja*. The system has worked well and the cultivation of *gānja* in the States has long ceased to exist. The States of Gāngpur and Bonai obtain their supplies of Rājshāhi *gānja* from the Government treasury at Puruliā. In the case of the five Sambalpur States the *gānja* supplied is Khandwā *gānja*; it was till recently issued to them from Sambalpur; but is now being obtained by them direct from the Deputy Commissioner of Nimār. The States, however, must retail the *gānja* at a rate not lower than that prevailing in adjacent British territory. The right to sell *gānja* in the States is annually auctioned out to the highest bidder. **Gānja.**

As regards country liquor the outstill system is generally in vogue, and in the five Sambalpur States the outstill system with dependent shops is the rule. The outstills are annually put up to auction; the liquor is mostly distilled from *mahuā*. The policy aimed at is to have not more than one outstill or shop for every 30 square miles, and this standard is observed in most of the States; of late years there has been a remarkable reduction in the number of stills and shops to the great improvement in the general excise administration, the supply of purer liquor and the lesser prevalence of drunkenness; the reduction has been marked in the Gāngpur State where the number of stills has fallen from 220 in 1904 to 60 in 1908; similarly reductions have been effected with similar results in the five States transferred from the Central Provinces; in these States there were formerly a number of dependent shops attached to the outstills; reductions have been effected amongst the large Khond population of these five States. Formerly in some of the States the Chiefs levied an excise fee on the brewing of rice beer (*pachwai* or *hāndiā*) for home consumption; this was strongly opposed by the indigenous races who brew *hāndiā* and the tax has universally been abolished by the Chief and brewing for home consumption is allowed, but on no account may *hāndiā* be brewed for sale and no licenses for brewing *hāndiā* **Liquor.** **Rice beer.**

are given. In Mayūrbhanj and Nīlgiri the Madras contract system for the supply of country spirit was introduced in 1905. The local manufacture of country spirit was prohibited and the spirit was obtained from the liquor depôt at Balasore, and stored at the State liquor depôts at the prescribed strength and then issued to the retail vendors on payment of cost price and duty.

Toddy. The tapping of the *tāl* palm for toddy is not allowed by the Chiefs of most of the States and any income under the head of *tāri mahāl* is unusual.

Excise staff. The only States which maintain a regular excise staff are the States of Mayūrbhanj and Gāngpur; elsewhere the control of excise arrangements rests with the revenue officers and the police.

Zamīndāri excise arrangements. In all the States the control of excise arrangements in the zamīndāris rests with the Chiefs.

For the prevention of disputes and smuggling a neutral zone of three miles has been established on either side of the boundaries between British India and the States, and the boundaries between the States themselves.

Excise revenue. The total excise income for all the 24 States is reported at Rs. 1,00,020 for the year 1892-93, at Rs. 2,26,225 for 1901-02 and at Rs. 4,16,001 for 1907-08.

ADMINISTRATION OF JUSTICE.

Civil Justice. In the disposal of civil justice the Chiefs of all the States have full powers, being bound only to administer justice fairly and impartially. It is open to the Political Agent to advise the Chiefs where injustice or hardship has been done. The great majority of the suits tried are below the value of Rs. 50. The average annual number of suits for disposal during the three years 1905-06 to 1907-08 was 17,105.

Criminal Justice. Criminal cases mainly consist of ordinary burglaries and thefts; dacoities take place occasionally but there are seldom any cases of rioting. Dacoity and robbery are as a rule exceptional, but certain limited areas bear an unenviable reputation for this class of crime: the wild and inaccessible hill tracts to the south of the Kālāhandī State on the border of the Jaypur zamīndāri in the Madras Presidency are subject from time to time to more or less severe outbreaks of dacoity: this area is a difficult one to control and bad characters frequently resort there. The Khonds who inhabit these parts are always ready to join in with any adventurous leader and plunder the timid cultivators of the plains: these dacoities are, however, mostly technical and are entered into by the Khonds more in the spirit of sport than from any addiction to violent crime. The Kols in the wilds of Bāmra and the western portion of the Bonai State will similarly, from time to time, band together and commit dacoity. Dacoity from agrarian troubles or other causes is rare, though from time to time rebellions, involving serious dacoity, have broken out amongst the indigenous races owing to opposition to some action of the State or to the pressure of the more civilised cultivators on the lands of these races. The average annual number of criminal cases reported to the police during the three years 1905-06 to 1907-08 was 7,768 in most of the States crime is now very fairly reported and these figures may be taken as a representative average.

The disposal of both civil and criminal justice has of late years shown a general improvement: suits and cases are disposed of with promptitude, findings and punishments are usually suitable and adequate, and this improvement is being steadily maintained.

The larger States of Mayūrbhanj, Keonjhar and Dhenkānāl are divided into subdivisions with an officer in charge and in some cases a second officer: in Bāmra the State is divided into three *tahsīls* with an officer in charge of each: this arrangement naturally makes for more efficient administration and prompter disposal of judicial business. In the States of Pātnā, Sonpur and Kālāhandī the leading zamīndārs and other prominent persons are invested with powers as Honorary Magistrates, sitting generally as benches: the zamīndārs also are sometimes invested with small civil powers.

POLICE. *Paiks.*

The creation of a regular police force in the States has been comparatively recent. In former times the *paiks* (feudal militia) served as the representatives of the law and order imposed by the Chiefs. This body of men, however, has always been a source of danger and trouble to the Chiefs and their influence has been more than once too strong for the Chiefs to resist: the *paiks* have always regarded their police duties as nominal and only performed these duties when and how it pleased them. The employment of *paiks* is now confined to guard duty at the Chief's residence, escort duty and appearance on occasions of pomp and ceremony and in their place it has become necessary with the general advancement of the country to introduce a regular police force: the *paiks* have accordingly been greatly reduced in number and their grants of land gradually resumed, except in the Kālāhandī State, where a very large body of these men are still maintained and made to assist the regular police in watching and patrolling the turbulent tracts of the south-eastern boundary.

Police force.

In 1907-08 the total police force in the States consisted of 418 officers and 1,936 men. In Keonjhar and Mayūrbhanj European officers were in charge of the police force. There has been a great improvement in the pay of the police of recent years and there are now trained and qualified officers in charge. The Chiefs send their own officers to the Police Training College at Rānchī for a course of instruction. In the larger States of Dhenkānāl, Gāngpur, Kālāhandī and Mayūrbhanj a large and well staffed police force is maintained and the police administration is very similar to that followed in British India. In the smaller States the police force is generally adequate and suitable to the requirements of the States, and in all cases regular rules are followed and suitable registers and forms maintained. The jealousy of earlier days between the police force of one State and another has very largely disappeared, and the State police now co-operate together for concerted action, regular inter-State co-operation meetings are held and inquiry slips as to the movements of bad characters regularly circulated : a set of mutual extradition rules has been adopted, and it is no longer possible for the criminal of one State to find a secure hiding in a neighbouring State.

In many of the States considerable attention has been paid to the proper housing of the police and excellent police stations and barracks are to be found.

Rural police. The rural police consist of the *chaukidars* who are remunerated with service lands: the *chaukidars* attend regularly on fixed dates at the police stations and are gradually being developed into a useful subsidiary aid to the police.

Military police. There are no regular military police in the States, but in most of the States a certain percentage of the force are armed with converted Martini-Henry carbines under the sanction of Government.

JAILS. The old fashioned State jails consisting of a few thatched huts surrounded with a mud wall are now of the past. All the States now possess fair to moderate jails and the management is usually fair. The States of Dhenkānāl, Gāngpur, Kālāhandī, Māyūrbhanj, Nayāgarh, and Patnā, possess excellent masonry jails, the jail of the Kālāhandī State affording accommodation for nearly 400 prisoners : there are good masonry jails in Bāmra, Barāmbā, Baud, Daspallā, Narsinghpur, and Sonpur : new jails are in course of erection in Athmallik, Hindol, Nīlgiri, Rairākhol and Tālcher. The general adoption of regular rules for the administration of the jails has resulted in late years in a very marked improvement in the management and discipline : sanitary arrangements are well attended to : regular diet is given and labour on a graduated scale enforced : prisoners' history tickets are duly maintained and a medical parade of all prisoners is held weekly, when tasks are changed according to the state of health of a prisoner : the State Medical Officer daily visits the jail and in several of the State jails there are now dispensaries and sick wards : under the rules a regular scale of punishment is prescribed and the punishments now inflicted are rarely inadequate or excessive. The majority of the labour done is extra-mural, but there is more regular indoor labour on set tasks than formerly : escapes are not very frequent, and in 1908 the total number was only 40 : this is noteworthy in view of the large amount of extra-mural labour done. The health of the prisoner is fair, and from 1906 to 1908 the total number of deaths was only 115. In all the States there is a Jail Superintendent and a Jailor in direct charge. The fly-shuttle loom is being rapidly introduced into all the jails and prisoners are sent to Bāmra, Dhenkānāl and Angul for training in the use of this loom.

PUBLIC WORKS DEPARTMENT.

With the exception of the two small States of Khandparā and Tigiriā, all the States now maintain Sub-Overseers in charge of their public works. In the States of Dhenkānāl, Keonjhar and Mayūrbhanj, regular Public Works Departments are maintained with qualified Engineers in charge, assisted by Overseers and Sub-Overseers. The States of Bonai, Gāngpur, Kālāhandī, Patnā, and Rairākhol employ the services of the Executive Engineer, Sambalpur district, who is known as the Agency Executive Engineer: in these States there are fine public buildings and works of considerable importance are undertaken : in order to secure efficiency and proper control the Public Works Department of each of these States is manned by qualified Overseers and Sub-Overseers. For the efficient management of the public works of the States of Hindol and Nayāgarh, which are under the administration of Government, a Supervisor is in charge of the Public Works Departments of these two States : the Chiefs of the Narsinghpur and Barāmbā States likewise employ the services of this officer: plans and estimates for works to be executed in the States in the neighbourhood of Angul and Cuttack, when under administration of Government, are sent to the Superintending Engineer, Orissa Circle, Cuttack, for professional scrutiny, and the same officer examines from time to time any plans and estimates on which the Chiefs of other States desire his opinion.

There are no canals in the States and the public works consist principally of public buildings, roads and bridges : there are excellent roads in several of the States: in most of the States there are excellent public courts and offices and good jails. Irrigation works on an extensive scale do not exist ; in Bāmra, Dhenkānāl and Mayūrbhanj, there are, however, some works of considerable size : in Bāmra, at a place called Sirgirā, the Chief has undertaken a large scheme which affords irrigation to 2,000 acres. Deogarh, the headquarters of the Bāmra State, boast of a water-supply obtained from a fine waterfall close to the town the water from which is carried through the town by pipes and standards have been erected at convenient centres : the town also is lit by electric light and the Chief has a telephone service to the headquarters of the three *tahsils*, to the railway station of Bāmra and to his irrigation works at Sirgirā. In Nayāgarh a programme of small irrigation projects has been drawn up and is being annually worked up to: the country of the Garhjāts lends itself very readily to these small but exceedingly useful works and of late years more attention has been paid to their developement.

For all the States famine programmes have been compiled, and the policy of gradually undertaking preventive works has been inaugurated. The villages in the Garhjāts are, however, for the most part well provided with irrigation tanks and small embankments, known locally as *mundā* : the nature of the country renders them a necessity, and in fact without them real rice cultivation would be impossible.

In 1907-08 the total expenditure on public works amounted to Rs. 8,03,879, of which Rs. 2,43,025 were spent on roads and Rs. 4,00,184 on public buildings. The principal expenditure incurred was by the States of Mayūrbhanj, Rs. 2,04,376; Keonjhar, Rs. 1,74,267; Kālāhandī, Rs. 60,240; Nīlgiri, Rs. 47,261; Nayāgarh, Rs. 45,668; Patnā, Rs. 41,219; Athmallik, Rs. 40,000; Dhenkānāl, Rs. 38,740; Bāmra, Rs. 27,855; and Gāngpur, Rs. 22,568. This expenditure was, however, above normal and was due to a certain extent to works being undertaken to provide labour owing to partial scarcity. The total expenditure in 1906-07 was Rs. 5,37,828. There is thus in the aggregate a considerable expenditure on public works, the expenditure annually showing a tendency to increase.

CHAPTER XII.

LOCAL SELF-GOVERNMENT.

MUNICIPALITIES.

THERE are three municipalities in the States, viz., at Bāripadā, the headquarters of the Mayūrbhanj State, and at Sonpur and Binkā, both in the Sonpur State. An account of these three municipalities will be found in the articles on the States of Mayūrbhanj and Sonpur.

CHAPTER XIII.

EDUCATION.

PROGRESS OF EDUCATION. EDUCATION is very backward, but in late years there has been steady progress, especially in primary education. In 1901 only 2·7 per cent. (5·3 males and 0·19 females) could read and write. In 1907-08 the total number of pupils in the primary stage, both in Primary and Secondary schools, was 47,468 against 22,662 in 1901-02. The increase is a satisfactory proof of the progress of primary education: this advance is partly due to the extension of the Government primary grant to most of the schools in the 17 States, which formerly comprised the Tributary Mahāls of Orissa, and partly to the better supervision afforded by the strengthened and better qualified supervising staff in all the States.

SECONDARY AND PRIMARY SCHOOLS. There were, in 1907-08, 3 High English schools, viz., at the headquarters of the Bāmra, Dhenkānāl and Mayūrbhanj States, with good boarding establishments attached; these schools are affiliated to the Calcutta University: 20 Middle English, 7 Middle Vernacular, 145 Upper Primary and 1,415 Lower Primary schools; the number of pupils in the High and Middle schools was 3,110, and there were 41,788 pupils in Primary schools. Besides these, in 1907-08, there were 5,409 pupils receiving instruction in 258 special, advanced and elementary schools.

One boy in every 5 of school-going age was in the primary stage in 1907-08 against one boy in every 11 of school-going age at the close of 1901-02. During the last few years there has been a growing demand for English education, with a view to gain admission to professional schools. The number of Middle English schools increased in 1901-02 by 4 and again in 1907-08 there was a further increase of 5 schools, and during the same period the number of Middle Vernacular schools declined by 5 in 1901-02 and by 5 in 1907-08.

FEMALE EDUCATION. The number of girls' schools in 1907-08 was 95 and 4,864 girls were under instruction; of this number, 3,180 girls were reading in boys' schools. In the 17 States, formerly known as the Tributary Mahāls of Orissa, the number of girls' schools has increased from 20 in 1901-02 to 48 in 1907-08 or by 140 per cent. Female education is gradually and slowly advancing and the appointment of qualified female teachers to these schools has done much to popularise female education and to keep girls attending school to an older age.

ABORIGINAL AND BACKWARD RACES.

In the States of Athmallik, Dhenkānāl, Kālāhandī, Keonjhar, Mayūrbhanj, Nīlgiri, Pāl Laharā, Pātnā and Sonpur there are special schools for the education of aboriginal and low caste pupils, and in 1907-08 the number of pupils attending these schools was 6,342. Besides the pupils attending the schools meant specially for them, 3,061 pupils of these races attended other schools along with the pupils of other races in 1907-08.

TRAINING SCHOOLS.

Towards the close of 1905-06 eight *guru*-training schools were started in the States of Athgarh, Athmallik, Dhenkānāl, Mayūrbhanj, Narsinghpur, Nayāgarh, Nīlgiri and Tālcher. These schools are entirely maintained and managed by Government agency: in these schools the teachers of the village schools are trained and monthly stipends are allotted for the purpose: a *guru*-training school has also been started at the headquarters of the Kālāhandī State at the cost of, and under the management of, the State.

FINANCES.

The total expenditure on education for the year 1907-08 was Rs. 2,50,000, of which Rs. 37,000 was paid by Government, Rs. 1,36,000 by the several States and Rs. 77,000 from fees and subscriptions. The expenditure shows a marked increase of recent years in comparison with the expenditure of 1903-04: in that year the total expenditure was Rs. 1,56,000, of which Rs. 20,000 was paid by Government, Rs. 85,000 by the several States, Rs. 44,000 was met from fees and Rs. 7,000 from subscriptions. The result is that during the last four years the total expenditure has risen by 60·3 per cent. and the increase has been 85·00 per cent. in the contribution made by Government; 60·00 per cent. in the expenditure from the revenues of the States and 50·98 per cent. from the income derived from fees and subscriptions. In the case of the 17 States, formerly attached to the Orissa Division, contributions towards education are made by Government, and free assistance is also given by deputing Sub-Inspectors, Deputy Inspectors under an Agency Inspector of Schools to assist these States and the States of Bonai and Gāngpur in regularly supervising the schools and providing for expert and qualified inspection. For this purpose these States are divided into circles with Sub-Inspectors attached, and a Deputy Inspector is in charge of each circle. In the case of the States transferred from the Central Provinces the cost of education is entirely borne by the State revenues and from fees, no contribution being received from Government: these States employ their own educational inspecting officers, and are assisted by the Agency Inspector of Schools.

The total expenditure on Primary schools for boys was Rs. 1,14,786 in 1907-08 against Rs. 74,754 in 1901-02: this increase is due partly to a larger contribution from Government as regards the 17 States, formerly included in the Orissa Division, and partly to an increased expenditure by the States.

The average cost of educating a boy in a Primary school amounted in 1907-08 to Rs. 2-15 per year. During the six years from 1896-97 to 1901-02 the percentage of expenditure on Primary schools for boys and girls to the total expenditure on public education was 64·7. In the village Primary schools the teachers receive the greater part of their remuneration in kind.

The number of schools, scholars, and the cost of education in the 24 States of Orissa in 1907-08 was as follows:—

SCHOOLS.					SCHOLARS.			Number of scholars of the several aboriginal races.	Percentage of boys at school to the boys of school-going age.	Percentage of girls at school to the girls of school-going age.	DETAILS OF EXPENDITURE.				
Public.															
Secondary.	Primary.	Special.	Private (Elementary).	Total.	Boys.	Girls.	Total.				Contributed by Government.	Contributed by the State.	From fees.	From other sources.	Total.
											Rs.	Rs.	Rs.	Rs.	Rs.
15,60	1,560	26	232	1,848	45,446	4,861	50,307	9,403	18·97	2·04	37,388	1,35,882	56,985	20,413	2,50,668

GAZETTEER

OF THE

ORISSA FEUDATORY STATES.

PART II.

STATES.

CHAPTER I.

ATHGARH STATE.

THE State of Athgarh lies between 20° 26′ and 20° 41′ N., and 84° 32′ and 85° 52′ E., with an area of 168 square miles. It is bounded on the north by Dhenkānāl State; on the east and south by Cuttack district; on the south the Mahānadī river forms the boundary between the State and the British district of Cuttack; and on the west by the States of Tigiriā and Dhenkānāl. The country is level, low-lying and very subject to inundation. The soil is fertile. The average rainfall for the six years from 1902-03 to 1907-08 was 53·50 inches. The headquarters of the State are at Athgarh. PHYSICAL ASPECTS.

This State is alleged to have originally extended on the east as far as *parganas* Cuttack Hāveli and Dālijorā; on the west up to Tigiriā; on the north from Kapilās to Gobindpur, Baldiābandh, Nadiāli, Krishnaprasād, and Paschimeshwar temple; and on the south to Bānki, Domparā, Matri, and Patiā. Kakhari and Tapankhand were annexed by the Mughal rulers, and neighbouring Chiefs encroached upon the State from all sides. Parājān and Bajrakot were given away as *Amruta-manohi* (religious) endowments about 106 years ago. The Rājā of Dhenkānal who married two of the daughters of the Chief of Athgarh obtained possession of most of the *mauzās* or villages of Majkuri Bisa, *i.e.*, from Kapilās temple *viâ* Krishnaprasād to HISTORY.

Paschimeshwar temple. The family of the Chief of the Athgarh State belongs to the Karan caste of Orissa, and its recognised title is "Srī Karan Bawārta Patnaik." The founder of the State was Nīlādri Bawārta Patnaik: he was the Bawārta or minister of the Purī Rājā, who conferred on him the title of Rājā, and gave him Athgarh as a reward for his services or, according to another account, as a dowry for marrying the Rājā's sister. The State is one of the ten States which entered into treaty engagements in 1803. From the time of the founder of the State up to date, twenty-nine Rājās are said to have held the *gadi*. The present Chief obtained in 1908, as a personal distinction, the title of Rājā Bahādur from the British Government. The emblem of the State is Rādhā Krishna.

THE PEOPLE. The population increased from 36,603 in 1891 to 43,784 in 1901; of the latter number all but 643 are Hindus. The most numerous castes are the Chasās (10,000), Sahars (6,000) and Khandaits and Pāns (5,000 each). The average density of the population is 260 per square mile. It is distributed among 192 villages, of which the principal is Athgarh, the residence of the Rājā and situated on the Cuttack-Sambalpur road, in 20° 31′ north latitude, and 85° 38′ east longitude. The village of Gobrā lies near the eastern border of the State, in 20° 35′ north latitude, and 85° 52′ east longitude.

The census report of 1901 returned the population at 43,784 souls, classified as follows:—Hindus—males, 21,701, females, 21,440, total 43,141, or 98·5 per cent. of the total population of the State; proportion of males to total Hindu population, 50·3 per cent. Musalmāns—males, 149, females, 112, total 261, or 0·6 per cent. of the population; proportion of males to total Musalmāns, 57·1 per cent. Christians—males, 200, females, 182, total 382, or 0·8 per cent. of the population. Population of all denominations—males, 22,050, females, 21,734, total population of the State, 43,784: proportion of males to total population, 50·4 per cent. Number of literate persons in the State is 2,100 or 4·8 per cent. of the total population. Averages:—Villages per square mile, 1·14; persons per village, 228; houses per square mile, 52·4; houses per village, 45·9; persons per house, 5. The 192 villages are classified as follows:—171 with less than five hundred inhabitants, 17 with from five hundred to one thousand inhabitants, 3 with from one thousand to two thousand inhabitants and 1 with from two to five thousand inhabitants. Between 1830 and 1840, a number of people in the Athgarh State embraced Christianity, and the Baptist Mission at Cuttack in 1841 obtained a lease of 10 acres of jungle lands from the Rājā of Athgarh near a village called Chhagān. There are now three Christian villages, Parbatiā, Kapatikiri and Arakhtāngar, with a population of nearly 400 souls, who live by agriculture as ryots of the Rājā, though they have their homesteads on Mission lands. In Parbatiā, there is a chapel and a boys' and girls' school. There are 5 Mission schools in the neighbouring Hindu villages.

PUBLIC HEALTH.

The State maintains at the headquarters a charitable dispensary known as the Diamond Jubilee Hospital in charge of a Civil Hospital Assistant. The number of indoor patients treated in 1907-08 was 6, and outdoor patients 7,439. Vaccination is making progress in the State and there were 2,089 primary vaccinations and 813 revaccinations in 1907-08.

AGRICULTURE.

The soil is fertile, but is liable to inundations from the Mahānadī. The cultivation consists chiefly of rice, sugarcane, of which very valuable crops are raised, pulses and millets. The country is for the most part open, and lends itself readily to cultivation: the villages are prosperous, rents are light and the cultivators are undoubtedly prosperous as a class, and excellent irrigation tanks and embankments are to be found in many of the villages. The Chief has opened an experimental farm and has done much to introduce the better classes of fine rice and the drought-resisting classes of *āus* paddy for high lands. There are no forests of real commercial value: the forest areas have long yielded to the spread of cultivation and cutting for export of fuel for sale in Cuttack.

RENTS, WAGES AND PRICES.

The average rates of assessment for 1st, 2nd and 3rd class rice lands per acre are Rs. 2-9-1, Rs. 2-4-11 and Rs. 2-0-9, respectively. During the period 1893-1902 the average daily wages of labour was:—superior mason, carpenter and blacksmith 4¾ annas each; common mason, carpenter and blacksmith 4 annas each; and cooly 2 annas. During the same period the average price of wheat, rice, gram and salt was 9 seers 15 chittacks, 18 seers 5 chittacks, 10¾ seers and 12¾ seers, respectively. In 1906 and 1907 a very marked rise in prices occurred owing to advantageous exports to outside areas, where high prices were prevalent: the cultivators of the State benefiting largely from the good prices obtainable for their produce. Prices here have risen about 50 per cent. in the last 15 years with the advent of the railway through Orissa and the facilities thus offered for the ready disposal of surplus stocks.

OCCUPATIONS, MANUFACTURES AND TRADE.

The chief occupation of the people is agriculture. In this State there is no manufacture or trade worth mentioning. The principal exported articles are food-grains, oil-seeds, fuel, bamboo, tree cotton and other minor forest produce, and the principal imported articles are iron, kerosene oil, piece-goods, spices, salt and thread.

MEANS OF COMMUNICATION. The State is traversed by the old high road from Cuttack to Sambalpur and the newly opened Cuttack-Angul-Sambalpur road. The Mahānadī river, which runs along the southern boundary, is readily navigable for large-sized boats, and great quantities of surplus grain, fuel and charcoal are thus cheaply and readily exported to Cuttack. There is a branch post office at the headquarters of the State.

LAND REVENUE ADMINISTRATION. The estimated land revenue in 1907-08 amounted to Rs. 35,620. No cesses are levied in the State and there are no zamīndāris. The land tenure system is the same as in other States of the group formerly known as the Tributary Mahāls of Orissa: the system is based on the village headman known as the *sarbarāhkār*, who receives a commission on the collection of rents: there are the usual grants to members of the Rāj family in way of maintenance and the usual service *māfi* or free grants to the *paiks* (State militia) and others, together with the ordinary religious *debottar* and *brahmottar* grants.

GENERAL ADMINISTRATION. The relations between the State and the British Government are regulated by the *sanad* granted in 1894, which was revised in 1908 and under which the State pays an annual tribute of Rs. 2,800, which is fixed: the Chief pays no *nazarāna* to Government on succession. The Chief carries on the administration of his State himself without any regular *Dīwān* (chief executive officer) though he is assisted by his relations, one of whom practically serves as *Dīwān*. The administration is on primitive and patriarchal lines, but is appreciated by the people. The total income in 1907-08 amounted to Rs. 53,375: the Chief has recently adopted a regular budget system.

Finances.

Forest. The forest revenue in 1907-08 yielded Rs. 2,778, and as already noted the forests are of little or no importance in this State. Excise yielded a revenue of Rs. 6,562. The number of civil suits for disposal was 892, all of a very petty nature, 88·5 per cent. being below the value of Rs. 50. In the year 1907-08 the number of cases reported to the police was 159. The police force consists of one Sub-Inspector, eight Head-Constables and 40 men: besides there are 335 *paiks* (State militia) holding service lands. The jail has accommodation for 10 prisoners and an extension of the jail is being undertaken. The daily average population was 10 in 1907-08. The State spent Rs. 6,340 on account of Public Works in 1907-08.

Excise. Civil justice. Crime. Police.

Jail.

Public Works Department.

EDUCATION. There are 80 schools with 1,264 pupils. The Middle English school, two Upper Primary schools, one Girls' school, one

Sanskrit *tol* and 62 Lower Primary schools are maintained from the State funds, and the remaining 12 Lower Primary schools are private institutions. There is also one Government *Guru*-Training school. The State spent Rs. 1,047 on education and received from Government a grant of Rs. 2,112 in 1907-08; it also enjoys the services of a Government Sub-Inspector and of the Agency Inspector of Schools.

CHAPTER II.

ATHMALLIK STATE.

PHYSICAL ASPECTS. THE State of Athmallik lies between 20° 37′ and 21° 5′ N., and 84° 16′ and 84° 48′ E., with an area of 730 square miles. It is bounded on the north by the State of Rairākhol; on the east by Angul district; on the south by the Mahānadī river, which separates it from Baud; and on the west by Sonpur and Rairākhol States. The country is for the most part covered with dense jungle, and a long range of hills clad with forest runs along its southern side parallel with the course of the Mahānadī. The country to the north of this range of hills rises to a fair elevation: the range is crossed by a picturesque defile which leads abruptly to the lower country on the south side of the range: between this range of hills and the Mahānadī river there is a belt of low land, fertile and opened up to cultivation, with an average breadth of 8 miles. There are deposits of graphite in this range of hills: iron ore of excellent quality is found universally over the State. There are no streams or rivers of any importance in the State. The fauna are the same as those met with in the other States of Orissa, and require no special notice. On the south-east of the State a tract of forest is reserved for elephant-catching operations: this tract joins up with the elephant forest in Angul. The Chief conducts elephant-catching operations generally about every third year: the catches do not usually average more than ten to fifteen animals. The average rainfall for the six years—1902-03 to 1907-08—was 53·16 inches. The headquarters of the State are at Kaintirāgarh.

HISTORY. The origin of the State is obscure. According to tradition, this State is said to have been founded by one Pratāp Deva who, with seven other brothers of the Rājā of Jaipur, came with their families on a pilgrimage to Purī. For some reason or other they had a quarrel with the Rājā of Purī, by whom two of the brothers were put to death. The remaining five brothers fled for their lives to the hills. The elevated plain known as Handapāgarh is, to the present day, renowned as the *garh*, or fortified residence of a Dom Rājā whom Pratāp Deva is alleged to have defeated. Pratāp Deva is said to have found a *handā* (metal vessel) in a tank which he was excavating there and gave the place and the State the name of Handapā. In course of time one of the Chiefs who held sway after Pratāp Deva divided the State into eight subdivisions and placed a Chief over each with a view of bringing the aborigines into subjection. Hence the State changed its name from Handapā to Athmallik. The Rājā of Angul considerably reduced the area of Athmallik State and included large tracts within the boundaries of Angul. Official records, however, show that till lately the State had no separate existence, and in the treaty engagement of 1804 it is mentioned as a tributary of Baud. It was treated as a separate State in the *sanad* granted to the Chief in 1894, the terms of which were identical with those contained in the *sanads* of the other Orissa Chiefs. The Chief was officially styled as the zamīndār of Athmallik, and was addressed as *sāmant*. In 1874, however, he was officially recognised as Rājā, which title was also made hereditary, and in 1890 the late Chief, Rājā Mahendra Deva Sāmant, was given the title of Mahārājā as a personal distinction on account of his able administration of the State. Baud and Athmallik belonged to what was formerly known as the South-Western Frontier Agency, from which they were transferred to the Orissa Division in 1837. The Chief's emblem is a *kadamba* flower (*Nauclea orientalis*) and his family is called the *kadamba-bansa*. Another version of the origin of the Athmallik State will be found in the article on the history of the Baud State.

THE PEOPLE. The population increased from 31,605 in 1891 to 40,753 in 1901, part of the gain being due to immigration from Baud and the Central Provinces. A great extension of cultivation has taken place in recent years, and the population is now nearly double what it was in 1881, but Athmallik is with the exception of Pāl Laharā, Bonai and Rairākhol, the most sparsely populated of all the Orissa States, the density being only 56 to the square mile. Of the total population all but 106 are Hindus. The most numerous castes are Chasās (8,000), Gauras (6,000), and Gonds, Pāns and Sudhas (4,000 each). There are 460 villages, the principal being Kaintirā, the residence of the Chief.

The population is classified as follows in the census report of 1901:—Hindus—males, 20,701, females, 19,946, total 40,647, or 99·7 per cent. of the population; proportion of males to total Hindus, 50·9 per cent. Muhammadans—males, 45, females, 36, total 81, or 0·2 per cent. of the population; proportion of males to total Muhammadans, 55·5 per cent. Other denominations—males, 15, females, 10, total 25, or 0·06 per cent. of the population; proportion of males to total 'others', 60 per cent. Total population of all denominations—males, 20,761, females, 19,992, total population of the State, 40,753; proportion of males to total population, 50·9 per cent. The number of persons able to read and write is 558 or 1·4 per cent. of the total population. Averages—Villages per square mile, 0·6; persons per village, 88·6; houses per square mile, 10·6; houses per village, 16·8; persons per house, 5·3. The census report returns the total number of villages in the State at 460, classified as follows:—457 with less than five hundred inhabitants, 2 with between five hundred and a thousand and only 1 with between one thousand and two thousand inhabitants.

The people are very wild and far more backward than the population of the neighbouring States of Baud and Sonpur and the district of Angul. They are content with inferior cultivation and prefer to spend much of their time in the forests of the State, hunting and living on forest produce.

PUBLIC HEALTH. The people are healthy and of fair physique. There is a dispensary at the headquarters with a Civil Hospital Assistant in charge and 4,295 patients were treated in 1907-08: an Ayūrvedic dispensary has also been opened by the Chief. The number of persons vaccinated during the year 1907-08 was 3,207, of which 1,350 were revaccinations: the operations are conducted by vaccinators trained in the Cuttack Training class and they are under a Sub-Inspector. The people being mostly denizens of the forests are strongly averse to vaccination.

AGRICULTURE. The crops are mostly coarse rice and other inferior grains, with a few oil-seeds: castor oil-seed, however, of excellent quality is largely grown in favourable years, on the clearings in virgin jungle soil, and from this crop the people are usually able to fully pay their rents and have money in hand. Irrigation is very little practised and cultivation is of the crudest: the people prefer to live on the abundant products of the extensive forests to labouring on the soil and improving their lands.

RENTS, WAGES AND PRICES. The average rates of assessment per acre for 1st, 2nd and 3rd class of rice lands are Re. 1-2-9, Re. 0-13-11$\frac{2}{3}$ and Re. 0-10-5 respectively. The average rate of assessment per acre for uplands is Re. 0-8-4 and the average rate of assessment per acre for homestead land is Re. 0-4-11. During the period 1893-1902 the average daily wage of labour was:—superior mason and carpenter, 8 annas each; common mason, 4$\frac{1}{2}$ annas; common carpenter, 4 annas; cooly, 2$\frac{1}{2}$ annas; superior blacksmith, 5 annas, and common blacksmith, 3 annas. During the same period the average price of wheat, rice, gram and salt was 8$\frac{5}{8}$ seers, 17$\frac{5}{8}$ seers, 10$\frac{1}{2}$ seers and 10$\frac{1}{2}$ seers respectively.

After 1903, there has subsequently ensued a marked rise in prices as in the other States, especially those situated on the Mahānadī, a ready highway for the export of surplus stocks.

The chief occupation of the people is agriculture, 66·6 per cent. of the total population being agriculturists: only 1·38 per cent. follow trade: 4·47 per cent. accept State, domestic and other services: 21·9 per cent. maintain themselves on labour: and the remaining 5·68 per cent. earn their livelihood from other sources. The State boasts no special manufactures: iron ore of good quality is smelted and sent down to Cuttack. The principal trade consists in timber, fuel, and jungle products, which are carried by boat: the forests have been leased for sleeper cutting and have now been nearly worked out of large trees: there is, however, one large tract of forest untouched, which is kept as a reserve for elephant-catching operations. There is a small trade in oil-seeds by pack-bullocks, but the greater part of the trade is river-borne: the forests supply nearly all the timber used for oars by the boatmen who work over the whole length of the Mahānadī. The principal imported articles are spices, salt, mill-made cloths, brass and bell-metal utensils, piece-goods and kerosene oil. **Occupations, Manufactures and Trade.**

The Cuttack-Sambalpur road runs through the northern portion of the State: a fair road from Kaintirā, the headquarters, joins up with the main road: it is a surface road and winds through the defiles in the hill range running parallel to the river. The Mahānadī affords a cheap and ready means of communication for the export of grain, timber and forest produce to Cuttack. There is a branch post office at the headquarters and the Imperial post crosses the river here and travels *viâ* Kantilo to Cuttack and *viâ* Baud to Sambalpur. **Means of Communication.**

The land revenue administration differs but little from that of the other neighbouring States of the group formerly forming the Tributary Mahāls. The State, however, has always been more in touch with the institutions prevailing in the Central Provinces: for this reason the village headman is a more prominent person than in the other States and his service lands (*bhogrā*) have not disappeared: a regular settlement based on a pole measurement has been made by the Chief. The land revenue demand is Rs. 25,770. **Land Revenue Administration.**

The relations between the Athmallik State and the British Government are, like those of the other States of the group formerly known as the Tributary Mahāls, governed by the *sanads* of 1894 and 1908. The State is liable to pay *nazarāna* on succession. The present Chief employs a regular *Dīwān* and carefully follows a budget system. The total income of the **General Administration.** **Finances.**

State was Rs. 77,823 in 1907-08; the tribute was formerly liable to revision every twenty years, but was made permanent in the *sanad* of 1894 and fixed at Rs. 730. The forest revenue yielded Rs. 45,670 in 1907-08. In 1907-08 the excise income amounted to Rs. 3,215. Civil suits are all of a very petty nature; in 1907-08, 80 per cent. of the suits were of Rs. 50 in value and less, the number of civil suits for disposal during the year being 148. Crime is light and not of a serious nature: only 73 cases were reported in 1907-08 to the police. The police force consists of one Sub-Inspector trained at Bhāgalpur, 5 Head-Constables, and 25 men: besides 335 *paiks* (State militia) holding service lands. There is a masonry jail with accommodation for 8 prisoners, but a new jail on modern lines with capacity for 35 prisoners is under construction. The State spent Rs. 40,000 on account of public works in 1907-08.

Forests. Excise. Civil justice. Crime. Police. Jail. P. W. Department.

EDUCATION.

In 1907-08 the number of schools in the State was 46, the number of pupils on the rolls being 1,163: there is a good Middle English school at the headquarters and also a girls' school: there are one Upper Primary school and 35 Lower Primary schools for boys in the State; there are besides 7 private schools. The Government *Guru*-Training school for teachers from the Baud and Athmallik States is located at Kaintirā. Education owing to the efforts of both the late and present Chief is making considerable headway in the State. The Chief spent Rs. 2,629 on education in 1907-08 and the State received an educational grant of Rs. 1,262 from Government in the same year.

CHAPTER III.

BAMRA STATE.

THE State of Bāmra lies between 21° 9′ and 22° 12′ N., and between 84° 8′ and 85° 13′ E. Its formation is extremely irregular, the northern part running up to a point into the Bonai and Gāngpur States; and two points also extend considerably to the westward, the one into the Lairā zamīndāri of Sambalpur district and the other into Tālcher State. It is bounded on the north by Bonai and Gāngpur States; on the south by the State of Rairākhol; on the east by Tālcher State and the State of Pāl Laharā, where it links up with the hill tracts inhabited by the Bhuiyās; and on the west by the Sambalpur *khālsa* and the zamīndāri of Jaipur or Kolābirā in Sambalpur. The extreme length north and south is about seventy-five miles, while the extreme breadth is about sixty-four miles. The total area is 1,988 square miles. The soil is light and sandy except in the immediate neighbourhood of the hills where it is loamy. There are some fine *sāl* (Shorea robusta) forests in this State; the hill ranges are well covered. Iron ore is to be found in abundance. The jungles produce a considerable quantity of lac, silk, cocoons, resin, bees-wax, and honey. The only river of note is the Brāhmanī. But for certain rocky obstructions that occur at one or two places timber might be floated down this river to the coast. On the southern border of the State, there is a fine range of hills with extensive plateau land rising in parts to an elevation of 2,000 feet. The descent from this plateau is sudden and very precipitous, the range of hills abutting close upon the Sambalpur border, near Gourpāli. PHYSICAL ASPECTS.

The climate is malarious owing to the large forest areas, but the cultivated tracts are salubrious. The average rainfall for the six years from 1902-03 to 1907-08 was 65·46 inches.

The headquarters of the State are at Deogarh and there are two *tahsīls* (subdivisions) with headquarters at Kuchindā and Bārkut.

The Bāmra State originally formed one of the Sambalpur and Patnā or Garhjāt groups, the Chiefs of which were at first independent; but were subsequently held in subordination to the HISTORY.

Mahārājā of Patnā, the most powerful of their number. In 1865 the Chief received from the British Government an adoption *sanad*, and in 1867 a *sanad* defining his status as a Feudatory Chief was granted. The State was transferred to Bengal from the Central Provinces in October 1905.

The family is Gangabansī Rājput; it does not appear to be in possession of any authentic traditions antecedent to *Sambat* 1602 (A.D. 1545): according to tradition the first Rājā of Bāmra belonged to the Rāj family of the Patnā State, and was stolen from his home and made Chief of the Bāmra State by the Bhuiyās and Khonds.

The present Chief succeeded to the *gadi* in 1903: his father, Sir Bāsudeo Sudhal Deva, obtained the title of K. C. I. E. The emblem of the State is a *sankh* (conch shell).

THE PEOPLE. According to the census of 1901 the population of the State amounted to 123,378 against 22,456 in 1866, and an increase of 18 per cent. since 1891. The population is classified as follows:—Hindus—males, 62,030, females, 58,962, total, 120,992 or 98·07 per cent. of the total population: proportion of males in total Hindus, 51·3 per cent. Musalmāns—males, 229, females, 118, total 347 or 0·28 of the total population: proportion of males in total Musalmāns, 65·99. Animists—males, 994, females, 1,031, total 2,025 or 1·6 per cent. of the total population. Christians—14.

In 1901 the number of villages in the State was 931, and there was one town, Deogarh, with a population of 5,702. The 931 villages are classified as follows: 907 with less than five hundred inhabitants, 21 with from five hundred to a thousand, and 3 with from one to two thousand. Averages—villages per square mile, 0·41; persons per village, 126; houses per village, 23·8; persons per house, 5; houses per square mile, 11·5.

The principal non-agricultural castes are Brāhmans, Rājputs, and Mahāntis, while agriculture is carried on by Chasās, Gonds, Khonds, Agariās, Kaltuyās, Sudhas, and Dumāls. About 77 per cent. of the population speak Oriyā and 18 per cent. the Oraon and Mundāri dialects. In 1901, 4·06 per cent. of the population were returned as able to read and write. The principal castes and tribes are Chasās, Kisāns, Gauras and Gandās: the Gonds and Bhuiyās are also numerous. The people are well-to-do for the most part, especially the regular cultivating classes: the wilder tribes who practise *dāhi* cultivation (clearing and burning forest tracts) and live to a great extent on jungle products are naturally not so well off.

PUBLIC HEALTH. The State possesses three dispensaries, viz., at Deogarh, Kuchindā, and Bārkut each with accommodation for indoor patients.

The dispensaries are in charge of Civil Hospital Assistants and an officer with the qualifications of an Assistant Surgeon is the Medical Officer of the State. In 1907-08 the number of patients treated was 21,188: vaccination work is in charge of a special Inspector: the State pays the vaccinators and itself collects a small charge for every case of successful vaccination: in 1907-08 the number of primary vaccinations was 2,931 and of revaccinations 580. Fever is the usual complaint; cholera and small-pox epidemics occur from time to time.

AGRICULTURE.

As elsewhere in these parts, rice is the staple produce; oil-seeds, pulses, cotton, and sugarcane are also cultivated. At Balam, about 10 miles east of Deogarh, the headquarters of the State, the Chief has started an excellent home-farm: here are to be seen threshing machines, rotatory saws and sugar-mills, driven by steam power: on the farm various varieties of crops are grown and experiments made: there is a large vegetable market garden attached: at Sirgirā close to Balam a large irrigation reservoir has been built irrigating a considerable tract of country. The villages are well cultivated and there are 974 irrigation tanks in the State. In the open areas of the State large and prosperous villages with good tanks for irrigation are commonly met with. Famine occurred in 1900 after a very widespread failure of the crops: the State, however, is not, unless under very exceptional circumstances, liable to severe famine.

RENTS, WAGES AND PRICES.

The average rates per *mān* (about $\frac{2}{3}$ of an acre) for 1st, 2nd and 3rd class rice lands in Deogarh *tahsīl* are Rs. 2-15-1, Rs. 2-6-9 and Re. 1-11-4, respectively, and in Kuchindā *tahsīl*, Re. 1-14-2, Re. 1-7-11, and As. 10-5, respectively. The average rate per *mān* for *gorā* or uplands is Re. 0-12-6 in Deogarh *tahsīl* and As. 9-8 in Kuchindā *tahsīl*. A regular assessment of the land based on a soil classification has been made. In late years the average daily wage for a mason, carpenter, blacksmith and ordinary cooly has been As. 2-9, As. 3, As. 2-3 and As. 2, respectively. In late years the average rate for rice, *mūga*, *bīrhi*, wheat and salt per rupee has been 18 seers, 16 seers, 20 seers, 8 seers and 17½ seers, respectively. The opening up of the country by the advent of the Bengal-Nāgpur Railway has enabled the farmers to dispose of surplus stocks at handsome profits with a consequent general rise in prices.

OCCUPATIONS, MANUFACTURES AND TRADE.

Nearly 74½ per cent. of the total population are agriculturists: 12½ per cent. of the population follow industries: 5 per cent. follow various professions: only 1 per cent. are engaged in commerce: and others serve as field labourers and personal servants, etc. Keoline pottery, sugar and weaving are the principal manufactures. At Sirid, a village on the main road between Bāmra and Deogarh, there are saw-mills for cutting logs into railway sleepers: these mills give employment to many workmen and the timber business of the State employs a large number of hands as sawyers and carters. Principal exports are rice, pulses, oil-seeds, iron, timber, forest produce and catechu: and principal imports are mill-spun piece-goods, salt, sugar, spices and brass utensils.

MEANS OF COMMUNICATION. There is a good road from the Bāmra railway station on the Bengal-Nāgpur line to Deogarh, the headquarters, about 58 miles in length. This road carries a considerable amount of the large sleeper traffic of the State, especially from Sirid. The road continues from Deogarh as a fair surface road to the Tālcher border: from Deogarh to Balam there is a good road 11 miles in length, on which there is one steel girder bridge. The old Sambalpur-Midnapore road traverses the State: this road is no longer of the importance it formerly was as the direct means of communication with the State: it is, however, bridged throughout the State over the small streams by rough, but strong, timber trestle bridges. The village roads are fair surface roads, and there is a road from Deogarh to the border of the Rairākhol State running on to Rāmpur, the headquarters of that State. The Bengal-Nāgpur Railway passes through the north-eastern corner of the State with two stations, Garpos and Bāmra, within its borders. The Brāhmanī river forms a means of communication for small open boats, but the presence of rocks and rapids renders the transport of goods on any large scale impossible. There are rest-houses at Bāmra station, Kuchindā and Sirid. A telephone line runs from Bāmra railway station to Deogarh, and from Deogarh to Bārkut, the headquarters of the *tahsīl* (subdivision) of that name and to Sirgirā. The Imperial post plies in the State, with sub-post offices at Bāmra, and Deogarh and branch post offices at Kuchindā and Bārkut, and letter boxes in the school houses at the principal villages. There is a telegraph office at Bāmra.

LAND REVENUE ADMINISTRATION. For the purposes of land revenue administration the State is divided into three *tahsīls*, or subdivisions with a *Tahsīldār* in charge of each. The *tahsīls* are Kuchindā, the most highly cultivated area of the State, in the north-west, the Sadar or Deogarh *tahsīl*, and the Bārkut *tahsīl* to the south-east. The land revenue demand is about Rs. 65,500 and settlement operations are in progress: the land revenue system is very similar to that prevailing in the neighbouring States of Rairākhol, Sonpur and Patnā. The land revenue demand is divided into fixed and fluctuating collections: the fluctuating collections are derived from new villages opened up and waste lands brought to cultivation. The rule is that new lands are generally allowed to be held five years free of rent. This collection also includes the assessment on *dāhi* cultivation. The area under *dāhi* is measured by the Forest Department and the rate charged is Re. 1-9 per *mān* (about ⅔ of an acre). The Pauriās or hillmen as in Bonai, are the people who practise this form of cultivation; the Chief is trying to localise and keep within prescribed limits this reckless and wasteful form of cultivation by compelling the Pauriās to apply for sanction for any area they burn and this is then checked by the Forest Department. There is a famine fund amounting now to Rs. 30,000: the people receive advances at moderate interest for improvements.

Land cess. A land cess is levied only from the people who live in Deogarh town, as they all hold their lands there rent-free. It is levied at a rate varying from one anna six pies to four annas per rupee according to the character of the *māfi* or free grant. The money is spent on the repairs of the town roads. **School cess.** The school cess is assessed at a quarter of an anna per rupee of rent according to the old settlement of 1877; it was not increased by assessing it on the rental obtained in the last settlement. ***Tikā* and *nazarāna*.** The *gaontiās* pay Re. 1 on the occasion of the *suniyā* (Oriyā new year in Bhādraba (August-September)) and the Paush Pūrnimā (December-January).

***Māfi* grants.** There are the usual grants to members of the family of the Chief for their maintenance, also *paik* (feudal militia) and other service lands, and religious grants. **Village administration.** The villages in the State are held by (1) *gaontiās*, (2) *pradhāns*, (3) *garhatiās*. No distinction is made between the first two classes. In the Deogarh *tahsīl* the headmen of the villages are called *gaontiās* or *sarbarāhkārs*, and in the Kuchindā *tahsīl*, *pradhāns* or *sarbarāhkārs*. The conditions of forfeiture are bad behaviour, failure to pay the rents, leasing or mortgaging the village or the *bhogrā* (village service lands enjoyed by the headman) lands. The *bhogrā* lands vary from 12 to 20½ per cent. of the cultivated lands of the village. *Rasad* or rations to State officers on tour are supplied on regular payment: in the village leases or *pattās* are entered a minute account of all heads of payments, *māfis* (exemptions) and duties. When a son succeeds his father as head of a village, he has to pay for mutation; only a son or an adopted son can inherit.

Feudal tenures. *Garhatiās*. The *garhatiās* are the headmen of the *paik* (militia) villages of the State; these villages have to render watch and guard on the palace when the Chief is away: they also have to assist in suppressing riots if called upon. In consequence they render no *bethi begāri* (free labour). Mr. Chapman, Political Agent, wrote of the feudal tenures in the Bāmra State as follows:—Though the necessity for military service has passed away, the whole system of the feudal tenure by which it used to be maintained still exists. Round the sites of the ancient *garhs* or forts which are mostly situated at vulnerable points on the border, such as Tārang on the boundary between the Bāmra and Rairākhol States and Garpos on the boundary between the Bāmra and Gāngpur States, are clustered colonies of men-at-arms called *paiks*. From ten to thirty *paiks* are located in a village. The head of the *paiks* in each village is called the *garhatiā* or *garh-naik*. He is also generally the *gaontiā* of the village. Besides his *bhogrā* land he receives a drawback of Rs. 6 per annum from his *jamā* for each *paik* for whom he is responsible. The *paik* is entitled to enjoy this amount of land rent-free in the village. The *garh-naik* also enjoys some Rs. 10 to Rs. 13 worth of land rent-free as such. He has an officer under him called the *dalbeherā* or captain who also enjoys *māfi* land. Over each group of 100 *paiks* is the *sardār* who generally enjoys one or more villages rent-free and receives a monthly pay of Rs. 5. In return for these remunerations the *sardār* and *garh-naiks* are bound to produce their *paiks* whenever called on by the Rājā. There is a great assembling of the *naiks* and *paiks* at Dasharā time when they compete for prizes in shooting and running before the Rājā. Their offices are hereditary. There seems to be no recognized head of the men-at-arms for the whole State corresponding to the *senāpati* in Kālāhandī. The duties of the *naiks* and *paiks* are now restricted to forming the Rājā's body-guard when he moves about the State, to carrying out certain police duties and conveying the *dâk*. Villages where *paiks* are located are known as *paiki* villages. The *paiks* and all the tenants of such villages are excused from all payments in kind. They pay all their rent in cash. The *sardār* is not responsible for the land revenue of the villages in his charge. His sole duty is to exercise supervision over the *garh-naiks* and *paiks*. The Gond community is presided over by headmen called *barihā* who in some cases hold several villages as their *jāgirs*. They are the intermediaries between the Rājā and the Gonds in all caste matters. There are other *jāgīrdārs* holding groups of 4 or 5 villages scattered over the State.

Rakumāt. *Rakumāt* or payment in kind is levied from all villages, except from *garhati*, *lākhirāj* and *brahmottar* villages. It has been regularly assessed and is entered up in detail in the *kistibandi* (demand register). The payment is made into the State granary (*bhandār*). It consists of paddy (unhusked rice), *chāul* (rice), *mūga*, *til* (sesamum), *ghī* (clarified butter) and *birhi*.

The relations between the State and the British Government are regulated by the *sanad* of 1867 and the State pays a tribute of Rs. 7,500 which is liable to revision and was last assessed in 1909 for a period of thirty years. The Chief administers the State, with the assistance of three *Tahsīldārs* as already noted, and there is also a *Naib* (Assistant) *Tahsīldār* at Kuchindā; these officers also exercise criminal and civil powers, and there are Honorary Magistrates who render assistance in the disposal of criminal cases. The Chief exercises full criminal powers, but sentences of death require confirmation by the Commissioner of the Orissa Division. For the disposal of criminal and civil business regular courts are maintained. The total income of the State in 1907-08 was returned at Rs. 1,68,481. A regular budget system is followed in the State and the finances are carefully administered. **GENERAL ADMINISTRATION.** **Power.** **Finances.**

In 1907-08 the forest revenue amounted to Rs. 32,637, excluding the revenue from sleeper operations. The State forests have been separated from the village or *khasrā* jungle. There are ten protected trees in this State, viz., *sāl* (Shorea robusta), *bijā* (Pterocarpus marsupium), *khair* (Acacia Catechu), *bandhan* (Ougeinia dalbergioides), *harar* (Terminalia Chebula), *mahuā* (Bassia latifolia), *kurum* (Adina cordifolia), *kendu* (Diospyros melanoxylon), *kusum* (Schleichera trijuga) and *sisū* (Dalbergia Sissoo). As regards the *khasrā* jungle, the villagers are allowed to use it, but are not allowed to destroy it uselessly and the prohibited class of trees cannot be cut from it without informing the Forest Department. The cultivators pay a commutation fee or *halpanchā* to cut and remove any kind of timber, except the prohibited class: non-agriculturists pay half an anna per head-load. The rate charged for dry timber of the prohibited class is two annas per cubic foot in Deogarh *tahsīl* and four annas in Kuchindā *tahsīl;* except under special permission no green timber of the prohibited kind may be cut. As regards destruction of the forests by the people the measures adopted are effective, and it is but rarely that instances are seen of the clearing of patches of forest with trees ringed and boles burnt for raising catch-crops on *gorā* or uplands. All persons, whether foreigners or people of the State, pay a grazing tax if they keep milch-cattle; the rate is one anna per cow and two annas per cow-buffalo to people of the State and four annas and eight annas respectively to outsiders. The people of the State get their fuel and also their supply of *chhan* (thatching) grass and *panāsi* (*sabai*) grass included in the commutation fee. If, however, **Forests.**

fuel or grass is exported, a tax is charged. There is a considerable quantity of *panāsi* or *sabai* grass in the State, but there is no export of it on any scale.

Regular licenses are issued for felling and removing timber of the reserved classes. The forests are in charge of a trained forest student from Dehra Dun, assisted by two subordinates trained in the neighbouring Government forest reserves in Singhbhūm: demarcation of the reserved forests has been undertaken and the cutting of fire lines is progressing and the forest blocks are being divided up into coupés for regular felling. The State of recent years has entered upon a more scientific and regulated system of dealing with the forests.

Excise. The State obtains its supply of opium through the Sambalpur treasury and Khandwā *gānja* is obtained from Nimār. The State charges the licensed vendors with the cost of transit; *gānja* is sold at Rs. 5 per seer. There is no regular excise staff, but the State officers and the police watch the sale of exciseable articles.

Market monopoly. The markets are leased out only in the Kuchindā *tahsīl*; elsewhere in order to encourage trading in the less developed tracts no assessment is imposed. Every tenant who attends the bazar or market for sale purposes pays 1½ pies, but fish and meat sellers are exempted. Local shopkeepers who expose goods for sale in the market pay 3 pies per market day. Foreign traders who visit the market for sale pay 1 pie per rupee if their sale is under Rs. 20 and 3 pies per rupee if it exceeds Rs. 20.

Pātki. A tax or *pātki* is imposed on industrial classes; the rate is higher than in the Bonai State, but the people are much better off. The rates per annum are, Pāns and Gandās (who weave) Rs. 2-2, Bhandāris (barbers) Re. 1-4, Kewats (dealing in parched rice) annas 12, Khātis (blacksmiths) annas 8, Kharurās (brass workers) annas 8, Lakharās (who make bracelets of lac) annas 8, Guriās (sweatmeat-sellers) annas 12, Khairās (preparers of catechu) Re. 1, Ghantrās (bell-makers) annas 8, Kāmārs (iron smelters) Re. 1-4, Jhorās (fishermen and gold-washers) Re. 1-4, Telis – one seer of oil for each pressing machine worked by them.

Civil Justice. Crime. Police. In the year 1907-08 the total number of civil suits for disposal was 378, out of which only 11·4 per cent. were for sums exceeding Rs. 100. During the year 1907-08 869 cases were reported to the police. The police force is in charge of a Superintendent, with two Inspectors under him and a regular staff of officers and men: the system followed is similar to that in force in the Central Provinces, but the system of surveillance of bad characters and criminals has recently been remodelled on the lines followed in Bengal.

Jails. There is a good masonry jail at headquarters where regular labour is imposed and discipline enforced. There is a large workshop where weaving on improved methods is taught to the prisoners under a trained expert; excellent cloth of various patterns and good *darīs* are manufactured: the flyshuttle loom and English made handlooms are in use: pottery work is also taught to the prisoners: other kinds of labour are lime-burning, brick-making and the oil-mill. There is also a small sub-jail at Kuchindā. The average daily jail population in 1907-08 was 92.

Public Works Department. The State possesses some good public buildings; the best being the jail and High school at the headquarters. The total expenditure incurred on account of public works in 1907-08 was Rs. 27,855.

EDUCATION. The number of schools regularly maintained by the State in 1907-08 was 33, and besides a large number of aided private schools (*pāthsālās*) impart simple instruction in the villages. There is a High English school at Deogarh. There is a girls' school at the headquarters. The number of pupils in 1907-08 in all the schools was 4,536. There is a special school for the education of Gandās at the headquarters. In 1907-08 the State spent Rs. 7,162 on education.

CHAPTER IV.

BARAMBA STATE.

PHYSICAL ASPECTS. THE State of Barāmbā lies between 20° 21′ and 20° 31′ N., and 85° 12′ and 85° 31′ E., with an area of 134 square miles. It is bounded on the north by the Hindol State; on the east by the Tigiriā State; on the south by Cuttack district and Khandparā State (the boundary line being formed by the Mahānadī river); and on the west by the Narsinghpur State. Kanakā peak (2,038 feet), the highest point of a hill range of the same name, is situated on the northern border of the State.

The country for the most part is open and flat and the soil is very fertile: the tract along the Mahānadī river is constantly liable to inundation and the riverain villages are frequently damaged by large deposits of sand and silt. The only hills of any importance are those on the northern border of the State. The average rainfall for the six years—from 1902-03 to 1907-08—was 53·43 inches. The headquarters of the State are at Barāmbā.

HISTORY. The history of the Barāmbā State is alleged according to the family tradition to commence from the year 1305 A.D. with Hatakeswar Rāut, a famous wrestler who served Kishor Narsingh, the Rājā of Orissa, and in recognition of his valour was presented with two Khond villages by name Sankha (conch shell) and Mohuri (pipe) on the north bank of the Mahānadī river, three miles south of the present headquarters. These two villages were then owned and inhabited by Khonds. Hatakeswar drove them away and settled in Barāmbā, which has since been the residence of all the Chiefs of the State. The area of the two villages when they were presented by the Orissa Rājā in all probability never exceeded four square miles. The founder, however, extended the limit of his possession to about eight square miles before he died, leaving his younger brother Malakeswar Rāut to succeed him.

The second Chief, Malakeswar Rāut, who held his *gadi* for 18 years, extended the limit of the State to Ogālpur, about three miles west and five miles south-west of Barāmbā. He discovered the temple of the goddess Vattārikā or Bruhadambā or Baramā at

Ogālpur, and out of respect for this goddess named the State after her. Jambeswar Rāut, the fourth Chief, who held his *gadi* from A.D. 1375 to 1416, conquered the Khond Chief of Khārodh, eight miles north-west of Barāmbā, and annexed his lands (about 20 square miles), thus raising the area of the State to about 36 square miles. The fifth Chief, Bholeswar Rāut, conquered the Khandait or Chief of Amātiā, six miles west of Barāmbā, and extended the limit of the State to Ratāpāt, eight miles west of the headquarters, and the present boundary between the Barāmbā and Narsinghpur States. It was during the time of this Chief, who held his *gadi* for 43 years (from A.D. 1416 to 1459) that the farthest western limit of the State was reached. His successors increased their possessions to the east of the headquarters, but made no attempt to extend the State further on the west. Kānhu Rāut, the sixth Chief, held his *gadi* for 55 years (from A.D. 1459 to 1514), and extended the limit of the State to Mahuliā, about five miles east of Barāmbā. Nabīn Rāut, the ninth Chief, held his *gadi* for 23 years (from A.D. 1537 to 1560). During his time the State attained its largest limit from Ratāpāt in the west, to Bidhārpur in the east, 18 miles, and from the range of hills separating Hindol from Barāmbā to the banks of the Mahānadī, about eight-and-a-half miles, the present limit of the State. During the time of the twelfth Chief, Krishna Chandra Mangrāj, who held the *gadi* from A.D. 1635 to 1650, the Marāthās invaded the country; the Chief acknowledging their supremacy was required to pay a tribute of 6,335 *kāhans* of cowries per annum. Padmanāva Bīrabar Mangrāj Mahāpātra, the seventeenth Chief of the State, was a weak Rājā; he held the *gadi* from A.D. 1748 to 1793. During the first part of the period during which he held his *gadi* the Rājā of Khandparā invaded the State, drove out the Chief, and remained in possession of the State for nearly 13 months. Rājā Padmanāva sought for and obtained the assistance of the Rājā of Khurdā, and recovered possession of the State. In the year 1175, the Rājā of Narsinghpur invaded the State and took possession of two of its important forts, Khārodh and Ratāpāt. The Rājā was powerless to expel the invaders, so he appealed to the Marāthās, and with their assistance and intercession was able to regain possession of the forts. This account is taken from the family traditions, but there are no authentic records.

It seems that the Mughals never exercised direct supremacy over the Chiefs of this State. The Marāthās however did so, and there are letters extant which show that they fixed the annual tribute of the State from the year 1776 to 1778 A.D. and collected the same directly from the Chief. There are also three other old letters of interest in the records. In one of these the Marāthās intimated their having recovered the Ratāpāt *garh* (fort) from the Narsinghpur Rājā; in another they required the presence of the Barāmbā Rājā to settle a boundary dispute between Barāmbā and Narsinghpur; the third is addressed to the Rājā of Narsinghpur, and contains the decision of the Marāthā Government regarding the possession of Khārodh and Ratāpāt. The State has no *farmān* either from the Mughals or from the Marāthā Government. The emblem of signature is a dog metamorphosed into a lion, a heraldic monster that took its origin in a story belonging to the time of the first founder, when a dog killed a tiger.

THE PEOPLE. The population increased from 32,526 in 1891 to 38,260 in 1901, of whom 37,441 are Hindus. A few Buddhists are still found in one or two villages. The most numerous castes are Chasās (11,000) and Pāns (4,000). The population is contained in 181 villages, and there are 285 persons to the square mile.

The population is classified as follows:—Hindus—males, 18,393, females, 19,048, total of Hindus 37,441, or 97·8 per cent. of the population; proportion of males in total Hindus, 49·0 per cent. Musalmāns—males, 60, females, 56, total of Musalmāns, 116 or 0·3 per cent. of the population; proportion of males in total Musalmāns, 51·7 per cent. Christians, *nil.* Other denominations—Buddhist—males, 360, females, 343, total, 703 or 1·8 per cent. of the population; proportion of males in total others, 51·2 per cent. Total population of the State 38,260; proportion of males in total population, 49·1 per cent. The number of persons able to read and write is 1,675 or 4·4 per cent. of the total population. Averages—villages per square mile, 0·74; persons per village, 211; houses per village, 43·8; houses per square mile, 59·1; persons per house, 4·8. The census report of 1901 returns 167 villages, with less than five hundred inhabitants, 13 with from five hundred to a thousand, and one with from one to two thousand.

PUBLIC HEALTH. There is a dispensary at headquarters in charge of a Civil Hospital Assistant: 2,926 patients were treated in 1907-08: this figure includes 2 indoor patients: besides this the Vaccination Sub-Inspector treated 1,298 patients. Vaccination work is in charge of a special Civil Hospital Assistant, who renders medical aid in the interior, and attends to village sanitation. In the year 1907-08 the number of primary vaccinations was 756 and re-vaccinations, 588.

The soil is very fertile, and the lands are well cultivated. The principal crop is paddy, of which several good varieties are grown: in most of the villages, there are fine mango groves: sugarcane is extensively cultivated, and is a very valuable and paying crop to the people of the State. **AGRICULTURE.**

The assessment of rent is light. The average rate per acre for uplands being Re. 0-11-4 for *padar* land and Re. 0-3-1 for *toilā* land and for the three classes of rice land, Rs. 2-12-11, Rs. 2-2-6 and Re. 1-2-8. The rate of daily wages during the ten years from 1893 to 1902 has averaged as follows: superior mason, 5⅓ annas, common mason, 3¾ annas; superior carpenter, 6 annas, common carpenter, 3 annas; cooly, 1¾ annas; superior blacksmith, 6 annas, common blacksmith, 2¾ annas: the rate of wages has remained practically stationary during this period. The average price of wheat, rice, gram and salt during the same period has averaged respectively 12½, 22½, 21¾ and 10 seers per rupee. **RENTS, WAGES AND PRICES.**

Nearly 75 per cent. of the total population live on agriculture, and of the remainder nearly 10 per cent. follow commerce. The State possesses no particular manufactures or trade. A colony of Buddhists inhabiting the village of Māniābandha weave silk *sāris* and silk cloth of fine texture and artistic patterns: the cloth is well dyed. The trade consists in the export of grain, pulses, molasses, oil-seeds, timber, bamboos, firewood, and other forest produce to Cuttack. The principal imported articles are spices, mill-cloths, salt, kerosene oil, iron, brass and bell-metal utensils. Bi-weekly trading fair is held at Māniābandha which is situated on the Mahānadī. **OCCUPATIONS, MANUFACTURES AND TRADE.**

The Mahānadī affords excellent water carriage, and logs of timber and bamboos are floated down the river to Cuttack and Purī districts. A good fair-weather road connects Barāmbā with Narsinghpur on one side and Tigiriā on the other, and joins the old Cuttack-Sambalpur road above Sankarpur in the Dhenkānāl State. **MEANS OF COMMUNICATION.**

There are four branch roads, viz.: Sasāng road towards Khandparā, 3 miles in length; Abhimanpur-Bhāupur road towards Dhenkānāl, 3 miles; the Bāngarsingā road, 6 miles in length, towards Bānki in the Cuttack district and the Gopīnāthpur road to Baideswar in Cuttack, 3 miles in length. There is a branch post office at the headquarters.

The land revenue administration follows the same system as in the other States of Orissa. The village headmen, known as *sarbarāhkārs*, hold their villages for the period of settlement and are remunerated by a cash commission on the village rental. The *sarbarāhkārs* formerly enjoyed service lands for their duties as **LAND REVENUE ADMINISTRATION.**

headmen and collectors of rent. The headman is responsible for the rent of the village and he cannot obtain from the State a certificate against defaulting tenants until he has paid in all the dues. The last settlement was concluded in 1906-07 during the period the State was under the administration of Government. The land revenue demand in 1907-08 was Rs. 30,469.

GENERAL ADMINISTRATION. The relations between the State and the British Government are governed by the *sanads* of 1894 and of 1908. For several years the State was under Government management owing to the minority of the Chief, but the administration has recently been handed over to him. **Finances.** The State yielded a revenue of Rs. 41,149 in 1907-08 and pays a tribute of Rs. 1,397 to the British Government. **Forests.** A regular Forest Department has been organised under a trained Forester: wasteful felling has been controlled and regular forest rules introduced together with a fuel cess levied at one anna per acre of cultivated lands. The forest income in 1907-08 was Rs. 3,537. **Excise.** The revenue from excise amounted in 1907-08 to Rs. 1,524.

Civil justice. The number of suits instituted during the year 1907-08 was 136. **Crime.** There were 242 cases reported to the police in 1907-08: and there is practically no heinous crime. **Police.** The police force consists of one Sub-Inspector, three Head-Constables and 16 constables besides *paiks* (State militia) and *chaukīdārs* (village watchmen). **Jails.** The State possesses a suitable masonry jail with accommodation for 24 prisoners: the daily average population in 1907-08 was 11·57.

Public Works Department. A considerable expenditure on public works was incurred in 1906-07, viz., Rs. 17,932; the expenditure was chiefly on irrigation embankments, tanks and the upkeep of the roads: the department is under the charge of a qualified Overseer. In 1907-08 the expenditure on public works was Rs. 6,264.

Education. The schools in the State consist of one Middle Vernacular, three Upper Primary, including one girls' school, fifty-five Lower Primary and one Sanskrit *tol.* There are also three private schools. The number of pupils attending was 977 in 1907-08: there has been a steady improvement in the popularity of education throughout the State. The State receives a grant-in-aid for primary education from Government.

CHAPTER V.

BAUD STATE.

THE State of Baud lies between 20° 13′ and 20° 53′ N., and 83° 35′ and 84° 48′ E., with an area of 1,264 square miles. It is bounded on the north by the Mahānadī river, separating it from the Sonpur and Athmallik States; on the east by the Daspallā State; on the south by the Khondmāls; and on the west by the Patnā and Sonpur States, from which it is separated by the Tel river. PHYSICAL ASPECTS.

The southern boundary is formed by the Khondmāls, which consist of high mountain ranges and highlands, between which and the Mahānadī river lie the fertile plains which now constitute the area under the Chief of the Baud State. The country consists of a long strip of level country running parallel with the Mahānadī, with gradual undulating rises to the hill ranges which form the Khondmāls. The natural features of the country lend themselves to irrigation, the hills on the southern border forming a natural watershed from which many small streams find their way to the Mahānadī: the principal of these streams are the Bagh and the Meherani. The hills on the southern border and the country along their foot are thickly covered with forest, in which *sāl* (Shorea robusta) largely predominates. The country except the tract in the close proximity of the Mahānadī is unhealthy. The principal mountain peaks are: Bandigārā on the southern border, 3,308 feet; Bānkonithudi, in the north, 2,080 feet; Siānangā, in the west, 1,917 feet. The average rainfall for the six years—1902-03 to 1907-08—was 51·40 inches. The headquarters of the State are at Baudgarh.

It is not known by whom the State of Baud was founded, there being no historical account to throw light on the subject. It is alleged that the State was bounded on the north by Bāmra and Angul, both of which are said to have belonged in ancient times to the Purī Rājā; on the south by Gumsur and Bara Kimedī; on the west by Amai river in the Patnā State; and on the east by Kamaimohan in Khandparā. The State was formerly reckoned to be 120 *kos* (240 miles) in length and breadth, but in course of time certain portions of it were HISTORY.

dissevered from the original, viz., (1) from Kamai to Udandi on the east; (2) from Amai to the Kharag river in the south-west corner; (3) from the Bāghnadī to the Meherani on the west; (4) Athmallik State (as it exists at the present time) on the north; and (5) the Khondmāls on the south. The above disintegrations are alleged to have taken place as follows:—

During the time of Rājā Siddheswar Deva a strip of country called Daspallā, and extending from Kamaimohan near Kantilo to Udandimohan in the east of the State, belonged to Baud. Its distance from the headquarters rendered it impossible for the Rājā to administer successfully. To relieve the people of that portion of the country from the difficulties and inconveniences which they had to put up with in coming on trifling affairs to the headquarters, the Rājā, in 1420 of the *Shakābdā* era, *i.e.*, in 1498-99 A.D., made a gift of this portion of his territory to his uterine younger brother, Nārāyan Rai, on the condition that he should govern it under the orders of the Rājā, and that only cases of minor importance should be disposed of by him, those of greater importance being sent up to the Chief. This condition Nārāyan Rai fulfilled for some time, but gradually began to exceed his powers by disposing of serious cases himself. The Rājā hearing this, sent for his brother, who in fear of punishment took refuge with the Rājā of Khandparā, to whom he made over possession of the tract extending from Kamai to midway between Khandparā and Daspallā. A council of *sardārs* (headmen) and people was called by the Chief of Baud and it was unanimously resolved to recover possession by force. Instead of carrying out this resolution, the Rājā sent emissaries to Nārāyan Rai, who appears for some time to have again complied with the conditions on which he held the grant and to have returned to allegiance. Nārāyan Rai, however, again gradually relaxed his obedience, and after the death of Rājā Siddheswar Deva gradually asserted, and practically obtained his independence, though it was never formally admitted by the Baud State.

The strip of country lying between the Kharag river, on the west of Baud and Amaimohan was given in 1521 (*Shakābdā*) *i.e.*, 1599-1600 A.D., by Rājā Madan Mohan Deva to his two daughters as a maintenance grant on their marriage, reserving, however, full authority over the area in all matters of administration. All cases from this tract were for a long time committed to the Rājā for trial, but there being no fixed rules for the administration, and the Rājā relying too much upon his sons-in-law they gradually asserted their independence and eventually paid homage to the Chief of the Patnā State to whom they were related: no hostile action was taken against them but their independence was at no time recognised by the Rājā of Baud.

In 1780-81 A.D. the Rājā of Baud obtained a loan from the Sonpur Rājā. For the liquidation of this debt he made over *pargana* Pancharā, lying between Bāghnadī and the Meherani. A dispute arose as to the possession of this tract and it was settled by the Superintendent of the Tributary Mahāls, who gave the *pargana* to the Sonpur Rājā.

The State which is at present known as Athmallik is alleged to have been once a part of Baud, and not an independent State. Two forts, named Dumbā and Handapā, are said to have been established by a former Rājā of Baud and the names of these forts are still familiar. Dumbā was in Baud and Handapā in Athmallik. For the collection of rents in that portion of Baud which lay to the south of the Mahānadī the Khonds and Sudhas were appointed *sarbarāhkārs* (headmen) of *muthās* (fiscal division of the Khonds) and a similar arrangement was in force for the tract lying to the north of the river and known as Athmallik, where a single *sarbarāhkār* was in charge of the collections. The only difference was that the former being in charge of comparatively small areas were called *sardārs*, while the latter was called *sāmanta*, on account of the greater importance of the charge. There was no material difference between them, nor was the *sāmanta* of Athmallik vested with greater powers. The Athmallik *sāmanta* was *sardār* of eight *māliks*, just as there are in Baud officers called *Sātmālik* and *Bāramālik*, who are in charge of seven and twelve *muthās*, respectively. On the death of a *sarbarāhkār* or *sāmanta* his successor on paying a *nazar* was recognised receiving a *sārī* (a piece of cloth) from the Rājā in return. In former days Athmallik apparently had no distinct *purohit* (priest and spiritual guide) of its own, but under the orders of the Rājā of Baud one used to go there from Baud. On the British conquest of Orissa the Chief went to Sambalpur to make his submission and have his tribute settled. The Sāmanta of Athmallik also went to Sambalpur and got a separate tribute fixed for Athmallik on the ground that it was an independent State.

In the treaty engagement of 1804, the Chief of the State is mentioned as the Rājā of Baud and Athmallik. The then Chief, Rājā Biswambhar Deva, apparently tendered his submission later than those Chiefs with whom treaty engagements were entered into in the first instance in 1803. Baud forms the western extremity of the group of the States formerly known as the Orissa Tributary Mahāls, and it awaited the result of the resistance offered by the Marāthās at the Barmūl Pass, in the State of Daspallā. On the 2nd November 1803, Major Forbes forced the pass and routed and dispersed the Marāthās. The Chief of Baud immediately submitted. A treaty engagement was entered into with him on the 3rd March 1804, some of the terms of which differ from those stipulated with ten of the Chiefs in 1803. Till 1837, the State formed part of what was then known as the South-Western Frontier Agency. The State was originally liable to a re-adjustment of its tribute after every 20 years, the last of which was made in 1875, but the *sanad* of 1894 has fixed it permanently.

The separation from Baud of the Khondmāls, over which the Chief of Baud possessed a merely nominal jurisdiction, was due to the Khonds of Gumsur lead by the renowned Chakra Bisoi having colluded with the Khonds of Baud and created disturbances which the Rājā was entirely unable to quell. The Chief failed to put down the practice of human sacrifices (Meriāh) then prevailing amongst the Khonds. He, therefore, in 1835 made over that part of his State, which was only nominally under his control, to the British Government, and it has since been incorporated with Angul into a British district. From the time of the last Brāhman Rājā Gandhamārdan Deva, who held his *gadi* in 403 (*Shakābdā*), *i.e.*, 481-482 A.D., up to the present day, it is said that there have been 44 Rājās. Gandhamārdan Deva is said to have continued on the *gadi* from 403 to 470 (*Shakābdā*), *i.e.*, 481-482 A.D., to 548-549 A.D., when one Anang Bhanj succeeded him, giving up the title of "Bhanj" and assuming that of "Deva."

This Anang Bhanj, it is said, was one of the two sons of Braja Kishor Bhanj, the younger brother of Biswambhar Bhanj, Rājā of Keonjhar, who was a contemporary of Rājā Gandhamārdan Deva of Baud. His father, Braja Kishor Bhanj, quitted Keonjhar, owing to some misunderstanding between himself and his elder brother, the Rājā of Keonjhar, settling with his family at Kuturi; on his death in 452 (*Shakābdā*), *i.e.*, 530-531 A.D., his widow with her two sons left the place and settled at Baud. The then Rājā of Baud who was childless adopted both children and gave the widow a maintenance allowance, Anang Deva thus obtaining the *gadi* of the Baud State. The Rājās of Baud showed themselves loyal to the Mughal and Marāthā rulers and received at their hands titles of distinction. The Baud, Daspallā, Keonjhar, and Mayūrbhanj Rāj families belong to the same stock, claiming descent from the solar race, and are held to be high caste Kshattriyas. The Chief has no distinct family title, but the surname of Deva is generally used. The emblem of the State is a peacock.

THE PEOPLE.

The population decreased from 89,551 in 1891 to 88,250 in 1901. The falling off is due, partly to the prevalence of epidemic disease and the general unhealthiness of the climate, and partly to the emigration of many migratory Khonds during the scarcity which occurred in 1900. The inhabitants are distributed among 1,070 villages and the density is 70 persons to the square mile. Of the total population 87,988 claim to be Hindus, but many of them are really Hinduized aborigines. The most numerous castes are the Gauras (23,000), Khonds (15,000), Pāns (9,000), Sudhas (7,000) and Chasās (4,000). The Khonds are giving up their primitive customs and beliefs and endeavouring to amalgamate with their Hindu neighbours. The Khonds of Baud are for the most part those members of the tribe who have for many generations back deserted their highland homes and settled down in the plains: they have taken to regular plough cultivation, but still supplement this by raising catch crops on the hill sides, where they cut and burn the light forest. The distinction between the Khond of the plains and of the highlands is very marked and real and is particularly noticeable in the neighbouring State of Kālāhandī where there is a large population of Khonds. The Khonds of the plains have given up their own language which they now scarcely understand and amongst themselves talk Oriyā: they do not eat, drink or intermarry with the Khonds of the hills: the distinction is locally well recognised. The population is classified as follows:—Hindus—males, 43,935; females, 44,053; total of Hindus, 87,988, or 99·7 per cent. of the population; proportion of males in total Hindus, 49·9 per cent. Musalmāns—males, 113; females, 63; total 176, or 0·19 per cent. of the population; proportion of males in total Musalmāns, 64·2 per cent. Christians—3. The number of other religions (Animists) is only 83, while the total population of the State is 88,250. The number of persons able to read and write is 1,425, or 1·6 per cent. of the total population. The people for the most part are very backward, poor and improvident: the villages along the Mahānadī are an exception and many of them are large substantial villages with very prosperous inhabitants. Averages:—Villages per square mile, 0·85; persons per village, 82; houses per village, 16·7; persons per house, 5; houses per square mile, 14·2. The 1,070 villages in the State are classified as follows:—1,062 with less than five hundred inhabitants, 6 with from five hundred to a thousand, 1 with from one to two thousand, and 1 from two to five thousand.

PUBLIC HEALTH. The country is unhealthy and is frequently visited by severe outbreaks of cholera introduced by pilgrims from Purī travelling by the main road along the Mahānadī. The State maintains a charitable dispensary at the headquarters with a small indoor ward and a relief ward for indigent pilgrims. The dispensary is in charge of a Civil Hospital Assistant, and in 1907-08 the number of outdoor patients treated was 6,071, and 27 indoor patients were admitted. The people of this State are very averse to vaccination, but the prejudice is being gradually broken down: in 1907-08 there were 1,942 cases of primary vaccination, but revaccination is practically unknown. The people suffer largely from malarial fever and bowel complaints.

AGRICULTURE. The land is fertile and the country readily lends itself to the construction of reservoirs and irrigation embankments, and the State is fairly well provided with small irrigation works and wells. The principal crop of the country is rice, which is very extensively grown in the open country along the Mahānadī: castor oil, *arhar* and gram are the other main crops and turmeric is also grown in the hills on the southern border.

RENTS, WAGES AND PRICES. The assessment is light, the average rates per acre for first, second and third class rice lands being Re. 1-9-0, Re. 1-2-9 and Re. 0-12-6, respectively, and for *āt* or uplands, Re. 0-8-4. During the decade from 1893 to 1902 there has been a slight tendency for the wages of skilled labour to fall; the average rate of wage during this period has been as follows:—superior mason, 4⅓ annas, common mason, 3⅓ annas; superior carpenter, 4⅓ annas, common carpenter, 3⅓ annas; cooly, 1¾ annas; superior blacksmith, 3½ annas, common blacksmith, 2½ annas. During the same period the average price of wheat, rice and salt has been 12¾ seers, 25¾ seers and 7¼ seers, respectively, showing a tendency to rise.

OCCUPATIONS, MANUFACTURES AND TRADE. There are no special occupations or manufactures carried on in the State. In ordinary years the produce of rice, food-grains and oil-seeds is in excess of requirements and a considerable trade is carried on by traders, who come from Cuttack in the rainy season and export the excess produce on boats down the Mahānadī: in the cold season carts work their way up from Cuttack and even from as far south as Ganjām and trade in *rāshi* (sesamum): turmeric, brought down from the Khondmāls, is also exported in large quantities: there is also a fair trade in forest products such as lac, myrobalans, bamboos and small timber for rafters; sleepers are also floated down the river to Cuttack. The principal imported articles are spices, salt, piece-goods, cloths, brass utensils and kerosene oil.

MEANS OF COMMUNICATION.

The Mahānadī, on the northern, and the Tel river on the western, boundaries of the State, offer excellent facilities for water carriage : by the former route considerable quantities of grain, bamboos and sleepers are carried to Cuttack in the rainy season. The main road from Cuttack to Sambalpur along the southern bank of the Mahānadī traverses the entire length of the State : trade follows this route from December onwards till the break of the rains. The road is maintained by the British Government and there are rest-houses at convenient distances throughout its length. There are no other roads in the State which is very defective in its communication with the interior. The imperial post plies both ways to Cuttack and Sambalpur from Baudgarh, the headquarters of the State.

LAND REVENUE ADMINISTRATION.

The land revenue demand is Rs. 29,043. In 1874, the Assistant Superintendent of the Tributary Mahāls made a summary settlement of rents and *pattās* were issued : this was done to settle the troubles between the Chief and the Khonds. The first regular settlement is now in progress. The land revenue system is closely akin to that of the other States of the group formerly known as the Tributary Mahāls of Orissa: the *sarbarāhkār* is the local rent collector and is rewarded by a commission ; this State being the most westerly of the States formerly known as the Tributary Mahāls of Orissa has always been more in touch with the customs prevailing in the States round Sambalpur and in consequence the *bhogrā* lands assigned to the *sabrarāhkār* have not become merged in the general village lands and though assessed to rent are held by the *sarbarāhkār* for the time being : the prohibition against the transfer, or mortgage by a *sarbarāhkār* of his village and by a tenant of his holding are likewise more clearly recognised and enforced. This State still shows traces of the former possession of the soil by the Khonds: in the *pattās* there are frequently found grants of more villages than one to persons designated as *muthā-māliks* or *muthā-sarbarāhkārs*: the word *muthā* means a Khond fiscal division and the terms above are applied to headmen who are appointed to collect for more than one village: in such cases the commission allowed is usually more liberal than that granted to the *sarbarāhkār* of a single village as the *muthā-mālik* usually employs *sarbarāhkārs* under him to whom he pays commission and keeps one or two villages in his own personal charge. The village *chaukīdār* (watchman) has grants of land averaging about 3 acres and there are the grants to the usual village servants ; these service lands are of course excluded in assessing the rental. The *sarbarāhkārs* obtain their villages generally for five years, and renewal is granted on the payment of a bonus or *nazarāna.*

GENERAL ADMINISTRATION. The relations between the State and the British Government are regulated by the *sanad* of 1894 which was revised in 1908 and the Chief exercises the powers of a magistrate of the first class. The Chief is bound to pay *nazarāna* to the British Government on succession. The State is administered personally by the Chief assisted by a *Dīwān.* **Finances.** The income of the State in 1907-08 was returned at Rs. 95,364 : an annual tribute of Rs. 800 is paid to the British Government. The State contained some fine **Forests.** forests on the southern and south-eastern borders, but these have been largely exploited by timber contractors and until recently, when a trained Forester has been appointed, no check was placed on wasteful and reckless felling: in 1907-08 the forests **Excise.** yielded an income of Rs. 47,404. The excise revenue yielded Rs. 10,609 : opium is obtained from the Government treasury at Angul and *gānja* from the nearest licensed Government *golādār.* **Justice.** The total number of civil suits for disposal in the year 1907-08 **Crime.** was 342. Crime is petty and heinous crime is extremely rare. The number of cases reported in 1907-08 to the police was 109. **Police.** The police force of the State consists of two Sub-Inspectors, one of whom has been trained at the Bhāgalpur Police Training School, ten Head-Constables and 59 constables. The principal police stations are at Baudgarh, the headquarters, Ghantāparā on **Jail.** the Pātnā-Sonpur border and Manomundā on the Tel. There **Public Works Department.** is a good masonry jail with accommodation for sixty prisoners. In 1907-08 the average daily population was 29. The State spent Rs. 8,576 on public works in 1907-08.

EDUCATION. The State maintains a Middle English school, 6 Upper Primary and 19 Lower Primary schools: there are besides 15 private schools: of these private schools 5 are advanced Lower Primary schools and 10 elementary *pathsālās* :—these schools are attended by 1,434 pupils ; there is a special school for girls at the headquarters with a qualified female teacher, and two more in the interior : the Government grant to the State for education in 1907-08 was Rs. 334, and in addition it enjoys free the services of a Government Sub-Inspector.

CHAPTER VI.

BONAI STATE.

PHYSICAL ASPECTS.

THE State of Bonai lies between 21° 39′ and 22° 8′ N., and 84° 30′ and 85° 23′ E., with an area of 1,296 square miles. It is bounded on the north by Gāngpur State and Singhbhūm district; on the east by Keonjhar State; and on the south and west by Bāmra State. Bonai is shut in on all sides by rugged forest-clad hills intersected by a few passes or gorges, which connect it with the surrounding States. The space within is not one extensive valley, but is interspersed here and there with hills. Most of the hills are densely wooded to the summit, and except at the regular passes are inaccessible to beasts of burden. The principal peaks are Mānkarnācha (3,639 feet), Bādāmgarh (3,525 feet), Kumritār (3,490 feet), Chheliātokā (3,308 feet), Kandādhār (3,000 feet), Bichākāni (2,970 feet), Jangrā (2,677 feet) and Raipīri (2,606 feet). Hog, bear, tiger, leopard, elephant, deer and peafowl are met with in the forests. The State enjoys an unenviable reputation for the number of man-eating tigers with which it is infested. The Brāhmanī, the only large river, flows from north to south through the centre of the State. It receives the drainage of the surrounding hill-streams, and waters a beautiful and spacious valley containing large groves of mango and other fruit-trees. The only real cultivation to be found lies along the valley of the Brāhmanī, which divides the State into two parts. On either side of the valley rise vast hill ranges with occasional cultivation in a few of the valleys. The road to Bonai starts from the Pānposh railway station on the Bengal-Nāgpur Railway and lies for about twelve miles in the Gāngpur State, passing through alternate jungle scrub and rice lands until Bānki, a police station in the Bonai State, is reached.

After leaving Bānki the road commences to rise quickly and enters the heavy forest, and eventually ascends by a high *ghāt* known as the Champājharan pass. The pass is said by the people to be named after the *champā* trees which grow on the summits of the surrounding hills, the flower of this tree being used in the worship of Mahādeo. The road then again enters the forest, and after ascending a high pass known as Barghāt drops down to the Kurhādī stream, which at this point enters the Brāhmanī. The scenery along the Kurhādī stream is extremely fine: the stream runs fast and clear falling in cascades along its boulder-strewn course and forming deep pools and eddies: on both banks it is closely shut in by towering forest-clad hills. From this stream and also from the Brāhmanī the Jhorās (gold-washers) obtain gold in small quantities. The people also obtain a little iron from the hills in these parts for their own agricultural uses. From this point the fertile valley of the Brāhmanī is reached, and the next important village is Dārjin on the banks of the Brāhmanī, situated just below a magnificent gorge. From here to Bonaigarh the road following the course of the Brāhmanī, passes over a low plateau, on which are situated a large number of prosperous villages. After crossing the Brāhmanī, Bonaigarh is reached. The village of Bonaigarh, the headquarters of the State, lies on rising ground by the banks of the Brāhmanī, and the *garh* or residence of the Chief itself looks over the river. The village itself consists of one broad street rising up to the *garh* with a line of shops and houses on each side. The *garh* itself lies at the head of this street.

Travelling south-west from Bonai, a region of vast hill ranges, forest and jungle is met with, extending up to the borders of the Gāngpur and Bāmra States. These forests have only been slightly exploited for tusser and lac. Between these forest ranges and the Brāhmanī there is, however, a fair quantity of cultivated lands dotted here and there with isolated hills. Considerable deposits of lime-stone in nodular form are found in this tract. Crossing the river on the southern border of the State, following up the other bank, a similar tract of fertile land is found between the river bank and hill ranges.

The tract of cultivated lands extends up to Khuntgāon, where the Gond *jāgīrdār*, a feudal service tenure-holder, the *mahāpātra* resides. In the southern portion of the State the *tāl* palm, which is but occasionally met with to the north, is fairly abundant. From Khuntgāon there extends to the north-east, to the borders of Singhbhūm and Keonjhar, vast hill ranges covered with dense jungle. Proceeding from Khuntgāon to Koira towards the Singhbhūm border it is necessary to cross high hill ranges, and the tracts over them are almost impassable for horses. The journey is a most arduous one, and on all sides is found evidence of the presence of wild elephants, tigers, and bears. These tracts are mostly inhabited by Pauri Bhuiyās who practise *dāhi* cultivation. There is scarcely a tree of any dimension worth speaking of to be found, though the hills are covered with dense jungle. After crossing the Dhaulāghāti pass round the shoulder of the Chheliātokā range, a small valley with regular cultivation is met. There is then another long and inaccessible ascent over the Khatiyābhāngan pass to the valley in which Koirā lies. It is from these tracts that the greater part of the tusser and lac is brought. The scanty population living in this area consists for the most part of Pauri Bhuiyās and a few Gonds. At Koirā there is a fine open valley well watered, and here are situated some thriving villages. From Koirā the same hill ranges and forests, but not so rugged and wild, continue in a north-westerly direction. There are a few scattered Pauri Bhuiyā villages here and there relying on jungle produce and cultivation on the hill sides for a living. The valley of the Brāhmanī is again met with in the neighbourhood of Balāeng, and from here to Pitāgāon on the west bank of the Brāhmanī on the border of the Gāngpur State regular valleys and cultivation extend on all sides. The average rainfall for the three years from 1905-06 to 1907-08 was 56·06 inches.

Bonai was ceded to the British Government in 1803 by the treaty of Deogāon by Raghujī Bhonslā, to whom it was restored by a special engagement in 1806. It reverted to the British Government under the provisional agreement concluded with Mādhujī Bhonslā (Appā Sāhib) in 1818, and was finally ceded by the treaty of 1826. The State is ordinarily administered, subject to certain restrictions, by the Rājā, who is required to pay a yearly tribute of Rs. 500 and a *nazarāna* (duty) on succession and to render military service in time of war. Indra Deva, the grandfather of the present Chief, received the title of Bahādur for his services in suppressing the Keonjhar rising: at the same time his Bhuiyā zamīndār and two Gond *jāgīrdārs* were presented with swords and shields. During the minority of the present Chief the State is under the direct management of Government. The State was transferred from the Chotā Nāgpur Division and included in the group of the Orissa States in October 1905. HISTORY.

The family of the Chief claims a mysterious and foreign origin. They say that they came from Sākaldwīp or Ceylon, and that the founder of the family was abandoned by his mother under a *kadamba* (*Nauclea cadamba*) tree. Being thus on the point of falling into the hands of an enemy, the infant was rescued by a peacock, which swallowed him, and kept him in its craw until the danger was past. In gratitude for this service the peacock was adopted as the family emblem. In reference to their early connection with the *kadamba* tree, the Chiefs describe themselves as *kadamba-bansī* Rājputs. Looking, however, to their position as Chiefs over powerful Bhuiyā vassals, who hold the bulk of the land, command the militia of the State, and claim the right of conferring the *tīkā* or token of investiture on the Chief, it is probable that the Rājā of Bonai was originally only the tribal head of the Bhuiyā clan. The Chief of this State on succession, like the Chief of the Pāl Laharā State, always takes his grandfather's name.

THE PEOPLE. The recorded population increased from 32,120 in 1891 to 38,277 in 1901, the growth being due partly to a more accurate enumeration and partly to the country having been rendered more accessible by the Bengal-Nāgpur Railway. The inhabitants are contained in 217 villages, the most populous of which are situated in the central valley along the banks of the Brāhmanī; for the whole State the density is 30 persons to the square mile. The State is the most sparsely populated of all the States in Orissa. The population is classified as follows:—Hindus—males, 13,712, females, 12,659, total, 26,371 or 68·8 per cent. of the total population; proportion of males in total Hindus 52 per cent. Musalmāns—males, 46, females, 23, total 69 or 0·18 per cent. of the total population; proportion of males in total Musalmāns 33·3 per cent. Christians—92 or 0·24 per cent. of the total population. Animists—males, 6,193, females, 5,552, total 11,745 or 30·6 per cent. of the total population. The number of persons able to read and write is 373 or 0·97 per cent. of the total population. Averages:—Villages per square mile, 0·16; houses per village, 29·4; houses per square mile, 4·92; persons per village, 176; persons per house, 6. The State contains 217 villages—200 with less than five hundred inhabitants; 13 with from five hundred to one thousand inhabitants and 4 with from one thousand to two thousand inhabitants. The population is chiefly of Dravidian origin, the most numerous tribes being Bhuiyās, Gonds, Hos, Khariās, Mundās and Pāns. The Bhuiyās and Gonds are the most influential classes; they have always shown a very independent attitude towards the Rājā, and rebellions of the Bhuiyās and of the Gonds have taken place. The headman of the Bhuiyās, who is called *sāont*, claims the prerogative of bestowing on the Rājā the *tīkā* or sign of investiture, a claim which is, however, not recognized by the Chief. The two headmen or leaders of the Gonds are respectively called *mahāpātra* and *dandpāt*. The *sāont*, the *mahāpātra* and the *dandpāt* are the only three fief-holders or sub-proprietors under the Rājā, each possessing several villages and having to render military service to the Rājā if required, besides paying him a fixed yearly rental. There is some immigration of Kols, Mundās and Oraons from Singhbhūm and of Kaltuyās (Kolthās) and Agariās from Sambalpur. The Kols and Oraons take leases of jungle-clad tracts and gradually reclaim them, and the area under cultivation is thus being rapidly extended. The Kaltuyā settlers are very industrious and intelligent cultivators, and have done much to improve the prosperity of the villages in which they have settled by banking up the hill streams for irrigation.

Of the Dravidian races the Bhuiyās are by far the most numerous; they numbered 6,428 in 1901; there are two distinct divisions, the Bhuiyās of the plains, and the Pahāri or Pauri Bhuiyās of the hills. The Bhuiyās are the dominant tribe in most parts of Bonai, and were probably the earliest settlers in the country. They hold fiefs under the Rājā, and form, with the Gonds of South Bonai, the organized militia of the State. The Bhuiyā of the plains has virtually lost all touch with his wilder brethren of the hills, with whom he does not intermarry and has adopted Hindu customs to a large extent. Hardly any other class of subordinate holders have fixed proprietary rights in the soil; and there can be no doubt that the Rājā of Bonai had originally no right to exercise any authority until he had received the *tīkā* or token of investiture from his Bhuiyā vassals. Besides their organization as a semi-military body, the Bhuiyās derive great power from their position as priests of the oldest temples and shrines. Colonel Dalton writes that "This custom has no doubt descended in Bhuiyā families from the time when Brāhmans were not, or had obtained no footing amongst them, and when the religion of the land and the temples were not Hindu. The temples are now, indeed, dedicated to Hindu deities, but there are evidences that they were originally occupied by other images. At some of these shrines, human sacrifices were offered every third year; and this practice continued till the country came under British rule." **Bhuiyās.**

The Bhuiyās of Bonai have lost all traces of their original Dravidian tongue, and speak Oriyā. The Pahāri or Pauri Bhuiyās of the hills retain, however, many characteristic customs of the race.

Next in influence to the Bhuiyās come the Gonds (5,707), also a Dravidian tribe, who inhabit the south of Bonai bordering on the State of Bāmra. The two leading members of this tribe, called respectively *dandpāt* and *mahāpātra*, hold fiefs on terms of military service under the Chief. The Gonds in Bonai have become thoroughly Hinduized, and know no language but Oriyā. They **Gonds.**

hold an inferior social position and rank with the low castes of Doms and Ghāsīs.

Jhorās. The Jhorās are included as a Dravidian race and are believed to be of Gond extraction. Their employments are gold-washing, boating, and fishing, in pursuance of which they live during the dry weather in temporary huts on the sands of the Brāhmanī river. They numbered 285 in 1901.

Khonds. A small sprinkling of the Khond tribe (730) is found in Bonai. They probably immigrated from the State of Baud, but have long occupied a servile position in Bonai as farm labourers, and have lost all the typical characteristics of their race.

The Kolarian tribes of Bonai all speak dialects of Ho or Mundā, except the Kisān or Nāgeswar, who use Oriyā. They represent themselves as immigrants from Chotā Nāgpur proper, or from Singhbhūm. They are worse looking and worse off than their brethren in those districts, and are probably the wilder members of the tribe, who have retreated before the advance of civilization.

The Hindu population of Bonai consists for the most part of well-known castes, and requires no special comment. The Brāhmans are cultivators and farmers. They employ a large number of the Gandās and other low castes as farm labourers, and treat these servants with studied indignity. The mere presence of a Gandā is regarded as pollution, and no Brāhman will enter the *Gandāparā*, or quarter of the village which is allotted to that caste.

Kaltuyās. The most noteworthy caste among the Hindus of Bonai is the Kaltuyā (Kolthā) (1,138 in number). They are found in Sambalpur, Bonai, Kālāhandī, and Patnā, and occupy in all places a very similar position as most respectable and substantial cultivators. The Kaltuyās of Bonai have markedly Aryan features, with hazel or grey eyes. Rāma Chandra, the seventh *avatār* (incarnation) of Vishnu, is their favourite deity. The Bonai Kaltuyās call themselves Rāmānandiās, followers of the Vishnuvite teacher of the thirteenth century who proclaimed the equality of castes. But they also worship at a temple erected to Rādhā and Krishna by a Rājā of Bonai, who appears to have been a votary of the love-worship introduced in 1520 by Vallabha Swāmī. The elders of the caste say that they came originally from Mithilā, which they left in the days of Rāma, and settled in Sambalpur. Six generations ago they emigrated from Sambalpur into Bonai, where they have remained ever since.

The following notice of the Bonai Kaltuyās is given by Sir W. Hunter in his Statistical Account of the Chotā Nāgpur

States and is taken from Colonel Dalton in his *Ethnology of Bengal*:—"They form a considerable portion of the agricultural population of Sambalpur, and appear as the best cultivators and most substantial people in Bonai. I found them occupying villages together with Gonds and Khonds; but these, the probable representatives of the aborigines of the place, had nearly all fallen into the position of farm servants to the Kaltuyās, who had large substantial, well-stocked farmyards, and very comfortable houses. I was freely admitted into their domiciles, and the women and children were all presented to me. They afterwards came to my tent and sat there. The *pardāh* system of excluding females was entirely unknown to them. Though, doubtless, best part Aryan in blood, there is, I think, a slight deterioration arising from admixture with the less comely aborigines. Their colour varies from coffee to tawny yellow. The mouths are well formed, though large; eyes generally large, full and clear, many hazel. I especially observed that many of the fair sex were distinguished by well-marked eyebrows and long eyelashes. The noses are not aquiline or prominent, but there is no remarkable deficiency of nasal bone, though this feature is often inclined towards the pug species. They have straight foreheads, but a want of breadth across the temples which takes from the oval of the face. The men show moustache and beard, but little whisker. They are well proportioned, and about the average height of Hindus in the Lower Provinces. The Kaltuyās generally allow their girls to grow to maturity before they give them away in marriage."

Material condition.

The material condition of the people of Bonai is fairly prosperous. The social customs followed are those of the Orissa Province. The dress of the better class of girls consists of a long silk scarf called a *kaupin*, wound round the loins; if the girl be adult, it also covers the bosom, leaving the legs bare to the hipjoint. Married women wear ampler garments; and on the whole, the Hindus of Bonai, and the best of the Bhuiyā and Gond races, dress very respectably. Women dress their hair neatly with silver ornaments, hair-pins, and pendants. The people on the whole are comparatively well-to-do. Their condition cannot of course be compared to that of the more advanced and civilized races of this Province. They have sufficient for their wants, which are few, and appear an exceedingly happy and contented set. There is, however, a marked difference between the condition of the people living along the valley of the Brāhmanī and those dwelling in the jungle and forest tracts. The villagers met with along this valley bear a decidedly prosperous appearance : the houses are large and for the most part well built and well cared for. These villages are conspicuous objects in the landscape, nestling under groves of graceful tamarind trees, with large homestead lands attached to each house : these homestead lands are heavily manured and covered with rich crops of *sarguja* with its bright yellow flowers gleaming in the sun or with heavy crops of castor oil-seed and sugarcane : these lands are strongly palisaded with timber, which is available for the cutting only, as a protection against the ravages of wild animals. The villages themselves are remarkably neat and clean, and free from the suggestion of squalor. The paths through the villages are wide, and as the soil is of laterite are clean and free from mud. The people themselves are very decently clad in home-made raiment. The villagers possess considerable herds of cattle and buffaloes. The people, however, are extremely backward and have practically no knowledge at all of what goes on outside their own villages : they scarcely ever leave the limits of their own villages ; and of the villagers of the interior, there are very few who have seen or ever heard of Rāurkelā railway station. The same remarks apply to the Gond villages. The Gonds in this State rank next in importance to the Bhuiyās. Though the greater number of the Gonds are centered in the villages belonging to the two Gond *jāgīrdārs*—the *dandpāt* and *mahāpātra*, they are by no means confined to these villages, and are found scattered about in hamlets in many Bhuiyā villages. The Gonds, however, are a more jungly race than the Bhuiyās, and dwell as a rule nearer the jungle area.

Almost in every village are to be found small settlements of Pāns, or Tāntis as they prefer to be called : in 1901 they numbered 3,358. These people weave the clothes for the village community ; there are also the village plough-maker and potter who work for two or three villages in the neighbourhood. In fact the villages are self-contained and self-managed.

There are very few villages in the vast hill and forest tracts to the west and north-east of the State. The so-called villages are for the most part nothing but hamlets consisting of less than 10 houses as a rule. Here live the wild Pauri (Pahāri) Bhuiyās and the Hos. These people from their method of livelihood are of course considerably worse off than the people living along the valley of the Brāhmanī, and their general condition is in marked contrast to their more favourably situated brethren. Their raiment consists of a scanty cloth round the loins and in some cases a body wrap ; their ornaments, a few glass beads strung round the neck. Their wants, however, appear to be of the simplest, and they apparently prefer the life of the jungle to any regular cultivation and settled abode. They eat mostly a grain, *gangāi*, and *kodo* and *makai* (Indian-corn), and supplement these with various jungle products and game when they can kill it. They raise crops of *makai* (Indian-corn) on clearings in the jungle on the hill sides, and have formerly done immense damage. The people are of course backward and have not developed the wants bred by civilization; but taking everything into consideration, they are fairly well off. They are extremely unthrifty, and in reaping their paddy content themselves with cutting the ears only, afterwards cutting any straw they want, but wasting a great quantity by turning their cattle in to graze on the standing stubble. Fuel is readily accessible, so too timber for their houses and agricultural purposes. The valley of the Brāhmanī, where the greater proportion of the population lives is fertile, and in ordinary years the yield of the crops is abundant.

The necessities of life can be cheaply obtained: of luxuries few are known except opium and a considerable consumption of *hāndiā* or *pachwai* (rice beer). This can be brewed free for home consumption. The supply of opium and *gānja* is limited to two maunds of each per annum. The Bhuiyās are freely addicted to the consumption of opium and *gānja*, especially the former, giving it even to children of three years of age. The jungle tribes take both drugs when they can obtain them. The Bhuiyās, though confirmed opium eaters and smokers, also consume a fair quantity of country liquor. The people are virtually shut off from civilization with its attendant increased wants.

Putting aside differences of caste and race, there is a very general level of equality amongst the people of this State. There are no zamīndārs in the ordinary sense of the term, and the difference in the size of holdings is not marked. The people are free from debt except for occasional small loans amongst themselves, and the money-lender is conspicuous by his absence.

The people appear healthy, and epidemics are said to be rare amongst them. Fever and spleen appear to be the chief complaints. The people themselves show no sign of suffering to any serious extent from malarial fever and their physique generally is good. There is a dispensary at Bonaigarh at which 9 indoor and 9,270 outdoor patients were treated in 1907-08: a dispensary is under construction at Koirā in the centre of the Bhuiyā tract: vaccination is in charge of a Civil Hospital Assistant with paid vaccinators under him: no fees are levied. Vaccination has hitherto been exceedingly unpopular and revaccination unknown: special efforts of late have been made to PUBLIC HEALTH.

induce the people to accept vaccination, and in 1907-08 there were 1,882 primary vaccinations and 582 cases of revaccination.

AGRICULTURE. The general character of the cultivation in Bonai is the same as in the other States. The principal crops grown in the State are:—cereals, rice; green crops—*kulthī, mūga, arhar, bīrhi, barai,* or *rambhā;* oil-seeds—*til* (sesamum), *sarisha* (mustard), and *sarguja.*

Rice cultivation. The regularly cultivated area is confined to the valley of the Brāhmanī river with a few small scattered areas in valleys lying between the hill ranges. Three regular rice crops are grown in Bonai,—*gorā dhān* or highland rice, autumn rice, and winter rice. Highland rice or *gorā dhān* is sown at the commencement of the rains in June or July, and reaped in September. The autumn rice crop is sown in June on the higher levels of the terraced slopes, and reaped in October. The winter rice is grown on the lower terraces and in the drainage hollows. It is sown in July in a nursery, and sometimes transplanted but generally sown broadcast. The crop is reaped in November. This crop is estimated to yield from eight times to ten times the amount of seed sown.

The principal crop of the State is the winter paddy. Early *āus* paddy is grown in some parts along the river-bed, but as a crop it is of no account. The chief kinds of rice grown are as follows:—*Sonākharikā, muktākeri, metrai, sītābhoga, rādhābhoga, tulsī, lakshmībhoga, sunāgundi, rāutgulī, bhajnā, kantākeri, kaintrāi, jhagrī, mālbamhini, gangātiriā, baidyarāj, badarās, pārāpakhiā, kīsrimundi, bhuskā, jhuntri, kuntāru* and others. These are reaped from October onwards.

A fourth rice crop, called *dāhi dhān,* is grown on forest land by the hill tribes. For this no ploughing is required, but the trees are cut down and burned on the land, and the ashes are mixed up with the surface soil. The seed is put in as soon as the rain commences. The outturn of the *dāhi* crop is very prolific, and it is not surprising that the forest tribes cling to this mode of cultivation with considerable tenacity. After two years, however, the land is exhausted, and a fresh piece must be prepared.

Other crops. Other crops are—*Kāngo, suān, kodo, gangāi* (*thalāri*), *māndiā, bīrhi* (*urid*), *kulthī* (two kinds—*bāli* or *kalā kulthī* and *kulthī* itself), *mūga, barai* (a kind of *mūga*), *buta, arhar, rantılā* (or *sarguja*), *rāshi* (sesamum), mustard, *jarā* (castor seed), *rāhāri, kumā, balijā, kuhā, ākhu* (sugarcane).

The most productive of the pulses is *bīrhi,* next come *kulthī, mūga, barai* and *badi* or *rambhā.* The pulse called *arhar* or *rahar* is grown on hill-sides by the wilder tribes, whose principal crop it forms. The oil-seeds—*til*, *sarisha*, and *sarguja*—are grown plentifully; and oil is also extracted from the *kusum* (*Schleichera trijuga*) and *mahuā* (*Bassia latifolia*) trees.

Boitālu or *kakhāru* (pumpkin), *baigun* (brinjal), *sāru* (Arum colocasia), *kachu*, *masiā*, *turāi*, *mendhāsinghā*, *kundru*, *kankro*, *rambhāchhuin*, *khirā* (cucumber), *karlā*, *sajināchhuin*, *kandamūla* (sweet potato), *kharbhuj*, *chalanā*, *panasa* (jack fruit) and plantains. Veget-ables.

No trustworthy statistics as to the outturn of crops are available. No regular land measures were formerly known in Bonai; that is, the local unit of measurement had no reference to any definite superficial area, but only to the quantity of seed which would usually be sown on the land. Thus a *khandi* of land is the amount of land which should receive half a maund of seed, an amount which obviously varies with the crop, season, and soil. But in 1880-81 Mr. Hewitt, who was then Commissioner of Chotā Nāgpur, fixed a unit by having a maund of rice sown in the presence of the Rājā and the tenants. The rates of rent on the *bighā* so ascertained (2,500 square yards) were fixed at one rupee for first class lands, 12 annas for second class and 8 annas for third class. In accordance with the custom of the country only rice lands were assessed. The average yield of the autumn crop on the area sown with half a maund of seed would be about twenty maunds, while the produce of the winter crop would be from thirty to thirty-five maunds. Outturn of crops.

In the Pābari *pargana* amongst the hill Bhuiyās agricultural holdings are assessed on the number of *hals* or ploughs that they contain. The local *hal* of Bonai is very large, containing seventeen *khandis* ($8\frac{1}{2}$ maunds). Despite the classification made in 1880 a cultivator when asked how much land he holds, still states the number of ploughs he possesses or number of *khandis* required to sow his land.

Irrigation to any general extent is not practised. In a few cases hill streams are dammed to irrigate rice crops. The only other crop which is irrigated is sugarcane, which is grown on the homestead lands by sinking a well or if possible by raising water by the ordinary lifts from any available tank.

The rates of assessment for 1st, 2nd and 3rd class rice land per acre are Re. 1-15-0, Re. 1-7-3 and Re. 0-15-6 respectively. The average rate of assessment for *nayābādi* land (land newly brought under cultivation) per acre is Re. 0-5-6. Rates of wages in Bonai are still determined by custom nor have money payments been usually adopted. It is extremely difficult to induce the RENTS, WAGES AND PRICES.

people to take up regular paid labour, four annas a day fails to attract labour for ordinary road earthwork: there is ample labour to be obtained by working as sawyers and carters for the two large timber firms, but practically no local labour is forthcoming and both skilled and unskilled labourers have to be imported from outside. The only system of obtaining local labour is the *begāri* (free labour) system of forced labour for State work rewarding the labourers with their daily allowance of two seers of rice per head. The daily rate of wages paid to imported labour is, superior mason one rupee four annas, common mason or carpenter twelve annas each and local wages when labour can be obtained for cash payment are nominally, cooly three annas, woman and boy two annas, thatchers three annas, common blacksmith four annas. The price of the best cleaned rice was returned by the Commissioner in 1873 at 27 *tāmbis* or seers for the rupee, of common rice 54 seers for the rupee, and of unhusked coarse paddy, 108 seers for the rupee. The price of common rice during the decade from 1893-1902 averaged 18 seers per rupee. The proximity of the railway to the State has undoubtedly given the cultivators a far better market for their produce.

OCCUPATIONS, MANUFACTURES AND TRADE. There are no special manufactures, trades or occupations in the State. *Asan* (*Terminalia tomentosa*) trees are found in great abundance, and large quantities of wild tusser silk cocoons are exported from Bonai. Artificial culture of the tusser worm has, however, made but little progress, as the mass of the population consider it an impure occupation, and none but the lowest castes, such as Doms, Ghāsīs, Pāns, and Gonds will engage in it. Silk cocoons and stick lac are the most valuable of the jungle products. Kerosene has penetrated as far as Bānki and Bonaigarh and tobacco is brought on pack-bullocks. The cheap continental-made blanket is in evidence, and a small trade is done in foreign-made glass beads, bracelets, looking glasses, etc.

The jungle tribes collect the tusser, lac, myrobalans (*harirā*), *sabai* grass, and other jungle products for the contractors dealing in these articles and receive payment in cash or kind. Cotton is cultivated to a considerable extent, but for local consumption only. Cotton thread from Calcutta is beginning to find its way even into the interior. In a few villages it has already ousted the locally produced article. Thus the Pāns round Koirā complain that formerly the people used to cultivate the cotton and bring it them to spin. Cotton is still, however, extensively grown and the village Pāns weave it and up to the present the great proportion of the cloth woven is from locally grown cotton.

Ropes of excellent quality are made by the jungle tribes from the creeper known as *siāli* which is found in abundance in the forests. The chief village industries are (1) weaving, (2) bamboo mat and wicker work, (3) the making of brass pots and pans, (4) iron-smelting, (5) gold washing and (6) the making of vessels of soap-stone for domestic use. **Industries and mineral resources.**

Weaving is done by men of the Pān (or Gandā) and Hansi castes and only coarse cotton cloths are woven. The hand-loom used by both castes is the same, but the cloths turned out by the Hansis are somewhat finer than those woven by the Pāns. Cloths are woven only for the local market. Bamboo mat and wicker work is done by the Turi, Dom and Khond castes. The Turis do by far the finest work. The Doms make the bamboo wicker trunks, called *petrās*, the better kind of baskets in domestic use, and bamboo and palm-leaf mats and fans, while cheap and rough mats and baskets are made by the Khonds.

Brass and bronze vessels and dishes, of all the usual forms in domestic use are made by men of the Kansāri caste. They make also the brass ornaments, such as anklets, bracelets, rings, etc., worn by women of the poorer classes. The work is usually of a very rough description and commands only a local market. Iron smelting is done by men of the Kāmār caste from iron ore picked up on the surface, and excellent iron is produced. All the domestic and agricultural implements used throughout the State are made from this iron. Gold-washing is done by the Jhorā caste, men and women alike sharing in the work. The gold is obtained from the sands in the bed of the Brāhmanī river and its tributary streams. The earnings of a Jhorā washer will average about 3 annas a day. Though the quantities of gold obtained in this way are small, probably most of the gold ornaments worn by people in Bonai are made of gold obtained locally from the Jhorās. A unique industry is that of the manufacture of vessels of soap-stone or *khari* for culinary and other domestic use. This industry is practised by men of the Bhumij or Bhandwāl caste. Two varieties of stone are found in Bonai. One is an opaque variety of a greyish-white colour known as *dudh-khari:* the other variety is of a greenish tinge and of a hyalescent or semi-crystalline character and is known as *ainlā-khari* being the more highly prized of the two. Very neat vessels of all the usually domestic shapes and sizes are turned out of this stone. The vessels are first scooped or chiselled out of the stone and are then turned on a lathe. These stone vessels are greatly prized locally and have acquired a reputation abroad. They find a modest market in the neighbouring states.

MEANS OF COMMUNICATION. With the exception of the road to Bānki, there are no regular roads in this State. At the best there are a few bullock-tracks, and travelling is a most difficult and slow process. Formerly carts could scarcely proceed from the railway to Bonaigarh owing to the difficulties of the road through the Champājharan pass: the pass has, however, been recently opened out by blasting and through communication for carts is no longer a difficulty: a good road from the line of rail to the headquarters is now under construction. The river is not navigable owing to rocks and rapids: small dug-outs work up and down, but it is unsafe for boats carrying merchandise and attempts to float sleepers down the river have ended in wreckage and failure. There is a branch post office at the headquarters. The Imperial post plies *viá* Pānposh.

LAND REVENUE ADMINISTRATION. The current land revenue demand in 1907-08 was Rs. 9,534. The assessment is very light and the demand is regularly and easily collected. The land revenue administration differs but little from that of the neighbouring States of Gāngpur, Keonjhar and Bāmra. Land is plentiful and whole village communities frequently abandon their holdings for new sites and in consequence the individual is careless of his rights in the land. The advent of the railway through Gāngpur is however changing this state of affairs, and under the security of administration there has been a noticeable improvement and development of the larger villages, especially in the valley of the Brāhmanī. A settlement was supposed to have been completed in 1880. The Commissioner Mr. Hewitt commenced the work by laying down a unit of land measurement as already described, and by measuring and assessing a few villages in the presence of the Chief who undertook to carry on the work on similar lines: the work of actual measurement was, however, at once abandoned by the people and the ordinary measurement by sight adopted taking Mr. Hewitt's *bighā* as the rough estimate for this chance estimate by observation. There has thus been no regular land settlement, but a regular survey and settlement of the State is about to be undertaken by Government agency. An allowance of about two acres of land is allowed by the State for the maintenance of the village *kotwāls* or *chaukīdārs* (watchmen) and no *chaukīdāri* tax is paid.

Cesses. Besides the rent, the cesses paid are in the case of purely agriculturists only the school and *halpanchā* cess (or fuel cess). The school cess is only collected from the *khālsa* villages, *i.e.*, the villages belonging directly to the Chief's domain and is not paid by the *sāont* zamīndār or Gond *jāgīrdārs*. The *halpancha* (or fuel cess) is levied at the rate of four annas per plough, and the tenant can cut as much timber of the species unreserved as he chooses for this payment from the unreserved portions of the jungles assigned to his village, which are usually of considerable size. The artisan classes, such as the cultivators of the tusser cocoon (*kuā*), pay a cess (*dālkati*) of one rupee per house; the gold-washers (Jhorās) and the Pāns engaged in weaving pay a cess (*pātki*) of one rupee per house or per loom; potters, one rupee per house; braziers, etc., pay similar cesses. These artisan classes pay no rent for their house sites.

Zamīndārs. In this State there is only one zamīndār, the *sāont* or head of the Bhuiyās. He has a small zamīndāri in the south of the State on the east bank of the Brāhmanī. He pays a small quit-rent of eighteen rupees per annum for his zamīndāri and appoints the headmen in his villages. The State, however, leases out the liquor shops in the zamīndār's estate. Besides the *sāont* there are in the south of the State the two Gond *jāgīrdārs* (military fief-holders) holding twelve villages each on the west and east banks of the Brāhmanī. In addition to their rent they pay a police cess at three annas in the rupee, the profits on *mundikats* (trees left on a clearing in the jungle), as regards the *jāgīrdāri* villages, is divided equally between the *jāgirdārs* and the State.

Khorposhdārs. There are none of importance. Various members of the Rāj family have a few villages here and there for their maintenance. They are but petty personages and their relations with the Chief are amicable.

Headmen. Except in the zamīndāri and *jāgīrdāri* villages headmen are appointed by the State. The headman or *gaontia* is purely a *thikādār* (farmer): he does not hold the *bhogrā* (service) lands free of rent; these are assessed in the general *jamā* or rental of the village, but are however the best in the village. Their duties are to collect the rents of the village for which they receive two annas in the rupee commission; to arrange for *begāri* (free labour); to appoint the *kotwāl* (village watchman) subject to approval of the State (*i.e.*, they nominate), and see that two *bighās* of land are reserved for his maintenance: their offices are generally held from father to son, but of course no such reservation is made in their *pattās* (leases) by the terms of which they usually are given the lease of a village when and until a fresh lease is made: in some cases the period of lease is fixed, in others not. In case of default they forfeit the lease. The headmen are substantial persons; they get their commission, hold good lands in the village and reap the profit from the rent of all new lands brought under cultivation during the period of their leases and get a certain amount of *begāri* or free service from their tenants.

GENERAL ADMINISTRATION. The relations of the Chief with the British Government are regulated by the *sanad* granted in 1899 and re-issued in 1905 when the State was transferred to the Orissa Division. Under the *sanad* of 1899 the Chief was formally recognized and permitted to administer his territory subject to prescribed conditions, and the tribute was fixed for a further period of 20 years, at the end of which it is liable to revision. Powers and jurisdiction. The Chief is under the general control of the Commissioner of Orissa whose advice he is bound to follow as regards all important matters of administration, including the settlement and collection of land revenue, the imposition of taxes, the administration of justice, arrangements connected with excise, salt and opium, and disputes in which other States are concerned. The criminal powers at present exercised by the Chief are to pass sentences of imprisonment up to 5 years and of fine to the extent of Rs. 200, but sentences of imprisonment for more than 2 years and of fine exceeding Rs. 50 require the confirmation of the Political Agent. The State is now under direct management by Government: the local officers are a Superintendent and an Assistant Superintendent as the head executive officers of the State.

Finances. The total revenue was in 1907-08 Rs. 93,759 and the tribute is Rs. 500 per annum.

Forests. There are valuable forests in the State which have for several years been worked by two European Timber Companies. There has been no actual demarcation of State and village forests, but the felling of prohibited classes of timber is strictly enforced and the Forest Department now guard against the wanton destruction of forest areas for upland cultivation and catch crops: a trained Forester is about to be appointed. The *sāl* (*Shorea robusta*) forests are extensive: it is however difficult to export the timber and attempts made to float sleepers down the Brāhmanī have failed owing to the rapids and rocks with which the river abounds until it enters the Tālcher State. Timber is accordingly carted from a considerable distance to the railway line. The forests are also full of *āsan* (*Terminalia tomentosa*), *piāsāl* (*Pterocarpus marsupium*), *sisū* (*Dalbergia Sissoo*) and *kusum* (*Schleichera trijuga*). The minor forest products consist of lac, tusser cocoons and *sabai* grass (*Ischœnum Angustifolium*) and are leased out to contractors. In 1907-08 the forest revenue yielded Rs. 67,088. Excise. In the year 1907-08 the excise revenue amounted to Rs. 6,054. Civil Justice. The total number of civil suits for disposal in the year 1907-08 was 107: the litigation was of a petty nature, having reference chiefly to small money claims and land disputes.

Police. There is a regular police force consisting of 1 Sub-Inspector, 5 Head-Constables and 29 constables: besides this staff there is a reserved police force of 9 men and 1 Sub-Inspector: there are also the village *chaukīdārs* or *gorāits*, 108 in number. As already stated there are feudal tenures held by Bhuiyās and Gonds: these feudatories form a sort of rural militia and are available for police duty in the State.

Jail. The jail in Bonaigarh affords accommodation for 31 prisoners.

Public Works Department. There is a regular Public Works Department under the Agency Executive Engineer with a Sub-Overseer locally in charge: the most important work now in hand is the construction of a good road from Pānposh on the railway to Bonaigarh, a distance of 38 miles. In the year 1907-08 Rs. 13,727 was spent on account of public works.

EDUCATION. Education is exceedingly backward and the State being inhabited by very wild aboriginal races scattered amongst the hill ranges and forests it has not been possible so far to spread education: the people are adverse to sending their children to school and making them attend regularly. In 1907-08 there were 13 Lower Primary schools and one Upper Primary school and the number of pupils attending was 492. A special State Sub-Inspector has been recently appointed with a view to improve the standard of the existing schools and endeavour to open others. The State also enjoys the services of the Agency Inspector of Schools, and there are signs that the cause of education is likely at last to make progress.

CHAPTER VII.

DASPALLA STATE.

PHYSICAL ASPECTS. THE State of Daspallā lies between 20° 11′ and 20° 35′ N., and 84° 29′ and 85° 7′ E., with an area of 568 square miles. It is bounded on the north by Angul district and Narsinghpur State, from the latter of which it is separated by the Mahānadī river; on the east by Khandparā and Nayāgarh States; on the south by the Madras district of Ganjām; and on the west by the Baud State. The principal peak is Goāldes (2,506 feet) on the north on the right bank of the Mahānadī.

The Mahānadī marks on the north the boundary line, except for a short distance, where the State extends to the north of the river and the boundary is conterminous with the British district of Angul. The State is divided into two parts—Daspallā proper, to the south of the Mahānadī, which comprises the original area of the State; and Jormuha Daspallā, a small tract to the north of the Mahānadī, which was formerly a part of the tract known as the Angul State, but annexed by conquest. On the west and south the State is covered by some fine hill ranges, but there are no peaks of any special height. These ranges are covered with dense forest, especially to the south, where there are large tracts of valuable *sāl* (Shorea robusta) forest. The rest of the State is open country undulating with a gradual slope from the southern hills to the Mahānadī and the country readily lends itself to irrigation. The State is famous for the magnificent and picturesque gorge of the Barmūl pass in the north-west corner of the State: at this spot the Mahānadī suddenly narrows down from its wide course and enters the gorge, sweeping along through the pass which in parts is not more than a quarter of a mile wide: on either side hills tower up precipitously from the river bed, clad with dense forest to their peaks, with rugged scarps standing out in bold relief: the channel scoured out by the volume of water tearing through the gorge is of great depth and is a magnificent sight in the rains: in the cold and hot seasons the depth of the channel provides a long expanse of water gleaming blue and clear in the sun, stretching out before the eyes like a lake surrounded by mountains: the contrast is enhanced at this time of the year when at either end of the gorge the Mahānadī has dwindled away to a few isolated currents running shallow between vast reaches of arid sand. The average rainfall for the six years—from 1902-03 to 1907-08—was 57·28 inches. The headquarters of the State are at Kunjaban.

Daspallā is said to be a corruption of Jaspallā, meaning a village or number of villages acquired by conquest. The State was established about 516 years ago by Sāl Bhanj, one of the brothers of the then Rājā of Baud. The boundaries of the State at the time of its foundation cannot be ascertained. It is said that Sāl Bhanj had some family quarrel in consequence of which he went to Purī to visit Jagannāth. On his return the then Chief of Nayāgarh took pity on him and gave him shelter at Barmūl. The Rājā of Khandparā joined the Chief of Nayāgarh in helping Sāl Bhanj. The latter gave him a part of his State named Koradā, five *kos* (ten miles) in area, and the former gave him an equal area and made him the Rājā thereof. Nārāyan Bhanj, the successor of Sāl Bhanj, conquered some of the Khond villages. The next Chief named Padmanāv Bhanj conquered that part of the State which is now called Khond Desha. The area of the State being thus extended, the Rājā of Nayāgarh tried to get back the portion of his State, which had originally been given to Sāl Bhanj, and eventually succeeded in doing so. This part was called Purunā Daspallā. Padmanāv Bhanj after the restoration to Nayāgarh of Purunā Daspallā defeated a Khond Chief or Mallik and established his capital at Kunjaban *garh*, the present headquarters of the State. The two succeeding chiefs attempted to wrest from the Rājā of Angul the tract known as Jormuha; but before the fate of the war was decided the matter came to the notice of Raghujī Bhonslā who deputed an officer to settle the dispute, and in 1776 A.D. gave a *sanad* for Jormuha to the Rājā of Daspallā. The twelfth Chief of this family, Krishna Chandra Bhanj, conquered the Khond *zilās* (tracts) named Na-saghar and Bāisipalli. None of the Chiefs have any *farmān* from the Mughal or Marāthā rulers. The Chief is commonly known as the Rājā of Jormuha Daspallā. No tribute is paid for Jormuha by virtue of a concession granted by the Marāthās in consideration of the Rājā supplying, free of all cost, all the timber annually required for the Jagannāth cars at Purī. It was at the Barmūl pass that the Marāthās made their last unsuccessful stand against the British in 1804. The emblem of the State is the peacock. HISTORY.

The population increased from 45,597 in 1891 to 51,987 in 1901, of whom 51,903 were Hindus, the most numerous castes being Khonds (12,000), Pāns (8,000), Chasās (7,000) and Gauras THE PEOPLE.

(5,000). The density is 92 persons to the square mile. The inhabitants are contained in 485 villages, of which the chief is Kunjaban, the headquarters of the State, situated 14 miles from the Cuttack-Sonpur road. The population is classified as follows:—Hindus—males, 25,733, females, 26,170; total of Hindus, 51,903 or 99·8 per cent. of the population of the State; proportion of males in total Hindus, 49·7 per cent. Musalmāns—males, 70, females, 11; total of Musalmāns, 81 or 0·16 per cent. of the total population; proportion of males in total Musalmāns 86·4 per cent. Christians 3. The number of persons able to read and write is 876, or 1·7 per cent. of the total population. Averages—Villages per square mile, 0·85; persons per village, 107; houses per village, 22·03; houses per square mile, 18·8; persons per house, 4·8. The majority of the aboriginal tribes are Khonds, who form 23·7 per cent. of the population. Of the 485 villages there are 475, with less than five hundred inhabitants, 9 with from five hundred to a thousand, and one with from one to two thousand inhabitants. The people are backward, fairly well off, but very improvident.

PUBLIC HEALTH. The country is not unhealthy, except in the forest tracts, where malaria is prevalent. The average ratio of births and deaths per thousand of the population for the ten years from 1893 to 1902 was 16·90 and 14·20 respectively; fever and bowel-complaints account for the principal number of deaths. There is a charitable dispensary at the headquarters in charge of a Civil Hospital Assistant; the dispensary has accommodation for indoor patients; in 1907-08 the total number of patients treated and the average daily attendance were 5,429 and 24 respectively. The people are strongly adverse to vaccination and the average annual number of primary vaccinations during the 10 years from 1893 to 1902 was only 282: since then the department has been placed in the charge of a special Vaccination Inspector, and in 1907-08 there were 1,543 primary vaccinations and 660 revaccinations: the hostile attitude towards vaccination is slowly giving way.

AGRICULTURE. The soil is fertile and the open country between the southern hill ranges and the Mahānadī is well cultivated, and there are several prosperous villages. The agricultural population is indolent and as elsewhere the system of cultivation is of the roughest and the produce obtained is nothing like what the soil is capable of yielding: transplantation of rice is but rarely practised. The crops are the same as in the neighbouring State of Baud, and nothing has so far been done to introduce fresh varieties of paddy or new crops. The soil, however, yields in abundance, and the people usually have large surplus stocks for export:

small reservoirs and embankments for irrigation are commonly met with. The total area in 1902 of the State in acres was 363,520, of which forests occupied 243,549 and 31,135 acres were not fit for cultivation: culturable waste other than fallow amounted to 49,219 acres, fallow 2,258 and net cropped area 37,359 acres and area cropped more than once 3,150 acres.

RENTS, WAGES AND PRICES. The assessment is light and the average rate of rent per acre of first, second and third class rice lands is Rs. 2-2-4, Re. 1-12-4 and Re. 1-7 respectively and for *āt* or uplands, Re. 0-9-0. The average rate of wages during the ten years 1893 to 1902 has shown a general tendency to rise; the average daily rate during this period has been as follows:—Common mason 7 annas 8 pies; superior carpenter 5 annas 8 pies; common carpenter $3\frac{3}{4}$ annas; common blacksmith 5 annas; the services of superior masons and blacksmiths are not available. The average price per rupee of wheat, rice and gram during the same period has shown a tendency to rise and has averaged $8\frac{1}{2}$ seers, $20\frac{1}{2}$ seers, and $14\frac{7}{8}$ seers respectively.

OCCUPATIONS, MANUFACTURES AND TRADE. This State has no special manufactures or occupations calling for notice. In the rainy season and up to January large quantities of food-grains, oil-seeds, bamboos, small timber and forest produce are carried by boat down the Mahānadī to Cuttack. As in the case of other *Garhjāt* States principal imported articles are salt, spices, mill-cloths and kerosene oil.

MEANS OF COMMUNICATION. The Mahānadī river forms the natural and readiest line of communication. The Cuttack-Sonpur road maintained by Government runs through the State parallel to the river; there are rest-houses along the road at easy distances. The State maintains one good surface road about 14 miles in length from the headquarters at Kunjaban linking up with the Government road. There are two inferior surface tracks leading to the Nayāgarh and Khandparā States. There is a post office at the headquarters and the post plies *viâ* Kantilo.

LAND REVENUE ADMINISTRATION. The system of the land revenue administration is similar to that of the neighbouring States and requires no detailed mention. There are no zamīndāris in the State. No cesses are levied. The last settlement was made in 1898 by pole measurements known as the *dastika-padikā* or a pole measuring 10 feet $5\frac{1}{3}$ inches. The current land revenue demand in 1907-08 amounted to Rs. 31,828.

GENERAL ADMINISTRATION. The relations between the State and the British Government are regulated by the *sanad* of 1894 which was revised in 1908 and the powers enjoyed by the Chief are those of a magistrate of the first class. **Powers.** The Chief is assisted by a *Dīwān* in the disposal of public business. **Finances.** The total income of the State is estimated at about Rs. 71,644 and an annual tribute of Rs. 661 is paid to the British Government. The chief sources of income in 1907-08 excluding land revenue were from the forests, Rs. 22,464 and from excise, Rs. 3,537 : reckless felling was formerly the custom in the valuable forests of this State, but this has been stopped and no trees under 6½ feet in girth are now allowed to be cut. Opium and *gānja* are obtained under the same system as in vogue in the other States : the outstill system for supply of liquor is in force and the standard enforced is not more than one outstill for every 30 square miles, and the number of outstills is in fact actually smaller. The total number of suits for disposal in 1907-08 was 265; 55 per cent. of the suits were of a petty nature being below the value of Rs. 50. The number of cases reported to the police in 1907-08 was 78 and serious crime is a rare occurrence in the State. The police force consists of one Sub-Inspector, 11 Head-Constables and 25 constables: besides these there are 210 *chaukīdārs* (village watchmen) and a *paik* militia of 112 men. There is a small masonry jail at head-quarters with accommodation for 25 prisoners : regular labour is exacted from the convicts, who are employed on weaving with a fly-shuttle loom, on oil-pressing and extramural work of road making. In 1907-08 the daily average population was 18·73. There is no regular Public Works Department. The State, however, spent Rs. 8,321 on public works in the year 1907-08.

Forests. Excise. Civil justice. Crime. Police. Jail. Public Works Department.

EDUCATION.

The State maintains a Middle English, two Upper Primary, 43 Lower Primary schools and a Sanskrit *tol*. The number of pupils on the rolls in 1907-08 was 851. Education is very backward and the State received in 1907-08 a grant of Rs. 279 towards education and also enjoys free of cost the services of the regular inspecting staff of Government officers. In 1907-08 the State spent Rs. 2,658 on education.

CHAPTER VIII.

DHENKANAL STATE.

THE State of Dhenkānāl lies between 21° 11′ and 20° 31′ N., and 85° 10′ and 86° 2′ E. It is bounded on the north by the Pāl Laharā and Keonjhar States; on the east by the Cuttack district; on the south by Athgarh, Tigiriā and Barāmbā States and on the west by Hindol State, Angul district and Tālcher State. The State comprises a total area of 1,463 square miles according to the Topographical Survey of 1857 and contains 968 villages and 2 towns. The river Brāhmanī traverses it from the north-west to the south-east for a length of 68 miles, roughly dividing it into two halves. The northern half is more jungly and sparsely populated than the southern. The State is interspersed with hills of which the most important are the Ranjanāgurā and the Anantpur ranges to the north and the Kapilās range to the south-east, and it is intersected by numerous hill-streams which generally flow into the Brāhmanī or its principal tributary, the Ramiāl. The Kapilās hill has an elevation of 2,239 feet and on the summit is a bungalow for the Chief's summer residence with a hill-road leading up to it. The general slope of the State is from west to east and from north to south; the country is undulating and contains a large number of fertile valleys and the soil varies from a rich loam to the gravely detritus of the hill slopes. Less than a third of the State has been brought under cultivation and the forest area covers nearly a thousand square miles, of which the reserved area amounts to 264 square miles. The undulating character of the country specially lends itself to easy irrigation by constructing *bandhs* or dams for the storage of rain water. The forests are rich in *sāl* (*Shorea robusta*), *āsan* (*Terminalia tomentosa*), *piāsāl* (*Pterocarpus marsupium*), *sisū* (*Dalbergia Sissoo*), *mahuā* (*Bassia latifolia*) though of an inferior growth and generally of an immature age. Mica deposits have been discovered in different parts of the State, limestone is also found; iron is smelted according to the primitive method by the Lohurās of Parjang and gold dust in very small quantities is collected by washing the sands of the Ramiāl, the gold thus obtained being of the purest quality. The rainfall averages 58·21 inches: the PHYSICAL ASPECTS.

M 2

summer months are very dry and the temperature rises to 106°. The town of Dhenkānāl, the headquarters of the Chief, contains a population of 5,609 souls, and has good public and other buildings and roads, most of which are metalled and well-aligned. A telegraph line connects it with the town of Cuttack, 24 miles off. The other important centre is Bhuban situated on the Brāhmanī in the extreme east with a population of 6,788 souls and noted as a centre of trade.

HISTORY. The State of Dhenkānāl has no authentic record from which any information as to its origin or history can be gathered. The State is said to derive its name from an aborigine of the Savar caste, named Dhenkā Sawara, who was in possession of a strip of land, about a couple of miles in area, upon which the present residence of the Chief stands. There still exists to the west of the Chief's residence a stone, commonly known as the *Dhenkā Sawara Munda* (head), to which worship is rendered once or twice in a year. About the middle of the 17th century, one Singha Bidyādhar, a scion of the then Khurdā (Purī) Rāj family, is said to have conquered the country and founded the State. Legend relates that the conquered Savar, when put to death, prayed that his head should always be worshipped. Singha Bidyādhar was probably one of a number of petty Chiefs who were known as *sāmantas* or subordinate Chiefs. In an old palm-leaf record it is stated that he was *jāgīrdār* of Hodā Karamul, the *bisa* or *pargana*, about 15 or 16 miles to the north of the headquarters of the State. There are in the Dhenkānāl State a number of places with the prefix of *Garh* such as Garh Siulā, Garh Besaliā, Garh Dom Rājā Katak, Garh Ganpur, and so on. In these there exist even to the present day, ruins of buildings, stone pillars, tanks, wells, and parts of ditches, etc., which show that the places so known were once the seats of petty or semi-independent Chiefs, *i.e.*, of a *sāmanta*. There is also in the State a place known as Bhīm Nagarī, where it is said that the well-known Orissa Chief Ananga Bhīma Deva, who held the *gadi* in the 12th century, was born. This fact is believed to have been recorded in the old palm-leaf records (Mādalā Pānji) of the Purī temple. The old temple of Chandra Sekhar on the Kapilās hill was built by Rājā Pratāprudra Deva of Orissa in the 16th century. There are no records to show the original limits of this State or the various changes in its boundaries. The tradition has, however, been handed down from generation to generation, that the State which originally consisted of one small strip of land was gradually enlarged by the conquests made by Singha Bidyādhar and his successors from the surrounding Chiefs. The largest acquisitions were made during the time of Trilochan Mahendra Bahādur from 1756 to 1798 A.D. He was a powerful Chief, and received the title of Mahendra Bahādur from the Purī Rājā, his predecessors having been designated only as Sāmanta Singha or Bhramarbar Rai. He obtained a *farmān* or *sanad* from the Rājā of Orissa. There is still extant a little poem called *Samara taranga* (war wave), which contains a description of the waves of the war which swept over Dhenkānāl. Up to a very recent date, some of the neighbouring Chiefs acknowledged the supremacy of Dhenkānāl. The Rājā of Hindol especially did so by making an annual present of sweets called *muān*. The present Chief's grandfather, Bhāgīrathī Mahendra Bahādur, was an enlightened Chief, and was made a Mahārājā in 1869. He was heirless, and adopted the youngest brother of the present Chief of Baud, the family thereby taking rank as high caste Kshattriya. He died in 1877 and was succeeded by his adopted son, Dīnabandhu Mahendra Bahādur, who died a minor in 1885. His son, the present Rājā Sura Pratāp Mahendra Bahādur, is the twentieth in descent. The emblem of the State is a fish.

The total population of the State according to the census of 1901 is 273,662 souls, classified as follows:—Hindus—males, 131,465 and females, 134,285, total, 265,750 or 97·1 per cent. of the population of the State; proportion of males in total Hindus 49·5 per cent. Musalmāns—males, 431 and females, 318, total, 749 or 0·28 per cent. of the population of the State; proportion of males in total Musalmāns 57·5 per cent. Animists—males, 3,496 and females, 3,636, total, 7,132 or 2·6 per cent. of the population of the State; proportion of males in total Animists 49·02 per cent. Christian – 18. Proportion of males of all classes in total population 49·04 per cent. Average density of population 187 per square mile. Averages—Villages per square mile, 0·66; persons per village, 269·9; houses per square mile, 36·7; houses per village, 55·5; persons per house, 5·1. Number of literate persons in the State is 9,392 or 3·43 (males, 3·33 and females, 0·10) per cent. of the total population. In this State there are two towns and 968 villages: the villages may be classified as follows:—1 village with from two thousand to five thousand inhabitants, 30 with from one to two thousand inhabitants, 113 with from five hundred to one thousand inhabitants, 824 with less than five hundred inhabitants. The population is ethnically divided as follows:—Aboriginal tribes 42,281 or 15·5 per cent. of the population, of whom the Savars are by far the most numerous (21,438); semi-Hinduised aboriginals 55,861 or

THE PEOPLE.

20·4 per cent. of the population, the Pāns forming the great majority (45,825); Hindu castes and people of pure Hindu origin 174,740 or 63·8 per cent. of the population, the most numerous castes being Chasās (51,116), Gauras (18,369), Khandaits (15,761), Brāhmans (11,541), Telis (10,290), Kewats (9,178) and Tāntis (6,788). Musalmāns 749 or 0·28 per cent. of the population. The large percentage of the Brāhman population compared with the other Garhjāt States is accounted for by the fact that the previous Chiefs of Dhenkānāl and more particularly Mahārājā Bhāgīrathī Mahendra Bahādur, the grandfather of the present Chief, and an enlightened ruler and lover of Sanskrit literature, made extensive grants of *lākhirāj* (rent-free) lands to learned Brāhmans and induced them to settle down in the State with a view to raise the standard of public morality. The *lākhirāj* grants amount to 110 square miles, about half of which consists of forests. The Pāns, 16·8 per cent. of the total population, are very numerous and though some of them own lands having settled down to a life of honest toil, a large number still retain their traditional cattle-lifting and pilfering propensities.

PUBLIC HEALTH. The climate of the State is dry and healthy, except that of the jungle tracts, some parts of which are malarious. In average years tanks and wells supplemented by irrigation reservoirs supply drinking-water to the people in the interior. In years of drought these sources dry up and the supply becomes deficient. Some of the villages are insanitary and the habits specially of the lower classes are very unclean. The aboriginal tribes still live largely on jungle roots. The diseases most prevalent are dysentery, diarrhœa, malarial fever, venereal diseases and skin diseases of various kinds. There are two charitable dispensaries entirely maintained by the State, one at headquarters and the other at Murhi, the headquarters of the Baisingā subdivision. The former is under a first grade Assistant Surgeon and the latter under a Civil Hospital Assistant; a lady doctor is attached to the former and there is a separate zanāna (female) hospital. Both the dispensaries are doing good work and increasing in popularity. The average number of patients annually treated is 27,240. The total number of patients treated in 1907-08 was 32,320. The annual expenditure of the State on these medical institutions averages Rs. 8,684, including the cost of the vaccination establishment under a Civil Hospital Assistant, who acts as a peripatetic village doctor and distributes medicine gratis to the villagers in the recess season. In 1907-08 the number of primary vaccinations, was 7,407 and that of revaccinations, 3,817. The State also employs a passed Veterinary Assistant to give occasional help to the villagers, when epidemics among cattle are reported.

Vital statistics are collected by the Police. The marginal figures compare the birth and the death-rates per mille for the last 3 years.

Year.	Birth-rates.	Death-rates.
1905 ...	18·65	16·82
1906 ...	16·47	18·40
1907 ...	22·01	21·96

There are epidemics of cholera and sometimes of small-pox of varying severity and confined to different parts of the State every year. The average number of deaths per annum from snake-bite is 24 and the number killed by wild animals is 29. Rewards are offered for the destruction of wild animals.

AGRICULTURE.

The population of the State is essentially agricultural; but the methods of agriculture are still primitive and there is great room for development. The cultivated area is 457 square miles or less than a third of the total area of the State. The rents are undeveloped, the average rent per acre being Re. 0-10-6 for all kinds of lands taken together. The total cultivated and occupied area according to the last settlement of the State completed in 1901-02 is divided as follows:—

Class of land.	Area in acres.	Percentage of each class.
Sārad or winter rice	131,873	46·8
Toilā or sloping highland	66,081	23·4
Culturable waste	29,437	10·4
Bāzefasal or miscellaneous crops	17,330	6·1
Biāli or autumn rice	9,776	3·5
Dofasal or twice-cropped area	8,362	3·1
Homestead	7,098	2·4
Orchards	8,676	3·1
Uncultivable tanks, reservoirs and ridges ...	3,186	1·0
Sites of temples and buildings	183	0·1
TOTAL ...	282,002	100

The area under rice cultivation is 170,454 acres as under:—

Description of land.		Area in acres.	Gross out-turn in maunds.	Average outturn in maunds.
Sārad ekfasal	... ...	131,873		
„ *dofasal*	... ...	839		
Total	...	132,712	288,816	18
Biāli ekfasal	... ...	9,776		
„ *dofasal*	... ...	7,521		
Total	...	17,297	121,079	7
Dālua or spring paddy	...	445	4,895	11
Sāthiā or *Toilā* paddy	...	20,000	80,000	4
GRAND TOTAL	...	170,454	2,594,790	15

Manuring is practised on a small scale but rotation of crops is not generally practised. The principal crop in this State is the monsoon paddy. It is a bumper crop if the rain is seasonable and well distributed. In bad years it requires irrigation for which the State from its physical character is well adapted. The tenants construct reservoirs by throwing up dams across water-courses at a moderate cost in primitive fashion. The area under jute is inconsiderable. Sugarcane is largely grown and the people have taken to the better varieties introduced by the State. Tobacco is grown on alluvial lands and near homesteads. *Rāshi or til* (sesamum seed) is extensively cultivated on highlands with a comparatively poor soil and is largely exported from the State. The State maintains an agricultural demonstration farm and a sericultural farm under an expert for the benefit of its tenantry and better results may be expected when these institutions come to be more appreciated by the people. There is an almost unlimited scope for the development of the agricultural resources of the State.

NATURAL CALAMITIES.

The State is subject to visitation of floods and drought. The riparian tracts on both sides of the rivers Brāhmanī and the Ramiāl, covering an area of nearly 500 square miles, are liable to flood. The floods in ordinary years do not cause much harm. In years of exceptional rains they are destructive to crops. The loss caused by the floods is recouped by a bumper winter crop if it is not followed by an unusual drought.

Drought is a more serious calamity in the State on account of the undulating nature of the country, the surface soil being highly porous. The areas most exposed are the extensive uplands in the north and the west of the State comprising an area of about 226 square miles; but in years of severe drought the greater part of the State is affected excepting the low lands and such other areas as are protected by *bandhs*, tanks and natural springs. Irrigation schemes large and small are therefore of cardinal importance to the State and their value is recognised. The well-to-do cultivators have small *bandhs* or embankments of their own and the State has invested a large sum of money in making a number of large reservoirs. But much remains to be done in this direction and the lack of capital and enterprise of the people is a serious drawback. The State devotes a portion of its income every year to irrigation projects, which ought to be highly reproductive in this State.

RENTS, WAGES AND PRICES.

The average rates of rent per acre for the different kinds of crops are:—(1) *Sārad* or winter rice, Re. 1-0-8; (2) *Biāli* or early rice, Re. 0-5-9; (3) *Bāzefasal* (miscellaneous crops), Re. 0-7-1; (4) *Dofasal* (twice-cropped areas), Re. 1-5-9; (5) *Toilā* or uplands at the foot of hills, Re. 0-2-1. There are 9 rates for *sārad* lands (winter rice), varying from Rs. 2-1-4 to Re. 0-6-3 per acre: average rates of assessment for 1st, 2nd and 3rd class winter rice lands per acre are Re. 1-13-2, Re. 1-0-8 and Re. 0-8-4 respectively. There are 5 rates for *biāli* land (early rice), varying from Re. 1-4-10 to Re. 0-4-2 per acre. Average rate of assessment per acre of *āt* or *biāli* land is Re. 0-12-6. The rents realised by the *lākhirājdārs* from their tenants are about 27 per cent. higher, while under-tenants usually pay half of the produce as rent. All classes of tenants are protected from illegal exactions by the record-of-rights framed at the last settlement and cannot be forcibly evicted. Rents have, with few exceptions, remained stationary for the last 30 years, in spite of the marked rise in the price of rice, the staple food-grain, within the State and the increased facilities for export provided by the Cuttack-Angul Road, which passes through the southern and most populous half of the State. The opening of the Bengal-Nāgpur Railway has given a further and marked impetus to the trade of the State.

In the town wages are paid in cash at Re. 0-2-0 per diem for unskilled and Re. 0-4-0 to Re. 0-6-0 for skilled labour. In the interior of the State wages are still paid in kind, and there has been little change in the rates for the last 30 years. Agricultural labourers get on an average about Rs. 2 to Rs. 2-8 per month. The daily wages of other classes of labourers are:—carpenter, 6 annas; blacksmith, 5 annas; stone-cutter, 5 annas;

mason, 5 annas; painter, 4 annas; thatcher, 4 annas; cartman, with cart, 8 annas.

The following table exhibits the average of prices current of the principal food crops during the periods 1882-83 to 1891-92, 1892-93 to 1901-02 and from 1902-03 to 1907-08:—

Year.	Quantities per rupee by the seer of 80 tolas.							
	Paddy.	*Birhi.*	*Müga.*	*Arhar.*	*Kulthi.*	*Chanā.*	*Barguri.*	Wheat.
1882-83 to 1891-92 ...	53	18	14	17	32	27	19	11
1892-93 to 1901-02 ...	49	17	16	19	29	26	27	12
1902-03 to 1907-08 ...	44	17	14	15	27	25	21	13

OCCUPATIONS, MANUFACTURES AND TRADE.

Occupations.

Of the total population of 273,662 souls, 11,541 or 4·21 per cent. are Brāhmans who are either *lākhirājdārs* or cultivators (Māstāns); 2,065 or 0·75 per cent. are Kshattriyas who are mostly *jāgīrdārs;* 2,393 or 0·87 per cent. are Karans or persons of the writer class; 19,401 or 7·08 per cent. are traders; 22,727 or 8·3 per cent. are artisans; 71,168 or 26·01 per cent. belong to the cultivating classes; 95,368 or 34·85 per cent. are labourers of different classes; 47,744 or 17·44 per cent. follow other miscellaneous professions and 1,255 or 0·46 per cent. are Bairāgis and other mendicants. Most of the persons enumerated above are largely dependent on cultivation in addition to their other occupations, which are generally of a subsidiary nature; broadly speaking, the total population of the State may be divided into agriculturists and labourers, of whom the former preponderate over the latter. The Māstān Brāhmans mostly cultivate their own fields, while the *lākhirājdārs*, *jāgīrdārs*, traders and other well-to-do tenants cultivate their lands with the help of servants. There are few tenure-holders or middlemen in the State, except a few large *jāgīrdārs* and *lākhirājdārs.*

Manufactures.

The principal articles of local manufacture are brass and bell-metal utensils, cotton and tusser cloths, iron, lac and catechu. The manufactures are on a very small scale.

Trade.

Food-grains, pulses, molasses, oil-seeds, hides, bell-metal utensils and forest produce are the principal articles of export from the State, while the chief imports are piece-goods, cotton yarns, salt, kerosene oil and spices. Trade is undeveloped and confined mainly to agricultural and forest produce.

MEANS OF COMMUNICATION.

The Cuttack-Angul road runs for 36 miles within the State and this section is maintained from State revenues; it passes through the town of Dhenkānal. The road is metalled, and, with one exception, bridged throughout and is an important trade route. The State expended Rs. 98,000 on this road, including the construction of four road-side bungalows. There are seven other roads connecting the town of Dhenkānāl with the subdivisional headquarters and other places of importance in the interior. The total length of the roads maintained by the State is 168 miles, of which 62 miles are metalled: 14 miles of the old unmetalled Cuttack-Sambalpur road lie within the State, and are maintained by Government. About Rs. 17,000 is annually spent by the State on repairs to its roads and the public works are supervised by a competent Engineer and his staff. There are other parts of the State remaining to be opened out, and a number of village roads, connecting the important villages with the State roads, are needed. No road-cess or tolls of any kind are levied.

Besides the roads, the river Brāhmanī which flows through the State and is navigable for about eight months of the year is extensively used for boat traffic and for floating down timbers and bamboos. The Ramiāl is also used for this purpose, though to a much less extent, as it is not navigable for more than four months.

POSTAL COMMUNICATION.

There is postal and telegraphic service between Dhenkānāl and the town of Cuttack on one side and Angul on the other. There is also daily postal communication between Dhenkānāl and Murhi, the subdivisional headquarters. All these are Imperial lines.

LAND REVENUE ADMINISTRATION.

The State deals directly with the tenants; there are no middlemen. Rents are collected by *sarbarāhkārs* appointed by the State, who retain 10 per cent. for their remuneration and pay in the balance into the Rāj treasury. The small *tanki* or quit-rent due from certain *lākhirājdārs* is collected by their headman or *mukaddam* and paid in direct. The revenue is payable in two equal instalments, viz., on the 15th of April and the 15th of January, and the *sarbarāhkār* is allowed to collect it from the ryots 15 days in advance. Under the terms of his agreement, the *sarbarāhkār* is responsible for short collections though equitable considerations are made for sufficient reasons and the State undertakes to collect the rents due from the defaulters for the *sarbarāhkār's* benefit where he is unable to do so. There is a record-of-rights, and therefore no uncertainty about the tenants' rental. The latter has no saleable rights in his holding, no mortgages or transfers without the permission of the State are recognised and the revenue demand is a first charge on the land. In cases of persistent default the tenant is evicted after notice and his lands resettled by the State; such cases are very few in practice, and the *sarbarāhkār* is not authorised to evict; he merely submits a list of defaulters. The *sarbarāhkārs* are too many; several of them are, in the absence of better men, incompetent and devoid of influence; and their remuneration is meagre in many cases, though the scale is liberal. By the fusion of some of the *sarbarāhkāris*, as they fall vacant, with others, a steady attempt is made to improve matters as far as possible.

The revenue demand stood at Rs. 25,409 only before any settlement of the State was attempted and its collection was most uncertain. The first settlement was made in 1846-47 by the grandfather of the present Chief and resulted in an assessment of Rs. 34,621; a settlement made in 1883-84 yielded Rs. 78,769, the settlement of 1901-02 gave an assessment of Rs. 1,26,680: the increase in 55 years thus amounted to Rs. 1,01,271.

The last settlement was made during Government management of the State at a cost of Rs. 93,826 and took seven years to complete.

The revenue is easily collected and few certificates have to be filed. The current gross land revenue demand, inclusive of the *sarbarāhkārs*' commission and the quit-rent paid by the *lākhirājdārs* is Rs. 1,50,878.

GENERAL ADMINISTRATION. The *sanad* of 1894, which was revised in 1908, regulates the relation between the State and the British Government, to whom the State pays a tribute of Rs. 5,099. The State was under Government management for 29 years during the minority of the Chief and of his father and the spirit of British administration modified to suit local requirements has been introduced. The Chief was placed on the *gadi* on the 12th February 1906 on his attaining majority and has continued the administration on approved lines. He has a *Dīwān*; there are two Assistants. One of the Assistant *Dīwāns* is the Subdivisional Officer in charge of the Baisingā subdivision. Appeals in all civil suits heard by the Assistant *Dīwāns* lie in the first instance to the *Dīwān* and the second appeals are preferred to the Chief. There are no Honorary Magistrates.

Finances. In 1907-08 the total income of the State was Rs. 2,52,970. The State has a considerable sum invested in Government funds.

Forests. There is a staff of 2 officers and 36 guards under a trained Dehra Dun Forester for the conservation of the State forests. In 1907-08 the forest revenue amounted to Rs. 31,765. **Excise.** The excise revenue yielded Rs. 16,750 in 1907-08. **Civil justice.** The number of title suits per annum is 312 and that of money suits 1,559.

Average crime per annum is 1,351 or 0·50 per cent. on the total population, cognizable crime being 0·22 per cent. The State is divided for administrative purposes into two subdivisions, 2 thānas and 5 outposts. The strength of the police force consists of 18 officers and 84 men under an Inspector. The State has a fine two-storied jail with accommodation for 180 prisoners, administered on British lines at the headquarters of the State, and also a sub-jail at Murhi, the headquarters of the Baisingā subdivision, with accommodation for 28 prisoners. In 1907-08 the daily average jail population at both the jails was 181·7. The Assistant Surgeon of the State is the Superintendent of the jail. The Public Works Department of the State is placed under an experienced officer of the rank of a Civil Engineer. In 1907-08 the State spent Rs. 38,740 on account of public works.

Crime. Police. Jails. Public Works Department.

The State expends about 5·00 per cent. of its income annually on education. It maintains a High English school located in a building, one of the finest in the Garhjāts. The cost of the upkeep of the school is Rs. 4,956. The fee collections amount to Rs. 332. There are 233 Primary schools including 27 advanced and elementary private schools in the State. The total cost of education in 1907-08 was Rs. 23,756 of which Rs. 10,385 was contributed by the State, Rs. 3,310 by Government, Rs. 9,039 by school fees and the balance was met by subscriptions.

EDUCATION.

The different kinds of schools in the State with the number of pupils receiving instruction in each are given below :—

CLASS OF SCHOOLS.	No. of schools.	No. of pupils.	REMARKS.
High English school ...	1	186	
Upper Primary schools ...	13	545	
Lower Primary schools ...	193	3,122	Includes one *Makhtab* with 14 pupils.
Sanskrit school ...	1	20	
Guru-Training school ...	1	10	
Private schools ...	27	134	
Total ...	236	4,017	

The number of boys of a school-going age is 20,311 of whom 3,573 or 17·5 per cent. are receiving instruction. Attention is paid to the teaching of girls and the children of backward or aboriginal tribes. There are one Upper Primary and 14 Lower Primary schools for girls and the total number of girl-pupils is 444. There are 5 Lower Primary schools for backward tribes with 60 pupils. The schools are inspected by two Sub-Inspectors and one Inspecting Pandit.

Education has slowly advanced in this State. Technical education has been started by the Chief. Two students are taught sericulture at the State farm and weavers are taught the use of different kinds of improved hand-looms at the State workshop. One student has been sent to Japan to learn practical chemistry and sugar refining, and two have been sent to the Rājshāhī Sericultural school.

CHAPTER IX.

GANGPUR STATE.

THE State of Gāngpur lying between 21° 47′ and 22° 32′ N., and 83° 33′ and 85° 11′ E., with an area of 2,492 square miles, is bounded on the north by Jashpur State and Rānchī district; on the east by Singhbhūm district; on the south by Sambalpur district and Bonai and Bāmra States; and on the west by Raigarh State in the Central Provinces. Gāngpur consists of a long undulating table-land about 700 feet above the sea, dotted here and there with hill ranges and isolated peaks which rise to a height of 2,240 feet. In the north the descent from the higher plateau of Chotā Nāgpur is gradual, but on the south the Mahāvīra range springs abruptly from the plain in an irregular wall of tilted and disrupted rock with two flanking peaks, forming the boundary between Gāngpur and the State of Bāmra. PHYSICAL ASPECTS.

The tutelar deity of this hill is a favourite object of worship with the Bhuiyās and other aboriginal tribes, and offerings to him are made in the form of a stone in the *sara* or sacred pool at its foot. The highest hills in Gāngpur with distinctive names are:—(1) Man, 1,935 feet in height; (2) Andiābirā, 1,455 feet; (3) Bilpahāri, 1,333 feet; and (4) Sātparliā, 1,341 feet. The country for the most part is open and well cultivated: on the northern border, however, is found the thick jungle of the Tarai, lying at the foot of the Chotā Nāgpur plateau: on the southern border also there is heavy forest linking up with the forest-clad ranges of the Bonai State. The average annual rainfall is 60·95 inches.

The principal rivers are the Ib, which enters the State from Jashpur and passes through it from north to south to join the Mahānadī in Sambalpur, the Sankh from Rānchī, and the South Koel from Singhbhūm. The two latter meet at Pānposh in the Nāgrā zamīndāri in the east of Gāngpur, and the united stream, under the name of the Brāhmanī, flows south into the plains of Orissa. The confluence of the Koel and Sankh is one of the prettiest spots in Gāngpur, and it is said by local tradition to be the scene of the amour of the sage Parāsara with the fisherman's daughter Matsya Gandhā, the offspring of which was Vyāsa, the reputed RIVER SYSTEM.

compiler of the Vedas and the Mahābhārata. A temple has recently been erected at this spot and attracts a considerable number of pilgrims. These rivers are practically dry from the end of the cold weather till the rains, and there is no systematic navigation on them. Their beds abound with great boulders and constant barriers of massive rock, forming in the cold and hot weather large deep pools, the sanctuary of quantities of fine fish. Small boats ply on both the Brāhmanī and the Ib and in the rains descend the Ib to its junction with the Mahānadī. The country is dissected with numerous smaller streams, some of them of considerable size : in the rainy season these hill streams sweep down in seething torrents rendering communication with the interior at this period of the year almost impossible.

Diamonds have occasionally been found in the sands of the Ib river, and gold-washing is carried on in most of the rivers and streams by Jhorā Gonds, who thus gain a precarious livelihood. An extensive coal-field is situated in the Himgīr estate, and is now about to be worked. Limestone and iron occur throughout the State in great abundance, especially in the north-east; near Bisrā on the Bengal-Nāgpur Railway there are limestone quarries on an extensive scale ; the quarries are connected by tramway with the main line: the lime is of high quality and has established itself in the Calcutta market: the industry is an important one and employs a large number of hands. Manganese is also found at various places in the State, and a concession for working one of the deposits has been granted and 2,000 tons of ore were raised in 1908. There is every prospect of the manganese industry developing into importance. Work has also been commenced in the dolomite deposits, which are said to be extremely rich and extensive.

The headquarters of the State are at Sundargarh, 19 miles by a good road from the Jharsagurā railway station on the Bengal-Nāgpur line.

HISTORY. The State was once under the suzerainty of Sambalpur, which formed part of the dominions of the Marāthā Rājās of Nāgpur. It was ceded in 1803 to the British Government by the treaty of Deogaon by Raghujī Bhonslā, Rājā of Nāgpur, but was restored to the Marāthā Rājā in 1806. It reverted under the provisional engagement with Mādhujī Bhonslā (Appā Sāhib) in 1818 and was finally ceded in 1826. In 1821 the feudal supremacy of Sambalpur over Gāngpur was cancelled by the British Government and a fresh *sanad* granted to the Chief. In 1827, after the permanent cession, another *sanad* was granted for a period of five years, but this was allowed to run till 1875 before it was renewed. The next *sanad* was granted to the Chief in 1899. The State was transferred from the Chotā Nāgpur to the Orissa Division in 1905.

The relations of the Chief with the British Government are regulated by the *sanad* granted in 1899, which was re-issued in 1905, with a verbal change due to the transfer of the State to Orissa and the appointment of a Political Agent to advise and assist the Chief. The dominant race in the State is the Bhuiyā: the Bhuiyās of Gāngpur retain no tradition of having ever been governed by a Rājā of their own tribe. They allege that for some time a Chief of the Kesarī or lion dynasty of Orissa bore rule in Gāngpur; but this line died out, and the people stole a child of the Sikhar family from Sikharbhūm or Pānchet and elected him as their Chief.

The present Chief, Rājā Raghunāth Sikhar Deva, is aged 57, and succeeded to the *gadi* in November 1858, when he was a minor. Lāl Gajrāj Sikhar Deva, his uncle, was appointed *sarbarāhkār* during his minority, and held his office till January 1871, when the present Chief took over charge of the State.

During the administration of the present Chief, there was a serious disturbance twelve years ago among certain *gaontiās* (village headmen) and *naiks* (feudal militia). The discontent had been smouldering for some years until in February 1897 it took the shape of open revolt by the malcontents which culminated in a series of dacoities and a general blackmailing of the villages in the disturbed tracts. It was at length found necessary to depute the Deputy Commissioner of Singhbhūm with an armed body of British police to assist the Chief in restoring order and in arresting the insurgent leaders. The general administration of the State, however, has been greatly improved by the appointment in 1900 of a *Dīwān* (chief executive officer) with judicial and executive powers. The emblem of the State is the deity *Jagdalā*.

THE PEOPLE.

In 1872 a census was taken by the Chief, and the population was estimated at 73,667 souls, inhabiting 13,977 houses. In 1891 the population was recorded as 191,440 and in the census of 1901 the recorded population was returned at 238,896: this increase and development being due to a considerable extent to the advent of the Bengal-Nāgpur Railway, which traverses the south-eastern portion of the State for about 70 miles. In 1901 the number of villages was found to be 806 against 601 in 1872 and the density of population to be 96 persons to the square mile against 30 in 1872. The population is steadily on the increase. The population is classified as follows:—Hindus—males, 74,717 females, 71,832, total, 146,549: proportion of males in total, Hindus, 50·98. Animists—males, 44,971, females, 43,978, total, 88,949: proportion of males in total Animists, 50·6. Musalmāns—males, 901, females, 739, total, 1,640: proportion of males in total Musalmāns, 54·9. Christians—males, 903, females 855, total, 1,758. The number of persons able to read and write is 3,077, or 1·3 per cent. of the total population. Average number of villages per square mile, 0·32; persons per village, 296; houses per square mile, 16; houses per village, 48·4; persons per house, 6. The 806 villages may be classified as follows:—686 with less than five hundred inhabitants, 102 with from five hundred to one thousand inhabitants, 15 with from one to two thousand inhabitants, and 3 with from two to five thousand inhabitants. The most numerous tribes are the Oraons (47,000), Gonds (37,000), Khariās (26,000), Bhuiyās (24,000) and Mundās (19,000). The Agariās (7,000), a cultivating caste, claim to be descendants of Kshattriya immigrants from Agra. A branch of the German Evangelical Mission, with its head-quarters at Kumārkelā, has been at work since 1899 and has made several converts. The Roman Catholic Jesuit Mission established in the Biru *pargana* of Rānchī claims many converts in the State, chiefly among the Oraons. In both the feudal and farming villages, the priests of the aboriginal deities, called variously *kālo*, *baigā*, and *jhānkar*, hold a position of considerable influence and rank next to the village head whether *naik* or *gaontiā*. The *gaontiās* are usually Aryans, either Brāhmans, Goālās, Telis, or Agariās; but the local priest must be drawn from the aboriginal races. His duties are to decide, boundary disputes, to propitiate the gods of the mountain and of the forest, and to adjudicate in charges of witchcraft. In Gāngpur, Hindus of the highest castes are as much under the influence of these superstitions as the aborigines themselves. It was admitted to Colonel Dalton that before the States came under British rule, a human sacrifice was offered every third year before the shrine of Kālī at Sundargarh, where the present Chief resides. A similar triennial offering was made in Bāmra and Bonai States, and Bhuiyā priests officiated at all three shrines.

Bhuiyās. Of the Dravidian races the Bhuiyās are by far the most numerous, amounting to 24,000 in 1901. They are the dominant tribe in most parts of Gāngpur, and were probably the earliest settlers in the country, as might be inferred from their holding fiefs under the Rājā, and being the special priests of the aboriginal gods. The head of the Bhuiyā vassals is the *mānjhi* of Tiliā or

Sargipāli, an estate situated in the north-west corner of Gāngpur, and so cut off from the rest of the State by a range of hills, traversed by a narrow and difficult pass, that it appears to belong properly to Jashpur. These hills are the boundary of the Oriyā language, which is spoken throughout the rest of Gāngpur to the south of the range, but gives place to Hindī on the north. The *mānjhi* claims to be the head of the Bhuiyās in Gāngpur, and as such to have the sole right of conferring the *tilak* or token of investiture on the Rājā of the State; but the custom of giving the *tilak* is now no longer recognised by the Chief. On the south-east of Gāngpur, the large estate of Nāgrā, stretching from the borders of Singhbhūm to beyond the Brāhmanī river, is held by another Bhuiyā feudatory under the title of *mahāpātra*, and is bound to attend with a contingent of armed followers or *naiks* when summoned by his superior lord. Several of his villages are held by these *naiks*, all of whom are Bhuiyās, on feudal sub-tenures, similar to that of the *mahāpātra* himself. In the south of Gāngpur, there is the *garhatiā* or military fief-holder of Himgīr. Both he and the *garhatiā* of Ergā are bound to render military service, but their tenures are more like ordinary zamīndāris than those of the *mānjhi* and *mahāpātra* mentioned above. There are five other Bhuiyā feudatories in Gāngpur, but their estates are small. One of them is the *garhatiā* of Sarapgarh, a fief which derives its name from a cave, said to be occupied by a snake family, which the rural population have for ages worshipped.

The Gonds, including the Jhorās or gold-washing and diamond-seeking branch of the tribe, numbered 37,000 in 1901; but, as in Bonai State, their social position is low. The name Jhorā, more properly Jhoriā, is said to be derived from *jhodī* or *jhorī*, a brook. **Gonds.**

Oraons (47,000) who are all immigrants from Chotā Nāgpur. The majority of them serve as agricultural labourers, and although there is abundance of land to be had for the clearing, make no attempt to improve their position. **Oraons.**

A small sprinkling of the Khond tribe is found in Gāngpur. They probably immigrated from the State of Baud, but have long occupied a servile position in Gāngpur as farm labourers and have lost all the typical characteristics of their race. **Khonds.**

Among the Hindu population the pastoral tribes are the most numerous. All of them are skilled agriculturists, though not so good as the Agariās, who are the most thriving cultivators in the State. The following description* of this caste **Agariās or Agoris.**

* This account is reproduced from Sir W. Hunter's description of the Gāngpur State.

is quoted from Colonel Dalton's *Ethnology of Bengal*:—"According to their own tradition, they are called Agariās from having come from Agra. They were there, they say, Kshattriyas; but having been subjected to some persecution by the ruler of the State, they left it, and taking up new lands in a new country, cast aside their sacred thread, the badge of the twice-born, with all its privileges and obligations, and took to the plough. Their appearance favours their pretensions to be of good blood. Tall, well-made, with high Aryan features and tawny complexions, they look like Rājputs; but they are more industrious and intelligent than the generality of the warrior caste. The women are spared from all outdoor labour, but are not secluded, and have their own share of industrial avocation as well as household duties. They spin their own cotton and give the yarn to the weavers, who return it to them in piece-goods. They are all decently, and even handsomely, clothed, and have a good store of silver ornaments. The girls are betrothed at a very early age, but remain in their fathers' houses till they grow up into women, so one of the evils of early marriage is avoided. I made inquiries amongst a number of young girls, and found that all above seven years old were betrothed, and wore the silver ornaments which had been given to them when they became engaged. At the marriage a Brāhman priest officiates; but it must be a Brāhman from the North-Western Provinces. They do not employ the Utkala Brāhmans. They have only one priest for a large tract of country, who goes his round and marries them all periodically. They are orthodox Hindus in most customs, but they allow widows to re-marry, and they bury the dead; but at any time when the bones are dry, the principal joints and part of the skull are taken up, and conveyed by the representative of the deceased to the Ganges. This service is often neglected. My informant told me that his father's, grandfather's and great-grandfather's bones were all in the ground and on his conscience. The bones taken are called *ashta-ashtānga* as representing the eight parts of man. The young girls, though betrothed, appear to enjoy great liberty. Some of them are very pretty, bright-looking creatures, of reddish light-brown complexion; fine glossy long black hair, very bright eyes, remarkable for the clearness of the conjunctive membrane, slight flexible graceful figures, teeth white and regular, faces not disfigured by paint, and no *godni*, or marks of tattooing, except on the hands and legs. The hair is very long and elaborately dressed, secured by a large silver ornament. I have seen among them many pairs of grey eyes, and long eyelashes are a prevailing feature.

There is among all classes in Gāngpur a widespread and deep-rooted belief in witchcraft. It is equally dreaded by the wildest and by the most civilised of the people; and I have had before me proceedings in several cases, in which it appeared that Agariā women had been badly treated, to drive the spirit out of them or make them give up the black art. I have been told that in Gāngpur there are old women, professors of witchcraft, who stealthily instruct the young girls. The latter are all eager to be taught, and are not considered proficient till a fine forest tree, selected to be experimented on, is destroyed by the potency of their *mantras* or charms; so that the wife, a man takes to his bosom, has probably done her tree, and is confident in the belief that she can, if she pleases, dispose of her husband in the same manner, if he makes himself obnoxious."

PUBLIC HEALTH.

The country is malarious, but of late years there has been a tendency to improvement owing to the extensive opening up of the land to cultivation consequent on the advent of the railway: foreigners suffer severely from malaria, but the jungle tribes, who form a considerable proportion of the population, are moderately immune. There is a good dispensary at the headquarters, Sundargarh, at which indoor and outdoor patients are treated: this institution is in charge of a Medical Officer with the qualifications of an Assistant Surgeon. At Pānposh in the Nāgrā zamīndāri on the Bengal-Nāgpur Railway, there is a smaller dispensary, in charge of a Civil Hospital Assistant, with accommodation for indoor patients. The total number of indoor patients treated in 1907-08 was 132, and of outdoor patients 17,628. Of late years, special attention has been given to vaccination, which has never been popular amongst the aboriginal races: in 1907-08 the number of vaccinations effected was 8,686, and revaccination totalled 12,788. The work is done by vaccinators paid by the State and is supervised by an Inspector of Vaccination. No fees are charged to the people.

AGRICULTURE.

The soil of Gāngpur is extremely productive in the Ib valley towards the south, and here the skilful and industrious Agariās make the most of their land. In the northern portions, which are occupied chiefly by Dravidian tribes, the soil is less fertile and the cultivators are at a disadvantage, owing to the ravages of wild animals and to their own ignorance and want of energy. The Bhuiyās, indeed, are not far inferior to the Hindus in the means and appliances of agriculture. Their cattle are strong, and they have learnt the use of manure; but they have no idea of combining to carry out schemes of artificial irrigation. Each man makes his own petty dam to water his fields; Agariā villagers, however, construct, in concert with their farmer or headman, reservoirs to irrigate large areas, and display considerable engineering skill.

The principal crops grown in Gāngpur are rice, sugarcane, oilseeds and tobacco. Tobacco is grown only for local use, and is not exported, but is of fine quality. Sugarcane grows luxuriantly, and the molasses extracted are highly esteemed and exported to great distances. The substitution of inferior crops for superior ones has not taken place to any appreciable extent: the inferior kinds of cereals are grown in Gāngpur as in other States, not because they are preferred to the better kinds, but because they are harvested at convenient seasons—are supposed to give less difficulty to cultivate by the ignorant aboriginal tribes who are strongly conservative and adverse to any change. There are, despite the large extension of cultivation of late years with the advent of the railway, considerable stretches of culturable waste land, some of which have never been tilled.

The condition of the cultivators is, on the whole, prosperous. The soil is fertile, prices are low, and the land assessment is very light. No rent is paid for the vast tracts of upland cultivation and in return *begāri* or free labour is rendered to the State and certain *panchās* or contributions in kind are paid. The railway has added enormously to the prosperity of the people and given them a ready market for surplus stocks and forest products. The pinch of severe distress is almost unknown: the better classes have ample stocks and the aboriginals and landless classes live, at most times, to a very large extent, on the products of the forests.

Rents, wages and prices.

There has been no regular settlement of this State and the rent is paid according to seed capacity: land which requires 4 maunds of paddy for sowing pays Rs. 3-14-6 in cash, 30 seers of rice and 3 seers of *birhi* in kind. During the period 1901 to 1902, the average daily wages of labour were:—superior mason, 8 annas; common mason, 3 annas 2 pies; superior carpenter, 10 annas 8 pies; common carpenter, 5 annas 4 pies; cooly, 2 annas 2 pies; superior blacksmith, 10 annas 8 pies; and common blacksmith, 5 annas 4 pies. It is extremely difficult to obtain paid daily labour and the two large timber companies and the limestone quarries in the State have to import the majority of their labour: the cultivators are well off and the landless field labourer obtains sufficiently good remuneration in kind from the farmer and prefers irregular labour eked out by the spoil of the chase or the numerous edible products of the jungle to regular hours and good cash wages. During the period 1893-1902, the average price of wheat, rice and gram was $11\frac{7}{8}$ seers, $16\frac{5}{8}$ seers and $12\frac{7}{16}$ seers respectively.

OCCUPATIONS, MANUFACTURES AND TRADE.

The principal occupation of the people is agriculture, 84·5 per cent. of the total population being agriculturists : 10·8 per cent. follow industry : 1·1 per cent. engage themselves in trade : only 0·4 per cent. follow professions. There are no indigenous manufactures in the State. The village weaver makes the cloth required by the people and ekes out a precarious livelihood owing to the competition of mill-spun goods. There are the lime quarries at Bisrā and two large timber companies with their headquarters at Raurkelā and Kalungā on the line of rail ; there is also a press for *sabai* grass at Bisrā, whence the compressed bales are exported : the manganese quarries also employ a considerable amount of labour. The principal articles exported are cotton, sesamum, lac, honey, arrow-root (*tikhur*), catechu and wax ; and the principal articles imported are salt, sugar, piece-goods, spices and kerosene oil.

MEANS OF COMMUNICATION.

There is only one good road in the State, the road from the headquarters, Sundargarh, to the Jharsagurā railway station; half of the road lies within the State and half in the district of Sambalpur ; the road is bridged throughout except at the large Sapâi nullah, where a good ferry is maintained. A large and substantial bridge is, however, in course of erection. There is a fair surface track with small wooden bridges from Kumārkelā or Rāj Gāngpur, an important village on the line of rail, to Sundargarh : a surface track continues north from Sundargarh to Loākarā, on the Ib in the Jashpur State. In the Nāgrā zamīndāri a good road, some 13 miles in length, is under construction from Pānposh on the railway line to Bānki, just across the border in the Bonai State : this road will be continued through to Bonaigarh. Elsewhere the only means of communication are tracks used by pack-bullocks and the solid wheeled country carts, known as *sagars*. Communications are defective, but are gradually improving. The traffic in the interior is carried almost entirely by pack-bullocks or by coolies, and in the rainy season is at a standstill. In the rains small boats carry goods down the Ib to Sambalpur. There are combined post and telegraph offices at Sundargarh, the headquarters of the State, Pānposh and Kumārkelā, and branch post offices at Kanikā, Bisrā and Kalungā.

LAND REVENUE ADMINISTRATION.

Sir W. Hunter in his statistical account of the Chotā Nāgpur States describes the village system in Gāngpur as follows :—

"Villages in Gāngpur are held either on feudal tenure or on farming leases. The feudal tenures date back to the early times, when the vassals of the Chief received grants of land, in consideration of rendering military service and making certain payments in kind. These payments were gradually commuted to a quit-rent in money, but the service conditions were rigidly enforced. When the Rājā went on a journey, his military fief-holders were obliged to accompany him with their *naiks* or lieutenants in charge of villages and *paiks* or foot soldiery. A few of them are armed with matchlocks, but the majority have only axes and bows and arrows. As the purchasing power of money decreased, the *māl-guzāri* or rent paid by the fief-holders and the heads of villages under them proved insufficient to meet the growing expenses of the Chief. Thus, demands for extra contributions arose. Neither fief-holder nor village head nor foot soldier, however, admit that there has been any enhancement of rent. This they claim to pay at the old rates, and take a separate receipt for, as *mālguzāri*, while the extra contribution is paid as *panchā*, *māngan* or cess, and the two are never consolidated. The *paiks* or foot soldiers pay rent to the *naiks* or village headmen at fixed rates, which average about half of those paid by tenants, who owe no service: the *paiks* of Gāngpur belong to the Bhuiyā tribe.

"All the other villages, whether belonging to the Chief's demesne lands (*khālsa*) or not, are held by small farmers called *gaontiās* under a simple lease-hold tenure for a term of from three to five years, which shows no signs of becoming hereditary, and is not usually held by any of the indigenous tribes. The *gaontiā* pays a stated annual rent, and is remunerated by the surplus collections from the tenants on account of new lands brought into cultivation and by certain *bhogrā* or service lands held rent-free. The yearly rent is very seldom changed; but whenever the lease is renewed, the *gaontiā* pays a bonus, which is supposed to represent the enhancement of value due to improvements or extension of cultivation within the currency of the lease. Under this system there has been little or no interference with the individual cultivators: they assist the *gaontiā* in the cultivation of his *bhogrā* (service) lands. The land measure, however, is based, as in Chotā Nāgpur proper, not on a specific superficial area, but on the amount of seed sown. On the occurrence of births, marriages, or deaths in the Rājā's family, the villagers are called on for extra contributions."

At the present time the employment of the paiks as a State militia has ceased and in the Gāngpur State there is no longer any body of men officially recognised as *paiks*: though service conditions are no longer enforced, the distinction between rent (*mālguzāri*) and cesses (*panchās*) is still, however, well recognised in the villages formerly granted as feudal tenures.

In the *gaonti* villages besides the priest of the aboriginal deity, who ranks next to the village headman, the only other recognised official is the *gorāit* or *chaukīdār* (village watchman). *Gaontiās* are *ex-officio* police officers; and the *gorāit*, besides being the village messenger, is also the assistant of the *gaontiā* in all matters connected with police or the detection of crime. Villages in the State are classified as *kut* and *akut* villages. The *kut* villages are those where a rough estimate by the eye has been made of the cultivated lands, and are practically entirely held by *gaontiās*: the *akut* villages are those in which no eye measurement has been made, and the head of these villages is usually known as a *ganjhu*: he is usually the original clearer of the soil or a direct descendant. The superiority of the position of a *ganjhu* over a *gaontiā* is shown by the fact that the former pays nothing in case of inheritance during the currency of his lease, whereas the latter has to pay regular fees for mutation. The foundation of administration rests very strongly in Gāngpur on the village headman. In this State these headmen have acquired by prosperity a very strong position and are fully capable of maintaining their rights against the Chief or feudal tenure-holder under whom they hold: this is especially marked in the Nāgrā zamīndāri, where many of the *ganjhus* have actually asserted claims to the forest in their villages and tried for years to style themselves *shikmī* (under) zamīndārs. The custom in the neigbouring States of the Sambalpur district is that a *gaontiā* should not hold more than 20 per cent. of the total cultivated land as *bhogrā*, village service lands; in Gāngpur, however, the village headmen, in many instances, owing to weak administration in the past, possess far more than this and are in consequence very wealthy and influential personages in the villages.

The land revenue demand in 1907-08 amounted to Rs. 22,586. There has been no regular settlement in the State, the first regular survey and settlement ever undertaken has recently commenced. Hitherto the villages have been divided, as already stated into two classes, viz., *kut* (surveyed by eye measurement) and *akut* (unsurveyed by eye measurement). In the *kut* villages a very rough and ready estimate of the quantity and class of lands is made by a body of five arbitrators, who examine the village, and make a rough estimate of area and quantities of the various classes of land merely by the eye; the system is locally known as *nazar-paimās*. The unsurveyed or *akut* villages are mostly those which have been more recently reclaimed from forest areas and the holders of these villages are generally the original clearers of the soil. *Panchās* or cesses of various kinds are levied in addition to the land revenue and are larger in the *akut* than in the *kut* villages.

GENERAL ADMINISTRATION. The relations of the Chief with the British Government are regulated by the *sanad* granted in 1899, which was re-issued in 1905 with a few verbal changes due to the transfer of the State to Orissa. Under this *sanad* the Chief was formally recognized and permitted to administer his territory subject to prescribed conditions, and the tribute was fixed for a further period of 20 years, at the end of which it is liable to revision. The State is liable to the *nazarāna* rules on succession. The Chief is under the general advice of the Commissioner of Orissa, or other officer specially authorized by Government, as regards all important matters of administration, including the settlement and collection of land revenue, the imposition of taxes, the administration of justice, arrangements connected with excise, salt and opium, and disputes in which other States are concerned; and he cannot levy import and export duties or transit dues, unless they are especially authorized by the Lieutenant-Governor.

Powers. The Chief is permitted to levy rents and certain other customary dues from his subjects, and has in criminal matters the powers of a Sessions Judge, sentences of death, however, requiring confirmation by the Commissioner of Orissa. The Chief's eldest son exercises powers, equivalent to those of a first class Magistrate, with the exception of the power of whipping: the Honorary Magistrate at Pānposh similarly exercises first class powers and deals with all cases from the Nāgrā zamīndāri. Appeals from the Honorary Magistrate lie to the Political Agent.

Finances. The income derived from excise, together with that from stamp duty and other minor heads, meets the expense of administration under all heads except forests and the surplus expenditure on education: the income from excise and stamps forms the public purse; the land revenue, income from forests and miscellaneous sources are kept by the Chief for the administration of those departments, and from these sources the Chief makes additional grants, in excess of the income received from the school cess, to meet the growing needs of education in the State. The total income of the State from all sources was Rs. 3,30,477 in 1907-08.

Forest. The estates of Himgīr and Nāgrā and certain portions of the *khālsa* or Chief's own domain, contain stretches of *sāl* (Shorea robusta) forest which have been worked since the opening of the Bengal-Nāgpur line through the State. The forests have, however, been recklessly exploited on all sides and little or no timber of any size is now left, except in the *khālsa* along the Tarai of the Rānchī plateau. The destruction has been so great that tho forests of Himgīr, Kinjīr and Nāgrā have been entirely worked out: a policy of forest reservation is now being put in force with a properly trained Forester in charge. It will be possible to resuscitate many of the areas and by careful working plans to keep up a regular source of income for the State, but it will necessarily be many years before any large supply of timber will again be available. The forest income in 1907-08 amounted to Rs. 28,018. The chief jungle products are lac, tusser silk, resin, catechu, all of which are collected from the jungles by the aboriginal races and impure Hindus, such as Gandās and Ghāsīs. There is also a large number of edible roots and indigenous drugs, the following twenty-nine being the most important :—(1) *Kantālu*, (2) *Khaukondā*, (3) *Tusarduā*, (4) *Basrā* or *Pitālu*, (5) *Kundukandā*, (6) *Kulhiā*, (7) *Cherengā*, (8) *Irbāi* or *Nakwā*, (9) *Nāgaliā* or *Chiktā*, (10) *Sanlangā*, (11) *Buti*, (12) *Barhā kandā* (13) *Simalī kandā*, (14) *Palsā kandā*, (15) *Khamāl kandā*, (16) *Masiā* or *Gharbasiā*, (17) *Chhelchuchī*, (18) *Sāru*, (19) *Barhālendi sāru*, (20) *Lāmgadī sāru* or *Pepchī*, (21) *Sankh sāru*, (22) *Tamā sāru*, (23) *Kandmūl* or *Sakarkand*, (24) *Gachh-kandmūl*, (25) *Keo kandā*, (26) *Saigā*, (27) *Keshri kandā*, (28) *Singrā*, and (29) *Sāluk* or *Vent*.

The administration of this department has been greatly improved of recent years. Five years ago there were 220 out-stills in the State, but the number has been reduced to 60, and still further reductions are under the consideration of the Chief. There is a regular excise department, with trained Sub-Inspectors. The result has been a very considerable improvement in the management of this department, the decrease of drunkenness and the supply of wholesome liquor to consumers. The revenue in 1907-08 amounted to Rs. 1,02,393. In the year 1907-08 the total number of civil suits for disposal was 327. The number of cases reported to the police in 1907-08 was 579. The police administration of this State has of late years been greatly improved and the force is now organised on the lines of the police in British India: the rules and procedure in the Bengal Police Code are closely followed. The force is under the general control of the *Dīwān*, with the eldest son of the Chief as Superintendent of Police, assisted by an Inspector, whose services have been lent from the British Police. The advent of the railway and the opening up of the country has rendered a properly trained police force an essential. There are eleven police-stations and outposts, and the force consists of 1 Inspector, 10 Sub-Inspectors, 12 Head-Constables and 120 constables maintained at a cost of Rs. 18,000 per annum ; there is in addition a *chaukīdār* (village watchman) in each village, who is remunerated by a grant of land.

Excise. Civil justice. Crime. Police.

Jails.

There is a well-built jail at the headquarters, Sundargarh, with accommodation for 114 prisoners. The jail is managed on modern lines and is efficiently administered. At Pānposh there is a small sub-jail where prisoners sentenced by the Honorary Magistrate to periods not exceeding three months are confined. The zamīndārs pay an annual contribution for the cost of prisoners coming from their estates.

EDUCATION.

There is a Middle English school at Sundargarh: the school building is a fine one with hostel attached. There is also a Vernacular Middle school at Ujalpur accommodated in a good house with a hostel attached. Of the 26 Primary schools in the State 7 are Upper Primary schools and 19 Lower Primary schools. The number of pupils reading in the Middle English school in 1907-08 was 128. In 1907-08 there were 1,724 boys and 126 girls reading in all the schools. There are two separate girls' schools maintained by the State with a staff of female teachers in charge. Education is very backward, but the Chief takes considerable interest in education and is trying to popularise it with his people and steady progress is being made: he has recently obtained the services of the Agency Inspector of Schools and employs a State Sub-Inspector of Schools. There is a school cess levied in the State at two annas and a half per rupee of rent. The State spent Rs 12,860 on education in 1907-08.

CHAPTER X.

HINDOL STATE.

PHYSICAL ASPECTS.

THE State of Hindol lies between 20° 29′ and 20° 49′ N., and 85° 6′ and 85° 30′ E., with an area of 312 square miles. It is bounded on the north and east by Dhenkānāl State; on the south by Barāmbā and Narsinghpur States; and on the west by Angul district. The northern area of the State is open country, but to the south consists of a wild and tangled range of hills known as the Kanakā range, rising to over 2,000 feet high: the range forms the barrier between Hindol and the State of Narsinghpur. The State, especially the southern half, is notoriously unhealthy and malaria of a very virulent type is common. The average rainfall for the six years—1902-03 to 1907-08—was 52·53 inches. The headquarters of the State are at Hindol.

HISTORY.

The State of Hindol was according to family tradition founded by Uddhab Deva Jenāmani in the time of the last independent Rājā of Orissa, Mukunda Deva Hari Chandan, *i.e.*, about A.D. 1560. The family name for some generations was Deva Jenāmani or Deva Mahāpātra, but has now been changed to Mardrāj Jagadeb. It is said that Hindol is a corruption of Hidambaka, the name of a semi-aboriginal who was once Chief of this tract. It originally comprised only the Iswarāpāl and Dudurkot *zilās* (tracts), about one-fourth of the present area. The largest extension of territory was made during the time of the sixth Rājā who extended his possessions by conquest up to the village of Bānspātnā near the Dhenkānāl capital. The Rājā of Dhenkānāl waged war, however, with the eleventh Rājā of Hindol, and reduced the limits of the latter State. About A.D. 1660, the fourteenth Rājā waged war with, and took possession of some parts of the Narsinghpur State, founding the present capital of Hindol. The emblem of the State is a dagger.

THE PEOPLE.

The population increased from 37,973 in 1891 to 47,180 in 1901, part of the increase being due to an accession of new settlers. It is contained in 234 villages, one of which, Hindol, is the residence of the Chief; the density is 151 persons to the square mile. Of the total population less than two hundred are non-Hindus. The most numerous castes are Chasās (11,000) and Pāns (7,000). The population is classified as follows:—Hindus—males, 23,229, females, 23,755, total of Hindus, 46,984, or 99·5 per cent. of the population; proportion of males in total Hindus, 49·4 per cent. Musalmāns—males, 117, females, 79, total of Musalmāns 196, or 0·3 per cent. of the population; proportion of males in total Musalmāns, 59·6 per cent. Christians—*nil.* Population of all denominations—males, 23,346, females, 23,834; proportion of males in total population, 49·4 per cent. Averages—Villages per square mile, 0·75; persons per village, 201; houses per village 40·6; houses per square mile, 30; persons per house, 4·9. The number of persons able to read and write is 1,668 or 3·5 per cent. of the total population. Of the 234 villages in the State there are 212 with less than five hundred inhabitants, 19 with from five hundred to a thousand, and 3 with from one to two thousand. The State is shut in on all sides by neighbouring States, and has no ready means of communication by river with more advanced places: the people are in consequence very backward and improvident: living, on the other hand, is cheap and their wants are few and simple.

PUBLIC HEALTH.

The tract of country comprised in this State is notoriously unhealthy except towards the more open parts to the north. The drainage is bad and malarial fever is rife. There is a charitable dispensary in charge of a Civil Hospital Assistant at the headquarters where, besides 13 indoor patients were treated 3,622 outdoor patients received medical aid during 1907-08: a small indoor ward is attached to the dispensary, but the accommodation is poor, and new buildings are in course of erection. Vaccination is in charge of a special Civil Hospital Assistant who also attends to village sanitation and renders medical assistance in the interior: the number of primary vaccinations performed in 1907-08 was 2,813, headway has now been made amongst the aborigines of this State who formerly strongly opposed vaccination. In the year 1907-08 the number of re-vaccinations was 164.

AGRICULTURE.

The country in the northern portion of the State is open and cultivation is general and there are some prosperous villages: in the southern portion of the State the cultivation is inferior and in this part the aborigines practise *dāhi* (clearing and burning the forest) cultivation to a considerable extent: rice is the principal crop, but there are no special varieties, and so far nothing has yet been done to introduce improved methods of cultivation and better varieties of seeds or new crops. Excellent oranges are grown at the headquarters and the climate of the southern hills appears favourable to their cultivation. The State generally is in a backward condition and the system of cultivation is poor. Out of a total acreage of 262,071 acres, forests occupy 111,697 acres and unculturable waste 85,730 acres.

RENTS, WAGES AND PRICES.

The average rate per *mān* (or about $\frac{2}{3}$rds of an acre) for first, second and third class rice lands is Rs. 2-10-9, Rs. 2-0-4 and Re. 1-5-4, respectively, and for uplands, Re. 0-6-3. Wages during the ten years from 1893 to 1902 have risen all round: the average daily rate for this period is: superior mason, $7\frac{3}{4}$ annas, common mason, $4\frac{3}{4}$ annas; superior carpenter, 13 annas, common carpenter, $4\frac{1}{2}$ annas; cooly, $2\frac{1}{2}$ annas, superior blacksmith, 8 annas, common blacksmith, $2\frac{1}{2}$ annas. During the same period the average price of wheat, rice, gram and salt has remained stationary and averaged $9\frac{3}{4}$ seers, 27 seers, $41\frac{1}{2}$ seers and 8 seers, respectively.

OCCUPATIONS, MANUFACTURES AND TRADE.

The principal occupation of the people is cultivation. The State possesses no trades or manufactures of importance: the ordinary requirements of village life in this backward tract are supplied by the village artisans: brass utensils are imported from Cuttack and Kantilo in the Khandparā State; the other principal imported articles are spices, salt, cloths and kerosene oil.

MEANS OF COMMUNICATION.

The old Cuttack-Sambalpur high road runs through the State in a south-easterly direction, and small quantities of country produce are thus brought to the Mahānadī and there sold to travelling merchants. A branch road $7\frac{1}{2}$ miles in length, connects the main road with the headquarters. The other roads in the State are Narsinghpur to Hindol, 2 miles in length, Hindol to Angul 6 miles. The total length of metalled roads is 3 miles and unmetalled 20 miles. There is a post office at the headquarters.

LAND REVENUE ADMINISTRATION.

The system of land revenue administration is the same as in the other States of the group formerly known as the Tributary Mahāls of Orissa; the *sarbarāhkārs* (village headmen) being remunerated by cash commission for collecting the rents. There are the usual grants of service lands to *chaukīdārs* (village watchmen), village servants and the ordinary rent-free and religious grants. The last settlement was made in 1901 and expires in 1911: the land revenue demand is Rs. 52,962.

GENERAL ADMINISTRATION.

The *sanad* of 1894, which was revised in 1908, governs the relations between the State and the British Government. The State is now, owing to the minority of the Chief, under Court of Wards and is directly administered by a Superintendent appointed by Government and exercising the powers enjoyed by

Finances. the Chief. The State has an estimated income of Rs. 66,753 and pays an annual tribute of Rs. 551 to the British Government. The State is encumbered with considerable debts accumulated by the late Chief. Forests. The forests are not productive and contain no large quantity of valuable timber and in 1907-08 yielded only Rs. 5,458. Excise. The excise revenue in 1907-08 yielded Rs. 1,886: opium and *gānja* are obtained in the usual manner through Government agency and the excise arrangements generally are modelled on those followed in British India.

Civil justice. The total number of suits instituted during the year 1907-08 was 125: the percentage of the suits under Rs. 50 in value was 78·4. Crime. There is little heinous or serious crime in the State. Police. In 1907-08 150 cases were reported to the police. The police force consists of a Sub-Inspector, 5 Head-Constables and 37 constables. There are three police stations in the State.

Jail. The jail accommodation is bad and a new jail is under erection. In 1907-08 the daily average population was 36.

Public Works Department. The Public Works Department is under the Public Works Supervisor of the Wards' States assisted locally by a Sub-Overseer and suitable public buildings have yet to be erected.

EDUCATION. The State maintains one Middle Vernacular school, 3 Upper Primary and 66 Lower Primary schools. The number of pupils on the roll in 1907-08 was 1,547: of the Lower Primary schools, 11 were entirely maintained by the villagers, and the rest were aided by the State. There are two separate schools for girls. The expenditure on education by the State in 1907-08 amounted to Rs. 1,434 and the Government contribution, to Rs. 765: the State also receives the assistance of inspection by Government educational officers. Education is backward but steady progress is being made.

CHAPTER XI.

KALAHANDI STATE.

THE State of Kālāhandī or Karond lies between 19° 3′ and 20° 28′ N., and 82° 32′ and 83° 47′ E. It is bounded on the north by the Patnā State; on the east by the Jaipur zamīndari and Chinnā Kimedi in the Vizagapatam and Ganjām districts of the Madras Presidency; on the south by the Jaipur zamīndāri; and on the west by Jaipur, Bindrā Nawāgarh, and Khariār in the Raipur district of the Central Provinces. The area of the State is 3,745 square miles. PHYSICAL ASPECTS.

The Kālāhandī State is divided into two distinct areas, the plain country and the hill tracts or *dangarlā* as they are locally named. The plain country is undulating and for the most part closely cultivated with an area of 2,330 square miles; the general elevation of this tract is about 900 feet above sea level; it is intersected here and there by hill ranges and isolated peaks, but contains a large area of cultivated lands. It is occupied largely by the Kaltuyās, clever and capable agriculturists, and fine embankments and tanks are no uncommon feature. A certain number of Khonds are also to be met with; these people have left their hill fastnesses and settled down to plough cultivation. The plain area stretches away from the Tel river, south for about 40 miles and to the east it includes a large portion of the Rāmpur-Madanpur zamīndāri. From Bhawānīpātnā, the headquarters of the State, the plain country sweeps round on the west through Junāgarh, and runs southward to the Jaipur border, forming a regular valley between the uplands of the *dangarlā* and the high hills of Jaipur and Khariār in the Raipur district of the Central Provinces.

Five miles south-east of Bhawānīpātnā the *dangarlā* country commences; it covers a vast area of about 1,415 square miles on the eastern side of the State, and extends southwards to the Jaipur border: of this hill area 238 square miles are in the direct possession of the State and the remainder 1,177 square miles form the hill zamīndāris of the State. This tract rises in a series of precipitous hill ranges from the plains. The path, by which the ascent on the Karlāpāt side is made is quite impracticable even for *sagars* (solid wheeled carts), and in many parts is impossible for horsemen. The hill-sides are covered with dense *sāl* (Shorea robusta) forests, and it is not until the open valleys at the higher elevation are reached that cultivation is met with. These valleys are extremely fertile, and are splendidly watered, being intersected by perennial streams. Here and there patches of regular rice cultivation are met with and crops of wheat, but for the most part the country is given over to *dāhi* cultivation or *jhūming*.

The hill tracts of the State form a conspicuous landmark in the scenery and the wild precipitous ranges, which mark their border, stand up from the plains like a vast wall and are visible for many miles. There are fine open valleys from about 2,800 to 3,200 feet above the sea level: rising from these valleys are great hill ranges running due north and south, the tops of which are plateau lands covered with long grass: the larger of these are some ten miles long with a breadth varying from half to two miles and water is available close to their summits. The principal plateau lands are the Karlāpāt, Kāshipur, Rāmpur-Thuāmūl ranges and the Bafliāmāli hill, a fine plateau on the border of the Kāshipur and Mahulpātnā zamīndāris: these in parts reach an elevation above sea-level of 4,000 feet and over. The State was visited in 1856 by Lieutenant C. Elliot, Deputy Commissioner of Raipur and his account of the State, which gives a detailed description of the country is quoted with corrections:—The country is high, lying near the foot of the main line of the Eastern Ghāts and partaking of the watersheds, both of the Mahānadī and Indrāvatī, which last, with several tributaries and sub-tributaries of the first, rise within its limits; it is well supplied with water, and in some parts (as Thuāmūl, Kāshipur, Karlāpāt and Lānjīgarh, etc.) the soil is enabled to yield two crops of rice within the year. The hills are chiefly plutonic, and independently of two or three considerable ranges detached hills of greater or less size are interspersed throughout the State; the light alluvial soil washed from their slopes is rich, fertile, and easily worked, yielding heavy crops of almost every description. Further in the open country the soil approaches more to the character of black cotton soil, mixed with lime nodules, and occasionally alternating with red gravel, but all is capable of cultivation, and gives good returns for labour well expended. The population is thinly distributed however and the tracts of waste-land are extensive. The hills are for the most part well-wooded except where the process, called *dāhi*, has been practised. In the hill tracts of the State the hillside have been recklessly cleared of forest by the Khonds, who burn the forest for cultivation: the hill sides, however, leading up to the valleys and plateau lands of the hill tracts are densely covered with fine and valuable forest, especially in the Rāmpur-Madanpur zamīndāri, where the hill tracts are more open and the ascent is more gradual. The tree most commonly met with in the State is the *sarai* or *sāl* (Shorea robusta) and attains to very large dimensions: trees of over 8 feet in girth being not uncommonly found. On the south-west border of the State on the border of the Khariār zamīndāri, there is a small quantity of good sized teak, and this tree is found at other places in the State, but mostly along the banks of the Tel river. The orange, though not indigenous, is here cultivated in considerable quantities, and produces very fine fruit. The trees have been introduced from Nāgpur and grow luxuriantly in the Kāshipur and Lānjīgarh zamīndāris, where the fruit ripens in December and April: the orange also flourishes in the open tracts of the State, but not so freely as in the cool moist climate of the hill zamīndāris: plantations of considerable size have lately been planted out in the zamīndāris named above with a view to an export trade so soon as the railway enters the State.

The principal range of hills in the Kālāhandī State is contributed by the Eastern Ghāts, and, though in some places disconnected, runs from north to south, and rather west through Madanpur, Karond, and Lānjīgarh, in the south of which last zamīndāri the range divides the main branch proceeding south through Jaipur to Gunpur; and the other, broad and mountainous, winds towards the west through Karlāpāt and Thuāmūl; again dividing, one branch running west into Bindrā Nawāgarh and the other south to join the original range. It receives names at different points from the villages near its base, the highest elevations being Bankāsāmo (4,182 feet), Karlāpāt plateau (3,981 feet) and Tikrigurā (3,683 feet). Small hills are also interspersed throughout the State. The rivers are for the most part small, and are all tributaries of large rivers. Those most deserving of notice are the Indrāvatī rising at Thuāmūl in the Rāmpur-Thuāmūl zamīndāri, a tributary of the Godāvarī; the Tel, a tributary of the Mahānadī; and the Hātī which rising in the Mahulpātnā zamīndāri falls into the Tel. The Rāul rising in the hills of the Rāmpur-Madanpur zamīndāri joins the Tel. The scenery along the banks of these streams during their course through the hills, especially on the Indrāvatī and the Rāul is exceedingly fine and varies from wild raging torrents sweeping over steep bare rocks, to placid stretches of deep pools with the stream swirling in eddies between rich meadow land, verdant with grass and banks overhung with willows.

The average rainfall for the six years from 1902-03 to 1907-08 was 55·83 inches.

The climate is far from healthy and is notoriously malarious. In the hill area of the Rāmpur-Thuāmūl zamīndāri, the climate is delightfully cool, even in the hottest months rarely rising above 84° in the shade and falling as low as 74° in the morning; during the winter the cold is intense. Being near the Ghāts, the rains are regular and abundant, during which season fever prevails, particularly amongst new arrivals and those unaccustomed to the climate and food of the country. The water of the rivers and wells is good, but a custom obtains which pollutes the water of the tanks, and renders it unfit for drinking purposes. Universally throughout the State the people are in the habit of anointing their bodies with oil and turmeric as a prophylactic against cold and fever, and from washing in the tanks the water becomes so much defiled that persons making use of it for any length of time are very liable to fall sick. The rivers are few and far between and the supply of water from this source is limited. Wells are but rarely met with except at the headquarters of the State and of the zamīndāris and some of the principal police stations. The water of the small hill rivulets is deadly being saturated with the stagnation of decayed vegetable matter. Though cholera is not unknown, its visits are not frequent, nor its ravages great. There are considerable and extensive deposits of aluminium on the plateau lands of the hill area and good graphite is also found and traces of coal deposits are found in a few places.

HISTORY. It is alleged that the dependency of Karond or Kālāhandī was formerly an independent State, paying no tribute to any power, but eventually came under the dominion of the Marāthās, and in the days of Raghujī Bhonslā a *takoli* of Rs. 5,330 was assessed and regularly paid. The State was not one of the Garhjāt States which composed the cluster under Pātnā and Sambalpur, but was a tributary chieftainship, owing formerly allegiance to the reigning Marāthā family of Nāgpur. It is not improbable that Karond or Kālāhandī was one of those States which together with Patnā, Sambalpur and others were restored to Nāgpur in 1806, after the treaty of Deogāon in 1803 had deprived Raghujī Bhonslā of his eastern possessions, but there is nothing to corroborate this view. When the Province of Nāgpur lapsed in 1853 to the Crown, Karond came under the jurisdiction of the British Government and was subsequently created a Feudatory State. The Rājā of Karond used annually up to 1854 to receive a *khilāt* from Government of Rs. 490 in value deducted from the *takoli*, but this is now no longer given.

The dependency of Kālāhandī is said to have formerly belonged to a family of Gangabansī Rājputs, the last member of which named Jagannāth Deva, having no male issue to succeed him, sent in the year 1008 A.D. for one Rugnāth Sāi Deva, the younger brother of the then Rājā of Shatranjigarh in Chotā Nāgpur and gave him his daughter in marriage, together with the right of succession to the dependency. This Rugnāth Sāi Deva, a Nāgbansī Rājput, was the first member of the present family which has ever since uninterruptedly held possession of the dependency. In 1881 a dispute as to the succession arose, and the Khonds broke into open rebellion and committed many excesses attended with bloodshed. The disturbance was repressed, and in 1882 a British officer was appointed as Political Agent, with headquarters at Bhawānīpātnā to manage the State.

Subdivisions. Some considerable changes have taken place in the divisions of the dependency since it was first acquired by the present family. It originally consisted of fourteen *garhs* (forts) to which four more, those of Kāshipur, Mahulpātnā, Chandragiri and Bisangiri were subsequently added, having been ceded in the year 1715 A.D. by Burhā Biswambhar Deva, Rājā of Jaipur. These four *garhs* (forts) were added to Thuāmūl by the Karond (Kālāhandī) Rājā in the same year, making the number of *garhs* (forts) included in the Karond (Kālāhandī) dependency amount to eighteen. Of these, thirteen *garhs* (forts) have, at different times, been bestowed as appanages on members of the family, forming five zamīndāris, the particulars of which are shewn below.

Thuāmūl zamīndāri. The zamīndāri of Thuāmūl, which was composed in 1856 A.D. of seven *garhs* (forts) is the largest; it is situated on the south of Karond (Kālāhandī). It originally consisted of only two *garhs* (forts), and was last granted in the year 1685 A.D., by Rai Singh Deva to his son Padman Singh, the *takoli* being fixed at Rs. 300 ; the Māndibisi *garh* (fort) was afterwards transferred to it from Karlāpāt, and lastly the four *garhs* (forts) of Kāshipur, Mahulpātnā, Chandragiri and Bisangiri, when ceded, as before stated, by the Jaipur Rājā in 1715 A.D., were added to Thuāmūl and the *takoli* raised to Rs. 700.

Lānjīgarh zamīndāri. The zamīndāri of Lānjīgarh composed of three *garhs* (forts) is situated on the south-east of Kālāhandī.

Karlāpāt zamīndāri. The zamīndāri of Karlāpāt originally consisted of two *garhs* (forts) Karlāpāt and Māndibisi, but the latter having been, as before stated, transferred to Thuāmūl, the former alone remains and is situated to the south of Kālāhandī adjoining Thuāmūl. The zamīndāri was last granted by Rai Singh, the 11th Rājā of Kālāhandī, to his youngest son Padman Singh on a *takoli* of Rs. 500.

Madanpur zamīndāri. The zamīndāri of Madanpur comprising the *garh* (fort) of that name, is situated to the north-east of Kālāhandī adjoining Patnā, Baud, and Chinnā Kimedi. It originally consisted of five *tāluks*, namely, Madanpur, Mohangiri, Taprang, Urlādāni and Baskā, but on account of the inability of the zamīndār to manage this last, he was deprived of it by Rājā Fateh Nārāyan Deva, and it was incorporated in the dependency and a reduction of Rs. 100 was made from the *takoli* of Rs. 300 formerly paid. The zamīndāri was last granted to Hatai Singh by the 19th Rājā of Kālāhandī, Biswambhar Deva, whose descendant Harihar Singh held it after him.

All these zamīndāris were granted originally as maintenance grants and have each of them on more than one occasion been regranted and their areas changed by various Chiefs. The Thuāmūl family is divided into an elder and younger branch: the head of the former succeeding to the title of Pāt Rājā, the head of the latter to the title of Thāt Rājā. Disputes arose from time to time between the two Rājās and between Karond and Jaipur occasioned by the claims of the latter to supremacy over the *pargana* of Kāshipur, a part of Thuāmūl. The Nāgpur Government determined to separate Thuāmūl from Karond. The zamīndāri of Thuāmūl was separated from the dependency of Karond in 1863 under the orders of Government in consequence of the Chief being unable to put a stop to the constant quarrels between the Thāt and Pāt Rājās. But as the same violent enmity was kept up between the two Rājās notwithstanding, it was subsequently in 1866 found necessary to divide the zamīndāri into two portions. Thuāmūl, with the *garhs* (forts) of Mahulpātnā, Depur and Bisangiri, was made over to the Pāt Rājā, while the Thāt Rājā was awarded Kāshipur, with the *garhs* (forts) of Māndibisi and Chandragiri. The Thuāmūl portion was, by desire of the people generally, re-attached under sanction to Karond, while Kāshipur for some time remained a separate zamīndāri, but was eventually also re-attached to Kālāhandī.

The emblem of the State is a cobra.

THE PEOPLE. The population, according to the census of 1901, numbered 350,529 souls. The population is classified as follows:—Hindus —males, 140,034, females, 139,622, total, 279,656 or 79·8 per cent. of the total population; proportion of males in total Hindus,

50·07 per cent. Musalmāns—males, 266, females, 238, total, 504 or 0·14 per cent. of the total population; proportion of males in total Musalmāns, 52·8 per cent. Animists—males, 35,770, females, 34,586, total, 70,356 or 20·07 per cent. of the total population; proportion of males in total Animists, 50·8 per cent. Jains—11. Christians—2. Number of literate persons in the State is 6,129 or 17·5 per cent. of the total population. Averages—Villages per square mile 0·59, persons per village 159, houses per square mile 17·95, houses per village 30·6, persons per house 5. The 2,198 villages in the State may be classified as follows:—Villages with from 2,000 to 5,000 inhabitants, 1; villages with from 1,000 to 2,000 inhabitants, 14; villages with from 500 to 1,000 inhabitants, 99; and villages with less than 500 inhabitants, 2,084. According to an estimate made in 1856 the population was 50,000. The principal castes in the State are Khond (103,086), Dom (62,462), Ahīr (59,120), Gond (31,770), Paik (13,598), Māli (9,230), Savar (9,053), Teli (5,971), Kumhār (5,827), Sundi (5,264) and Rājput (5,090). About two-sevenths of the population are Khonds, whose restless disposition seldom allows them to remain long in the same spot. Practically speaking, the whole hill area of the State is in possession of the Khonds, with whom reside a certain number of Doms, who act as servants to the former. The total number of Khonds in the State is 103,086. The open area of the State is occupied by the ordinary cultivating classes, who are very well off: in all villages there are settlements of Gandās and Doms, who perform the scavenging work of the village and also serve as labourers.

In the most southerly portion of the State on the borders of Jaipur in Madras, a tribe known as the Bhatrās is met with: this tribe is in the Kālāhandī State practically only found in the Mahulpātnā zamīndāri: they are said to have come from the Bastar State: the tribe is given over to agriculture in which they are experts: the members are well off, and both men and women are gaily dressed in bright raiments: at the time of the festival of the *Holi* the men of the village in a body go forth from daybreak to night-fall on large hunting parties to the forests: on their return at night there is a general entertainment in the village when the women join them in dancing and revelry: part songs are sung, the men sitting on one side and the women opposite. The songs always open with an invocation to the crow and call for a blessing on the hunting excursions and the men in stanzas relate the exploits of the day, and the women in their turn sing stanzas of praise and congratulation, if the day's hunting has been successful, but if a failure, hold up the men

Bhatrās.

to ridicule. The festal garb of the men on these occasions consists of a tunic round the loins, not unlike a kilt and two brightly coloured strips of cloth fall from the waist between the legs in front and behind reaching below the knee: their heads are gaily adorned with bright turbans and peacocks' plumes, and in their hands they carry short staves of bamboos split and bound at the ends: as they dance they beat time by hitting these staves together: the dance is generally a circular one, and as the dancers move round, they break into parties of fours, who clash their staves together in time to the music; when the bar changes, two of the party move on to the next group of four, and this change being effected all round the circle, there is constant movement and the dance is lively and pleasing: except on this one occasion the Bhatrās as a body do not give way to revelry or drink and are a most industrious race.

Khonds. The Khonds are virtually the sole occupants of the inaccessible hill tracts and prefer to eke out their livelihood by the less arduous system of *dāhi* cultivation or *jhūming*; the sides of the hills which rise from these valleys bear eloquent testimony to this destructive system of cultivation. In this country the Khonds have for years reigned unmolested, paying a mere nominal rental for their villages, or, more correctly speaking, for their *jhūming* areas (*padās*): they are an exceedingly independent race, and they make no hesitation in showing that they resent the appearance of any stranger in their midst, especially of one in authority. The principal crop grown by them is *māndiā*; turmeric is also grown on a small scale, but they supplement their resources largely from the jungles. No Khond ever appears in any way hard up for food. They also keep stores of grain hidden away in caves and make use of this when out on hunting expeditions. These are the real Khonds who still preserve their own language and customs intact; their dialects differ corresponding to the dialects spoken in Gumsur and Kimedi and is in many cases interspersed with Telugu. The Khonds of Kālāhandī are *Kutiā* Khonds. In the course of time, however, a considerable number have settled down in the more open country and taken to regular cultivation, these are known as *Kachhariā* Khonds, while the hill Khonds style themselves *Pahāriā* or *Dangriā* Khonds: the former are gradually more and more assimilating Hindu customs and no longer eat, drink or intermarry with their brethren of the hills: they have dropped their own language and speak Oriyā, and like the *Dihariā* Khorwās of Jashpur and Sirguja, they pretend to have no longer any connection with the *Pahāriā* Khonds of the *dangarlā*. The *Kachhariā* Khonds form about three-fifths of the

Khond population of the State. The following description of the Khonds of Kālāhandī was given by Lieutenant C. Elliot, Deputy Commissioner of Raipur, writing in 1856. This description gives an accurate account of this tribe, the only difference now being that the Khonds of the open country have become more separated from their hill brethren and have more fully adopted Hindu customs: the account is as follows:—"The *Kachhariā* Khonds differ slightly in custom, depending chiefly on their relative positions, and though this may be supposed to have determined their division, yet they do not intermarry, or hold much intercourse one with another. They are described as peaceable, loyal and industrious, generally being cultivators. They have no distinctions of caste, each house providing for its own domestic arrangements. Their clothing generally consists of a single cloth and in some rare exceptions a turban. They worship the same gods as the hill Khonds, marry one wife, and their ceremonies are conducted by the *mānjhi* of the village, or one of the elders of the tribe. There appears to be nothing specially observable regarding them except that they seem to be a race in disposition and under circumstances highly favourable to efforts for their improvement. The Hill Khonds on the other hand appear to possess the characteristics and qualities of all savage hill tribes, quick of observation, suspicious, sensitive, exceedingly trustworthy, fond of ornaments, and primitive in their habits. Their villages consist generally of one long wide street of double bamboo and thatched houses, having each a door of access in front and a door of escape in rear; their cultivation is entirely in the hills, and they have only lately begun to evince a desire to locate themselves in the more healthy plains, attaching themselves in most cases to some larger village, at a distance from which they construct their own quarter, as near to the foot of the hills as possible. They pay no tax whatever, their only contribution being a sheep or some small present at the Dasharā. The gods worshipped by both tribes of Khonds are represented by two sticks of unequal lengths inserted in the ground without any tenement or temple.

"The names locally given are Dhurnī or earth and Dhurma (the judge of departed souls) and the offerings, which usually consist of arrack and live animals, as fowls, sheep, buffaloes, etc., (and until very lately, there is no doubt human beings) are simply placed in front of the idol upon the ground. In their food they are wholly indiscriminate, and cook in old earthen vessels which they prefer to new ones, and which they obtain from the villagers of the open country when they bring the produce of their jungles, as turmeric, chillis, tobacco, oil-seeds, *kāndol* (a large variety of pulse) and edible roots, of which there are several kinds resembling the yam and very palatable, to exchange for salt, cloths, etc."

The practice of human sacrifice referred to in this account has long since ceased. Assessments have now been imposed at nominal rates on the *jhūming* areas (*padās*); these assessments were recently revised and enhanced without opposition and the hill Khonds are slowly but surely advancing and falling more into line with the more civilized races. The Khonds claim the right of placing the Chief on his *gadi* and until this has been done the Chief is not formally recognised by them: this custom is similar to that in vogue amongst the Bhuiyās of Keonjhar and Bonai States. Lieutenant Elliot in his report thus describes the ceremony:—

"The ceremony observed on the installation of a new Rājā is curious and appears worthy of mention. There is a place called Jugsāipātnā about 24 miles east of Junāgarh, where it is said a large village formerly stood (probably at one time the principal town of the dependency) but now covered with jungle. Near this, lives a Khond family the eldest member of which is called the *pātmānjhi*; when the Rājā dies, his funeral rites are performed and his corpse disposed of by the orders of his successor who does not take part in the ceremony: after the due completion of these offices, the zamīndārs and principal persons in the dependency assemble at Jugsāipātnā for the purpose of installing the young Rājā, which ceremony is conducted in the following manner. The *pātmānjhi* or Khond above mentioned having seated himself on a large rock at Jugsāipātnā, dressed in rich cloths given him for the occasion, a rich cloth is thrown over his lap on which the young Rājā sits while his turban is tied by the *Bāghe Pātar* or *Dīwān*, all the zamīndārs and principal persons present holding the turban cloth. The zamīndārs and others then present their *nazars* (gifts) in token of obedience to their ruler. The origin of the custom of celebrating the ceremony in the lap of a Khond is attributed to a covenant said to have been entered into between some former Rājā and the Khonds of the country, but unfortunately the legend has been lost; it does not appear that this particular Khond exercises any authority over his tribe." The description above given represents traditional custom, but omits to notice an important feature, namely, that the Chief must marry a Khond girl. This marriage ceremony is performed by presenting a girl to the Chief who immediately returns her to her parents and the tribe by the Khond system of divorce, whereby a fine is paid by the husband to the tribe for divorcing his wife.

The following description of the other castes found in Kālāhandī is taken from the same report.

The Bhuliās and Kostās are both weavers, the former of cotton and the latter of *kosā* or tusser silk. Their language is Oriyā, but they do not intermarry. The Bhuliās are said to have emigrated from the Dhamtari and Dhamdā in Chhattīsgarh. The caste of Mālis or gardeners is here divided into two, both distinct, their members not intermarrying with each other, the one called Pandrās earn their livelihood by the sale of *churā* or parched rice, and the other called Koslās cultivate vegetable gardens. The Dosis or astrologers are few and illiterate, but satisfy the superstitions of an ignorant and credulous population. They wear Brahmanical threads, though not Brāhmans, and speak Oriyā. Their mode of proceeding in practising their vocation is simple. When any person comes to consult him, the astrologer takes a small quantity of rice in his hand and having counted out the grain in parcels of eight or any smaller number, the remaining grains under that number are referred to the pages of a book, counted from the end according to the number of the seeds, the words written on the page being the answer to the question proposed. On examination of the book, written in Oriyā on palm leaf, of one of these functionaries, the very convenient arrangement was found adopted, of having a favourable and an adverse sentiment on each page, which are used at discretion or as prompted by the liberality or otherwise of the applicant. The Bāngtis are only found in Junāgarh and their employment is confined to catching fish, though they also cultivate. The Kandrās are basket-makers working in bamboo, which is split and woven into mats and baskets. The Kaltuyās are a race of cultivators nearly allied to Mālis but of a distinct caste. They cultivate generally, but their special province is the cultivation of the sugarcane and preparation of sugar. The Dorās are cultivators, serving also as soldiers and their language is Telugu, differing in this respect from the common language of the country and indicating their origin as from the south-east. The Bankās are soldiers, or *paiks*, but use the Oriyā language. The Sauriās are an ignorant, rude, uncivilized race, in progress much on a level with the Khonds. They are cultivators and speak Oriyā, having the privilege, as before stated, of wearing the Brahmanical thread. The Kamārs are basket-makers and *shikāris* or hunters: their number is small. The Sāmpuās are mendicants who travel about the country exhibiting snakes as

Bhuliās and Kostās.

Mālis.

Dosis.

Bāngtis.

Kandrās.

Kaltuyās

Dorās.

Bankās.

Sauriās.

Kamārs.

Sāmpuās.

their name implies. They speak Oriyā and are few in number.

Doms. Doms are found throughout the length and breadth of the dependency, their numbers being considerable. Their language is a corruption of Oriyā and they weave cloths in addition to other employments of a meaner denomination connected with the village. Their duties are the same and the race appears to be identical with the Doms of Hindustān; they correspond in every particular to the *dhers* or out-castes of the village, though not aborigines.

Bhois. The Bhois or bearers found here speak Telugu; they are few in number and confined to Junāgarh.

PUBLIC HEALTH. The country is very malarious and unhealthy to new comers: permanent inhabitants of the State however suffer only to an ordinary degree from fever and bowel complaints: from time to time there are small cholera epidemics, but small-pox visitations owing to the universal and effectual vaccination of the people are very rare. There are five dispensaries in the State each provided with accommodation for indoor patients: these dispensaries are situated at Bhawānīpātnā, Junāgarh, and at the headquarters of the Rāmpur-Thuāmūl, Kāshipur, and Mahulpātnā zamīndāris: they are in charge of Civil Hospital Assistants and the Medical Department of the State is under a qualified Medical Officer: at the headquarters there is a separate female dispensary with a lady doctor in charge: the dispensary at Mahulpātnā has only just been opened. In 1907-08 the number of patients treated was 66,277. Vaccination is free and is very thoroughly carried out and at the present time there is little or no opposition to vaccination, though it is not popular: in 1907-08 there were 15,799 cases of primary vaccination and 12,525 of revaccination. The vaccination operations are supervised by two Vaccination Inspectors under the control of the Medical Officer.

AGRICULTURE. In the open area of the State there are many large and prosperous villages with highly cultivated lands. In the hill area cultivation is almost confined to the burning of the hill sides by the Khonds, except at the headquarters of the hill zamīndāris where rice and wheat are cultivated alternately. The valleys of the hill country are intersected with perennial streams issuing from the plateau land just above and fine crops of wheat are raised by means of natural irrigation by the zamīndārs and in those villages where the members of the zamīndārs' family happen to reside. The Khonds however confine themselves in these parts to growing *māndiā* and turmeric on the hill sides where they have cleared and burnt the forest. The best cultivators in the plains are the expert Kaltuyā cultivators and the small tribe of Bhatrās. The regular cultivating classes make very large profits annually by the sale of produce to merchants who flock to this State in large numbers to export rice, *rāshi* (sesamum) and other cereals, and very large sums of money pass through the post office on this account. In the southern portions of the State a variety of spring rice is harvested in April. A vast change has come over the State during the last fifty years: the population has increased from 80,000 to 350,000 and the soil has come under the plough and the open country is now highly cultivated and well irrigated with fine tanks and embankments. Wheat is grown on the highlands of the hill zamīndāris: special efforts of late years have been made to extend the cultivation of this crop and water mills have been obtained to enable the cultivators to grind the wheat locally. The State has never suffered from any general or serious failure of the crops, and even in 1900 when all the neighbouring country was severely affected, Kālāhandī knew only a slight scarcity. Nothing can illustrate better the change which has taken place than the following quotation from Lieutenant C. Elliot's report of 1856:—

"The productions of the Karond dependency, though various, are none of them of a very superior quality, or in such quantities as to admit of exportation, the greater part of them being consumed within the limits of the State. They may be thus enumerated—Rice, *kutki*, *māndiā*, *kodo*, *gulji*, *mūga*, *urid*, *kandol*, *kulthī*, *sarso* (mustard), *til* (sesamum), *erāndi*, sugarcane, cotton, and tobacco. Wheat and several kinds of pulse, common in other parts, are not cultivated here, though the soil is admirably adapted for them, and gram is produced to a very limited extent. There appears to be no obstacle to their introduction, further than that they do not form articles of consumption by the inhabitants."

The lands are classified as follows:—(1) *Bāhāl*, 1st-class lands; (2) *Bernā*, 2nd-class lands; (3) *Māl* or *bedā*, 3rd-class lands; (4) *Bhatā* or *āt*, uplands. There are also *barchhā* or sugarcane plots and the homestead land or *bāri*.

Land measures. The local measure is the *sukā*, which is not fixed, but means the area sown by two or three *putis* (4 or 6 maunds) of seed. The whole village area is estimated to contain so many *sukās*; 4 *sukās* = 1 *khuri* or the area sown by 8 to 12 *putis* (16 to 24 maunds) of seed. The villagers also speak of the *puti paran*, 20 *māns* (2 maunds) of seed grain as the amount sown in a *puti paran*.

RENTS, WAGES AND PRICES. The average rates of assessment per acre for 1st, 2nd and 3rd class rice lands are—Re. 1-4, Re. 1 and Re. 0-10, respectively, and the average rate of assessment per acre for *āt* or uplands is 2 annas. In the hill tracts the Khonds pay a mere nominal sum for their *jhūming* areas (*padās*). Labour is almost entirely paid for in kind and averages about 2 annas a day for a man and 1 anna 6 pies for a woman. There are three classes of field labourer in this State, viz., (1) *Bāhābandā* (2) *Barshikiā*, (3) *Bhutiār*. The first class take an advance of money from their employer and do not leave his service until the amount is paid; they receive one *puti* (2 maunds) of unhusked rice per mensem, and on the occasion of the Paush Pūrnimā a gift of 4 *putis* (8 maunds) of *dhān* (unhusked rice) and three pieces of cloth. *Barshikiās* are labourers engaged in the month of Māgh (January-February) for one year; the usual rate is Rs. 4 per annum and one *puti* (2 maunds) of *dhān* (unhusked rice) per mensem, and at the close of the year four *putis* (8 maunds) of *dhān* (unhusked rice). The last class are merely day-labourers who receive two *māns* (8 seers) of unhusked rice daily.

Skilled labour receives comparatively high wages, as it is all imported: mason, 8 to 12 annas per diem; carpenter, 6 to 12 annas per diem; blacksmith, 6 to 12 annas per diem; brick-layer, 5 to 6 annas per diem; brick-moulder, 4 to 6 annas per diem; sawyer, 6 annas per diem; *gharāmī* (thatcher) 5 annas per diem; tile-moulder, 6 annas per diem; bamboo basket and mat maker, 3 annas per diem; painter, 6 annas per diem; tailor, 14 annas per diem. Rice and food-grains are cheap, and when the price of common rice rises to 13 seers per rupee, prices are held to be high. During the three years, during which period there has been an exceptionally brisk export trade, from 1905 to 1907, the average price of rice, *mūga*, wheat, sesamum seed, mustard seed, *urid*, gram, *kodo*, *arhar*, *māndiā* and salt was $17\frac{5}{16}$ seers, $13\frac{5}{16}$ seers, $11\frac{5}{16}$ seers, $23\frac{5}{16}$ seers, $17\frac{5}{16}$ seers, $15\frac{5}{16}$ seers, $15\frac{5}{16}$ seers, $29\frac{5}{16}$ seers, 16 seers, $22\frac{11}{16}$ seers, and 12 seers, respectively.

The scale of measure in use is—

2 *Gidhās*	= 1	*Solā*.
2 *Solās*	= 1	*Adā*.
4 *Adās*	= 1	*Mān*.
20 *Māns*	= 1	*Puti*.
4 *Putis*	= 1	*Pastamā*.
2 *Pastamās*	= 1	*Purug*.

The *gidhā* is equal to 4 chittacks, one *solā* is equal to half a seer, and an *adā* to a seer of 80 *tolahs*.

OCCUPATIONS MANUFACTURES AND TRADE. The occupation of the people of this State is almost entirely agricultural, 76·6 per cent. of the total population living on agriculture; 16·9 per cent. earn their livelihood by industry;

0·94 per cent. accept personal and domestic services; 0·79 per cent. accept State and village service; 0·32 per cent. follow professions and 0·25 per cent. live on commerce. The only manufactures are those of the ordinary village requirements—weaving, plough-making, blacksmith's works and the construction of solid wheeled carts or *sagars*. Brass utensils are imported: most of the import trade comes into the State from Pārbatīpur in Madras and consists chiefly of salt, tobacco, spices, superior cloth, saltpetre, kerosene oil, wheat and brass utensils. There is, as already stated, a very heavy export trade in grain from the State: the principal exported articles at present are rice, pulses, oilseeds, cotton, gram, hides, lac and other forest produce, and it is expected that the advent of the railway will give a large impetus to trade and render the exploitation of the forests possible. There are large trading centres at Junāgarh about 16 miles south of the headquarters and at Bhawānīpātnā: at the latter place there is a considerable settlement of traders, who have built masonry houses and shops and carry on a brisk trade in the sale of cloth and purchase of grain.

MEANS OF COMMUNICATION.

The State is very well provided with good roads. The Raipur main road runs across the State and is bridged over the smaller streams. There is a good surface road from Bhawānīpātnā to the borders of the State on the Tel river: the length of the road is 34 miles with two rest-houses at Kasurparā and Utkelā: this road continues through the Patnā and Sonpur States to Sambalpur: another good surface road runs due south from Bhawānīpātnā to Ampāni and Jaipātnā in the Mahulpātnā zamīndāri *viā* Junāgarh with rest-houses at Junāgarh Chārbāhāl, Ampāni and Jaipātnā, the headquarters of the Mahulpātnā zamīndāri: about 30 miles from Bhawānīpātnā this road bifurcates one branch going to Jaipātnā and the other to Ampāni: a good gravelled road has been constructed at considerable expense over the difficult Ampāni *ghāti* and carts can now ply between Naurangpur in Jaipur and Kālāhandī. From Bhawānīpātnā there is a good road with wooden bridges running north to Depur about 13 miles in length. There are also good village roads: the hill tracts are provided with fair roads. There is an inspection bungalow at Bhawānīpātnā. The railway runs as far as Pārbatīpur, 46 miles from the border of the Kāshipur zamīndāri. The public works of the State are in charge of the Agency Executive Engineer. There is a sub-post office at Bhawānīpātnā in direct communication with Sambalpur, and there are letter-boxes at the headquarters of all the zamīndāris and in the important villages in the interior. The mail to Madras runs *viā* Junāgarh, Koksarā and Ampāni and the mail to Raipur in the Central Provinces runs *viâ* Khariār.

LAND REVENUE ADMINISTRATION.

The State is divided into two areas, the *khalsā* area (1,415 square miles) and *dangarlā* which belongs partly to the *khālsa* (238 square miles) and the rest (2,092 square miles) of it to the hill zamīndāris and the plains areas belonging to the zamīndāris at the foot of the hills of the *dangarlā* tract: in the former the State is the landlord and collects the rent through the agency of village rent-collectors known as *gaontiās*. In the zamīndāris the zamīndārs are the landlords and pay to the State a *takoli*, which is liable to revision from time to time. The land revenue collection of the State in 1907-08, including the zamīndāri *takolis*, was Rs. 99,385. The land revenue is readily collected and the assessment is light. The principal revenue officers of the State are a *Tahsildār* and *Naib-Tahsildār*: there is a permanent Settlement Department in charge of a Superintendent of Land Records with a regular staff of *kānungos* (Revenue Inspectors) and *patwāris*: the system of settlement in the plains area is similar to that of the Central Provinces and the records are maintained and annually revised. The last settlement was concluded in 1904. This was a regular settlement: in the *dangarlā* area of the *khālsa*, which contains 271 villages, a lump assesment was made. In the regularly settled area the assessments were based on the soil factor and soil unit systems.

The settlement expires in 1911. Settlements have been made by the State on behalf of the zamīndārs in all the zamīndāris. The villages are leased out to *gaontiās* (farmers) for the period of the settlement; *pattās* have been given to all *gaontiās* setting forth in detail the payments due from the village and reserving lands for the village servants and personal residence by the *gaontiās* in their villages is insisted upon. There are no tenure-holders such as the *Umrās* found in the Patnā State: these intermediate tenure-holders disappeared many years ago and there are now only zamīndārs or *khorposhdārs* and *gaontiās*; the rights of the latter are regulated by rules under which many of the *gaontiās* have been given protected status and every encouragement is given them to expend time and labour in improving the villages and earning the protected status and loans are given for land improvement purposes. There is a large body of *paiks* (State militia) in the State, 446 in number, each of whom enjoys rent-free 10 *putis* of land as service-tenures; besides there are the usual *māfi* (rent-free) grants, *brahmottar*, *debottar* and maintenance grants: these *māfi* (rent-free) grants are usually assessed to a small quit-rent (*tanki*) at each settlement. Rents are taken entirely in cash. The zamīndāris are situated in the hill tracts, where the cultivation may be said to be almost entirely *jhūming*; there has been no regular settlement of such lands and *patwāris* are not needed. *Nazarāna* (bonus) is taken on leasing out a village to a new *gaontiā*. The *gaontiā* taking a village for the first time has to pay this *nazarāna*, but when it is renewed with him from time to time he pays nothing.

GENERAL ADMINISTRATION. The relations between the State and the British Government are regulated by the *sanad* of 1867, which was revised in 1905 when the State was transferred to the Orissa Division. The Chief possesses full powers in criminal matters, but capital sentences have to be submitted to the Commissioner of the Orissa Division for confirmation. **Powers.** The State is now under administration of Government and its affairs are managed by the Political Agent. There is a Superintendent and an Assistant Superintendent, assisted by a staff of revenue officers as mentioned before: the Superintendent exercises the powers of the Chief, except that sentences passed by him exceeding seven years are required to be submitted to the Political Agent for confirmation: the Assistant Superintendent exercises the powers of a first class Magistrate. There are good and commodious offices at headquarters and the various branches of the administration are in charge of qualified and capable officers. **Finances.** In 1907-08 the total income of the State was Rs. 2,32,868. The State pays an annual tribute of Rs. 16,000 to the British Government: the tribute is liable to revision.

Forests. There are valuable forests in the State especially in the Rāmpur-Madanpur, Lānjīgarh, and Karlāpāt zamīndāris and in parts of the *khālsa*. In the plains area the State reserve forests have been separated at the time of settlement from the village forests, but were not demarcated: the work of demarcation is now in progress and an officer from the State, sent to the Singhbhūm Division for training, is in charge of the work. Successful efforts have been made to persuade the Khonds to confine their *jhūming* operations to their old and recognised *padās* and to leave the top third of all hills unfelled to secure a seasonable rainfall: this the Khonds have at last agreed to and the work of demarcation of reserved forests in the areas thus exempted is being rapidly pushed on in the hill tracts of the zamīndāris. Cutting in the forests goes on under the license system and regular rates are in force. In the *khālsa* area, the tract under direct administration of the State, the agricultural classes pay a commutation fee (*nistār-patti*) of 3 annas per plough, which allows them to cut for agricultural and domestic needs all trees which are not included in the list of reserved species: they are however allowed to cut *sāl* (Shorea robusta) sufficient for their ploughs and agricultural requirements. Grazing fees are levied from outsiders who send in cattle in considerable number to graze in the hot season. No charge is made from residents of the State, unless the cattle are taken into the State forests. The total receipts of the State under this head amounted to Rs. 27,260 in 1907-08.

Excise. The State obtains its supply of opium from the Sambalpur Treasury on the same conditions as the other States transferred from the Central Provinces and *gānja* is obtained from Nimār: the opium and *gānja* shops belong entirely to the State, but in the case of liquor shops the zamīndārs are allowed to make their own excise arrangements. The Khonds are large drinkers and the village still is a regular institution: of recent years endeavours have been made to reduce the number of liquor shops throughout the State and a very considerable reduction has been made: the Khonds tap their sago palms (*salpi*) free: the headman of each Khond village pays a small sum for the village still: the arrangement is an amicable one with the headman, who divides up the amount amongst the villagers who use the still. The excise receipts of the State amounted to Rs. 28,538 in 1907-08.

Civil justice. The total number of civil suits for disposal in 1907-08 was 493, of which 85 per cent. were for sums under Rs. 50 in value.

Crime. Crime is heavy in this State and being on the borders is the resort of many refugees, especially in the wild tracts of the Eastern Ghāts: severe outbreaks of dacoity are not uncommon and a strong and efficient police force has to be maintained. The Khonds and Doms of this tract are always ready to join in with any adventurer on a plan of dacoity and look upon it as a kind of sport not unlike their hunting parties: the average number of all kinds of cases is generally about 900 per annum.

Police. The police are in charge of a British Inspector of Police: the civil police consists of one Inspector, two Sub-Inspectors, 14 Chief Constables, 51 Head-Constables and 268 constables, with a civil reserve of one Chief Constable, 3 Head-Constables and 29 men. From time to time it has been necessary to locate special police on the borders: of the force 68 men are drilled and trained in the use of arms: the force is well paid and is fairly efficient. The zamīndārs formerly maintained their own police, but this has, as elsewhere, been abolished: the police force is entirely appointed and controlled by the State. In former days the *paiks* rendered both military and civil services acting as a crude police force : the *paiks* still number 446 and are still organised under regular officers, viz., *senādhyaksha* (Commander-in-Chief) 1, *sardārs* (equivalent to captains) 4, *naiks* (equivalent to *sūbahdārs*) 30, *naliā* sepoys (armed with antiquated muzzle-loading country guns) 334, drummers 25, *gauras* or luggage carriers 52, total 446. The distribution of the above force according to caste is as follows:—Brāhmans 3, Rājputs 2, Paiks 150, Dhakud Paiks 21, Bankā Paiks 164, Karan 17, Bairāgi 1, Teli 1, Mālis 2, Bhandāri 1, Gauras 11, Gonds 3, Moslems 2. The Commander-in-Chief is called *Senādhyaksha.* He gets *salāmi* or *nazar* on the day of the *Dasharā* festival at 8 annas from each *sardār* and *naik*, and at 4 annas from each *naliā* sepoy. In lieu of the services rendered, 29 villages have been assigned free of revenue to the force. There is a fine masonry jail at headquarters well managed and well appointed: there is accommodation for over 300 prisoners and the jail is worked on the model of jails in British India. In the year 1907-08 the average daily number of prisoners in the jail was 353. The Public Works of the State, *khālsa* and zamīndāris, are supervised by the Agency Executive Engineer, Sambalpur, the Public Works Department being under a State Overseer. The total expenditure on this account in 1907-08 was Rs. 60,240.

Jail.

Public Works Department.

EDUCATION.

Education is in charge of a State Deputy Inspector of Schools and the officers of the State regularly inspect and visit the schools. The villagers themselves construct and repair the schools in the interior. In 1907-08 there were 58 schools in the State, including 10 private institutions: these consist of a Middle English school at the headquarters, 1 Upper Primary boys' school, 49 Lower Primary schools including a girls' school and a separate school for low caste children and 6 elementary schools (*pāthsālās*): the number of pupils on the rolls was 4,860, of whom 393 were girls; the State expends about Rs. 10,000 a year on education: there is a good hostel attached to the Middle English school. The State enjoys the services of the Agency Inspector of Schools.

CHAPTER XII.

KEONJHAR STATE.

PHYSICAL ASPECTS. THE State of Keonjhar lies between 21° 1′ and 22° 10′ N., and 85° 11′ and 86° 22′ E.; it is the third largest of the Orissa States, having an area of 3,096 square miles. It is bounded on the north by Singhbhūm district; on the east by Mayūrbhanj State and Balasore district; on the south by Cuttack district and Dhenkānāl State; and on the west by Dhenkānāl, Pāl Laharā and Bonai States. Keonjhar is divided into two widely dissimilar tracts, Lower Keonjhar being a region of valleys and low lands, while Upper Keonjhar consists of mountainous high lands. The mountain summits appear from the low lands as sharp peaks with narrow ridges, but in reality there are extensive tablelands on their summits fit both for pasture and for tillage.

Wild ranges of lofty hills and dense jungle form the boundary between Keonjhar and the neighbouring States of Dhenkānāl, Pāl Laharā and Bonai. This range is the watershed of the rivers Baitaranī on the north, and Brāhmanī on the south. From the eastern side of this range a large plateau extends to Mayūrbhanj and Singhbhūm on the one hand and to the borders of Lower Keonjhar on the other, varying in height from 800 feet to 1,500 feet. With the exception of isolated hills and undulating tracts this vast plateau is generally open, comprising nine *parganas* or *dandpāts* (fiscal divisions) and occupied by large and influential villages and numerous hamlets; it is well watered by streams which in the rains are raging torrents, hurrying to discharge their waters into the Baitaranī. The source of the Baitaranī is at Gonāsikā, where a temple has been built: in the early part of its course it flows as a hill stream due north till it reaches the Singhbhūm border where it abruptly turns to the south, forming the boundary between this State and Mayūrbhanj State for a certain distance and then entering into Keonjhar borders increases rapidly in width and flows out into the Cuttack district passing to the north of Jājpur town. The range of hills in which the Baitaranī rises, develops on the south-east into lofty peaks and wide ridges till it strikes the Sukindā border, a zamīndāri in the Cuttack district, when turning north it forms a belt across the State to the Baitaranī, negotiable only by a few well-known passes.

Below this belt and east of it is Lower Keonjhar consisting of the Anandpur subdivision called Athgarh. For the first 10 miles this tract emerges in a gentle slope from the belt of hills, and then spreads out into an open plain towards the Cuttack district, flanked by two long ranges of hills to the Sukindā and Mayūrbhanj borders. This tract differs little from the neighbouring districts of British India, containing little jungle, but dotted with a few low isolated hills; it is well cultivated and thickly populated.

The watershed which runs from the north to south in the shape of a crescent is the home of primitive tribes, chief among them being the Bhuiya and Juāng. On the west of this range there is one *pargana* and the zamīndāri of Kāliāhattā which unlike the plateau on the other side is of no particular elevation. Though the valleys consist of rich alluvial soil, the uplands consist mainly of loose stones and boulders, intersected here and there by hill streams which eventually discharge their waters into the Brāhmanī.

The highest and best known peaks are Gandamardan (3,477 feet), six miles from the headquarters with a wide ridge on the top. Mānkarnāchā on the Bonai border (3,639 feet) with a plateau in its neighbourhood and the Gonāsikā peak (3,219 feet), Thākurānī (3,003 feet), Tomāk (2,577 feet) and Bolat (1,818 feet).

The average rainfall for the six years—from 1902-03 to 1907-08 was 53·74 inches. The climate is exceedingly malarious. The headquarters of the State are at Keonjhargarh.

HISTORY.

The early history of Keonjhar is fragmentary. If tradition and the papers in the possession of the State can be trusted, Upper Keonjhar and Mayūrbhanj formed part of a State called Hariharpur. Keonjhar became a separate State about 1128 A.D. From that date down to the present time, there have been 37 Chiefs.

In 1098 A.D., one Jai Singh, son of Mān Singh, a Kachuā Rājput of the solar race and a Chief of Jaipur in Rājputāna, came on a pilgrimage to Purī, where he married the daughter of the then ruling Gajapati Chief of Purī, receiving as a dowry the territory of Hariharpur, which comprised modern Mayūrbhanj and Upper Keonjhar. Of this union two sons were born, the elder being called Adi Singh and the younger Jati Singh. Adi Singh early in life showed prowess in the field subduing a troublesome petty Chief called Mayūradhwaja, for which service he received the title of "Bhanj" (*Bhanjan* to break) from the Gajapati ruler, which surname has remained in the two families of Keonjhar and Mayūrbhanj. Their father divided his territory of Hariharpur among them before his death; the first forts erected by these two brothers were Adipur in Mayūrbhanj and Jatipur in Keonjhar, both on opposite banks of the Baitaranī. Later the younger brother moved to a more central spot eventually settling at a place called Kendujhar which has been corrupted into Keonjhar. Kendujhar means the *kendu* (ebony) tree and *jharā* or *jhar* a spring. Keonjhar thus originally formed part of Mayūrbhanj, but about two hundred years ago the tribes of this part, finding great difficulty in going to Mayūrbhanj to lay their grievances before their Chief, separated and installed the brother of the Mayūrbhanj Rājā as their Chief. The Bhuiyā tradition is that they stole the boy Chief from Mayūrbhanj, but it was probably a case of necessity which brought the young Chief to the fastnesses of his State. There is no doubt that the Bhuiyās played an important part in the early history of this State as up to date a new Chief wins his way to the *gadi* through Bhuiyā ceremonials, being carried as a part of the ceremonies on the back of a Bhuiyā. There is nothing noteworthy in the history of the State till Rājā Gobind Bhanj, falling out with his father, joined the services of the Purī ruler and for his victory in the battle of Kānchī Kāverī (Kanjeveram, Madras Presidency) obtained as a reward on his accession to the *gadi* the zamīndāri of Athgarh, better known as the Anandpur subdivision, which still forms a part of this State.

The next additions to the State were the purchase of villages Raipur and Jujhpadā, by Pratāp Balabhadra Bhanj in 1751 A.D. This tract is now known as Jujhpadā in the map. From that time this isolated portion remained a part of the State and was recognized by the East India Company as such when making a treaty with Rājā Janārdan Bhanj.

The connexion of Pāl Laharā with Keonjhar dates from the year 1794 A.D. when Janārdan Bhanj married Krishnapriyā, the daughter of Munipāl and granddaughter of the Dowager Rānī Annapūrnā of Pāl Laharā, receiving the then zamīndāri of Pāl Laharā as a dowry. On the death of Krishnapriyā in 1825, the tenants of Pāl Laharā rose in rebellion and were subdued by her husband, but on presentation of a petition to Colonel Gilbert, Political Agent, the State was kept under attachment, and subsequently in 1830 it was decided that the tribute of Pāl Laharā should be paid through Keonjhar: from 1794 to 1826, the Rājā of Keonjhar had full authority over Pāl Laharā. At the present time the tribute of Pāl Laharā is paid direct to Government. The original annual tribute fixed by the East India Company for the State in 1805 was Rs. 2,976-11-11, inclusive of the tribute of Pāl Laharā. In 1858 the British Government, in recognition of loyal services, which the present Chief's grandfather Gadādhar Bhanj rendered in the revolt of Chotā Nāgpur and Sambalpur, reduced the tribute by Rs. 1,000: and the tribute now paid is Rs. 1,710-1-3.

Of the 37 Chiefs who have held the *gadi*, the following Chiefs deserve recognition:—Jati Bhanj, the founder; Rājā Gobind Bhanj, the warrior and victor of Kānchī Kāverī; Lakhmī Nārāyan Bhanj, the builder of the fine old temple of Balabhadrajī at the head-quarters of the State; and Narsingh Nārāyan Bhanj, who consolidated his State and subdued his rebellious tenants. Partāb Balabhadra Bhanj increased his State by taking over some rebellious *tāluks* (tracts) from the Mughal rulers. Janārdan Bhanj, who signed the treaty with the East India Company, his title of Rājā being recognised by the British Government; his Bawārta (chief officer of the State) made the first settlement. Prior to this, little or nothing is known of the administration of the State. The Chiefs conducted the administration in a patriarchal fashion. Gadādhar Bhanj was honoured with the title of Mahārājā and a reduction of Rs. 1,000 in his tribute for loyal services rendered during the Mutiny and his Bawārta, Chandra Sikhar Dhal, also received the title of Rai Bahādur with a personal pension of Rs. 200 per mensem. This Chief died in 1861 without legitimate issue, and on Government nominating his natural son to the *gadi*, a dispute arose as to the succession culminating in an insurrection of the Bhuiyā and Juāng tribes, which was only suppressed by the aid of British troops. The hill tribes again rebelled in 1891, as a protest against the oppressions of the minister, and the aid of British troops had again to be invoked before the rising could be suppressed. The late Chief received the title of Mahārājā in 1877 and was the first to make an attempt to open roads, erect buildings and to work on a budget system: he constructed the imposing revetment at Deogaon on the river Kusāi, in honour of the deity and as a protection to the village. In his time a rebellion again occurred among the Bhuiyās which was quelled by the British Government and a regular police force brought into existence. He died in 1905. The emblem of the State is a pea-fowl.

The following account of the disputed succession of the late Chief, which is of considerable interest as affording a good illustration of the peculiar relations which exist between the Bhuiyā and other aboriginal tribes of Keonjhar and the Rājās of the country, is taken from Sir W. Hunter's Statistical Account of the Orissa States.

On the 22nd March 1861, the Rājā of Keonjhar died at Tribenī, near Calcutta, leaving a widow who was childless, and two illegitimate sons by a *phulbihāi* concubine, who were named Dhanurjay and Chandra Sikhar. On the 3rd April the *Dīwān* or minister of Keonjhar reported that Dhanurjay had been placed on the *gadi* with the consent of the Rānī. On the 9th April, the Rājā of Mayūrbhanj represented that a grandson of his, named Brindāban, had been adopted by the late Rājā of Keonjhar, and that he was going to Keonjhar to instal the boy. The Superintendent of the Tributary States directed that the Mayūrbhanj Rājā should take no action in the matter; but the Rājā sent his grandson to Keonjhar, where the latter was secretly installed by the Rānī and some of the principal leaders of the State. The story of the adoption of Brindāban subsequently proved to be altogether untrue. The Rānī, however, abandoned the cause of Dhanurjay, if she had ever countenanced it, and supported the claim of the so-called adopted son Brindāban. She asserted that Dhanurjay was not the son of a *phulbihāi* or respectable concubine, but only the son of a slave-girl. The respective claims of Dhanurjay, the illegitimate son, and Brindāban, the adopted son, were closely investigated by the Superintendent of the Tributary Mahāls in accordance with the established rule, under which all claims to succession in these States are decided, as laid down by Regulation XI of 1816. The Superintendent decided in favour of Dhanurjay. The party in favour of Brindāban then appealed to the High Court at Calcutta; but the decision of the Superintendent was upheld by the Court, and the case dismissed. Finally, they appealed to the Privy Council in England, but with the same result. Meantime the decision in favour of Dhanurjay was confirmed by the Bengal Government, and the Rānī was informed that Dhanurjay was recognised as Rājā of Keonjhar. An establishment out of the State funds was sanctioned for Dhanurjay, who was still a minor; and the management of the State was left to a *Tahsīldār* and the *Dīwān*. Dhanurjay pursued his studies during his minority at Cuttack, whilst the Rānī continued to reside at the family house at Keonjhar.

Thus matters stood till January 1867, when Mr. Ravenshaw, the Superintendent of the States, reported to the Bengal Government that Dhanurjay would attain his majority in the following September, when the State might be made over to his charge. In

September, the Superintendent reported that he had made over charge of the State to Dhanurjay at Cuttack and proposed proceeding with him to Keonjhar, in order to instal him formally upon the *gadi*. Meantime, the Rānī petitioned that the installation might be postponed until the appeal before the Privy Council should be finally settled, or that, if he should be put into possession, security might be taken from him. Meantime, the Superintendent reported that the refractory Keonjhar dependents, who had hitherto opposed the succession of Dhanurjay, had tendered their unqualified submission to the young Rājā at Cuttack, and promised to be loyal and obedient to him. He therefore considered that this reconciliation would render it unnecessary for him to accompany the young Rājā to Keonjhar; and that it would suffice to send his Assistant with him as far as Anandpur, where Dhanurjay wished to remain before going to the family house at Keonjhar, in order to ascertain if the Rānī would accept him as the successor to the Rāj. The Superintendent expected that the Rānī would acquiesce; and when the reconciliation had been effected, he proposed joining the Rājā at Anandpur, and marching with him to Keonjhar, and there summoning the hill tribes to give in their adherence to Dhanurjay. It was also expected that the reconciliation of the Rānī with Dhanurjay would probably lead to the withdrawal of the appeal to the Privy Council. Subsequently seven or eight hundred heads of villages and office holders arrived of their own accord at Cuttack, and escorted the Rājā to Anandpur, accompanied by the Superintendent's Assistant. The Superintendent retained one refractory *sardār* at Cuttack, and considered that there was only one other individual who was openly hostile to the installation of Dhanurjay, a *sardār* of the hill tribes named Ratnā Nāik, who was said to have declared in favour of Brindāban.

On the 1st November, it was evident that the Rānī was carrying on secret communications with the hill tribes. These people occupy a tract to the westward of Keonjhar, and mainly consist of two tribes, the Juāngs and the Bhuiyās. The latter are the more numerous, and moreover claimed a right to instal each Keonjhar Rājā separately after their own fashion. The principal leader of the Bhuiyās was Ratnā Nāik, already mentioned; and it appeared that, ever since the death of the late Rājā in 1861, this man had supported the Rānī in her efforts to set up Brindāban. The Rānī now threatened to leave Keonjhar if the young Rājā Dhanurjay came there; and it was expected that the Bhuiyās and Juāngs would raise a disturbance if the Rānī quitted the family house. The Superintendent, therefore, directed his Assistant to proceed to Keonjhar and deliver a letter to the Rānī, and also to explain to the hill chiefs that the Rājā was desirous that the Rānī should reside in the family house, but that, if she was determined to leave, she would be properly escorted wherever she pleased to go. On arriving at Keonjhar, the Assistant found that the agents of the Rānī were fomenting disaffection. A large body of people, who were proceeding to Anandpur to tender fealty to the Rājā, were led away by one of the Rānī's servants into Mayūrbhanj. Meantime a large deputation of hill-men proceeded to Calcutta, and in December the Lieutenant-Governor granted an interview to a selected number who were chosen by themselves. The men said that they only wished to know what were the real orders of Government. In reply, they were told that Government intended to support Dhanurjay, unless the Privy Council decreed in favour of Brindāban. The deputation then declared that they would acknowledge Dhanurjay, and that they would make no disturbance; and they asked that the Rānī might receive her allowance through the Superintendent, and that the *Dīwān* of the State might not be allowed to do them any ill turn. They were promised the first point, and assured the protection of Government if they only kept peaceable. Strict orders were then sent to the Superintendent to warn the Rājā and his minister (*Dīwān*) to avoid giving any cause of complaint. The Superintendent, when he proceeded to Anandpur, found no traces of disaffection there. The Rājā was popular, and had been accepted by the village headmen; revenue collections were going on as usual, and all seemed fair. He heard, however, that there were large gatherings of hill-men in the neighbouring jungles, and that deputations were passing between them and the Rānī.

On the 5th December, the Superintendent arrived at Keonjhar with the Rājā, and reported that his journey had not been satisfactory. The people on the road were in alarm; no provisions had been supplied to his camp; and there were constant rumours of opposition. The headmen of the villages had gone off, either to the assemblages on the hills or with the deputation to Calcutta. On reaching Keonjhar he found the village nearly deserted, and the Rānī preparing for flight; and on remonstrating with the Rānī, she had removed into another set of rooms, which is equivalent in native ideas to beginning a journey. He obtained an interview with a party from the two hill tribes, the Bhuiyās and Juāngs, at which the Juāngs promised to accept Dhanurjay; but the general result of the meeting was that no definite answer could be given, until both tribes had held a conference together. Meantime the Superintendent found that the Rānī was perfectly implacable and impracticable. All the connections of the late Rājā accepted Dhanurjay, but the Rānī utterly refused to recognise him; and her influence was so considerable, that Dhanurjay, who had previously begged that she would remain at the family house, was now willing that she should leave Keonjhar.

In December, however, Mr. Superintendent Ravenshaw formally installed Dhanurjay amidst the abuse of the Rānī and her women. The ceremony was attended by many of the Juāngs, but not by the Bhuiyās, and was quite distinct from that of recognition by the hill tribes. The Superintendent had twenty constables with him, and he sent for twenty more to remain at Keonjhar with the Rājā after he left. He reported, however, that the people of Keonjhar had no grievance, save the objection, fomented by the Rānī, to the succession of the son of a concubine; and yet such a succession was in accordance with the custom of the States, and had occurred several times before.

In the same month, viz., December 1867, the Superintendent proceeded on a journey through the hills, and for some days found that the people were warmly espousing the cause of the Rānī and expressing their opposition to Dhanurjay. After a short while, he found that there was a manifest change in public opinion. Colonel Dalton, Commissioner of the neighbouring Province of Chotá Nāgpur, joined Mr. Ravenshaw; and the Chiefs who accompanied Colonel Dalton at once recognised Dhanurjay. An important section of the community, known as the Sāonts, also declared for Dhanurjay; the Juāngs followed, and ultimately the bulk of the Keonjhar tribes gave in their adhesion. The Bhuiyās, however, held out stoutly, being strongly under the influence of Ratnā Nāik, who was said to have been bound by an oath not to desert the cause of the Rānī. This opposition was of some importance, in consequence of the prescriptive right claimed by the Bhuiyās, of confirming the installation of a new Rājā by certain peculiar ceremonies. It was, however, expected that if the Rānī could be quietly removed from Keonjhar to Purī, the Bhuiyās would accept Dhanurjay.

On the 16th January 1868, the Rānī left Keonjhar, but halted seven miles off at the village of Basantpur, where she remained some days. Meantime the Bhuiyās assembled in the neighbourhood, and the Superintendent found that the jungle was full of Bhuiyās, armed with bows, arrows, and axes. Mr. Ravenshaw and his constables caught a hundred of them, and brought them into the presence of the Rānī, and asked her if she wished to bring all her so-called children into a similar predicament. At length the Rānī formally released the Bhuiyās from their oath, and consented to invest Dhanurjay with the usual insignia of her acquiescence in his succession, and to withdraw from all further interference. The captured Bhuiyās were released, and despatched with conciliatory messages to their fellow-tribesmen of the hills; and eventually the whole tribe, excepting Ratnā Nāik, renounced further opposition. Ratnā Nāik succeeded in making his escape, but he had created so much terror that the Bhuiyās themselves aided in pursuing him. He, however, succeeded in making his escape, but his influence seemed to have passed away. The Rānī, at the earnest entreaties of the Bhuiyās, who addressed her as their mother, returned from Basantpur to Keonjhar, and took up her abode in the palace. On the 13th February 1868 she was present at the installation of Rājā Dhanurjay by the Bhuiyās, and on the next day she conferred on the Rājā a *shiropā*, or token of her acknowledgment of his succession.

On the 17th February 1868, the final ceremony of "first-offering," in token of submission, was performed by the Bhuiyās and Juāngs. The Rājā was seated on a low *gadi* of cushions in the outer courtyard, and received the people, who flocked in with music playing and garlands round their necks. Each Bhuiyā headman in succession kissed the foot of the Rājā, and then pressed it to his forehead and ears. Offerings of pumpkins, plantains, and grain were then presented, and salutations were exchanged. The Juāngs followed the Bhuiyās, and separately made offerings and addresses to the Rājā. Each headman was then presented with a tusser silk turban and a suit of clothes; goats and fowls were provided, and the people celebrated the occasion with a general feast.

The succession seemed to be now finally settled. The Rānī decided upon remaining three months at Keonjhar, in order to support Rājā Dhanurjay by her presence, and then to proceed to Purī. A *panchāyat* or court of awards, consisting of her two brothers, the Assistant to the Superintendent, the Rājā, and his *Dīwān*, fixed her allowance at Rs. 600 per mensem. She asked for Rs. 1,500, which was nearly one-third of the then revenue of the State. Ultimately she was allowed Rs. 550 in cash, and villages yielding Rs. 50 per mensem. By the end of February all the police force, excepting twenty constables, was removed, and for two months the public tranquillity remained undisturbed.

About the end of April the Bhuiyās suddenly broke into insurrection under Ratnā Nāik and Nandā Nāik. They plundered Keonjhar bazar, and carried off the Rājā's *Dīwān* with a hundred of his partizans. They also disarmed the twenty constables and dismounted the Rājā's guns. According to their statement, the *Dīwān* had promised to place Brindāban upon the *gadi* within three months, if they would recognise Dhanurjay during the interval. It turned out, however, that they had a more substantial grievance ; for the *Dīwān* had found the partizans of Brindāban in power, and had turned them out to make room for his own relations. By this rising the whole country was disorganized, and all the wild clans joined in the insurrection. Dr. Hayes, the Deputy Commissioner of Singhbhūm, with a police force and body of Kols, immediately started for Keonjhar, which he reached on the 7th May, and found that the Rājā was regularly besieged by the wild tribes, who were armed with bows and arrows, axes, and swords. He at once released the Rājā from his position, by disarming the besiegers and turning them out of the fort. He then sent a written demand to the Bhuiyās for the surrender of their captives, but without effect ; and on making a detour into the hill country, the inhabitants fled at his approach. Subsequently further steps were taken to put down the rising, rescue the captives, and apprehend the two ringleaders, Ratnā Nāik and Nandā Nāik.

Orders were issued by the Bengal Government for the immediate advance of troops and police to Keonjhar. Colonel Dalton, the Commissioner of Chotā Nāgpur, who was known to possess great personal influence over the Chiefs of his province, was ordered to proceed to Keonjhar and take charge of affairs on the spot; while Mr. Ravenshaw was directed to devote himself to the task of throwing in supplies from the Cuttack side, and opening up communications from Anandpur. Colonel Dalton was unable to reach Keonjhar till the end of June. Active hostilities, however, were commenced in the last week of May. A party of police advancing from Anandpur were attacked on the 27th May, and had to fight their way back with the loss of their baggage. Another party of police, however, managed to force a passage *viâ* Dhenkānāl; and large reinforcements from the Chotā Nāgpur side reached Dr. Hayes throughout both May and June. Dr. Hayes succeeded in securing the people of the plains from the raids of the hill-men, who looted the villages which would not join them; but though he repulsed every attack upon his posts, he was not strong enough to retaliate, and could only shut up insurrection in the hills until succour arrived.

At the end of June, Colonel Dalton reached Keonjhar with a strong force, and at once proceeded to carry the war into the enemy's fastnesses. These lay in a wild hilly tract, covered with deadly jungle, which would have been pathless but for the water-courses, which were now filled by the heavy rains of June. It was here that the unfortunate *Dīwān* and other adherents had been carried by the insurgents. Small flying columns were sent out from Keonjhar fort, and they succeeded in releasing many of the captives and burning the villages in which they had been confined. Several disaffected leaders now submitted to Colonel Dalton; and it appeared from them that the captured *Dīwān* had been cruelly murdered by the hill-men soon after his capture. On the 10th July, the Bhuiyās made overtures of submission. Meantime Mr. Ravenshaw had completed his work on the Cuttack side, and reached Keonjhar just eight days after Colonel Dalton, and was associated with him in the management of affairs. Accordingly Colonel Dalton, in conjunction with Mr. Ravenshaw, insisted upon an unreserved surrender of the ringleaders and delivery of the captives, and would not agree to a suspension of hostilities for a single day.

About this time the neighbouring Rājās took active measures to support the British troops; and their acclimatized forces were of great assistance in beating up the inner fastnesses, and thus saving the health of our soldiers and police. The Rājā of Udaipur joined with a force of ten elephants, fifteen troopers (*sawārs*), and two hundred well-armed sepoys. The Rājās of Bonai, Pāl Lahāra, Dhenkānāl, and Mayūrbhanj also furnished contingents. On the 1st August twenty-five Bhuiyā leaders submitted to the Bonai Rājā, and twenty-five Juāng leaders surrendered in like manner to the Rājā of Udaipur. On the 15th August Ratnā Nāik was captured, with his principal coadjutor, Nandā Nāik.

This ended the rebellion. The trials which followed dealt leniently with men who, after all, had only acted according to their immemorial custom. Out of the mass of prisoners taken red-handed in murderous revolt, only six, who were the ringleaders or directly concerned in the cold-blooded murder of the Rājā's *Dīwān*, received sentence of death. About a hundred others suffered various terms of imprisonment.

THE PEOPLE.

It is probable that originally this State with the exception of the Anandpur subdivision was peopled only by aborigines; but with the advent of a Hindu Chief the Hindus of the plains gradually settled in the State. The population increased from 248,101 in 1891 to 285,758 in 1901, but is still very sparse, the density in the latter year being only 92 to the square mile. The inhabitants are contained in 1,938 villages, of which the most important are Keonjhargarh, the headquarters of the State with a population of 4,532 and Anandpur, situated on the Baitaranī river being the headquarters of the subdivision of that name. Averages:—Number of villages per square mile is ·63: number of persons in a village, 147: number of houses per square mile, 18·4: number of houses in a village, 29·5: number of persons in a house, 5·00: 7,348 persons or 2·6 per cent. of the total population are literate. Of the total population 246,585 are Hindus and 38,567 Animists, the most numerous castes being Pāns (31,000), Khandaits (29,000), Gauras (28,000), Hos (24,000), Bhuiyās (20,000), Kurmīs (17,000), Gonds (16,000), Bāthudis (13,000) and Khonds (12,000). Hindus—males, 123,803, females, 122,782; proportion of males in total Hindus, 50·2. Animists—males, 19,921, females, 18,646; proportion of males in total Animists, 51·7. Musalmāns—males, 342, females, 257, total, 599; proportion of males in total Musalmāns, 57·1. Christians—3. At present the aboriginal tribes are the Bhuiyā, the Bāthudi, Sāonti, Juāng, Kol, Kurmī, Santāl, Gond, Khandwāl, Khond, Savar and a small tribe of Pitās. The other castes consist of almost all the well known castes found in Orissa proper. The 1,938 villages may be classified as follows:—1,875 with less than five hundred inhabitants, 56 with from five hundred to one thousand inhabitants, 5 with from one to two thousand inhabitants, 2 with from two to five thousand inhabitants.

The Bhuiyā (20,000) is the second largest wild tribe in the State and the fourth largest in the Agency. The higher castes take water from them though they eat fowls and drink liquor and have no barber to shave them at death and birth ceremonies. They have peculiar customs at marriages. The village is governed under a patriarchal system: the village elders being looked upon as the first of equals. Their religion is practically one of blood. All their gods are devils who, if not appeased, will bring destruction; the good spirits are left alone and the Bhuiyās while embracing a certain set of deities unmistakably aboriginal, have supplemented it with deities of mixed and doubtful origin with a few derived from the Hindus. Though this pantheon consists of native and imported gods, yet their priesthood is confined to their tribe and hereditary priesthood exists among them. The oath is on a tiger skin and a little earth from an ant-hill. Trial by ordeal is a favourite mode of decision; the ordeals being very severe, either hot water or fire. Their festivals generally turn into orgies, coupled with coarse ribaldry among the women, especially maidens. Their rent is confined to a house and plough-tax, and Bhuiyās.

certain services. A detailed account of the Bhuiyās will be found in the general article on the States.

Juāngs.

The Juāngs are Sir W. W. Hunter's "Leaf Wearers of Orissa." They are more primitive than the Bhuiyās, with a dialect of their own though their numerals are in Oriyā, while the dialect is very limited in words, anything foreign being expressed in Oriyā. They have now taken to wearing cloths, though at certain religious ceremonies the priestess wears leaves, as this is considered the correct attire. They wear long brass ornaments in their nose and cover the neck and shoulders with beads. They are of a fair complexion, but their features are ugly and they are uncleanly in their habits. Their cultivation like the Bhuiyās is restricted to *jhūming* or burning the hill-side with perhaps a patch here and there of wet cultivation. They are considered a very low caste, but furnish the Rāj family with coolies when wanted on a long journey. Their rents consist of payment in kind and a few services.

Bāthudi and Sāonti.

Though the Bāthudis and Sāontis are aborigines there is nothing exceptional to note about their habits. They practise wet cultivation and are to be found all over the State, especially the central portion. There is very little crime among them. The Sāontis are considered a better caste than the Bāthudis and look to their chief, the Birajal Mahāpātra, for social and caste grievances. This Birajal has the unique privilege of riding in a *pālki* on State occasions and has quit-rent *jāgīr* (service) lands assigned to him. The title is hereditary.

Kol and Santāl.

The Kols and Santāls have migrated from Singhbhūm, Mayūrbhanj and Chotā Nāgpur. The histories of these people are well known and need no comment here. The Kols who have been in the State for generations have greatly degenerated, and are much addicted to crime. There is a marked distinction between the new comer and the older settlers. The Santāl village is easily recognised by the gaily painted walls and the formation of their houses. A thrifty and agricultural class, they are seldom found involved in a criminal case.

Gond.

The Gond is an immigrant from the Central Provinces wearing the Brahmanical thread, but is considered a low caste, his touch defiles. Their caste chiefs are called Mahāpatras and Singhs.

Khandwāl.

The Khandwāl is a low caste Goālā, who eats and drinks fowls and liquor, but makes a good tenant. Their social customs are very elastic.

All the above aborigines, except the Kol, Santāl and Juāng, wear the Brahmanical thread in imitation of the higher castes, but it is meaningless.

The Kurmī is an immigrant of Chotā Nāgpur and its neighbourhood. The first Kurmī settlement recorded was in 1848, but since then they have increased enormously. They are splendid jungle-clearers, spending money to irrigate and improve their lands: few of their villages being without an irrigation embankment. A Kurmī village can always be recognized by its thriftiness and the condition of its fields. They know how to turn every penny into account, and are prompt in payment of rent. They are, however, considered a low caste, drinking liquor and eating fowls. The women dress well and the vermilion mark on their foreheads is characteristic. They are litigious only when lands are encroached or entered upon; and they are rarely involved in criminal cases. KURMĪ.

There are a good many classes of Goālās in the State, the Aunlāpatiā being a class which has many revolting customs. Intestate property is divided among the caste, the Chief receiving a share. Their female orphans and widows are considered the property of the caste. Most of the Goālās are well-to-do. The Deshuā class alone shoulder the *pālki*. GOĀLĀ.

The climate of the State is malarious and very deadly to newcomers and even the inhabitants suffer greatly from malaria: outbreaks of cholera and small-pox are not uncommon. There are three dispensaries, one at the headquarters, one at Anandpur and one at Champuā: in 1907-08 the number of patients treated was 16,631 of whom 37 were indoor patients. Hitherto very little had been done for medical relief of the people: recently however a well qualified doctor with European qualifications has been placed in charge as Medical Officer of the State and there is also a lady doctor; the dispensaries, especially the indoor accommodation, are being greatly improved: similarly in former years little or nothing was done in the way of vaccination and the annual average for the years 1900-01 to 1906-07 was 6,888: in 1907-08 the number of vaccinations was, however, 11,781 of which 12 were secondary vaccinations: classes for training local vaccinators have been opened at the headquarters and the employment of local men as vaccinators has proved popular with the people and secondary vaccination will in the future progress: vaccination also has been made free and a special Civil Hospital Assistant placed in charge of the work, who also acts as a peripatetic doctor in the villages, where he also renders assistance in village sanitation. PUBLIC HEALTH.

The chief product of the State is the rice crop, both wet and upland; winter crops of almost all the cereals grown in Orissa are cultivated, the rich alluvial soil giving a very fair AGRICULTURE.

outturn. Sugarcane is grown chiefly in Lower Keonjhar and it is here that pumpkins and vegetables are extensively grown. In Upper Keonjhar pumpkins, beans and brinjals are also grown to a large extent. The implements of agriculture are inferior and heavy. In Upper Keonjhar the rice grown is generally of a finer quality than that sown in the plains. It comes into ear earlier and unlike the custom of the plains it is threshed as soon as it is gathered. This gives the rice a better colour and fresher taste. Among the poorer people, certain grasses yielding grain are sown on deteriorated lands to supplement their food before the rice is cut. Indian corn in Upper Keonjhar is an extensive crop, gives a very good outturn and is recognised as one of the staple foods. Tobacco is grown chiefly for home consumption. The leaf is coarse and pungent. Cotton is generally sown in Kurmī and Chasā villages, but very little attention is paid to this remunerative crop. There is a State experimental farm and endeavours are being made to introduce new crops and improved varieties of seed.

NATURAL CALAMITIES. The country suffers from drought upon an untimely cessation of the rains. In Upper Keonjhar, owing to the undulating character of the country and percolation a total loss of crops is scarcely possible, but in Lower Keonjhar this may be possible.

Floods do very little damage in Upper Keonjhar, but in Lower Keonjhar the Baitaranī and its large distributaries occasionally overflow their banks and destroy the crops in the neighbourhood. There is no record of any serious flood.

RENTS, WAGES AND PRICES.

Rents. The present settlement has fixed rates of rent for each description and class of land; produce rents have been abolished, except in the case of certain temple lands and the Juāng *pīrs* and *bethī* (free labour) has been regulated; due provision having been made that the labourer will get his hire.

The principle on which *sārad* (winter rice) lands in Upper Keonjhar has been assessed is as follows:—The *dandpāts* (fiscal divisions) have been divided into three groups, the villages in each group into three classes, and the lands in each village also into three classes. Thus there are altogether 27 rates for *sārad* land varying from Re. 0-12-6 to Re. 1-11-3 per acre. Besides these, special rates two annas less than the above were adopted in two *dandpāts* and in certain villages of other *dandpāts* in consideration of the inferiority of their lands, coupled with the poverty of the tenants. In Lower Keonjhar the subdivision of groups and classes of land is still greater. The *dandpāts* are divided into four groups, the villages in each group into three classes and lands into four classes. Thus giving a total of 48 rates varying from Re. 0-8-3 to Rs. 4-1-6 per acre.

Lands other than *sārad* are assessed at moderate rates:—Uplands from Re. 0-2-6 to Re. 0-6-2 and *pāl* or river side lands from Re. 0-9-10 to Re. 0-14-10 per acre respectively.

The other assessed classes of land are homestead lands, and *dāhi* (forest cleared and burnt). For sugarcane and betel groves in Lower Keonjhar special rates prevail. Betel groves are very limited and the rates were fixed with the consent of the tenants at Rs. 6-3 per acre. The table below shows the average rates for winter and upland rice lands:—

Tracts.	Average *sārad* (winter rice) rates.				Average *gora* (upland) rates.			
	1st class	2nd class.	3rd class.	4th class.	1st class.	2nd class.	3rd class.	4th class.
	Rs. A. P.	Rs. A. P.	Rs. A. P.	Rs. A. P.	Rs. A. P.	Rs. A. P.	Rs. A. P.	Rs. A. P.
Upper Keonjhar	0 9 0	0 8 0	0 7 0	...	0 2 6	0 2 0	0 1 6	0 1 0
Lower Keonjhar	1 2 0	0 15 3	0 12 10	0 10 3	0 8 4	0 6 3	0 4 2	0 2 1

The local land measurements are 16 *biswās* equal one *gunth*, 25 *gunths* equal one *mān* and 20 *māns* equal one *bāti* in Lower Keonjhar; in Upper Keonjhar the same measurements are in force but here 20 *gunths* equal one *mān*. In Upper Keonjhar a *mān* is equivalent to $\frac{4}{5}$ths of an acre and in Lower Keonjhar to half an acre.

Wages of unskilled labour vary from Re. 0-2-0 to Re. 0-3-0 per diem. The women's wages are Re. 0-1-9 to Re. 0-2-3 per diem. Skilled labour is at a premium and no fixed wage can be quoted as the majority of this kind of labour is imported and the wages vary with the demand, season and work. The skilled labour available in the State consisting of carpenters and blacksmiths and a few masons earns about Re. 0-4-0 per diem. For the last five years the average price of food-grains per rupee was as follows:—Unhusked rice 43 seers and 3 chittacks. Rice 16 seers and 8 chittacks. *Bīrhi* 13 seers and 15 chittacks. *Mūga* 8 seers and 4 chittacks. *Arhar* 13 seers and 9 chittacks. *Kulthī* 18 seers and 5 chittacks. Wheat 7 seers and 8 chittacks. *Barguri* 14 seers and 1 chittack. Molasses 7 seers and 9 chittacks. *Māndiā* 15 seers and 4 chittacks. The advent of the Bengal-Nāgpur Railway through the Cuttack district has caused a large rise in prices of late years and has enabled the agriculturists to dispose of surplus stocks and has

Wages and prices.

greatly enhanced the material prosperity of the people. Prices for sugar, salt, kerosene oil, spices, cloths and all such like imported goods are very high, in many instances double the price in the markets of the neighbouring districts of British India. It is hoped that with better communication this will soon be a matter of the past.

OCCUPATIONS, MANUFACTURES AND TRADE.

A small minority of the people are engaged in trade, while the mass find occupation in agriculture. Manufacture is limited to tusser cloths in Anandpur and a fine wire for the native guitar (*sitār*) made at the headquarters, but this work is dying out as there is no demand. Coarse cotton cloths, agricultural implements, stone ware, bamboo baskets with lids, bellmetal, brass pots for drinking water (*koruā*), and heavy brass ornaments are also manufactured.

Trade consists of the export of rice, oil-seeds, lac, tusser cocoons, cloth, hides, *mahuā*, horns, *sabai* grass, timber, fuel, honey and molasses. The hide and horns trade is in the hands of licensed Muhammadans from British India. Timber export is confined to a sleeper merchant and petty traders in the south of the State. The export trade is principally in the hands of petty outside *mahājans* (merchants), supplemented by a growing band of local people. The pack-bullocks carry salt and cotton goods for sale in the interior, and in return they take back harvest produce in the winter and dry months, when a brisk trade ensues. The Muhammadans of Chotā Nāgpur and others carry on trade by pack-ponies and deal in salt, cloth, oil, tinsel ornaments and beads, mirrors, cheap finery, tobacco, native drugs, match boxes, cotton yarn, spices, etc., etc. Mārwāri and other trading classes are finding their way in and have established shops at convenient centres and markets. The export of lac, rice and cereals is large. These are collected by traders at the various *hāts* (markets) and are now taken by carts to Cuttack and the neighbouring districts.

MEANS OF COMMUNICATION.

The State has no road available throughout its length for wheeled traffic: communication is at present defective, but roads and bridges are now under construction. Carts find their way however as far as the headquarters from the Singhbhūm border, but the rates are very high. A main road is now under construction from Champuā, the headquarters of the Nayāgarh subdivision on the Singhbhūm border to the Bengal-Nāgpur Railway at Vyās-sarovar in the south in the Cuttack district touching important villages *en route* and passing through the headquarters and Anandpur. There is also the old Midnapore-Sambalpur road, which has dwindled down to a track but still can be traced along its whole length. There are two other tracks in Upper Keonjhar, one running through the plains of the eastern plateau and another running from the headquarters to Anandpur subdivision parallel to the main road. There is a second class road from Anandpur to the Bhadrakh border in the Balasore district. Bungalows are to be found furnished on the main road.

The imperial post now plies from Jaintigarh on the Singhbhūm border to Keonjhargarh and thence to Anandpur there connecting with the line to Bhadrakh in the Balasore district. There is no telegraphic communication.

LAND REVENUE ADMINISTRATION. The headman or *pradhān* of each village in Upper Keonjhar is responsible for the collection of rent. He realises the same in three *kists* as follows:—

Māgh (January to February)	...	10 annas.
Baisākh (April to May)	...	4 „
Bhādrab (August to September)	...	2 „

For this he receives as remuneration two *māns* (nearly one acre) of land per *bāti* nearly 10 acres, *i.e.*, 10 per cent. He is responsible for the payment of the village rent in due time and is liable in default to have the dues realised from himself. In Upper Keonjhar there is the system of *Tahsīldārs* (rent collectors) with *Muharrirs* (clerks) under them, and peons. They collect the revenue from the headman in the *dandpāts* under them and pay it into the State treasuries. The commission paid to the *Tahsīldārs* for collection work is 10 per cent. of the village rental plus the pay of the *tahsīldāri* clerks and peons.

In Lower Keonjhar the *pradhāns* (village headmen) pay their rent direct to the treasury. The *pradhān* receives a percentage of Rs. 8 on the village rental for making these collections.

The Bhuiyā *pīr* settlement consists of a house and plough tax and rendering certain work at the residence of the Chief, also giving two he-goats to the deity at the headquarters. The Juāng *pīr* settlement consists of a payment in kind, certain duties in the residence of the Chief and one or two he-goats for certain religious ceremonies. The current land revenue demand is Rs. 2,51,102. Tenures consist of:—(1) *Khanjā* lands assigned as maintenance for members of the Rāj family. (2) *Debottar*, religious endowments. (3) *Lākhirāj*, or rent-free grants. (4) *Minhā*, an allowance of rent-free land in a tenant's holding for homestead at the rate of one *gunth* per *mān*, *i.e.*, 4 per cent. (5) Service tenures, such as grants to *paiks* (State militia), *chaukīdārs* (village-watchmen), etc., in lieu of cash payment. (6) *Tanki* or privileged rent-paying tenures. The zamīndāri tenures are two in number:—Kāliāhattā in Upper Keonjhar and Dhenkā in Lower Keonjhar. Both are ancient tenures dating back to a period long antecedent to British rule. Their history, if tradition be true, is that Kāliāhattā came over from Dhenkānāl, and Dhenkā was first ceded to this State in 1194 *Amli* or 1784 A.D., on account of the zamīndār's persistent default in payment of revenue. The settlement rents have been fixed for the cultivators and the zamīndārs pay the State as noted below:—Kāliāhattā 30 per cent., of the mufussil assets, and Dhenkā 40 per cent.

GENERAL ADMINISTRATION. The relations between the British Government and the Keonjhar State are regulated by the terms of the *sanad* of 1908. The State pays a tribute of Rs. 1,710-1-3 to the British Government.

Powers. In criminal matters the Chief exercises the powers of a first class Magistrate, viz., imprisonment up to two years, fine up to one thousand rupees and whipping up to thirty stripes: certain classes of offences, such as heinous crimes, are excluded from the jurisdiction of the Chief. These excepted cases are committed to the Court of a British Officer for trial. The present Chief who succeeded to the *gadi* in 1905, resigned in 1907, and the administration of the State has been taken over by Government. A Superintendent has been placed in direct charge under the Political Agent. The State is divided for administrative purposes into three subdivisions, viz., Anandpur, Keonjhar proper, and Nayāgarh, with Subdivisional Officers in charge: a regular judiciary and executive staff has been organised and also all branches and departments necessary for proper and careful administration. Active measures are being taken to develop the State which is in an exceedingly backward condition.

Finances. The income of the State in 1907-08 amounted to Rs. 3,79,130.

Forests. There is a Forest Department with a trained Forester in charge: in

Excise. 1907-08 the forest revenue yielded Rs. 28,227. The excise administration is modelled on lines similar to those in British India; the revenue from excise in 1907-08 was Rs. 9,464. The aboriginal tribes are allowed to brew rice beer for home consumption free and they indulge largely in this mild form of liquor

Civil justice. with the result that the excise revenue is low. In 1907-08 the total number of civil suits was 1,282; the cases were mostly of a

Crime. petty nature, below the value of Rs. 50. Crime is not heavy: in 1907-08 the number of cases reported to the police was 521. The

Police. police force has been recast and it consists of 1 Inspector, 1 Assistant Inspector, 7 Sub-Inspectors, 17 Head-Constables, 1 *Jamādār* and 153 constables under a European Superintendent of

Police. There are three jails in the State: the central jail at headquarters has accommodation for 50 prisoners, the two sub-jails at the subdivisional headquarters of Anandpur and Nayāgarh have each accommodation for 25 prisoners. The jails are, however, antiquated and new jails on modern lines are to be constructed. In 1907-08 the daily average jail population was 58·97. A Public Works Department has been organised with a State Engineer in charge, being assisted by 1 State Supervisor, 3 Overseers and 2 Sub-overseers: in 1907-08 the State spent on account of public works Rs. 1,74,267.

Jails.

Public Works Department.

EDUCATION.

To give an impetus to education two Government Sub-Inspectors have been assigned to the State and they are assisted by two State Inspecting Pandits. The educational work is supervised by the Agency Inspector of Schools under the Political Agent: since the administration of the State was taken over much has been done to improve education: the schools are being rapidly provided with suitable houses and equipped with furniture, and parents are being pressed to secure regular attendance of their children; five special schools have been opened amongst the Bhuiyās and four separate girls' schools started. In 1907-08 there were 164 schools in the State: there were two Middle English schools, 7 Upper Primary schools, 115 Lower Primary schools including 4 separate schools for girls, 1 Sanskrit *tol*, 3 special schools and 36 *pāthshālās*: and the number of pupils was 2,951 including 162 girls. In 1907-08 the State received a grant of Rs. 1,075 from Government for primary education. In the same year the State spent Rs. 8,055 on education.

CHAPTER XIII.

KHANDPARA STATE.

PHYSICAL ASPECTS. THE State of Khandparā lies between 20° 11′ and 20° 25′ N., and 85° 0′ and 85° 22′ E., with an area of 244 square miles. It is bounded on the north by the Mahānadī river, which separates it from Narsinghpur and Barāmbā States; on the east by the Cuttack and Purī districts; on the south by Purī district and Nayāgarh State; and on the west by Daspallā State.

The country along the Mahānadī is open and fertile; to the south and west are hill ranges, clad with fine *sāl* (Shorea robusta) and in the plains the country abounds with magnificent mango and banyan trees. The open country of the plains is healthy. The headquarters of the State are at Khandparā.

HISTORY. It is alleged that Sūryamani Singh, the youngest son of a former Rājā of Rewah, coming from Rewah founded the State of Nayāgarh. The Rāj family from its alleged descent from the Rewah Rāj family claims to belong to the Baghel class of Kshattriyas. Rājā Raghunāth Singh of Nayāgarh had two sons, the elder, Harihar Singh, became Rājá of Nayāgarh, and the younger, Jadunāth Singh Mangrāj, retained possession of four *garhs* or forts as his share in Nayāgarh. The name of the State (Khandparā) implies that it is made up of pieces (*khandus*) originally consisting of the four villages received in maintenance. In 1599 A.D. Jadunāth Singh Mangrāj is said to have defeated the Chief then holding sway over the country from Agalpur to Harichandanpur in Khāndparā and took possession of his territory. The successors of Mangrāj extended their dominions and strengthened the State of Khandparā which at one time extended on the east up to Bānki, on the west to Balarāmprasād in the Daspallā State, on the north to Kantilo, and on the south up to Jogiāpāli in Nayāgarh.

Rājā Jadunāth Singh Mangrāj, the founder of the Khandpara State, obtained the title of Mangrāj from the Mahārājā of Orissa. Another Rājā Banamāli Singh of Khandparā was a powerful Chief and assisted the Mahārājā of Orissa against the attacks of his enemies; he received as a reward the title of Bhāi Madarāj Bhramarabar Rai, which is employed by the Chiefs to the present day. During the time of Rājā Nīlādrī Singh Mardarāj Bhramarabar Rai, Raghujī Bhonslā, the Mahārājā of Nāgpur, presented the Rājā with a flag. When Orissa was conquered by the British, Rājā Narsingh Singh Mardarāj Bhramarabar Rai rendered assistance, and received an elephant and a cannon in recognition of his services. The emblem of the State is a tiger's head.

THE PEOPLE. The population increased from 63,287 in 1891 to 69,450 in 1901. It is contained in 325 villages, of which the most important is Kantilo, a large mart on the Mahānadī. The density is 284 persons to the square mile. The population is classified as follows:—Hindus—males, 34,758, females, 34,671: total of Hindus 69,429 or 99·9 per cent. of the population of the State; proportion of males in total Hindus, 50·96 per cent. Musalmāns—males, 15, females, 6: total of Musalmāns 21 or 0·03 per cent. of the population. Christians—*nil*. The number of persons able to read and write is 1,391 or 2·0 per cent. of the total population. Population of all denominations—males, 34,773, females, 34,677; proportion of males in total population 50·06 per cent. Averages—villages per square mile, 1·33; persons per village, 213; houses per village, 34·6; houses per square mile, 46; persons per house, 6·1. Of the 325 villages in the State there are 302 with less than five hundred inhabitants; 17 with from five hundred to one thousand; 4 with from one to two thousand; 2 with from two to five thousand.

The people are prosperous, and carry on a considerable export trade in grain and forest produce with Cuttack.

PUBLIC HEALTH. There is a small charitable dispensary at headquarters with an indoor ward: the number of patients treated in 1907-08 was 2,891. The State is subject to frequent visitations of cholera usually imported by pilgrims passing through the State on their return from Purī. Fever and bowel complaints are responsible for but a small proportion of deaths: during the period from 1893 to 1902, the average ratio per thousand of births and deaths was returned at 30·00 and 33·50 respectively. Vaccination is backward, and in 1907-08 the number of primary vaccinations was only 879 and that of revaccination was 18.

AGRICULTURE. The soil is very fertile, and the villages are prosperous, and the lands better cultivated than in the neighbouring States: the principal crop is rice. The total area of the State is 156,160 acres of which forests comprise 76,920 and 5,240 acres are not fit for cultivation: culturable waste amounts to 12,000 acres and fallow, to 25,000 acres. There are normally 30,000 acres under rice, 700 acres under sugarcane, *til* (sesamum) and mustard 200 acres each, cotton 150 acres, and jute 35 acres: millet, maize, *māndiā* and tobacco are also grown in small quantities.

Rents, wages and prices. The average rate per *mān* (two-thirds of an acre) of first, second and third class rice lands is Re. 1-9, Re. 1-2-9 and Re. 0-12-6 respectively and of uplands, Re. 0-8-0. During the period from 1893 to 1902 wages have risen about 14 per cent. and the average daily wage during that period has been as follows:—superior mason, $7\frac{3}{4}$ annas, common mason, $4\frac{3}{4}$ annas; superior carpenter, 4 annas, common carpenter, 3 annas; cooly, 2 annas; superior blacksmith, 6 annas, common blacksmith, 4 annas. During the same period, the prices of food-grain have remained practically stationary: the average price of wheat, rice, gram and salt has been $10\frac{1}{8}$ seers, $19\frac{1}{4}$ seers, 10 seers, and 12 seers respectively.

Occupations, manufactures and trade. The principal occupation of the people is agriculture. A considerable trade is carried on at Kantilo, which is noted throughout the States of Orissa for its brass utensils: it is situated on the south bank of the Mahānadī and is a regular emporium for traders from Cuttack who bring salt, spices and tobacco for exchange for cotton, wheat, clarified butter and oil-seeds, which are brought down the river from Sambalpur. The State possesses no other manufactures beyond that carried on in brass utensils at Kantilo.

Means of communication. The principal route of communication is the Mahānadī: the Cuttack-Sonpur road, maintained by Government, passes throughout the State running parallel with the Mahānadī: there is one State road from the headquarters to Kantilo: communications in the interior are very defective. There is a sub-post office at Kantilo at a distance of 7 miles from the headquarters.

Land revenue administration. The land revenue administration is similar to that prevailing in the other States of the group formerly known as the Tributary Mahāls of Orissa, but in Khandparā the prohibition against transfer and mortgage of holdings is not so clearly defined. There has been no land settlement since 1849. The current land revenue demand in 1907-08 was Rs. 25,548.

General administration. Finances. The relations between the State and the British Government are regulated by the *sanad* of 1894, which was revised in 1908. The Chief assisted by a *Dīwān*, administers the State. The administration is not developed. The estimated revenue amounted in 1907-08 to Rs. 49,795, and the State pays an annual tribute of Rs. 4,212 to the British Government. **Forest. Excise.** The latest returns show the forest revenue at Rs. 5,000: there is no regular forset department. Excise yielded in 1907-08 Rs. 2,884. The number of suits instituted during the year 1907-08 was 358. The litigation was mostly of a petty nature, 45 per cent. of the suits being below the value of Rs. 50. The number of cases reported to the police in 1907-08 was 66: crime for the most part is petty. The police consists of one Sub-Inspector, 3 Head-Constables and 38 constables. There is a small and incommodious jail. There is no regular Public Works Department. In 1907-08 the State spent Rs. 1,102 on account of Public Works.

Civil justice.

Crime.

Police.

Jail.

Public Works Department.

EDUCATION.

The State maintains one Middle Vernacular, 1 Upper Primary, 33 Lower Primary schools and a Sanskrit *tol;* besides there are 4 private schools. The number of children attending in 1907-08 was 675. There is a separate school for girls. The State receives from Government an annual grant for education and enjoys free the services of a Government Sub-Inspector. Education is very backward.

CHAPTER XIV.

MAYURBHANJ STATE.

PHYSICAL ASPECTS. THE Mayūrbhanj State is the most northerly and the largest of the States of Orissa. It lies between 22° 34′ and 21° 17′ N., and between 85° 40′ and 87° 10′ E., and is bounded on the north by the Midnapore and Singhbhūm districts, on the east by the Midnapore and Balasore districts, on the south by the district of Balasore and the States of Nīlgiri and Keonjhar, and on the west by the State of Keonjhar and the district of Singhbhūm. Mayūrbhanj State extends over an area of 4,243 square miles and presents every variety of soil and scenery. It abounds in rich valleys, but a vast extent still remains under primeval jungle. The central portion of the State is occupied by a group of hills about 600 square miles in area known as the Simlāpāl hills. The Meghāsanī hill, literally the "seat of clouds," which rises to a height of 3,824 feet, is situated in the southern extremity of this group. Sir William Hunter in his *Statistical Account of the Orissa Tributary States* speaks of this group as "the hitherto almost unexplored mountains of Mayūrbhanj, heaped upon each other in noble masses of rock from 3,000 to nearly 4,000 feet high, sending countless tributaries to the Baitaranī on the south and pouring down the Burābalang with the feeders of the Subarnarekhā on the north. The peaks are densely wooded to the summit, and except at the regular passes, are inaccessible to beasts of burden. The intermediate valleys yield rich crops in return for negligent cultivation." The description given above in the year 1877 remains true to this day. The ravages of wild beasts and its malarial climate have checked the growth of population in this tract and except for a few Khariā and Kol hamlets it remains practically uninhabited.

RIVER SYSTEM. The Mayūrbhanj State is watered mainly by the Burābalang, the Khadkāi, the Sālandī, and numerous other tributaries rising from the Simlāpāl hills which fall into the Baitaranī and the Subarnarekhā. The Burābalang rises from the Simlāpāl hills in lat. 21° 24′ N. and long. 86° 36′ E., and after receiving the flow of the two small streams Palpalā and the Chipat passes close to the town of Bāripadā. The banks of the river are steep and cultivated. The Jambhirā, Bāns and Bhairangī rise from the plains of the Sadar subdivision. The Khadkāi rises from the Simlāpāl hills and after a tortuous course westwards through the Bāmanghāti subdivision falls into the Subarnarekhā. The Khair and Bhandan are small hill streams which rise in the Simlāpāl hills and fall into the Baitaranī after a short westward course through the Pānchpīr subdivision. The Sālandī rises on the southern slope of the Meghāsanī mountain and meets the Dhāmra river near its mouth.

NATURAL DIVISIONS. The territory of Mayūrbhanj may be divided into three natural divisions. Running due north and south from the central group there are two ranges of hills of lesser elevation dividing the plains portion of the State into two halves, the eastern, which forms the Sadar subdivision, and the western: this latter is again subdivided into two portions, viz., the Bāmanghāti and the Pānchpīr subdivisions by another range of hills running in a westerly direction from the northern portion of the main central group; thus there are three distinct portions divided off from one another by hill ranges and drained by different rivers. The eastern or the Sadar subdivision slopes gently from the foot of the hills towards the sea and served as it is by innumerable hill streams forms an ideal country for irrigation. The western portion consisting of the Bāmanghāti and the Pānchpīr subdivisions is mainly a rolling plain rising and falling in gentle slopes and studded with innumerable rocky mounds and hills. The soil, specially of the northern or the Bāmanghāti subdivision, is very fertile and lends itself to extensive cultivation. Mayūrbhanj proper, that is to say, such portion of the State as is not included in Bāmanghāti and Nayābasan, consists of hills, jungles and valleys, the latter intersected by mountain streams; quite 1,000 square miles of Mayūrbhanj is composed of hills, the greater portion of which are as yet inaccessible to commerce, or are so unhealthy as to be habitable only by the rudest jungle tribes. Bāmanghāti consists of open plains, well cultivated and well watered during the rainy season by natural streams.

The approximate areas of the three subdivisions of the State are as follows:—(1) The Sadar subdivision including the central hill group, 2,800 square miles, (2) Bāmanghāti subdivision, 750 square miles and (3) Pānchpīr subdivision, 560 square miles.

GEOLOGY. A Geological Survey of the State was undertaken by the Chief: it was reported that the chief mineral wealth of the State consists in its iron ores, which are possibly among the richest and most extensive in India. They occur in all parts of the State, but specially in the Bāmanghāti subdivision. Usually they consist of hæmatite and limonite, but thick and rather extensive deposits of magnetite are met with at the foot and along the flanks of the Gurumaisāni hill, south-east of Kulaisilā, east of Sundal and also near Kotapiti in the Bāmanghāti subdivision. It is difficult to make even an approximate estimate of the quantity of available iron ores. But it would probably be no exaggeration to say, that a practically inexhaustible supply for several furnaces on a modern scale may be safely depended upon. The ores are easily accessible from the Sini-Kharagpur section of the Bengal-Nāgpur Railway. Limestone in the form of tufa occurs at several places in and close to the iron area.

Red and yellow ochres occur at places and are much used by the Santāls in painting their houses. Gold is washed for in the Subarnarekhā river on the northern border of Mayūrbhanj proper and in the Khadkāi and Barhai rivers in the Bāmanghāti subdivision. There is nothing specially noteworthy about these river washings. But at the head waters of the Barhai river about Kudarsāhi and Sāpgherā there is a tract about 2 square miles in extent, where almost the entire alluvium is found to be more or less auriferous. Some 50 families of gold-washers earn their living by gold-washing in this area. They just scrape off the surface soil which is usually the richest, owing, probably, in part, to its being periodically replenished by wash from the adjacent hills during the rainy season, and in part, to natural concentration *in situ* by rain water. Nuggets are occasionally met with, but the largest shown as found in the area weighed half a *tolā*.

The auriferous alluvium is of brownish colour, and is thinly spread over micaceous and trappean-looking schists referable to the transition series. It contains more or less gold down to a depth of about two feet. The richest placer deposits were found invariably to occur in the immediate vicinity of dioritic rocks with iron pyrites traversed by thin irregular veins of quartz. There are no quartz-reefs in the area, and it is a curious fact that, though there are good reefs outside the area, no gold is known to occur either in or near them.

West and north-west of Ruānsi and Gohāldangri washed by the Gadiā river and its feeder, and separated from Kudarsāhi-Sāpgherā ground by a low range of hills, there is another area of placer deposit of similar extent. The deposits here are at places 12 to 15 feet in thickness, and consist of rather gritty, brownish, stiff clay resting upon a coarse gravel bed about three feet in thickness. The red rock seen at places is greyish-white micaceous schist with thin veins of quartz. Nuggets weighing as much as two to three *tolās* are reported as having been recently found in the area under description. It supports some 20 families of goldwashers settled in it, besides casual visitors from Dhalbhūm.

Mica occurs extensively in Mayūrbhanj proper and in Bāmanghāti, but the plates obtained are small not exceeding two or three square inches. About Jamgoriā the plates obtained from the surface measured more than eight square inches but were necessarily in a much weathered condition. Excavations are in progress to test the quality of the mineral at depth.

Yellowish fossiliferous limestone occurs in the bed of the Burābalang river at Mohuliā, two miles south of Bāripadā. The clays which underlie the laterite about Bāripadā are generally very well suited for pottery.

Potstones, from which utensils are manufactured, occur at various places. Grindstones are made at Kulianā out of the quartzites of the transition series. Agate, flint, jasper, etc., occur in some profusion at places in the Bāmanghāti subdivision.

The average annual rainfall for the ten years 1897-98 to 1906-07 was 66·60 inches. The headquarters of the State are at Bāripadā.

HISTORY.

According to tradition the Mayūrbhanj State was founded some 1,300 years ago by one Jai Singh, who was a relative of the Rājā of Jaipur in Rājputāna. Jai Singh came on a visit to the shrine of Jagannāth at Purī and married a daughter of the then Gajapati Rājā of Orissa and received Hariharpur as a dowry. Of his two sons, the eldest, Adi Singh, held the *gadi* of the Mayūrbhanj State. The annals of the Mayūrbhanj Rāj family, however, say that Jai Singh came to Purī with his two sons, Adi Singh and Jati Singh, the elder of whom was married to a daughter of the Purī Rājā.

When returning home Jai Singh conquered Rājā Mayūradhwaja then holding the *gadi* of Bāmanghāti. In the vernacular almanac written annually in the Mayūrbhanj State, this Bāmanghāti is regarded ever since that period as the original place of residence of the Rāj family, and the State is called after Mayūradhwaja. In every State seal the design of a peacock was introduced as a family distinction. According to family tradition the limits of the State of Mayūrbhanj from the year 1538 A.D. up to the year 1831 extended to Bhanjbhūm and Khelor *parganas* in the north; to the Balasore district in the east; to the Nīlgiri State in the south-east; to the Baitaranī river in the south; and to Porāhāt and Dhalbhūm Rāj in the west. The area of the State has greatly decreased from what it originally was. *Pargana* Bhanjbhūm, which is in the neighbourhood of Midnapore town, was given to the Midnapore Rājās by Mahārājā Santāi Bhanj about the year 1556. *Pargana* Khelor was also given to them by Mahārājā Jagannāth Bhanj about the year 1643, and both are still in their possession. *Pargana* Nayābasan, which is also in the Midnapore district, became a revenue-paying *mahāl* of this Rāj from before the time of the Permanent Settlement of Bengal. Nīlgiri State was a subordinate zamīndāri of the Mayūrbhanj State up to the year 1728, since which year it has been separated and made independent of Mayūrbhanj. Four large *pīrs* of Bāmanghāti, named Thāi, Bhorbhoriā, Aulā and Lālghar, were, it is said, made over to the British Government by Jadunāth Bhanj, great-grandfather of the present Chief, during the Kol rebellion between the years 1830 and 1834. They are now part of the Kolhān in the Singhbhūm district. *Pīrs* Khāuchang and Haldipokhur, now in the Singhbhūm district, formerly formed parts of Bāmanghāti. The former was given to Abhirām Singh of Saraikelā. The latter, now a portion of the Dhalbhūm Rāj, was given to the Dhal Rājā.

No *farmān* or *sanad* from the Emperor of Delhi or from the Marāthās is available. It is alleged that in the time of Mahārājā Dāmodar Bhanj, a near relation of his was deputed to Delhi and there is said to have obtained a copper *sanad* from the Emperor. This *farmān* is not now, however, forthcoming.

The tribute of this State was fixed in 1812 at Rs. 1,001 on the then Chief of the State agreeing to forego his claim to levy a tax on pilgrims who had to pass through the State on their journey to and from Jagannāth. No treaty was concluded with this State in 1803 and 1804 as was done with the other States of Orissa and it was, therefore, not included in the list of States mentioned in section 36 of Regulation XII of 1805. When the British conquest of Orissa took place in 1803, Mayūrbhanj presented the then unique spectacle of a Rānī occupying the *gadi* in the person of Rānī Sumitrā Dei Bhanj.

On her death in 1811, the succession devolved on Tribikram Bhanj, an adopted son taken from the Keonjhar family. He executed two *ekrārnāmās* or agreements—one in 1812 and the other in 1815. On his demise, he was succeeded by his son Jadunāth Bhanj with whom a treaty engagement was entered into in 1829.

In 1866 the subdivision of Bāmanghāti was taken under the direct control of Government on account of the then Chief's mismanagement, but it was restored in 1878 to the present Chief's father, Mahārājā Krishna Chandra Bhanj Deva, who was an able and enlightened ruler. He was created a Mahārājā in 1877 for his efficient administration of the State and for his public liberality, the most prominent instance of which was his donation of Rs. 27,000 towards raising the Cuttack High School to the status of a College.

After his death in 1882, the State came under Government management owing to the minority of his son, the present Chief, Srīrām Chandra Bhanj Deva, who was placed in charge of the State in 1890. He received a liberal education, and is the most enlightened of the Garhjāt Chiefs. The administration of his State is carried on on British lines under his personal supervision. He was a guest of the Government at the Imperial Darbār held at Delhi on the 1st January 1903. The title of Mahārājā was, on the same occasion, conferred on him as a personal distinction. A gold Delhi Darbār medal was awarded to the Mahārājā and a silver medal to one of his *sardārs*.

THE PEOPLE.

The population of the Mayūrbhanj State is, according to the census of 1901, 610,383, of whom 303,266 are males and 307,117 females. The density of population is 144 per square mile. Bāripadā, the headquarters station, is the only town in the State containing a population of 5,613 persons. The rest of the population, viz., 604,770, are distributed over 3,593 villages, which may be classified as follows:—2 villages with from two thousand to five thousand inhabitants, 13 with from one thousand to two thousand inhabitants, 114 with from five hundred to one thousand inhabitants, 3,464 with less than five hundred inhabitants. The average number of villages per square mile is 0·84; persons per village, 169·83. The number of houses according to the census statistics of 1901 is 121,958 and the average number of persons per house is 5·00 and the average number of houses per square mile 47. The population of the State is rising rapidly as will be seen from the following table:—

Population at the census of 1872.	Population at the census of 1881.	Population at the census of 1891.	Population at the census of 1901.
258,680	385,737	532,238	010,383

The opening out of the State by roads and the security to life and property which the administration affords has led to rapid immigration from the congested districts in the neighbourhood. Large tracts of culturable waste and jungle lands which awaited exploitation acted as an inducement for immigration, and along with the rise in the population the cultivated area has also proportionately increased.

Ethnical division of the people.

The population is mainly Hindu consisting of 606,223 persons including Animists (93,485), the number of Musalmāns being 3,785, Christians 368, and others 7 only. Of the Hindu population, the aboriginal and semi-Hinduised tribes preponderate enormously over the purely Hindu population. The number of the principal aboriginal tribes who form 56·52 per cent. of the total population is as follows:—(1) Santāl 185,149, (2) Ho or Kol 67,768, (3) Bhumij 56,157, (4) Kurmī 35,968. The number of the principal semi-Hinduised tribes who form 16·4 per cent. of the total population is:—(1) Bhuiyā 31,753, (2) Bāthudi 28,128, (3) Pān 24,762, (4) Gond 6,280, (5) Khond 5,833, (6) Savar 1,873, (7) Kewat 1,485. The number of the principal Hindu castes who form 13·89 per cent. of the total population is:—(1) Brāhman 8,308, (2) Khandait 15,365, (3) Chasā 1,007, (4) Gaura 29,861, (5) Kāmār 10,880, (6) Kumhār 8,667, (7) Tānti 4,568 and (8) Teli 6,121. A population in which the aboriginal element preponderates is necessarily backward in education which is confined more or less to the pure Hindu element. The number of persons who can read and write is 13,115 or 2·14 per cent. of the total population, of whom 340 or 0·05 per cent. can read and write English.

Christian Missions.

At present there are two centres for Mission work in Mayūrbhanj, one at Bāripadā, the headquarters of the Mayūrbhanj State, and another at Nangalkatā, 8 miles from Bāripadā on the Bāripadā-Balasore road. The former belongs to the Baptist missionaries, and was started in 1894. The Mission which is called "The Mayūrbhanj State Mission Council" has obtained from the Chief a lease of 4·68 acres of land. The Mission at Nangalkatā belongs to the Roman Catholics.

Material condition of the people.

The great majority of the people are agriculturists and the prosperity and contentment of such a population depends mainly upon the rainfall and crops. The failure of crops in a single year means widespread distress. Since the great famine of 1866 the State has however been free from the visitations of famine or even of severe scarcity. With the opening up of the State by roads and the Mayūrbhanj State Light Railway, the prosperity of the people has steadily increased. Each year fresh jungles are reclaimed and the areas already reclaimed are improved and the holdings of the tenants are increasing in quantity and improving in productive quality year by year. This is specially noticeable in those tracts where jungles preponderate over the cultivated area, and testifies to the prosperity of the tenants. The fixity of tenures and the rights of occupancy conferred upon the tenant have materially contributed to his well being. The system of granting land improvement loans each year has also helped in the development of the State; the standard of comfort of the tenant has changed for the better and his purchasing capacity has increased. In the markets, articles of European manufacture find ready customers: umbrellas, towels, brass utensils and bell-metal ornaments are much in evidence amongst the aborigines. Trade and commerce, specially in timber and in minor forest produce, has increased enormously in recent years, and this has given employment to a large number of the labouring classes.

PUBLIC HEALTH.

The climate of the State is fairly healthy. The hill and the jungle tracts are however malarious. Fever is the most prevalent disease in the State and accounts for the largest number of deaths. Vital statistics are not kept except in the following localities:—

			Death rate per thousand, 1906-07.
Bāripadā town	...	...	34·45
Olmarā thāna	...	...	34·75
Baisingā "	...	...	29·72
Mordā "	...	...	16·00

Cholera epidemics break out in different parts of the State almost every year during the summer. Small-pox also occurs in epidemic form at intervals. Vigorous vaccination operations during the last 12 years have, however, minimized the ravages of this scourge.

The number of dispensaries in the State is six, distributed as follows:—(1) Bāripadā town, (2) Bahaldā, (3) Karanjiā, (4) Kuāmarā, (5) Bāngriposī, and (6) Mordā. These dispensaries are in charge of qualified Hospital Assistants. The Medical Department of the State is under the charge of a qualified Medical Officer of the Assistant Surgeon class. The number of indoor patients treated in the State dispensaries in 1907-08 was 272, and of outdoor patients 35,695. The daily average attendance of indoor patients was 14·07, and of outdoor patients 233·49. The number of persons vaccinated in that year was 24,109, and that of persons revaccinated, 261.

AGRICULTURE. Crops

The principal crops and their varieties grown in the State are—(1) cereals, (2) pulses, (3) oil-seeds, (4) root crops, (5) fibre crops, (6) sugarcane, (7) cotton, (8) tobacco, and (9) vegetables.

Cereals.

The cereals grown are rice and millets.

Rice.

The rice grown here is divided into two classes: *āman* (winter) and *āus* (early). The varieties of *āman* paddy are:—(1) *Champāisāli*, (2) *Baidyanāth*, (3) *Nāradi*, (4) *Ganjājatā*, (5) *Barasāli*,

(6) *Rakatbol*, (7) *Madnā*, (8) *Kalāsāru*, (9) *Haldiguri*, (10) *Gayābāli*, (11) *Dasrāgeli*, (12) *Dumerkūdi*, (13) *Jaldubi*, (14) *Berhāmāltā*, (15) *Bānsgajā*, (16) *Hātīpanjar*, (17) *Raghunāthbhog*, (18) *Gopālbhog*, (19) *Pānakhiā*, (20) *Mohanbhog*, (21) *Iswarjatā*, (22) *Pimpribās*, (23) *Rangani*, (24) *Kāntarangani*, (25) *Kashiphula*, (26) *Saharchampā*, (27) *Sundarphenā*, (28) *Mirjui*, (29) *Maināsāli*, (30) *Sārangiphula*, (31) *Kantākapur*, (32) *Chingrikayā*, (33) *Harnākayā*, (34) *Bhāluchari*, (35) *Charāināki*, (36) *Nariyāsol*, (37) *Dhuriā*, (38) *Tikāmuridiā*, (39) *Kāliā Simulkasi*, (40) *Agnisol*, (41) *Hemtarangi*, (42) *Lāl Simulkasi*, (43) *Berhākābri*, (44) *Sālgojā*, (45) *Thubirangi*, (46) *Karākachu*, (47) *Kadalmundi*, (48) *Mālati*, (49) *Kākurimanji*, (50) *Jaradā*, (51) *Khejurchangā* and (52) *Kalājirā*.

The outturn of *āman* rice varies from 8 to 20 maunds per *mān* according to the class of land, one *mān* of land being about ⅞ of a standard acre or 0·698 acres.

The varieties of *āus* rice are :—(1) *Geti*, (2) *Bhālukchumri*, (3) *Simulkasi*, (4) *Karni*, (5) *Ardkulā*, (6) *Tusku*, (7) *Tālchirā*, (8) *Ulsukai*, (9) *Chanāchitā*, (10) *Bāiganmanji*, (11) *Hātīpanjar*, (12) *Dudhniāli*, (13) *Kārtikgeti*, and (14) *Gorādhān*. The outturn is from 5 maunds to 8 maunds per *mān*.

Both the *āman* and *āus* rice are sown in Jyaistha (May-June), but the former is reaped in Paush (December-January), while the latter is reaped in Bhādraba (August-September). The *āman* rice is also transplanted in Srāban (July-August). The outturn of transplanted paddy is higher than that of sown paddy.

Millets. The varieties of millets are :—(1) *Gundlu*, (2) *Kāngu*, (3) *Kodo*, (4) *Bājra*, (5) *Jowār* black and (6) *Makā* (maize).

The average outturn of the millets is about 4 maunds per *mān*. They are generally sown in Asādh (June-July), and reaped in Bhādraba (July-August).

Pulses. The principal kinds of pulse grown in this State are :—(1) *Birhi* and *māskalāi*, (2) *Balijā mūga* and *krishna mūga*, (3) *Arhar*, (4) *Kulthi*, (5) *Khesāri*, (6) *Chanā* (gram), (7) *Rambhā*, etc. They are generally sown in Ashwin (September-October), and reaped in Agrahāyan (November-December). The outturn of these pulses is 4 maunds per *mān*.

Oil-seed. The principal oil-seeds grown in this State are :—(1) *Surgujā*, (2) *Til—bhādoi* and *māghi*, (3) Linseed or *tisi*, (4) Mustard-*Turi* and *Rāi*, (5) Castor.

The outturn of *Surgujā* is about 2 maunds per *mān* : and that of *til* is 2 to 2½ maunds per *mān* : the average outturn of *tisi* (linseed) is 4 maunds per *mān* : it grows in *āman* (winter rice) lands and is sometimes sown when the *āman* paddy is still standing on the land : the outturn of mustard is 1½ to 2 maunds per *mān.* The winter variety of castor yields a larger proportion of seed and oil than *bhādoi* castor. The yield of castor varies from 4 to 5 maunds per *mān.*

The principal root crops that are generally raised in this State are :—(1) Potato, (2) Dioscoria Sativa, (3) Cassava, etc. Root crops.

(1) Potatoes are grown in small quantities by a few well-to-do people in the town of Bāripadā and in the subdivisional headquarters. Some of the poorer cultivators of the interior have also commenced growing this crop on a small scale. The outturn of the Patna variety is from 30 to 40 maunds per *mān*, while that of the Nainitāl variety is from 30 to 50 maunds per *mān.*

(2) Dioscoria Sativa or *khamālu* is grown here as a garden crop. Besides this there are some crude roots which grow wild in the jungle such as *pānālu*, *tungālu*, *chunālu*, *sakarkandālu*, etc., and the majority of the wild tribes of this State live upon them in time of scarcity but they never cultivate these roots.

(3) Cassava.—Some of the tenants of the State grow sweet cassava which can be eaten raw; being a drought-resisting plant it can be planted at any season, which is a great advantage in famine prevention. The total outturn from the roots of cassava is nearly 200 maunds per *mān.*

The principal fibre crops grown are :—(1) Jute both Sirājganji and *deshi* and (2) Kanra. Fibre crops.

(1) Jute cultivation is generally increasing among the tenants of the State. Most of the cultivators grow it on their homestead lands for their own use, *i.e.*, for making ropes, etc., but some of the tenants cultivate it in *dāhi* land for profit, but the outturn is poor. The yield of jute is 3 to 4 maunds per *mān.*

(2) Kanra.—Bombay or Deccan locally known as hemp. It is superior to jute in every respect. Rocky and laterite soils which are not suitable for jute cultivation are well adapted for its cultivation. The average outturn of this fibre is 6 to 7 maunds per *mān.*

The varieties of sugar-cane grown are—(1) *Dhablā* (white), (2) *Khari* and (3) *Sāmsārā.* Sugarcane.

The outturn of *gur* (molasses) is nearly 20 maunds in addition to $2\frac{1}{2}$ maunds of clean molasses per *mān.*

Two varieties of cotton are generally cultivated, *khariā kapā* (annual) and *burhi kapā.* The average outturn of cleaned cotton varies from 10 to 15 seers per *mān.* The Sambalpur variety growing in the State Experimental Farm seems to be well adapted to this State. Cotton.

Tobacco.

Tobacco of inferior quality is cultivated by the poorer classes of the Bāmanghāti subdivision on homestead land for their own consumption. Five maunds of dry tobacco leaf on the average is said to be obtained by the cultivators from one *mān* of land (homestead) but a well grown crop is expected to yield 10 to 12 maunds per *mān*.

Vegetables.

The following vegetables are generally grown in this State:—(1) Brinjal, (2) Chillies, (3) Pumpkin, (4) *Kachu* or *sāru*, (5) Earth potato, (6) *Karalā*, (7) *Kundru*, (8) *Kākuri* (cucumber), (9) *Phuti*, (10) *Tarbhuj* (water melon), (11) *Bhendi* (okra), (12) Sīm (bean), (13) *Barbati* and (14) *Mūlā* (radishes).

Foreign vegetables such as cabbages, cauliflowers, etc., are grown on a very small scale by a few well-to-do inhabitants.

Agricultural implements.

The principal implements of agriculture in use are—(1) The plough—the local cost of the plough is Re. 1 each. (2) A beam used for breaking clods and levelling lands.—the average cost of a beam is Re. 0-6-0. (3) *Korol.*—It is generally used for levelling the field. The average cost of this implement is not more than Re. 1-14. (4) The *sagar* or solid wheeled cart—it is used for carrying manure to the field, and for carrying unthreshed paddy to the farmyard. The average cost of it is nearly Rs. 3. (5) *Bāngi.*—It is a carrying rod made of an elastic piece of wood or bamboo and is used for carrying seeds, etc. The cost of a *bāngi* is nearly As. 3. (6) *Buriā* or axe.—It is used for cutting wood, etc., and costs 2 to 4 annas. (7) *Bindhuni* or *nihan.*—An iron rod used for boring holes in wood, costing 2 annas each. (8) *Bārshī.*—It is a kind of axe larger and heavier than *buriā* used for making carts (*sagars*), etc., and costs 6 to 12 annas. (9) *Sābal.*—It is a heavy iron rod used for making holes in the soil. It costs Re. 1 each. (10) *Gainti* or pick-axe.—It is used for digging trenches and removing small stones; the cost is 10 to 12 annas. (11) *Dā* (sickle)—used for reaping paddy, etc., and costs 2 annas. (12) The spade or *kodāli* costs 12 annas to Re. 1-4 each. (13) *Ghāchikatā.*—It is a small spade used for removing paddy plants after the weeding has been finished from congested parts of the field to parts less thickly planted. It costs 1 to 2 annas. (14) Basket.—It is used for carrying manures, etc., and it costs 1 anna. The total cost of agricultural implements for one "plough" of land or 6 acres is about Rs. 12 approximately. Bullocks as well as buffaloes are employed in agriculture. The number of bullocks used for agriculture exceeds that of buffaloes by 98 per cent. A pair of buffaloes perform 50 per cent. more work than a pair of bullocks. The price of bullocks varies from Rs. 20 to Rs. 60 per pair, while a pair of buffaloes will cost Rs. 30

to Rs. 60. The cattle of the State have considerably degenerated on account of insufficient fodder supply. The fodder is sufficient on the grazing ground during the rainy season, but as soon as the rains are over the green fodder disappears and the cattle are fed on straw in insufficient quantities and are reduced to skeletons. They are not fed here on oil-cakes or grains. The supply of oil-cake is very limited. The estimated cost of cultivation per *mān* is Rs. 9-4-0.

As the outturn of paddy is 8 to 20 maunds per *mān*, the cultivator gets Rs. 24 to Rs. 60 per *mān* calculating the price of paddy at Rs. 3 per maund.

Manure and irrigation.

The manures used are cow-dung, ashes and silt of old tanks. The banks of tanks situated near the rice fields are cut through and the water is allowed to pass through the rice fields. There are two kinds of embankments—(1) embankments constructed across a sloping depression, between two ridges of upland. All the water that falls on the elevation during the rainy season flows down to the bottom of the depression, and is arrested by the embankments; (2) embankments raised across the stream diverting their water into artificial channels leading to the rice fields.

Rotation of crops.

Rotation of crop is seldom practised by the people. It is confined to uplands (*gorā*). On *berhā* lands some well-to-do and industrious cultivators sow *khesāri* in September before the paddy crop has been reaped. On *jal* lands which are very fertile, mustard or *mūga* is sometimes sown after harvesting the rice crop. Double crops are, however, raised by very few tenants of the State. The fertile uplands (*gorā*) are alternately cultivated with *gorā* paddy in one year and mustard, *surgujā* and *til* in the next. Maize or *makā* is sown with cotton, *arhar* with *gorā* paddy and *gangi* with *makā*. On very fertile *gorā* lands containing a large proportion of clay, gram is sown with mustard, but gram cultivation is extremely limited.

NATURAL CALAMITIES.

The State has not suffered much from natural calamities. There was a heavy flood in September 1900 and some damage was caused, but it was nothing compared to the loss of life and crops which occurred in the neighbouring district of Balasore. The great cyclone of May 1887 which passed over Orissa caused some damage, but its effect was very much less destructive in the State than in the British districts of Orissa. The only natural calamity which affects intimately the welfare of the people is deficient rainfall or its uneven distribution. Since the great Orissa famine of 1866 this State has been spared from another such visitation although scarcity, more or less severe, has occurred. Experience shows that favourable rainfall from the middle of June to the end of September, a fall of about 2 inches in October and half an inch early in November will suffice to mature the winter paddy, the staple crop of the State. If there is unusual fluctuations in the rainfall the winter paddy crop suffers. The main population of the State being aboriginals, who even in normal years supplement their food supply by fruits and roots taken from the jungles and whose standard of living is very low, a year of scarcity is tided over with comparative ease provided there is no failure of the edible jungle fruits and roots and the State comes forward to their help in proper time by opening relief works in the affected areas and in granting *taccavi* loans.

RENTS, WAGES AND PRICES.

The *mān* is the standard land measure; it is equivalent to 0·698 acre. The following table classifies the different average rates of rents per *mān* prevalent in the State according to the latest settlements:—

NAME OF SUBDIVISION.	Ist class winter paddy land.	2nd class winter paddy land.	3rd class winter paddy land.	*Aus* or early paddy land.	*Dāhi* or upland.	*Kalā* or homestead.
	Rs. A. P.	Rs. A. P.	Rs. A. P.	Rs. A. P.	Rs. A. P.	Rs. A. P.
1. Mayūrbhanj subdivision proper.	1 6 6½	1 3 1½	1 0 9	0 6 4	...	1 8 5
2. Bāmanghāti subdivision.	1 3 0	0 13 0	0 9 0	...	0 2 0	...
3. Pānchpir subdivision.	0 13 4	0 10 9	0 8 4	...	0 2 0	...

The average rates of assessment per *mān* for 1st, 2nd and 3rd class rice lands of the State taken as a whole are Re. 1-2-3½, Re. 0-14-3½ and Re. 0-11-4, respectively, and for uplands Re. 0-3-1.

The rise in the price of food-grains, especially rice, which has been observable during the last five years, has been a benefit to the cultivator. The rise in the price has enabled the cultivator to earn almost double the money which he used to get by the sale of the surplus stock of his grains in previous years. With this saving the cultivator has been able to buy cattle and indulge in luxuries. Many cultivators who used to be in a state of chronic indebtedness were enabled to pay off their debts. To the labouring classes the rise in the price of food-grains has not been an unmixed blessing, but the number of labourers who own no land at all is very small in the State, and even these labourers are paid in the mofussil not in cash but in kind. The labourers in the town of Bāripadā and those who are employed in sleeper operations or under traders and *mahājans* are paid in cash and not in kind, but in their case the rise in the price of food-grains has led to a rise in the rate of wage. The following table compares the prices of food-grains and the wages of labour during the last 10 years.

Price of food-grains during last 10 years from 1897-98 to 1906-07.

NAME OF ARTICLE.	SEERS PER RUPEE IN—									
	1897-98.	1898-99.	1899-00.	1900-01.	1901-02.	1902-03.	1903-04.	1904-05.	1905-06.	1906-07.
1. Paddy (unhusked rice)	36	48	48	50	50	60	60	50	40	19
2. Rice	16	24	20	20	16	18	16 to 24	14 to 22	10 to 13	8 to 10
3. *Birhi*	13	21	24	21	21	21	18	16	16	14
4. *Mūga*	12	20	20	15	20	16	16	14	10	8
5. *Arhar*	20	21	24	21	20	18	24	20	18	14
6. *Kulthī*	32	32	24	32	32	32	32	30	20	20
7. *Chanā*	16	12	16	13	16	13	16	14	12	10
8. *Gur* (molasses) ...	5	6	8	6	6	8	8	6	5	5
9. *Māndiā*	..	...	...	...	32	32	32	30	24	20

Daily wages of labour during last 10 years from 1897-98 to 1906-07.

KIND OF LABOUR.	1897-98 per head.	1898-99 per head.	1899-00 per head.	1900-01 per head.	1901-02 per head.	1902-03 per head.	1903-04 per head.	1904-05 per head.	1905-06 per head.	1906-07 per head.
Unskilled male labourer.	1½ a. to 2 as.	1½ a. to 2 as.	1½ a. to 2½ as.	1½ a. to 2 as.	1½ a. to 2 as.	1½ a. to 2 as.	2 as.	2 as. to 2½ as.	2 as. to 2½ as.	2½ as. to 3 as.
Unskilled female labourer.	1 a. to 1½ a.	1 a. to 1½ a.	1 a. to 1½ a.	1 a. to 1½ a.	1 a. to 1½ a.	1 a. to 1½ a.	1½ a.	1½ a. to 2 as.	1½ a. to 2 as.	2 as.
Skilled labourer such as carpenters, blacksmiths, tailors, masons, etc.	4 as. to 6 as.	4 as. to 6 as.	4 as. to 8 as.	4 as. to 8 as.	4 as. to 8 as.	4 as. to 8 as.	4 as. to 8 as.	4 as. to 8 as.	4 as. to 8 as.	4 as. to 8 as.

The majority of the population of the State are agriculturists. Even the labouring classes who earn their living by engaging in labour own a few *māns* of land for cultivation, and it can be said that over 97 per cent. of the population are agriculturists or engaged exclusively in agricultural labour. The non-agriculturists are confined to Bāripadā, the headquarters of the State, and to the subdivisional headquarters. Their number in the interior is infinitesimal. The only manufactures which are worth mentioning are the manufacture of coarse cloth

OCCUPATIONS, MANUFACTURES AND TRADE.

mostly by Pāns and of tusser fabrics by Tāntis in Olmarā *pargana* and in the Bāmanghāti subdivision. The aboriginal population show preference for coarse cloths locally manufactured as they are more durable and can stand rough usage better than the finer mill-woven counts. The manufacture of tusser fabrics formed an important industry formerly, but it is declining at the present moment owing to keen competition. The Tāntis who were formerly solely engaged in it are turning to agriculture. Owing to the opening up of the State by roads and by the Mayūrbhanj State Light Railway the manufacture of sleepers in the fine forests of the Simlāpāl hills has received an impetus and very large quantities of sleepers are being exported within the last few years. Cultivation of tusser cocoons and of lac is an important occupation of the aboriginal populations. These two industries which were in a decaying stage show signs of reviving. The important articles of export are paddy, rice, oil-seeds, forest produce, such as timber, tusser cocoons, lac, myrobalans, nux vomica, etc. The principal articles of import are salt, kerosene oil, cotton yarns and other fabrics, etc.

MEANS OF COMMUNICATIONS. The headquarters of the State is connected by a narrow gauge railway with the Bengal-Nāgpur Railway at Rūpsā. The line is 33 miles long and was constructed by the State. The total capital expenditure incurred up to the end of December 1907 was Rs. 7,17,144-1-10, and the line was opened to traffic in January 1905.

During the short time that it has been in existence the development of trade has been extensive especially in paddy, fire-wood and sleepers. Many traders from outside have established businesses in the State and others have gone in for reclamation of jungle lands for agricultural purposes along the railway line.

The total mileage of metalled roads was 149·50 miles and that of unmetalled roads 350 miles up to March 1908. The principal metalled roads are—

			Miles.
1.	Bāripadā-Balasore road	...	33
2.	Bāripadā-Bahaldā road	...	60
3.	Bisāi-Karanjiā road	...	43
4.	Bāripadā-Nayābasan road	...	24

The other unmetalled roads are principally feeders to the railway or the main roads. There are no navigable rivers in the State and except for timbers floated down the Burābalang river during the rainy season the river-borne traffic is *nil*. There is an Imperial sub-post office at Bāripadā, the headquarters of the

State, and branch post offices at Bahaldā, Karanjiā and Bisāi, and there are letter-boxes in important villages.

The special features of the land revenue system of the State are the village *padhāns* or headmen and the *pargana sardārs*. The land revenue of a village is collected by its *padhān* who is responsible for its payment in proper time to the *sardār*, who is again responsible to the State for the payment of the revenue of his *pargana*. These functionaries receive 10 per cent. of the village and *pargana* land revenue respectively as commission and pay the remainder of the revenue to the State. Thus 20 per cent. of the revenue is paid as collection charges and the balance 80 per cent. comes to the State. In the subdivision of Bāmanghāti the *padhāns* used to pay the revenue direct into the treasury without the intervention of the *sardārs* and were liable to make good any balance which remained in arrears. This system was introduced by Dr. Haye, the Deputy Commissioner of Singhbhūm, who held charge of the subdivision for a number of years up to 1878, as it was found that the *sardārs* in Bāmanghāti, who are mostly Santāls, either failed to pay the revenue in proper time or misappropriated it if collected. In the last settlement, however, which was completed in 1906, some of the intelligent *sardārs* have been invested with the power to make the collection in their *parganas* and others have been replaced by *Tahsīldārs* who are paid by a monthly salary. With the exception of two or three *sardārs* of Bāmanghāti, the others have been deprived of police powers which they formerly exercised. In the Sadar and the Pānchpīr subdivisions the collection is made in four *kists*, viz., the April-*kist*, 4 annas, the July-*kist*, 2 annas, the October-*kist*, 4 annas and the January-*kist*, 6 annas.

LAND REVENUE ADMINISTRATION.

Land revenue system.

The land revenue of the State is liable to re-settlement and settlement operations are a permanent feature of the land revenue administration as *pargana* after *pargana* is taken up in regular rotation for settlement and not the whole of the State at once. The *parganas* which have been denuded of jungle, and where there is little room for extension of cultivation have been cadastrally surveyed and the term of settlement is fixed at 20 years; *parganas* where the cultivated area is small and there is room for reclamation of jungle lands are surveyed according to the native method and the term of settlement is fixed at 10 to 15 years. In the Mayūrbhanj Tenancy Regulation provision is made for the record-of-rights and settlement of rents.

Land tenures.

Excepting the *sarbarāhkār* of Kaptipadā whose estate extends over an area of 200 square miles, there are no large land owners in the State. The *lākhirāj* tenures are divided into the following classes:—(1) *debottar*, (2) *brahmottar*, (3) *datta mahatrān*, and *datta pānpik*, (4) *bābuān jāgīrs* and (5) *paikān* and other *jāgīrs* or service tenures. The *debottar* lands are rent-free lands given to the Hindu deities whose number in the State is very large and include large *maths* presided over by ascetic *Mahants*. The *brahmottar* are grants made to Brāhmans, and include *sāsans* or *brahmottar* villages divided into a number of holdings and allotted to Brāhmans. These holdings are never escheated to the State: in the event of the *lākhirājdār* dying intestate, his holding is made over to another Brāhman. The number of *sāsan* and *bātikatiā* or individual *brahmottar* grants is very extensive in the State. The *datta mahatrān* or *datta pānpik* grants are made to persons other than Brāhmans. *Bābuān jāgīrs* are *lākhirāj* grants made to the relations and others belonging to the Chief's caste. *Paikān jāgīrs* are the service tenures granted to *paiks* or the ancient yeomanry of Orissa who formed a part of the military force of the Chief. The number of *lākhirāj* tenures in the State especially in the Sadar subdivision is very large. Most of these tenures are only partially rent-free, as 5 annas in the rupee is paid as *darbesi* and collection cess. The rent paying lands are known as *māl* or *hāsilāt* lands. According to the provision of the Mayūrbhanj Tenancy Regulation twelve years' possession gives the occupier a right of occupancy over his holding and he cannot be dispossessed of it, except in the due course of the law.

The current land revenue demand in 1907-08 amounted to Rs. 6,04,554.

GENERAL ADMINISTRATION. The relations of the State with the British Government are governed by the *sanad* of 1894, which was revised in 1908: the State pays a yearly tribute of Rs. 1,067-11-9, and is under the rules liable to pay *nazrāna* on succession.

For administrative purposes the Mayūrbhanj State is divided into three subdivisions, viz.—(1) the Sadar subdivision, (2) the Bāmanghāti subdivision and (3) the Pānchpīr subdivision. A Council has been established since the year 1892 with the Chief of the State as President and the *Dīwān*, the State Judge, the Superintendent of Police, the State Engineer and two non-official gentlemen as members. All legislative measures are passed by the Council, and the Budget is discussed in Council. The Chief with the *Dīwān* or any other member of Council whom the Chief may nominate form the Judicial Committee which hears appeals against the orders of all State courts according to the provisions of the law of the State. The *Dīwān* is the head of the Revenue Department including the settlement, agriculture, the zamīndāri and the Registration Departments. Under him is the Collector and a staff of Deputy Collectors and the Subdivisional Officers in their capacity as Deputy Collectors. The State Judge is the head of the judicial side of the administration, and has under him all the Magistrates, Munsiffs and Sub-Judge and the Subdivisional Officers in their capacity as Deputy Magistrates. In the subdivisions of Bāmanghāti and Pānchpīr, the Subdivisional Officers exercise both judicial and executive functions. The Superintendent of Police and the State Engineer are in charge of their respective departments, and deal direct with the Chief. The Chief Medical Officer, the Superintendent of Education and all other departments deal direct with the Chief, and are immediately subordinate to him.

Finances. The receipts and expenditure, excluding debts and deposits, for the year 1907-08 amounted to Rs. 12,14,895 and Rs. 12,09,592, respectively. The State has a reserve fund to meet emergencies of Rs. 11,67,700 invested in Government securities.

Forest. The forests of Mayūrbhanj State are distributed over the central group of hill ranges and the plains sloping to the east and west of those hills.

In this State the Forest Act is in force and the forests of the State are classified as reserved and protected. The area of the reserved forests is 1,054 square miles and that of the protected forests 741 square miles. To the former class belong the compact forests on the hills, and on a part of the plains, whereas the latter class is scattered all over the east of the plains area of the State and honey-combed with villages. A little over one-third of the area of reserved forests contains mature *sāl* in fair proportion and the remaining area contains poles in different stages of growth, intermixed with stray trees of full size here and there. The protected forests are composed mainly of *sāl* poles.

In former days the forests were not under systematic management. Timber contractors confined their fellings to the plain forests in the vicinity of Bāripadā and exhausted them leaving only poles. In 1894 action towards the systematic management of the extensive forests was taken. In the same year the services of Mr. C. L. Hatts of the Imperial Forest Service were lent to the State by Government. He drew up an exhaustive report of the forests of the State and prepared a preliminary working plan for a small portion of it, viz., for about 88 square miles. Thereafter a well organised Forest Department has been gradually formed to manage and control all forest matters on the model of forest administration prevailing in British districts. The cost of maintaining the Department which has been placed under a trained Forest Officer with an adequate staff, some of which are recruited from the Imperial Forest College, Dehra-Dun, is at present nearly Rs. 54,000 a year.

The present revenue from the sale of timber is Rs. 1,00,000 to Rs. 1,20,000.

The ryots of the State pay a fuel cess and in return they are allowed to remove dry fire wood from unreserved trees. In Bāmanghāti subdivision the ryots pay, besides the fuel cess, a special cess for which each cess payer is permitted to remove 2 *sagar* loads of bamboo and 10 dry *sāl* posts of 2 feet in girth annually. Concession has also been granted to each ryot to get free of charge trees of the unreserved species for house building and agriculture implements. They are also allowed the privilege of grazing their cattle free all over the protected forests, but in the reserved forests free pasturage is permitted only to adjacent villages within a radius of 2 miles. All ryots are also permitted to remove for their own consumption edible fruits, roots, bulbs tubers, etc.

Besides *sāl* the following principal timber trees grow in these forests :—*piāsāl* (*Pterocarpus marsupium*), *sissū* (*Dalbergia Sissoo*), *karam* (*Adina cordifolia*), *bandhan* (*Oujeinia Dalbergioides*), *gamhāri* (*Gmelina arborea*), *kendu* (*Diospyros melanoxylon*), *mahuā* (*Bassia latifolia*), *āsan* (*Terminalia tomentosa*). Among other common trees found in the forests of the State are mango (*Mangifera indica*), *jām* (*Eugenia Jambolana*), *chār* (*Buchanania latifolia*), *kasāphal* (*Terminalia chebula*), *kuchilā* (*Strychnos Nux-vomica*), *bāharā* (*Tarminalia belerica*), *semul* (*Bombax malabaricum*), *kusum* (*Schleichera trijuga*), *banyan* (*Ficus indica*), *pīpal* (*Ficus religiosa*), *dhao* (*Ausgeissus latifolia*), *arjun* (*Terminalia arjuna*), *aonlā* (*Phyllanthus emblica*), *champā* (*Michœlia champaca*), *koine* (*Stephegyne parvifolia*), *mānkarkendu* (*Diospyros embryoperis*), *siris* (*Albizzia lebbech*) and *rohini* (*Somida fabrifuga*). Among minor forest products are lac and tusser cocoon which are reared by the people of the State. Tusser cocoons are reared on *āsan* trees and lac on *kusum* trees. The ryots are permitted to rear lac on trees free of charge, and a duty of Rs. 2-8 per maund is levied from dealers. The revenue from these two sources to the State ranges between Rs. 25,000 to Rs. 30,000.

Prior to the systematic organisation of the Forest Department, *i.e.*, during the years 1884-1894, the annual revenue from forests never exceeded Rs. 30,000, but at present it is nearly Rs. 2,50,000 a year.

In the Mayūrbhanj State there is a regular excise staff and the Excise Department is in immediate charge of a Deputy Collector designated as the Excise Officer, under the control of the *Dīwān* of the State. Excise.

The chief sources of excise revenue are opium, *gānja*, country liquor, imported liquor, *bhāng*, *tāri*, *hāndiā* and *madat*. There are five methods of taxation, viz.:—(1) Retail license fees, (2) duty on actual quantity of article passing into consumption, (3) distillery fee, (4) license fees for preparation and sale of *hāndiā* at godowns and (5) license fees for sale of home brewed *hāndiā* at *hāts*.

The supply of opium is obtained from the Balasore Treasury and the *pattādārs* (licensed vendors) get their supply from the State Treasury. Opium. *Gānja* and *bhāng* are imported from Calcutta or Nowagāon under a pass granted by the State and countersigned by the Collector of Balasore. *Gānja* and *bhāng*. Country liquor is manufactured by the distillery system in the Sadar subdivision and the outstill system of brewing is prevalent in the other two subdivisions. Liquor. The distillery, opened at Bāripadā, is supervised by the Distillery Superintendent under the control of the Excise Officer. Imported liquor is sold in a shop at Bāripadā. The home manufacture of *madat* has been made penal to put a check upon the steady increase of opium smoking and nobody can smoke it except in a licensed den. *Madat*. The result has been a decrease in the number of *madat* smokers. During the four years 1904-05 to 1907-08 the average annual excise revenue and expenditure were Rs. 45,663 and Rs. 4,551 respectively; both the items are increasing year by year, the revenue and the expenditure during the year 1907-08 being Rs. 63,130 and Rs. 8,541 respectively.

The number of civil suits instituted during the year 1907-08 was 2,112. Civil justice.

In the year 1907-08, 1,864 cognizable cases were reported to the police, of which 240 were held to be false. Crime. Convictions were obtained in 530 cases, or 58·05 per cent. of the true cases sent up for trial, in which 1,691 persons were tried and 820 or 48·4 per cent. were convicted.

Total strength of the police force is 332, consisting of 59 officers and 273 men: there are 25 police stations and outposts. Police. Proportion of regular policemen to the square mile is 1 to 12·7 square miles, and to population is 1 to 1,838·5 persons. The annual cost of maintenance of the force is Rs. 15-7-6 per square mile and anna 1-8 per head of the total population.

Village police. *Chaukīdārs* and *chaukidāri* system.

There are 1,221 *chaukīdārs* in the whole State, out of whom 638 are in Mayūrbhanj proper (527 were appointed under Act VI of 1870 and 111 under Regulation XX of 1817), 401 in the Bāmanghāti subdivision and 182 in the Pānchpīr subdivision appointed under Regulation XX of 1817. Compared with the area and population there is one village watchman to 3·47 square miles of the area and one to every 499 persons of the population. Cost of maintenance of the *chaukīdāri* force is Rs. 6-9-4 per square mile of the area and 8 pies per head of the population.

Jails.

There is one main jail in the Sadar subdivision and two sub-jails in the Bāmaṇghāti and the Pānchpīr subdivisions. The jail staff consists of a Superintendent of jails, two Superintendents of the two sub-jails, 1 Jailor, 1 Assistant Jailor and 24 warders. The Subdivisional Officers of the two subdivisions are in charge of the sub-jails and are designated Superintendents of sub-jails. The Hospital Assistants of the two Subdivisional dispensaries exercise the functions of jailor in the sub-jails. The total jail population in all the jails in the State was 779 in the year 1907-08. The daily average number of prisoners was 128. The proportion of average daily jail population to entire male population is 1 to 2,369. The proportion of deaths to jail population is 1 to 153·1, and the average cost of maintenance per prisoner was Rs. 4-11 per month per head. The jail manufactures are generally rope-making, cloth-weaving and oil-pressing, etc. The total receipt was Rs. 1,983-4-3. The total charge was Rs. 1,470-15. The average earning per manufacturing prisoner was Rs. 2-8.

Public Works Department.

The Public Works Department of the State is in charge of the State Engineer, being assisted by a subordinate staff. In 1907-08 the State spent Rs. 2,04,376 on account of public works.

LOCAL SELF-GOVERNMENT.

The Bāripadā Municipality was established in 1905 with an area of 2 square miles: the number of rate-payers is 570. The Officers are 1 Chairman, 1 Vice-Chairman, besides 15 Commissioners, appointed by the Chief, of whom six are State officials and nine are non-officials, and the various classes of the community are adequately represented. The town is divided into six wards. The sources of revenue are latrine tax, registration fees of carts, revenue from ferries, pounds and markets and a State grant. The receipts and expenditure for 1907-08 were Rs. 10,870-12-2 and Rs. 7,587-3-9, respectively. The population in 1901 was 5,617, but has considerably increased since then.

The water-supply of the town is drawn from three rivers, wells and two big *bandhs* on its northern side and a large tank called the jail tank on the eastern side of the town which has been reserved for drinking purposes.

Conservancy. The conservancy establishment consist of 17 *mehtars* in the scavenging and road cleaning branch and of 31 sweepers in the latrine cleansing section, with one Inspector, one *jamādār* and one peon to supervise their works. The street sweepings and garbage are removed by refuse carts to distant corners of the town and reduced to ashes. The night-soil is deposited in regular trenching grounds at a distance of 3½ miles from the town.

EDUCATION. Secondary schools. The Bāripadā High English school: the total number of pupils on the rolls in 1899-00 was 112 and in 1907-08 was 271. Average daily attendance in 1899-00 was 53, and in 1907-08 it was 203. The cost of tuition per boy in 1907-08 was Rs. 19, of which the whole was paid by the State. Out of 271 pupils on the rolls, 258 were Hindus, six Muhammadans, six native Christians and one aborigine.

The number of Middle English schools in the State was 5. They registered 409 pupils at the end of the year 1907-08, and 251 in 1899-00. The average daily attendance was 232 in the year 1899-00 and 292 in the year 1907-08. The cost of educating each such pupil was Rs. 10-4. There is no Middle Vernacular school in the State.

Primary schools. The number of Upper Primary and Lower Primary schools for boys in the State during the year 1907-08 was 362. The total number of pupils attending these schools was 7,299, and the average cost of educating a pupil in any of these schools was Rs. 3.

Female education. The total number of girls' schools in the whole State was 5. The total number of girls attending was 124 in the year 1907-08. The number of girls attending boys' schools was 225. The average daily attendance was 81. The cost of tuition of each girl was Rs. 8-7 in 1907-08. Slow but steady progress is being made in female education.

A two years' course is followed, viz., 1st year's course—elementary drawing and carpentry; 2nd year's course—advanced instruction in carpentry, blacksmithy and fitter's works. Besides there are 2 Sanskrit *tols* and one *guru*-training and 9 private schools.

The expenditure from the State funds on account of education in all branches in 1907-08 was Rs. 35,541-8-4, or 2·9 per cent. of the gross revenue of the State. It is more by 0·3 per cent. than what it was in 1899-00.

CHAPTER XV.

NARSINGHPUR STATE.

PHYSICAL ASPECTS. THE State of Narsinghpur lies between 20° 23′ and 20° 37′ N. and 84° 58′ and 85° 17′ E., with an area of 199 square miles. It is bounded on the north by a range of forest-clad hills, which separate it from Angul district and Hindol State; on the east by the Barāmbā State; on the south and south-west by the Mahānadī river which divides it from the Khandparā and Daspallā States; and on the west by Daspallā and Angul district. The State is for the most part open and cultivated country with a few small ranges and isolated hills, except to the north where a range of fine hills separates it from the Hindol State. This northern range contains a large quantity of *sāl* (*Shorea robusta*) trees, which here attain to a considerable dimension. The climate, on the small plateau about 1,500 feet high on the crest of this range, is a welcome change in the hot season from the heated plains of the country below. The temperature in the hot season is high and the tract of country in the neighbourhood of the headquarters is very hot. The average rainfall for the six years—from 1902-03 to 1907-08—was 51·24 inches. The climate is healthy. The tract bordering along the Mahānadī is subject to frequent inundations, which leave deposits of sand, doing serious damage to the cultivation. The headquarters of the State are at Narsinghpur.

HISTORY. The State is alleged to have been founded by one Dharma Singh, about the year 1292 A.D. The State is said to have originally been in the possession of two Khonds, Narsingha and Para, from whom the name of this tract of country was taken. The area of the State has been from time to time curtailed of many portions by the Chiefs of Hindol, Barāmbā and Daspallā. None of the Chiefs ever obtained any *farmān* from the Mughals or Marāthās. The title "Mānsingh Hari Chandan Mahāpātra," was obtained by the fifteenth Chief, Dayānidhi Mānsingh Hari Chandan Mahāpātra, from the Mahārājā of Purī, to whom the State was subject. The emblem of the State is a scorpion.

THE PEOPLE. The population increased from 33,849 in 1891 to 39,613 in 1901, the density being 199 persons to the square mile. It contains 198 villages, the most important of which is Kānpur. Of the total population all but 158 are Hindus. The most numerous castes are Chasās (6,000) and Pāns (4,000). The population is classified as follows:—Hindus—males, 19,481, females, 19,974, total of Hindus, 39,455, or 99·6 per cent. of the population of the State; proportion of males in total Hindus, 49·3 per cent. Musalmāns—males, 89, females, 66, total of Musalmāns 155 or 0·3 per cent. of the population; proportion of males in total Musalmāns 57·4 per cent.; Christians—3. Proportion of males in total population, 49·4 per cent. Number of literate persons in the State is 3,309 or 8·4 per cent. of the total population. Averages—villages per square mile, 0·99; persons per village, 200; houses per square mile, 42; houses per village, 42·3; persons per house, 4·7. According to the census of 1901, out of the 198 villages in the State there were 179 with less than five hundred, 17 with from five hundred to a thousand, and 2 with from one to two thousand inhabitants. The people are prosperous, more advanced and their standard of living is generally higher than in the neighbouring States.

PUBLIC HEALTH. The country is healthy and the people do not suffer to any exceptional degree from fever: epidemics of cholera are, however, not uncommon. There is a dispensary, with an indoor ward, at the headquarters in charge of a Civil Hospital Assistant: the number of indoor and outdoor patients treated in 1907-08 was 45 and 5,627 respectively: there is a veterinary department attached to the dispensary and in the year 1907-08, 78 animals were treated. Vaccination is in charge of a special Civil Hospital Assistant, who also looks after village sanitation and gives medical relief in the interior where 312 patients were treated in the year 1907-08: the vaccinators employed are licensed local men, trained in the vaccination class of the Medical School at Cuttack; in 1907-08 the number of primary vaccinations was 1,352 and of re-vaccinations 1,871. Considerable progress has of late been made in overcoming the prejudices of the people against vaccination: during the period from 1893 to 1902 the average annual number of vaccinations was 464 and re-vaccination was almost unknown.

AGRICULTURE. The soil is fertile and the villages are many of them prosperous with well cultivated lands: the riparian villages are liable to inundation and deposits of sands and there are no embankments to resist the powerful floods of the Mahānadī. The principal crop is rice and in ordinary years there is an ample surplus stock for export: good crops of castor-oil, *arhar*, sugarcane and sweet potatoes are raised.

Rents, wages and prices. The average rate for ordinary first, second and third class rice lands per acre is Rs. 3-2-5, Rs. 2-13-5, and Rs. 2-8-4, respectively, and for uplands Re. 0-9-0. Wages during the ten years from 1893 to 1902 showed a slight tendency to fall, the average daily wage during this period was as follows:—Superior mason, 7⅓ annas, common mason, 4 annas; superior carpenter, 7⅓ annas, common carpenter, 3⅓ annas; cooly, 2 annas; superior blacksmith, 5¾ annas, and common blacksmith 2⅓ annas.

The run of prices during the same period has varied with the harvests, but there has been no noticeable tendency to a rise in prices: the average price during the period 1893 to 1902 of wheat, rice, gram and salt has been 12⅛ seers, 26 seers, 20⅜ seers and 10½ seers, respectively.

Occupations, manufactures and trade. There are no occupations, manufactures or trade in the State calling for special notice. Lac and cocoons are cultivated as usual throughout the State. A considerable trade, however, is carried on by exporting bamboos to Cuttack and a small amount of timber is also removed. The trade is mostly in grain, cotton, oil-seeds and molasses. The principal imported articles are spices, salt, cloth, piece-goods and kerosene oil.

Means of communication. The State is fortunate in its line of communication: the Mahānadī forms its frontage to the south and affords ready means of transport almost throughout the year. There is a good road from the headquarters to Barāmbā and a fair road, which passes over the steep northern range of hills, to Angul and Hindol. There is a post office at the headquarters.

Land revenue administration. The system of land revenue administration is the same as in other States of the group formerly known as the Tributary Mahāls of Orissa. The last settlement was made in 1898-99, when the State was under the Court of Wards. The land revenue demand is Rs. 37,983. The *sarbarāhkārs* are paid by cash commission and have no special service lands in the villages: steps have been taken to identify the old *sarbarāhkāri* service lands and assign them again to the village headmen: these lands in previous settlements were brought into the general assessment of the village.

General administration. The *sanad* of 1894, which was revised in 1908, lays down the relations between the State and the British Government. The State pays an annual tribute of Rs. 1,450 to the British Government. The State has been for some time under the direct administration of Government owing to the minority of the Chief, who has, however, recently been given charge of his State; he conducts the administration with the assistance of a trained

Finances. *Dīwān*. The estimated annual income is about Rs. 66,000.

During the period of management precise rules for the administration of the forests were drawn up and a regular Forest Department organised under a properly qualified Forester: a fuel cess at the rate of one anna per acre on cultivated lands has been introduced. In 1907-08 the forests yielded Rs. 7,031. **Forests.**

The excise arrangements are on the lines prevailing in British districts; the supply of opium and *gānja* is obtained from Government in the manner common to all the States of the group formerly known as the Tributary Mahāls of Orissa. In 1907-08 the excise revenue amounted to Rs. 2,442. **Excise.**

Civil suits are of a petty character and in 1907-08 the number of civil suits instituted was 131 of which only 30 suits were for values exceeding Rs. 50. **Civil justice.**

The majority of the crime consists of petty theft and burglaries and heinous crime is rare. **Crime.** The police force consists of one Sub-Inspector, 3 Head-Constables and 21 constables, the *chaukīdārs* number 186 and have service land; they annually receive at harvest a sheaf of paddy (unhusked rice) from each cultivator, and occasional meals and they enjoy the right to dispose of the hides of dead cattle. **Police.**

There is a jail with accommodation for 24 prisoners. The daily average population was 16·56 in 1907-08. **Jail.**

There is a Public Works Department in charge of a sub-overseer under the Public Works Supervisor employed for States under administration: money is annually assigned for improvements of tanks and irrigation. The State spent Rs. 9,961, on account of public works in 1907-08. **Public Works Department.**

The schools maintained by the State are one Middle Vernacular, two Upper Primary, 27 Lower Primary for boys and two Lower Primary for girls: there is also a Sanskrit *tol*. There is also one *guru*-training school. The number of pupils on the rolls in 1907-08 was 804, and the State expenditure on education was Rs. 1,998 and in addition there was the Government grant of Rs. 1,397. Education is backward, but more advanced than in the neighbouring States. **EDUCATION.**

CHAPTER XVI.

NAYAGARH STATE.

PHYSICAL ASPECTS. THE Nayāgarh State is situated between 19° 53′ and 20° 20′ N., and 84° 48′ and 85° 15′ E., with an area of 588 square miles. It is bounded on the north by Khandparā State and Purī district; on the east by Ranpur State; on the south by Purī district; and on the west by Daspallā State and the Madras district of Ganjām. A splendid range of hills, varying from 2,000 to 2,500 feet in height, runs through the centre of the State. The south and south-eastern portions of the State are very hilly and incapable of tillage, but elsewhere there are wide-spread tracts of highly cultivated lands. A chain of hills rising abruptly surrounds the southern and eastern boundaries of the State in the form of a semi-circle. The hill ranges are at places alternated by small peaks but the chain is nowhere broken: on the lower slopes thick forests of bamboos are found. In the valleys there are rich forests of timber. *Sāl* (Shorea robusta), *piāsāl* (Pterocarpus marsupium) and *sisu* (Dalbergia Sissoo) abound with *kendu* (Diospyros melanoxylon) and *gamhār* (Gmelina arborea). The silt from the hills is deposited annually with the setting in of the monsoon and furnishes rich material for the luxuriant growth of valuable trees. In the plain country the lands are all undulating and readily lend themselves to irrigation. The average rainfall for the six years from 1902-03 to 1907-08, was 56·47 inches. The State is traversed by numerous streams taking their rise in the hill tracts: these streams eventually discharge into the Kusumi which flows from west to east and thence to the north, meeting the Mahānadī in the Khandparā State. The streams are all fordable throughout the year except immediately after a heavy downpour when they come into sudden spate but fall again in the brief space of an hour or two. There are numerous natural springs in the northern part of the State, which protect this area from scarcity. The headquarters of the State are at Nayāgarh.

HISTORY. According to tradition the founder of the family was one Sūryamani Singh from Rewah in the Central Provinces. He established a *garh* (fort) at a place called Gunānati in Nayāgarh.

He was elected by the people of the country as their Chief and received from them in marriage a daughter of a Māli, *i.e.*, a gardener, who was the priest of the village goddess. On her death he married again, a Kshattriya bride, whose descendants have since held the *gadi* of the two States of Nayāgarh and Khandparā. Two or three generations afterwards the limits of the State were extended from Gunānati to the present capital of Nayāgarh. The fourth Chief established a *garh* (fort) at Nayāgarh, and still further extended his dominions. The twelfth Chief extended his boundaries by waging war with the Chiefs of Baud, Ranpur, Bānpur and Gumsur. He gave Nayāgarh to his eldest son, Khandparā to his second son, Lakshmīprasād to his third son: the third son dying heirless, Lakshmīprasād was again included in Nayāgarh, and the boundaries of Nayāgarh and Khandparā as then fixed have remained unchanged. The twenty-third Chief was the last of the lineal descendants of Sūryamani Singh. He held the *gadi* for 12 months, and was succeeded by Rājā Raghunāth Singh, a blood relation, who died without heirs in 1897, and on his death-bed authorized his younger Rānī to adopt a son. The present Chief was accordingly adopted from a family related by marriage. None of the Chiefs appear to have received any *farmān* from the Mughals or Marāthās. Raghujī Bhonslā, Mahārājā of Nāgpur, bestowed the gift of a flag on the Chief, and after the conquest of Orissa, the Chief, for the assistance rendered by him, received an elephant and a cannon. The emblem of the State is a tiger's head.

THE PEOPLE.

The total population of the State according to the census of 1901 is 140,779, or a density of 239 persons per square mile. Hindus constitute 95·18 per cent., Animists 4·40 per cent., and Musalmāns 0·42 per cent., of the total population: there are 9 Christians. Proportion of males of all classes in total population is 49·58 per cent. Hindus—males, 66,341, females, 67,654, total 133,995; proportion of males in total Hindus, 49·51 per cent. Musalmān—males, 356, females, 229, total 585; proportion of males in total Musalmāns, 60·85 per cent. Animists—males, 3,094, females, 3,096, total 6,190. The number of persons able to read and write is 12,013 or 8·5 per cent of the total population. Averages—villages per square mile, 1·3; persons per village, 181·6; houses per square mile, 49·3; houses per village, 37·4; persons per square mile, 239; persons per house, 4·9. The State contains 775 villages which are classified as follows:—734 villages with less than five hundred inhabitants, 32 with from five hundred to one thousand inhabitants, 7 with from soue thousand to two thousand inhabitants and 2 with two thousand to five thousand inhabitants. The people may be divided into the following general groups according to their] occupations:—(1) Agricultural (85,447), including Chasās, Sudhas, Golās, Telingās, Rājus, Bauris, Khadāls, and Pāns. They represent 60·7 per cent. of the total population. (2) Religious, Literary and Titular including Brāhmans, Ksuattriyas, Karans, Khandaits, Rājputs, Mālis and Vaishnavas. They represent 12 per cent. of the total population. (3) Traders (14,077), including Vaisya, Guriās, Kumutis, Telis, Sunris (or Sundis), Pātrās, Thoriās, Gandha Baniks and Baniyās. They form 10 per cent. of the total population. (4) Village servants (8,446), including Bhandāris, Kāmārs, Kumhārs and Dhobās. They constitute 6 per cent. of the total population. (5) General artisans (4,223), including Kānsāris, Tāntis, Kharurās and Khairās. They constitute 3 per cent. of the total population. (6) Miscellaneous (11,685) about 9 per cent. of the population follow minor occupations. All the castes, except the Brāhmans, Karans, Khandaits and Kshattriyas, have their respective caste committees which sit once or twice a year and decide all social and religious questions. The penalties inflicted by the committees are in the shape of fines, or corporal punishment. Widow-marriage obtains among all castes except the Brāhmans, Karans and Kshattriyas. The younger brother, if any, of a deceased husband has preference over others for the remarriage of the widow, and disparity of age is no bar to such re-marriage. A Khond widow will not however re-marry if she has got a son. The Kumutis and Telingās will only marry the daughters of their maternal uncles, failing which the latter's permission to any other marriage relationship has to be purchased at considerable cost.

The Khonds worship their village goddesses known as Suliās Brāhmandei, Sitalā and Tarkei. In the event of a villager being killed by a tiger or a leopard, the idol is, however, thrown away and replaced by another and the priest also is dismissed.

The people are by character exceedingly given over to litigation and intrigue. The condition of the people is, on the whole, good. The soil is very fertile, and yields to the cultivator a good income annually. The people are well off and gold earrings and necklaces are worn by many.

PUBLIC HEALTH. The State is hilly and the climate dry. The headquarters Nayāgarh, are, however, badly situated in a hollow, closely surrounded by hills and are in consequence very malarious. The rest of the State is more salubrious, but malaria is more or less universal. The people are ignorant of the elementary principles of sanitation. Houses are built with no arrangements for ventilation. The tank which provides drinking water is indifferently used for all purposes. Fever with enlargement of spleen, dysentery, and diarrhœa are the most common form of disease. Diseases of the lungs very seldom occur. Cholera breaks out in an epidemic form once in 3 or 4 years. Small-pox has been successfully combated by the introduction of vaccination. The hot months are the healthiest part of the year. With the setting in of the rains people suffer from dysentery and malaria. There are two dispensaries in the State with indoor accommodation, one at the headquarters and the other at Odgaon. In 1907-08 the number of patients treated was 18,637: this figure includes 24 indoor patients treated during the year. Vaccination is now general, and the practice of revaccination was recently successfully instituted: the total number of primary vaccinations and revaccinations was 5,516 and 5,148 respectively in the year 1907-08.

AGRICULTURE.

The total area under cultivation is 123,402 acres, which is about $\frac{1}{3}$ of the total area of the State. The area under cultivation is very much in excess of the actual requirements of the population. There is no likelihood of the pressure of the population being felt on agriculture in the near future. Nearly half the produce of the paddy (unhusked rice), if not more, is available for export in an ordinary year. Rice occupies 68 per cent. of the total cultivated area, and the soil is admirably suited for its cultivation. Of the miscellaneous crops *mūga*, gram, sugarcane, cotton and *kulthī* are the most important. *Mūga* is extensively sown on rice lands if there is a good rain in December. Sugarcane is mostly grown on lands in the immediate vicinity of village sites. Cotton is grown on high lands, but of poor quality. *Kulthī* is extensively grown by the Khonds and is one of their staple food stuffs. During recent years the intelligent tenants have taken to the cultivation of jute, wheat, potato, *burhi* cotton and ground nut: these crops promise to have a future before them. The State experimental farm has been successful in introducing these new crops to the tenants. Of the oil-seeds, *rāshi* (sesamum) is the most important, and of the millets, *māndiā*, *suān*, and *kuhuri*. *Suān* (*sāwān*) and *kuhuri* are grown on high lands and do not require much labour. They ripen in the course of six weeks from the time of sowing and stand the tenants in good stead in years of scarcity. They are easily digestible in the form of cakes and are a good substitute for rice, and are sown in May and reaped in July.

Sugarcane is the most paying of all the crops grown in the State. The heavy initial outlay and the want of permanent sources of irrigation stand in the way of extension of cultivation of this valuable crop. Cow-dung stored in open places exposed to the sun and rains is the principal manure used. It is used at the rate of 40 to 60 maunds per acre. Sixty per cent. of the population own plough-cattle. The cattle are small but sturdy, getting an abundance of fodder from the jungles and waste lands. Several irrigation works have been constructed by the State and a regular programme is being undertaken and rapidly pushed on.

RENTS, WAGES AND PRICES.

Rents.

Prior to the recent settlement there were 45 rates of rent per acre ranging from Rs. 6-4 to 0-1-0. They were too numerous and unworkable, and were reduced to 9 in the recent settlement. The highest rate per acre is Rs. 3-2-0 and the lowest Re. 0-6-3. The rates have been applied according to the produce of the land. An acre of double-cropped land yielding on an average 36 to 40 maunds of rice per annum has been assessed at the highest rate (Rs. 3-2-0) while an acre of land yielding not more than 8 maunds of rice has been assessed at the lowest rate (Re. 0-6-3). The average class of land of which the annual produce of rice was 20 to 24 maunds has been assessed at the rate of Re. 1-9-0. The rates of rent for lands growing miscellaneous crops only are three, viz., Re. 0-10-5, Re. 0-8-4 and Re. 0-6-3. The proportion which the rent of an acre of 1st class land bears to its gross produce is as 1 to 16, of the average class 1 to 21, and of the inferior class 1 to 26. The rents are light.

Wages.

There are five kinds of agricultural labourers:—(1) *Barsakiā* (one who serves throughout the year). He gets from his employer Rs. 20 in cash, a coarse country cloth valued at 8 annas, and a loan of 4 maunds of unhusked rice and Rs. 2 free of interest. He is not fed by his employer. (2) *Chhamāsiā* (one who serves his employer on every alternate day). He receives Rs. 10 in cash, one cloth valued at 8 annas, a loan of 2 maunds of unhusked rice and one rupee free of interest, and 8 seers of unhusked rice per diem when the rice crop is reaped. (3) *Chārimāsiā* (one who serves his employer on every 3rd day). He receives Rs. 7 in cash, one napkin valued at 4 annas, and 8 seers of unhusked rice per diem when the rice crop is reaped. (4) *Tinimāsiā* (one who serves his employer on every 4th day). He receives Rs. 5 in cash, one napkin valued at 4 annas and 8 seers of unhusked rice on every day the paddy is reaped. (5) The daily labourer earns 2 annas per diem. The first two classes are the most numerous.

Although the price of rice, the principal agricultural produce, has risen considerably by a brisk export yielding a substantial profit to the land-owners the wages of agricultural labour remain stationary. During the ten years from 1893 to 1902 wages for skilled labour have shown no tendency to rise and the daily wage has averaged as follows:—Superior mason, 8 annas; common mason and superior carpenter, 6 annas each; common carpenter and superior blacksmith, 4 annas each; common blacksmith, 3 annas. The reason is, that the supply of labour is much in excess of the demand, the labourers as a class remain contented with a subsistence allowance. The labouring class constitutes 22 per cent. of the total population.

Prices. The chief agricultural produce of the State is rice. The average price of unhusked rice during the decade (1887-1896) was 51 seers per rupee but rose to 36 seers during the last decade (1897-1906). During the ten years from 1893 to 1902 the average price of wheat, rice and gram has been $10\frac{7}{8}$ seers, $19\frac{9}{16}$ seers, and $15\frac{13}{16}$ seers respectively. The year in which the Bengal-Nāgpur Railway was opened in Orissa marks an epoch in the economical history of the State. A brisk export trade of rice with different parts of India dawned upon the State and the prices of rice have risen 70 per cent. in one decade. The rise of prices of the principal produce has contributed materially to the prosperity of the State by ensuring handsome profits to the tenants and increasing the value of the land.

OCCUPATIONS, MANUFACTURES AND TRADE. The religious and literary classes consisting of Brāhmans, Karans and Kshattriyas, who constitute 12 per cent. of the total population, do not as a rule turn their attention to agriculture and trade. Agriculture is the chief occupation of 60 per cent. of the total population, who have little or no secondary occupation to supplement their income from the land. The agricultural classes are all hardworking and show signs of increased prosperity. They are, however, very conservative and do not readily welcome any departure from their old system of cultivation. Ten per cent. of the population follow trade. Only 2 per cent of the population follow fishing as their occupation, and 6 per cent. is represented by washermen, potters, blacksmiths and menial servants.

Occupations.

Manufactures The principal commodities of local manufacture are cotton fabrics, tusser, brass and bell-metal utensils, saltpetre, and catechu. The Tāntis who number 3,497 in the whole State and some of the Pāns manufacture coarse cotton fabrics by hand-weaving. Only a very small number of Tāntis turn out tusser cloth. The cotton fabrics are very much in demand in the local markets specially by the low-caste people. The tusser cloths are exported to Purī and Cuttack. Kānsāris and Kharurās who number 724 turn out brass and bell-metal utensils. They are not of very fine polish, but still they command a large sale in the State. Khadāls manufacture saltpetre. The outturn is small and it is consumed in the State. Catechu is manufactured in the forest by the Khairās. Chains, buttons, sticks and statues of fine workmanship—all of ivory—are manufactured by a few families at the headquarters of the State. The ivory work has won admiration from all quarters.

Trade. The principal commodities of export are: (1) rice, (2) timber, (3) cotton, (4) oil-seeds, (5) hide, (6) horns of deer and buffaloes, and (7) minor forest produce. Rice occupies the foremost place in the export trade of the State. Trade in timber is carried on by local men and some merchants from Cuttack. The *sāl* (Shorea robusta) of Nayāgarh is considered the best in Orissa. Cotton is exported chiefly to Ganjām in the Madras Presidency. It is mostly grown by Khonds in the western part of the State bordering on Ganjām. Hides are exported to Calcutta. Among minor forest produce are included Nux vomica and *gundi* (Mallotus philippinensis) dye. They are chiefly exported to the Ganjām district. The import trade consists of cotton piece-goods, salt, kerosene oil, iron and fancy goods. They command a very good market in the State.

MEANS OF COMMUNICATION. There is no railway. There is a metalled road from the headquarters to Khurdā railway station on the East Coast Section of the Bengal-Nāgpur Railway. It is in good condition. Another metalled road ten miles in length to the Ranpur border is in course of construction. This road will connect with the line at Kāluparāghāt railway station. There are no navigable rivers in the State. There is an Imperial sub-post office at the headquarters of the State and the imperial post plies *viâ* Khurdā.

LAND REVENUE ADMINISTRATION. The land revenue of the State rose from Rs. 43,673 to Rs. 74,937 in the last settlement. The revenue is realised by the *sarbarāhkārs* of whom there are 885 in the State. They pay the revenue direct into the treasury. They receive ten per cent. commission or *mālikānā* and enjoy *jāgīr* (service) lands varying from 1 to 108 acres of land. The *sarbarāhkār* is held responsible for realisation of land revenue. There are four *kists*, viz., 15th November, 15th December, 15th January, and 15th February, and the revenue is paid in four equal instalments. If there are any defaulters the *sarbarāhkār* files a list of them after the *kist*, and steps are taken against them under the certificate procedure. The Superintendent of the State, the Assistant Superintendent and the *Kānungos* make periodical tours in the interior to check any illegal cesses or *abwābs* being realised by the *sarbarāhkārs*. There is no road or public works cess on the land. Printed cheque receipts are granted for the payment of rent, the counterfoils are kept by the *sarbarāhkār*; *sihā* (daily receipts), and *wāsil-bāki* (rent-roll) are also kept by the *sarbarāhkār* and every precaution is taken to prevent the *sarbarāhkār* defrauding the ignorant tenants.

GENERAL ADMINISTRATION. The relations between the State and the British Government are regulated by the provisions of the *sanad* of 1908, and the State pays a tribute of Rs. 5,525. The State is now under the administration of Government owing to the minority of the Chief. The administration of the State rests with the Superintendent who is guided by the instructions of the Political Agent; there is also an Assistant Superintendent. All important civil and criminal and rent cases are tried by the Superintendent, who is in immediate charge of the Public Works Department, Forest, Police, Jail, Dispensary, and Education. The Chief and the Assistant Superintendent help in the disposal of criminal, civil, rent and miscellaneous cases.

Finances. In 1907-08 the income of the State was Rs. 1,40,473 and the expenditure Rs. 1,35,105: the State has been cleared of debt and the finances are on a sound footing.

Forests. The forest staff consists of one Ranger, one Forester, one Assistant Forester and 23 guards: the receipts under this head in 1907-08 amounted to Rs. 20,308. **Excise.** The excise revenue amounted to Rs. 9,503 in 1907-08.

Civil justice. The number of civil suits for disposal during the year 1907-08 was 951, most of which were of a petty nature, 65 per cent. of the total number being for sums below Rs. 50 in value.

Crime. The number of cases reported to the police in 1907-08 was 73, of which more than 50 per cent. were petty theft.

Police. The police staff consists of 1 Sub-Inspector, 10 Head-Constables, 10 writer-constables, and 35 men. There is besides a staff of reserve police officers consisting of one *Jamādār* (Head-Constable) and 20 men.

Jail. There is a good masonry jail recently constructed on modern and sanitary lines affording accommodation for 46 prisoners. In 1907-08 the average daily population was 24·4. **Public Works Department.** For the Public Works Department there is a Sub-Overseer, the work being under the control of a Joint Supervisor of the Wards States: during the year 1907-08 Rs. 45,668 was spent on public works.

EDUCATION. There are one Middle English, three Upper Primary, two Model Lower Primary schools for aborigines only, maintained entirely from State funds. Besides the above there are 71 Lower Primary schools which receive annual aid from the State funds. There is one separate girls' school at headquarters and one in the mufassil. There is an Ayurvedic institution and a *guru* training school. The total number of boys and girls attending all the schools in 1907-08 was 1,427 and 79 respectively: thus 2·04 per cent. of the total male population attended the schools in 1907-08. Education is backward, but is making steady progress, and the intelligent section of the population are anxious to give a high English education to their boys. The total annual expenditure in 1907-08 on education was Rs. 9,369. In 1907-08 the State received a grant of Rs. 2,113 from Government for primary education.

CHAPTER XVII.

NILGIRI STATE.

PHYSICAL ASPECTS.

THE State of Nīlgiri lies between 21° 17′ and 21° 37′ N., and 86° 25′ and 86° 50′ E., with an area of 278 square miles. It is bounded on the north and west by the State of Mayūrbhanj, and on the east and south by Balasore district. One-third of the area is taken up by hills, some of which contain valuable timber. There is much land awaiting reclamation. Valuable quarries of black stone are found and there are also good granite quarries in the hills close to Nīlgiri, the headquarters of the State. The climate is hot in the summer, but tempered by breezes from the sea: the average rainfall for the six years from 1902-03 to 1907-08 was 64·38 inches. The headquarters of the State are at Nīlgiri, 13 miles from the Balasore railway station on the Bengal-Nāgpur line and five miles from the Trunk Road from Calcutta to Madras. Nīlgiri contains the residence of the Chief, a fine building picturesquely situated at the foot of a fine range of hills: the public buildings consist of a dispensary with indoor accommodation, a jail, courts and public offices, a Middle English school, a commodious circuit-house and combined post and telegraph office.

HISTORY.

As regards the origin of the Nīlgiri Rāj family it is alleged that the State was founded in 1125 A.D., by two brothers who came from Chota Nāgpur. During the time of the Mughals, the tribute of the State having fallen into arrear, *kilā* Mangalpurpatnā and Talmundā were made into separate *tahsīls*, and the area of the State was thus considerably reduced. In the time of the Marāthās the zamīndārs of *parganas* Mukharā, Khejurī, Armalā, Kudāi, and Bānchās, in the Balasore district managed to get some of the eastern villages of the State included in their zamīndāris. The Rājā of Mayūrbhanj, too, is said to have taken possession of some of the villages on the north-west boundary, and included them in his State. The thirteenth Chief Nārāyan Basant Birāt Bhujang Māndhātā received the title of Harichandan from the Mahārājā of Orissa, for having ably defended the celebrated goddess of the State (Udarchandī) and her temple, which had been built by the Mahārājā—from the inroads of Kālāpahār. The fourteenth Chief was honoured in 1596 A.D. by the Mughal Emperor Akbar Shāh for having assisted his Wazīr, Mān Singh, during the attack on the Pathāns on the bank of the Subarnarekhā river, and for having humbled the pride of the Athkhunta Bhuiyās in Nīlgiri.

The fifteenth Chief obtained in 1611 A.D. the title of Mardarāj for the assistance he rendered to the Mughals against the Pathāns on the bank of the Subarnarekhā. The thirtieth Chief received from the Marāthās the title of Fateh Singh Bahādur for having assisted Motirām, the Marāthā *Fauzdār* at Balasore, in his war against the Jāmkundā Bhuiyās. The present Chief, a brother of the Chief of Mayūrbhanj, obtained the *gadi* by adoption. The Chief is a Kshattriya. The emblem of the State is the flower *karallā*.

THE PEOPLE. The population increased from 56,198 in 1891 to 66,460 in 1901; it is contained in 466 villages, and the density is 239 persons to the square mile. The most important village is Nīlgiri. Hindus number 58,896, Musalmāns, 101, Christians, 161, and Animists, 7,302. The most numerous castes are Khandaits (15,000), Bhumijes (6,000), Brāhmans (5,000) and Gauras and Hos (4,000 each). A small Christian community belonging to the American Free Baptist Mission is established at Mitrapur, 11 miles west of Balasore town. The Mission was started in 1855: the Christian community at Mitrapur numbers 80: an Upper Primary school is maintained and is attended by Christians, Pāns and Santāls and is open to all without distinction, The population is classified as follows:—Hindus – males, 29,479. females, 29,417, total 58,896 or 88·6 per cent. of the population of the State; proportion of males in total Hindus 34·7 per cent. Musalmāns—males, 80, females, 21, total 101 or 0·15 per cent. of the population. Animists – males, 3,581, females, 3,721, total 7,302 or 10·98 per cent. of the population. The number of persons able to read and write is 3,660 or 5·5 per cent. of the population. The average number of villages per square mile is 1·6; persons per village, 142; houses per village, 28·6; houses per square mile, 47; persons per house, 49. Of the 466 villages in the State there are 455 with less than five hundred, 10 with from five hundred to a thousand, and one with from one to two thousand inhabitants. The people are well off for the most part and fairly advanced, at any rate in the southern and eastern parts of the State owing to their close proximity to Balasore and the line of rail.

PUBLIC HEALTH. There is a good dispensary with indoor ward attached at the headquarters: a medical officer with the qualifications of an Assistant Surgeon is in charge assisted by a Civil Hospital Assistant, who also looks after vaccination work, and there is also a qualified female Civil Hospital Assistant for female patients. The total number of patients treated during the year 1907-08 was 7,004. The eastern and southern areas of the State are not unhealthy, but fever as usual is prevalent in the hill and forest areas. The State suffers from time to time from severe epidemics of cholera. Vaccination is carried on by licensed vaccinators, but is not popular: it has however recently made progress and in 1907-08 revaccination was successfully undertaken. In 1907-08 the number of primary vaccinations was 2,228 and that of revaccinations, 597.

AGRICULTURE. The soil is fertile and in the open country to the south and east the lands are well cultivated and abundant rice crops are raised. The villages in this area are prosperous and tanks for irrigation are common : no special attempts to introduce better varieties of seed or new crops have been made by the State.

RENTS, WAGES AND PRICES. The average rent per acre of first, second and third class rice lands is Rs. 2-0-8, Re. 1-9-0 and Re. 1-2-9 respectively and of uplands, Re. 1-0-8. During the period from 1893 to 1902 there has been a decided rise in wages by nearly 50 per cent. in the case of skilled labour with a somewhat smaller rise for unskilled labour : the average daily wage during that period has been as follows: superior mason, 6½ annas, common mason, 4 annas; superior carpenter, 6 annas, common carpenter, 4 annas; cooly, 2 annas; superior blacksmith, 4½ annas, and common blacksmith, 3¼ annas. The rate of wages is now likely to increase further with the opening of the granite quarries. During the same period the prices of rice, gram and salt have remained practically stationary and have averaged 18¾ seers, 11⅝ seers and 10⅜ seers respectively.

OCCUPATIONS, MANUFACTURES AND TRADE. Of the total population more than half, *i.e.*, 55·5 per cent live by agriculture : 15·97 per cent. follow industrial pursuits and 10·4 per cent., professions: 9·9 per cent. are engaged in trade. From the quarries of blackstone found in this State a considerable quantity of stone cups, bowls and platters are manufactured and exported. The granite quarries of the State are now being worked and it is intended to export the stone to Calcutta for road metal: the quarries are connected with the line of rail at Balasore by a tramway. The principal imported articles are spices, mill-made goods, kerosene oil, salt, cotton yarn, iron and brasswares, and the principal exported articles are paddy, rice, soapstone, stoneware, tusser cocoons, myrobalan, timber, fuel, horns and hides.

MEANS OF COMMUNICATION. There is a good road from the headquarters linking up with the Madras Grand Trunk Road : by this route Balasore is

13 miles distant from the headquarters: a fair surface road runs up to the border of Kaptipadā, an estate in Mayūrbhanj with a rest-house close to the border: there is also a surface road to Mitrapur: there is a good bungalow for travellers at the headquarters. The headquarters of the State are connected with the Balasore town by a telegraph line and the imperial post runs to and from the headquarters *viâ* Balasore.

LAND REVENUE ADMINISTRATION. The land revenue system is similar to that prevailing in the other States: the land revenue demand is Rs. 53,689. The last settlement was completed in 1898. There are no zamīndāris in the State and no cesses are levied.

GENERAL ADMINISTRATION. The terms of the *sanad* granted in 1894, which was revised in 1908, regulate the relation between the State and the British Government: an annual tribute of Rs. 3,900 is paid. **Finances.** The State has an estimated income of about Rs. 1,37,000. **Forest.** In the year 1907-08 the forest revenue amounted to Rs. 12,555. **Civil justice.** Civil suits are numerous, but petty: the number of suits instituted in 1907-08 was 350. **Crime.** Crime mostly consists of petty theft and burglary. The number of cases reported to the police in 1907-08 was 225. **Police.** The police force consists of one Inspector, 3 Sub-Inspectors, 4 Head-Constables and 36 men. **Jail.** The jail accommodation is small and a new jail is about to be erected. In 1907-08 the average daily population was 13. **Public Works Department.** There is a regular Public Works Department and the State has good public buildings. In 1907-08 the State spent Rs. 47,261 on account of public works.

EDUCATION. In 1907-08 the number of schools in the State was 87, consisting of one Middle English school, 10 Upper Primary schools, 37 Lower Primary schools, two Sanskrit *tols* and one *Guru*-training school. The number of students on the rolls was 1,987, and the expenditure by the State amounted to Rs. 11,692 and the grant from Government was Rs. 2,347. The people are appreciative of the benefits of education and several of the Lower Primary schools are privately maintained. Special attention is paid to the education of the Santāls. There are two special schools for girls and one for aborigines.

CHAPTER XVIII.

PAL LAHARA STATE.

PHYSICAL ASPECTS.

THE State of Pāl Laharā lies between 21° 9′ and 21° 41′ N., and 85° 0′ and 85° 24′ E., with an area of 452 square miles. It is bounded on the north by the Bonai State; on the east by the Keonjhar State; on the south by the Tālcher State; and on the west by the Bāmra State. The east and north of the State are occupied by hills. A magnificent hill, Malayagiri (3,895 feet), one of the loftiest peaks in the States of Orissa, towers above the lesser ranges. The State is for the most part a region of wild hill ranges densely covered with forest in which *sāl* (*Shorea robusta*) abounds. The *sāl* forests are the finest in Orissa, but are, from the nature of the country, very inaccessible: towards the south on the Tālcher border there is a certain extent of open country dispersed with smaller hill ranges. The high hills to the north form the central portion of the mass of tangled hill ranges, which stretch into the Bonai and Keonjhar States. There are no rivers in the State, but numerous hill streams which frequently come down in heavy spate sweeping away the hamlets perched on their banks. The distinguishing feature of the country is the Malayagiri peak; the ascent is made from the south-western side and a rough hill-path has been made: the ascent is steep and prolonged, but presents no real difficulty to the transport of goods by hand. The path winds up over bold spurs with magnificent views of the plains of the Tālcher and Dhenkānāl States in the distance, and two ranges are climbed before the final ascent is reached. The actual summit is a narrow plateau nowhere more than half a mile wide and in parts less. It is formed by a depression on the top of the hill and is about half a mile long; at either end rise up two bold peaks of bare rock: the western peak is the actual summit of Malayagiri and rises almost precipitously: on its western and northern fronts it is quite inaccessible and falls away in a sheer precipice of many hundred feet: below to the west stretches out a fine range of hills running westwards in two parallel ridges with a valley between them, the level of the valley being about 1,500 feet: seen from above the range gives the appearance of a vast trough clad with dense forest : to the north-east the whole range of Malayagiri falls away precipitously : for a distance of nearly half a mile the hill on the south-western side slopes away fairly gradually and on this side would afford suitable sites for building but the area is limited : there is a spring near the top of the hill on the south-western side and a small reservoir has been constructed. The Chief has erected a small bungalow on the summit. The average rainfall for the six years from 1902-03 to 1907-08 was 60·07 inches. The headquarters of the State are at Pāl Laharā.

HISTORY. This State is alleged to have been founded by Santosh Pāl of Dharānagar, some time before the 18th century. The original limits of the State cannot be accurately given. During the 18th century the State appears to have attained its largest limits, consisting of 198 villages, 131 of which were subsequently forcibly taken possession of by the Keonjhar, Tālcher and Dhenkānāl Rājās, leaving under its sway only 67 villages, which now comprise an area of 452 square miles.

No Chief of Pāl Laharā is said to have obtained any *farmān* or *sanad* from the Mughals or Marāthās. The Chiefs of this State were formerly styled zamīndārs. The late Chief received from Government the personal title of Rājā Bahādur, in recognition of the services he rendered in suppressing the Bhuiyā rebellion in Keonjhar in 1867-68 A.D. In 1874 A.D. he was vested with the hereditary title of Rājā. No Mādalā Pānji or any family history of the Rāj family is available ; tradition, however, runs that Santosh Pāl was the founder of the present ruling family. He is said to have belonged to the Paumar Rājputs of Dharānagar. He went to Purī on pilgrimage with a body of followers, and while returning home was selected by the Savars, Khonds, Malhārs, and Jhorās as their Chief. He settled at Laharā and subdued the aboriginal tribes who were then contending among themselves for supremacy. He was called Pāl because the Savars concealed him under a heap of straw (*pāla*) while fighting with his followers, who were all defeated and put to death. From the official enquiries that were made during the settlement of the dispute that arose between the Mahārājā of Keonjhar and the zamīndār of Pāl Laharā regarding the supremacy of the former, it was stated that 52 generations had already held sway in Pāl Laharā up to A.D. 1778. During that year the Chief, Muni Pāl, died without male issue. After his death the management of the State remained for about 47 years in the exclusive hands of his mother, Anna Pūrnā, and of his illegitimate brother Nanda Pāl.

Anna Pūrnā died in A.D. 1815. Nanda Pāl acknowledged the supremacy of Keonjhar and remained in charge of the management of the State till he died in 1825. The people of Pāl Laharā after his death resisted the claims of Keonjhar, but being defeated, submitted a petition to Colonel Gilbert, the then Political Agent of the South-Western Frontier. Colonel Gilbert ordered the withdrawal of the Keonjhar force from Pāl Laharā, and allowed the people to select their own Chief. They chose one Baidya Nāth Pāl, one of the paternal uncles of the late Chief Muni Pāl, whose family has since held the *gadi* for three generations.

The titles of "Ganeswar Pāl" and "Muni Pāl" are assumed alternately by the successive Rājās of Pāl Laharā when succeeding to the *gadi*. The emblem of the State is a cobra.

The population increased from 19,700 in 1891 to 22,351 in 1901; it is distributed among 265 villages. The density is 49 persons to the square mile, or less than in any other of the Orissa States except Rairākhol and Bonai. Hindus number 20,770, Animists 1,540, and Muhammadans 41, the most numerous castes being Chasās (5,000) and Pāns (4,000). The leaf-wearing Juāngs are still met with in the outskirts of the Malayagiri range. They are extremely shy and retiring, but still wear their costumes of *asan* leaves in the more remote portions of this State and in some of the inaccessible recesses of the neighbouring hill ranges of Bonai and Keonjhar: the costume consists of a few leaves pinned together worn over the person by men and in the case of women an apron made of leaves is worn: no other covering is worn. The population is classified as follows:—Hindus—males, 10,134, females, 10,636, total of Hindus, 20,770 or 92·9 per cent. of the population of the State; proportion of males in total Hindus, 48·7 per cent. Musalmāns—males, 25, females, 16, total of Musalmāns 41 or 0·18 per cent. of the population; proportion of males in total Musalmāns 60·9 per cent. Christians—*nil*. Population of all denominations—males, 10,861, females, 11,490; proportion of males in total population, 48·5 per cent. The number of persons able to read and write is 518 or 2·3 per cent of the total population. Averages—Villages per square mile 0·58; persons per village 84; houses per square mile 11; houses per village 19·5; persons per house 4·3. Of the aboriginal tribes the Savars are the most numerous. The Bhuiyās inhabit the hills and high valley lands to the north which with the ranges stretching into Bonai and Keonjhar form their ancestral homes. The people are extremely backward, but contented, their demands are few and they live

THE PEOPLE.

for preference very largely on forest fruits and roots. There are 265 villages in the State, but in none does the population amount to five hundred.

PUBLIC HEALTH. The nature of the country renders it very unhealthy to strangers who suffer severely from malaria. The inhabitants suffer to a certain extent from malaria, but not to such a degree as would be expected, from the dense jungle and heavy rainfall. The vital statistics for ten years from 1893 to 1902 show the average ratio of births per mille as 18·38 and deaths 10·42, but little reliance can be placed on them. There is a small dispensary at headquarters with an indoor ward in charge of a Civil Hospital Assistant: 3,690 patients were treated in 1907-08. Vaccination is in charge of a special Civil Hospital Assistant who also renders medical aid in the interior and attends to village sanitation: 1,164 children were vaccinated in 1907-08; of this number 655 were primary vaccinations and 509 re-vaccinations. The aboriginal and backward tribes are very averse to vaccination.

AGRICULTURE. Agriculture is of the crudest. The system most popular is to cut the light forest in the hill sides, burn it and raise a crop on it for one or two years and then abandon the site. The Juāngs, in especial, practise only this form of cultivation and, endeavours are being made by grants of seed and bullocks to induce them to settle down to regular cultivation. The cultivation of the plain country is very inferior and every tenant as far as possible practises *dāhi* cultivation as well. The coarse varieties of rice are grown and also millets. The total acreage of the State is 289,280 acres, of which 262,352 are forests, unculturable waste 4,297; the normal area under crops is 16,982 acres, of which 9,810 acres are under rice: oil-seeds are normally sown on 3,250 acres, of which 1,400 acres are under linseed and 1,250 under *til* (sesamum); 400 acres are normally under *māndiā* and 600 under maize.

RENTS, WAGES AND PRICES. The assessment is light and the average rate for first, second and third class rice lands is Rs. 2-7-6, Rs. 2-1-4 and Re. 1-11-1, respectively per acre and for uplands, Re. 0-14-0 per acre. During the period from 1893 to 1902 the rate of daily wages has remained stationary and has averaged as follows: superior mason, six annas, common mason, four annas, superior carpenter, six annas, common carpenter, four annas, cooly, $2\frac{1}{2}$ annas, superior blacksmith, six annas, common blacksmith, four annas. The price of rice, gram and salt during the same period has shown no tendency to rise and the rates have averaged $25\frac{5}{8}$ seers, $33\frac{3}{16}$ seers and $7\frac{5}{8}$ seers respectively.

Occupations, Manufactures and Trade. The only occupations followed are the cultivation of lac and rearing of tusser cocoons, the collection of wild honey, myrobalans and other forest produce by the jungle tribes. Trade in the real sense there is none : a certain amount of timber is sold and exported and traders barter for the jungle products with salt, tobacco and spices.

Means of Communication. There is a good road from the headquarters south to Sibpur in the Tālcher State and the same road continues on the north-east to the border of Keonjhar : this portion of the road and its continuation due west to the border of the Bāmra State was formerly the old Sambalpur-Midnapore road.

There is a staging bungalow at the headquarters and at Kamār, an important village on the road to Tālcher. There is a post office at headquarters and the post travels *viâ* Tālcher to Angul.

Revenue Administration. The last settlement was made under Government direction in 1905-06 during the period the State was under Court of Wards : special care was taken to enforce the prohibition against sale, mortgage or transfer of holdings and to guard against the lands of aboriginals being leased out by the village headmen to the more advanced class of cultivators ; long rent-free periods are granted to clearers of new cultivation. The land revenue demand is Rs. 21,237, and is collected without difficulty : the Bhuiyās pay a house tax of Re. 1 per house per annum : besides this they pay in kind one *khandi* (35 seers) of *bīrhi* per house per annum.

General Administration. As in the case of the other States of the group formerly known as the Tributary Mahāls of Orissa the *sanad* of 1908 regulates the relationship between the State and the British Government. The State has for some years been on account of minority under Government management and has only recently been restored to the Chief, who conducts the administration with the assistance of a *Dīwān.* The Chief on succession is bound to pay *nazarāna* to the British Government. **Finances.** The State pays to the British Government a tribute of Rs. 267, and its annual revenue is about Rs. 38,000. The income of the State is very limited and its finances have to be very carefully administered. The State contains some of the finest *sāl* (*Shorea robusta*) forests in Orissa, and **Forests.** during the period of administration by Government a regular forest department was created under a qualified forest officer and detailed forest rules introduced: the forests were divided into reserved and protected and demarcation and survey has been practically completed. The finest range is that of Malayagiri. The forests yielded a revenue of Rs. 6,952 in 1907-08 and the

Excise. revenue is expanding. The excise revenue amounted to Rs. 1,630 in 1907-08. Civil justice. Institutions of civil suits are very few and the suits are of a petty nature; in 1907-08 the number of civil suits instituted was 22 only, of which 80·9 per cent were below the value of Rs. 50. Crime. Crime is exceedingly light: the number of cases reported to the police in 1907-08 was 121. Police. The police force consists of one Sub-Inspector, 4 Head-Constables and 14 constables. Jail. The jail has accommodation for 10 prisoners. Public Works. The State possesses the necessary public buildings, but only the courts and offices are masonry. The State spent Rs. 2,647 on account of public works in 1807-08.

EDUCATION. The State maintains an Upper Primary school at the headquarters and 32 aided Lower Primary schools. The total number of pupils reading in schools in 1907-08 was 577. The Upper Primary school at headquarters is a commodious building with a hostel attached. The Government grant amounted in 1907-08 to Rs. 360. Education is extremely backward and there is little or no demand for it by the people: under great difficulty parents are persuaded to send their boys to school and then constantly take them away to roam the forests.

CHAPTER XIX.

PATNA STATE.

PHYSICAL ASPECTS.

The State of Patnā, in Orissa, lies between 20° 9′ and 21° 4′ N., and between 82° 41′ and 83° 40′ E.; and is bounded on the north by the Borāsambar zamīndāri of the Sambalpur district; on the east by the State of Sonpur; on the west by the zamīndāri of Khariār, belonging to the Raipur district in the Central Provinces; and on the south by the State of Kālāhandī. The average length is about fifty miles long by as many miles broad, with an area of 2,399 square miles. The country is an undulating plain, rugged and isolated, with hill-ranges rising in various directions, a lofty irregular range forming a natural boundary to the north. The soil is for the most part light and sandy, about two-thirds of the whole area are under cultivation, the rest being for the most part forests and scrub-jungle. The main forest area of the State stretches along the western boundary starting from Bangomundā in the Patnā State and running parallel with the border of the Khariār zamīndāri, in the Raipur district and then turning to the north runs parallel with the Borāsambar zamīndāri of the Sambalpur district. This tract is broken by occasional clearings and small settlements, but is for the most part dense forest in which bamboo of excellent quality predominates and fine *sāl* (Shorea robusta), *sahāj* (Terminalia tomentosa), *piāsāl* (Pterocarpus marsupium), *dhaurā* (Lagarstæmia parviflora) and ebony (Diospyros melanoxylon), are the principal timber with *sāl* predominating. In the forests tiger, leopard, bison, bear, spotted and barking deer, *sambar* and mouse deer are met with. The finest compact forest area starts near Haldi, about 10 miles south-east of Bangomundā and stretches away to the south and east through Lapher, gradually thinning out till it meets the main road which runs south through the State from Bolāngir, the headquarters, to Kālāhandī: this tract contains *sāl* of fine quality in abundance. From Bolāngir to the Tel river large tracts of light forest extend to a considerable distance on both sides of the main road and contain some good *sāl*, *piāsāl*, *sahāj* and other timber, but are considerably broken up by cultivation, and there are some large villages located in this area, the principal being Deogaon and Saintalā. At a distance of 7 miles from Bolāngir there is a fine range of hills carrying excellent timber and the tract is kept as reserved forest: from this range rises the high peak Muktāi (2,259 feet): this peak is a conspicuous feature in the landscape for many miles from Bolāngir. The north-western boundary is formed by the magnificent range of hills known as Gandha Mardan, which separates the Patnā State at this point from the Borāsambar zamīndāri. On the northern crest of this range springs the famous stream which descends to the foot of the hill in fine waterfalls and finally issues forth to the plains at Narsinghnāth, a sacred and famous place of pilgrimage in the Sambalpur district: on the southern slope a similar stream issues from the crest of the range and is known as Harisankar, and at the foot of the hill, a few miles from the village Sargipāli in the Pātnā State, where the stream reaches the plains, there is a fine orange grove and temple, frequented by pilgrims. The crest of this range of hills is a fine plateau some ten miles long with an average height of 3,000 feet and rising as high as 3,234 feet. The principal rivers are, the Tel, which forms the boundary on the south-east between Patnā and Kālāhandī; the Ang, which divides Patnā from the Sonpur State on the north; the Suktel, and the Sunder.

The temperature is very much the same as that of the plains elsewhere; in the cool months the thermometer is often as low as 45° F. at daybreak, and at midday rarely rises above 80°. The hot months are from April to the middle of June, the thermometer rising then sometimes as high as 112° in the shade. The average rainfall during the 14 years from 1894-95 to 1907-08 was 52·18 inches. The climate in the more open areas of the State is healthy and the headquarters of the State are certainly salubrious. The forest areas are naturally malarious, and strangers moving through them or settling in their neighbourhood suffer greatly from fever, but the indigenous settlers are robust and healthy in appearance. Iron ore and graphite occur in the south of the State.

HISTORY. The Patnā State was formerly the most important of all the States attached to the Sambalpur district, and the head of a cluster of States known as the eighteen Garhjāts or forts. According to tradition one Ramāi Deva, of the Chauhān race, obtained the *gadi* of the Patnā State some 600 years ago. While the Chauhān family may perhaps have held their *gadi* for twenty-seven generations, it is hardly likely that this family dates back more than five hundred years, and an inscription on a stone discovered in the Patnā State throws light on this point. The inscription referred to bears the date 1253 of the Sālibāhana era (1351 A.D.) which was in vogue with the Chiefs of the Gangabansa family: and the inference is that at the date of the inscription, which is thus 557 years old, the Patnā State was held by Gangabansī Chiefs. It may, however, be accepted that the period, the Chauhān family held the *gadi* of the State, extends back for a period of not much less than five hundred years.

As to the families which preceded the Chauhāns, there seems reason for believing that the State was at one time under the Sūryabansī Rājās. There exists at the present time in fair preservation at Sālebhattā in the Patnā State an ancient temple dedicated to Birinchi Nārāyan Devatā, the sun-god. Images dug up on the spot establish the nature of the worship originally practised there, and the form of the images, as well as the design of the temple, tally precisely with those found in the temple at Baidyanāth, in the Sonpur State, which contains inherent evidence of being the work of Sūryabansī Chiefs. No archæological remains of more ancient date than those ascribed to the Sūryabansīs have been discovered either in Patnā or in the adjacent States, and tradition assigns to that family the earliest administration of Patnā.

Another curious fact is that at Rānīpur-Jhariā, in the south of the Patnā State a stone was found in one of the many ancient temples that exist there, inscribed with the name of Someswar Deva. Similar inscriptions appear to have been found in the Bastar State, and these facts would imply that the Bastar State and the southern portion of the Patnā State were formerly under one and the same Chief. More satisfactory evidence exists to show that at a comparatively recent period the Patnā State was under the sway of the Rājās of Vizianagram. Tradition among the Khonds asserts that they at one time paid taxes to the Rājās of Kalinga, which is to this day a common term to describe the Vizagapatam littoral. Moreover a copper lease or *tambā-pattā* granted by a former Vizianagram Chief to the ancient holders of the village of Bakatī in Patnā, and the discovery of a similar lease relating to a village in the Sonpur State go far to confirm the tradition that the Vizianagram Chief's power extended to Patnā. Chiefs of the Bhojbans family are also said to have held the *gadi* of Patnā for some time and the tank at Patnāgarh called the Bhawasāgar is attributed to them ; but tradition regarding them is vague.

Coming to more recent times it would appear that the Chauhān family which was inaugurated by Ramāi Deva was immediately preceded by a state of affairs under which the

Pātnā State was administered by eight joint superiors each of whom held power by turn for one day at a time, the eight Chiefs being each in charge of a *garh* or fort and their administration being called the *Ath-mālik*.

Representatives of these Chiefs are found even at the present day in Patnā, and though the living claimants may have but shadowy titles to represent the former Chiefs, the manner in which the *Ath-mālik* administration was succeeded by that of Ramāi Deva is described by local tradition with such detail as to bear the semblance of truth. As it is the turning point in the claim of the Chauhān family to be descended from the Rājput Rājās of Garh Shambar, it is worth mentioning.

It is said that one Hamīr Deva had fled from Garh Shambar and established himself at Mānikgarh fort in the hills of Khariār. On one occasion before proceeding to battle he took leave of his seven wives and told them that should he not return they would be apprised of his death by the homeward flight of some carrier pigeons. He failed to return and was never afterwards heard of; the return of the pigeons satisfied his Rānīs that he had fallen. Six of them drowned themselves in the pool called Rāmdarha near Narsinghnāth to the north of the Patnā State and the remaining Rānī was found wandering in the jungles near Rāmud on the border between Patnā and Khariār. She was kindly treated by her preserver, a Binjhāl: in due course she was delivered of a child—Ramāi Deva—who put an end to the *Ath-mālik gadi* by murdering the eight Chiefs and himself assuming supremacy over the eight *garhs* (forts) which he welded into the compact State of Patnā, and thus introduced the administration of the Chauhān family. The precise spot of Ramāi Deva's birth is still pointed out, and the circumstances under which it occurred are still described with interest by those conversant with Patnā traditions.

A detailed account of the Patnā family was written by Major Impey in 1863, from which the following sketch is abstracted.

The Mahārājās of Pātnā claim direct descent from a race of Rājput Rājās of Garh Shambar, near Mainpurī and trace it through thirty-one generations. It is alleged that Hitāmbar Singh, the last of these Rājās, offended the Rājā of Delhi and was killed; that his family had to abandon their country and fly in every direction; and that one of his wives who was at the time *enceinte*, found her way down to Patnā. Patnā was, it seems, at that time, represented by a cluster of eight *garhs* (forts) and the Chief of each *garh* took it in turn to hold powers for a day over the whole. The Chief of Khulāgarh received the Rānī kindly and in due time she gave birth to a boy, who was called Ramāi Deva. The Chief adopted him and eventually abdicated in his favour, and when it came to his turn to hold powers over the whole, he took the first opportunity of causing the Chiefs of the other seven *garhs* to be murdered and setting himself up as the Chief over the whole with the title of Mahārājā. He contrived to preserve his position through the influence that he obtained by a marriage with a daughter of the then Rājā of Orissa. Between the periods of Ramāi Deva and Baijal Deva II, the tenth Mahārājā or during a period of some 300 years, there was a considerable acquisition of territory made by Patnā, viz., the States of Khariār and Bindrā Nawāgarh on the west; Phuljhar and Sārangarh to the north; Bonai, Gāngpur and Bāmra to the north-east, which were all made tributary dependencies; while the zamīndāri of Rairākhol, as well as a tract of land to the eastward on the left bank of the Mahānadī, was annexed. A fort was erected in Phuljhar, and the Chandrapur *pargana* (tract), also on the left bank of the Mahānadī, was forcibly wrested from the Chief of Ratanpur. Narsingh Deva, the twelfth Mahārājā of Patnā, ceded to his brother Balrām Deva all such portions of his territories as lay north of the river Ang. The latter founded a new State (Sambalpur) which very soon afterwards by acquisition of territory in every direction became the most powerful of all the Garhjāts; while from the same time the power of Patnā commenced to decline.

Garh Shambar was the famous seat of Chauhān power in Rājputāna, while Mainpurī was apparently in the United Provinces of Agra and Oudh. The following account gives a fairly correct and accurate description of the Rāj family.

It appears from the Koshlānand, a local work on the history of the Patnā Rāj family, that Baijal Deva, the third Chief from Ramāi Deva, was the most powerful Chief and extended his dominions far and wide. He fought with Rām Chandra and Mahāling, Gajapatis of Orissa for six years. Bāmra was reduced to an annual tribute of 16 elephants. Gāngpur, Bonai, and other neighbouring States submitted without a fight, and Baud and Sirguja also submitted. It is said that 72 Chiefs were made tributary to Patnā by Baijal Deva I. Dhenkānāl was also subdued and the temple of the golden Mahādeo at Sonpur was built by him.

Batsarāj Deva, the successor of Baijal Deva I, was defeated by the Orissa Chief, who seems to have overrun the Patnā State and defeated its Chief. Nothing of importance happened in the time of the next six Chiefs.

The Chief Bhanjan Hīrādhar Deva was called to Purī by the Gajapati and made a prisoner for 10 months. Hīrādhar Deva then attacked Orissa with a very large army and defeated Rām Chandra Deva Gajapati and entered into a treaty with him.

It was about this time that there was a war with Bastar. The Rājā of Bastar was taken prisoner and put to death, and his brother was placed on the *gadi* of Bastar on the condition of his agreeing to pay an annual tribute of Rs. 30,000. A sister of the Patnā Mahārājā was at this time married to Mukunda Deva Gajapati of Orissa. Mahārājā Bhūpāl Deva, the 24th Chief from Ramāi Deva, granted the Jarāsinghā zamīndāri as a maintenance grant to his younger brother Jugrāj Singh. He also granted the Agalpur zamīndāri to his 6 sons for their maintenance.

In 1755 A.D. the State fell under the dominion of the Marāthās of Nāgpur, but was ceded to the British Government by the treaty of 1803 with Raghujī Bhonslā. It was restored to the Marāthās in 1806, and in 1818 reverted again to the British Government. On this occasion many dependencies of Pātnā were separated from it and made independent. The State was under the control of the Bengal Government till 1861, when it was included in the Central Provinces. Enquiries made between 1863 and 1866 into the status of the Chiefs and zamīndārs of the Central Provinces resulted in Pātnā being classed as a Feudatory State.

Mahārājā Hīrā Bajra Deva died in 1866 A.D. In 1869 owing to mismanagement there was a rising of the Khonds. It was suppressed, but it was believed that the Chief's brother Lāl Bishnāth Singh and his followers had committed many atrocities : for these crimes Lāl Bishnāth Singh was removed from the State, the Chief himself deposed and the State passed under Court of Wards in 1871. Mahārājā Sūr Pratāp Deva died in 1878 leaving no male issue. He was succeeded by his brother's son Rām Chandra Singh Deva who was educated at the Jabbalpur Rājkumār College. The Court of Wards' management was withdrawn in 1894: the Chief died on 8th June 1895. As he left no male issue he was succeeded by his uncle Mahārājā Dalganjan Singh Deva, who was born in 1856. In 1900 the State suffered severely from famine, and want of control led to a severe out-break of dacoity which extended into the Sambalpur district. A force of Government police had to be deputed to Patnā to suppress the outbreak.

The State was transferred from the Central Provinces and placed under the charge of the Commissioner of the Orissa Division on the 16th October 1905.

The family intermarries with Mayūrbhanj, Bāmra, Kālāhandī, Bastar and Baud. The emblem of the family is the *chakra* (quoit).

THE PEOPLE. The population of the State in 1901 numbered 277,748, composed chiefly of the agricultural classes. The most common Hindu castes are Brāhmans, Mahāntis, Rājputs, Agariās, and Kaltuyās (or Kolthās). The aboriginal tribes are the Gonds, Khonds and Binjhāls (Binjhwārs). The population is classified as follows:—Hindus—males, 113,110; females, 115,985; total 229,095, *i.e.* 82·5 per cent. of the total population; proportion of males in total Hindu population is 49·4 per cent. Musalmāns—males, 296; females, 216; total, 512, *i.e.*, 0·18 per cent. of the total population; proportion of males in total Musalmān population is 57·8 per cent. Animists—males, 22,991; females, 24,976; total 47,967, *i.e.*, 17·3 per cent. of the total population; proportion of males in total Animist population is 47·9 per cent. Christians—males, 71; females, 71; total 142. Jains—males, 20; females, 12; total 32. The number of persons able to read and write is 5,142 or 1·9 per cent. of the total population. The State contains 1,850 villages which may be classified as follows:—1,773 villages with less than 500 inhabitants; 69 with from 500 to 1,000 inhabitants; 7 with from 1,000 to 2,000 inhabitants and 1 with from 2,000 to 5,000 inhabitants. Averages—villages per square mile, 0·77; persons per village, 150; houses per village, 29·5; houses per square mile, 22·7; persons per house, 5·09. The density of population is 116 persons per square mile.

Of the earliest inhabitants of Patnā the aboriginal tribes of Binjhāls (who are said to have come from the Nīlgiris in Madras) and of Savars, appear to be the oldest and to have preceded the Khonds. The original home of the Khonds is said to have been in the hill tracts of Baud and Kimedi, and the order in which the successive Khond tribes travelled east and northward and the chief places they traversed on their route through the north-east of Kālāhandī in their migration towards Patnā are still mentioned in their ancient lore. The first immigration of the Khonds into Patnā is said to have occurred during the period of the Gangabansī Rājās, and to have continued late into the period of the Chauhān family. And the fact that some of the present leading Khond families in Patnā still intermarry in Baud and in the tracts said to have been traversed by the Khonds in the course of their movement eastwards, gives colour to their version of the events connected with their early immigration. The Khonds now found in the Patnā State have assimilated themselves in many ways to their Hindu brethren. They have taken largely to regular cultivation though at the same time they continue like all the people of these parts to practise *dāhi* cultivation. They have adopted the Oriyā language and do not take water from or intermarry with their wilder brethren living in the hill tracts of Kālāhandī and the neighbouring regions.

MISSION. The Baptist Missionary Society has a sub-station at Loisinghā: the mission was started in 1893. The mission in 1907 had one assistant missionary and one evangelist at work: the mission employs 12 school-masters in charge of day and Sunday schools and the number of scholars attending in 1907 was 234: the total Christian community of the mission numbers 1,371 souls with 350 church members: the work at present is almost entirely confined to the Gandā caste.

PUBLIC HEALTH. The country in the cultivated area is healthy and the people suffer as a rule from only the ordinary ailments. The forest tracts are feverish and malarial fever is common: the original settlers, however, are sturdy and robust and fever makes no great inroads upon them. The old headquarters of the State at Pātnāgarh are notoriously unhealthy, but this is due to the presence of a large number of abandoned tanks, which are stagnant and with no drainage. There is a fine dispensary at headquarters with excellent accommodation for males and females and a separate ward for low caste patients. The institution is in charge of an Assistant Surgeon and Civil Hospital Assistant and is well found with surgical instruments and medicines: in 1907-08 the number of patients treated was 25,819 and the daily average attendance was 144·8. The State is subject to periodical visitations of cholera. Of late years small-pox has been almost unknown in the State: this has been due to the energetic and universal system of vaccination and re-vaccination practised in the State: vaccination is entirely free and is supervised by an Inspector: in 1907-08 the number of primary vaccinations was 11,932 and of re-vaccinations, 21,045.

AGRICULTURE. The best cultivation of the State is found in the northern portion of the State, part of the Agalpur zamīndāri, and to the east and west of the main road from the Sambalpur district: from Bolāngir, the headquarters, southwards the country is largely broken by undulating forest land, for the most part unsuitable for cultivation, but here and there in this tract considerable areas of very fertile lands and prosperous villages are met with. The principal crop is rice: oil-seeds, pulses, sugarcane and cotton are, however, grown to a considerable extent and very rich crops of *til* (sesamum) are raised. In many villages good tanks and embankments exist: the fields are terraced and the country readily lends itself to irrigation. The cultivation practised is, however, not of a high order and the wasteful system of *dāhi* or *jhuming* is practised to a considerable extent. There is no experimental farm in the State and nothing has been done to introduce new crops or improve the quality of seed grain. The soils are classified as follows :—(1) *Khaliā.*—Hard white clay, sometimes mixed with lime concrete. It varies as follows :—(*a*) *Chāndi khaliā.*—White in colour and very hard. (*b*) *Gut khaliā.*—A white, hard and saline clay. (*c*) *Gengti khaliā.*—White and hard, mixed with lime-stone. (*d*) Ordinary *khaliā.*—Or agricultural clay. (2) *Bāhā.*—Sandy soil. If it is mixed with clay it is called *pandakāpithiā.* It is a good rice soil. (3) *Badmattā* or *kanhār.*—Black cotton soil. In the *Khondān* tracts (the southern area of the State inhabited mostly by the Khonds) it is called *malawā.* (4) *Pankuā* or *kachhariā* —Low lying land on the banks of rivers. (5) *Rugudiā.*—Gritty soil. **Kinds of soil.**

The classification of the land for assessment is as follows :—(1) *At.*—The high land which is dependent entirely on the rainfall for its moisture. (2) *Māl.*--Embanked land lying high on a slope. (3) *Bernā.*--Land lying along the main surface drainage and embanked. (4) *Bāhāl.*—The low lying land on the main surface drainage and embanked. When these four classes of land are situated beneath a tank they are known as irrigated *āt*, *māl*, *bernā* and *bāhāl.* (5) *Khāri.*—Manured land round the village site, and which receives the village drainage. (6) *Barchhā.*—Sugarcane land. These plots are generally prepared on *āt* or *māl* lands, and are irrigated from wells. The plot is alternately sown with cane and pulses or wheat occasionally. (7) *Bāri.*—Plots attached to the house and fenced in. **Land classification.**

The various kinds of rice, pulses, oil-seeds and vegetables grown in the State are :—(1) *At dhān*, of which the following varieties are grown :—(1) *Sitābhog*, (2) *Pandernuākhāi*, (3) *Bhudoshingeri*, (4) *Satkā*, (5) *Sariā*, (6) *Sankrā*, (7) *Dhobli* or *chāulimenjo*, (8) *Kalechi*, (9) *Palsāphul*, (10) *Kurāiphul*, (11) *Sukunābhātā* and (12) *Rāni* or *Lakshmīkajal.* These ripen in the months of Bhādraba and Dasharā (September). (2) *Māl dhān* the varieties grown being, (1) *Badkusma*, (2) *Karni*, (3) *Hiranjhutri*, (4) *Dāhikharkuili*, (5) *Sānbento*, (6) *Mālpathri*, (7) *Tāmbdiā*, (8) *Dāhipudinā*, (9) *Dāhichitri*, (10) *Jhuler*, (11) *Kankriā*, (12) *Sānkesri* and (13) *Bīramani.* These ripen between Dasharā and Kārttik (October). (3) *Bernā dhān*, this consists of the following varieties :—(1) *Dudhkhadikā*, (2) *Kālīkuji*, (3) *Bānko*, (4) *Rāisiri*, (5) *Kankriā*, (6) *Phuler* and (7) *Suāthunti.* These ripen in the month of Kartik (November). (4) *Bāhāl dhān*, there are **Rice.**

27 varieties known in the State, viz:—(1) *Bātrāj*, (2) *Baidyarāj*, (3) *Pathri*, (4) *Ruknibhog*, (5) *Raghusāi*, (6) *Goindi*, (7) *Rājgoindi*, (8) *Makarkām*, (9) *Nuniāpān*, (10) *Mahārāji*, (11) *Chināmāl*, (12) *Jhiliparāgi*, (13) *Sunāpān*, (14) *Samudrabāli*, (15) *Krishnakalā*, (16) *Rādhāballav*, (17) *Tulsikanthi*, (18) *Ratanchuri*, (19) *Hundā*, (20) *Sagardhuli*, (21) *Matiā*, (22) *Jalchingri*, (23) *Tentuliā*, (24) *Badkharkuili*, (25) *Haldigundi*, (26) *Charāiguri* and (27) *Agmāchhī*. These ripen in the month of December. The four kinds of paddy (rice) represent 58 per cent. of the total cropped area of the State. The paddy is mostly sown broadcast, and the sowings are known as (*a*) *Kharadi* which takes place before the break of the monsoon; (*b*) *Batri*, just after the rains have broken; (*c*) *Achhrā* or *gajrā*, this is the latest sowing. The seed which has previously been steeped in water and germinated, is sown broadcast. When the paddy sown broadcast is about six inches high, the land is again ploughed, this operation is known as *bihudā*. A certain quantity of *dhān* is also grown from transplanted seedlings.

Cereals. (5) Inferior kinds of cereals (millets) consisting of (1) *Gulji*, (2) *Jhāri*, (3) *Kodo*, (4) *Māndiā*, (5) *Kāngo*, (6) *Jowār* and (7) *Makai*. These cover 4 per cent. of the cropped area and ripen in August and September.

Pulses. (6) (1) *Bīrhi*, (2) *Kulthī*, both sown in August and September, and ripen in December; (3) *Mūga*, sown a little later than the sowing of *bīrhi* and *kulthī* and ripens in December; (4) *Arhar*, sown in June, and ripens in February; (5) Gram, this crop is sown very sparingly (it is sown in September), and ripens in February.

Cotton. (7) Cotton covers $2\frac{1}{2}$ per cent. of the cropped area, and is sown in June and ripens in December.

These crops, numbers 5 to 7, cover 12 per cent. of the cropped area.

Oil-seeds. (8) (1) *Til* (Sesamum) sown in July, and ripens in December; (2) Castor oil-seed sown in September, and ripens in March. These two crops cover 21 per cent. of the cropped area.

Sugarcane. (9) Sugarcane is but little grown in this State. It occupies only $\frac{1}{2}$ per cent. of the cropped area.

Vegetables. (10) (1) *Bhendi*, (2) *Sāru* (aroideal), (3) *Kākudi* (cucumber), (4) *Kakhāru* (pumpkin), (5) *Barbati* (cow-gram), (6) *Janhi* (Luffa acutangula), (7) *Lau* (bottle gourd), (8) *Baigun* (brinjal); these ripen in autumn: (9) *Semi* (beans), (10) *Kandamul* (sweet potato), (11) *Onion*, (12) *Garlic*, (13) *Chillies*, (14) *Dhaniā* (coriander-seed) and (15) *Bhājisag* (potherbs); these ripen in winter. Vegetables are few in number and cover only about $\frac{1}{5}$ per cent. of the whole cropped area and are sown in the gardens of the houses.

The State is liable to famine, of which the most disastrous on record is that of 1900. The southern and western areas of the State are especially liable to suffer on any untimely distribution or early cessation of the rains : these tracts are inhabited for the most part by aboriginals, the Khonds to the south in the Kondhan and the Binjhāls to the west, in the area known as Binjhálty. These aboriginal races are very indifferent cultivators and make no attempt to secure regular crops by constructing irrigation dams and reservoirs. Even in ordinary years they are extremely indifferent to their cultivation preferring to live very largely on forest products of fruits and roots and the pursuit of the chase. The northern and eastern area of the State is however fairly protected from any entire failure of the crops : the people of this part are skilled agriculturists and most of the villages possess dams and tanks for irrigation. The greater degree of protection enjoyed by the north-eastern area was markedly shown in the famine of 1900, when, though there was practically a cessation of the rains from August, the people of this part were able by irrigation to harvest a 65 per cent. crop and the Khonds and Binjhāls to the south and south-east only harvested a 30 per cent. crop. The great factor is the even distribution of the rainfall : in 1896 the rainfall 54·65 inches was in excess of the average, but there was a prolonged cessation after the sowings with the result that the rice did not germinate properly. In the following year 1897 there was considerable scarcity in the State, but no actual famine amongst the people of the State. There was however acute distress in some of the neighbouring States and a large influx of people in search of work invaded the State. Relief works were accordingly opened at the headquarters and private enterprise amongst the rich cultivators provided work for others by embanking fields and improving tanks. The State was however visited in this year (1897) by a very severe outbreak of cholera, which raged with great virulence, especially amongst the refugees who had fled to the State for employment and subsistence.

NATURAL CALAMITIES.

In 1899-1900 the rainfall was 7 inches below the average, but would readily have sufficed for the crops, but for its unfavourable distribution. Over 5 inches fell between March and May and was very useful for preparing the lands for the coming rice crop. The rains were favourable to the end of July, when they came practically to a cessation, except for a small fall in the early part of August, with a few scanty falls to the middle of September, when the rains ceased entirely. The crops yielded a 65 per cent harvest in the northern and eastern areas of the

State and 30 per cent. in the south and west : in the latter areas affairs were partially improved by the fact that the Khonds and Binjhāls had reaped good millet crops of Gulji, Māndiā and Sawā. By the end of September prices of food grains had risen largely and people began to wander over the State in panic, there being no reserve of stocks at command. In the middle of August rice was selling at 24 seers per rupee, but in September had risen to 20 seers and continued rising steadily to November : for the next three months prices remained stationary, but from February onwards again rose rapidly, reaching in July 5 seers per rupee. The position was rendered the more difficult by the almost entire absence of any reserve stocks : the year 1896-97 had been one of shortage and though the two succeeding years were good the people had sold off their surplus to make good their needs of former years : communications were defective and when the rainy season set in it was almost impossible to import rice except at prohibitive rates : the famine relief kitchens were kept supplied with great difficulty by importing from Kharagpur. A considerable import of *māndiā* however was obtainable from Ganjām and all classes alike were compelled to subsist on this to a great extent. The *mahuā* crop, which is of enormous value, especially to the aboriginal races, who form 33 per cent. of the population, was a failure, but the mango crop was fortunately a bumper one. A test work was opened soon after the close of the monsoon, but did not attract workers. It was not till March that people regularly came to the relief works, all of which took the form of tank excavations : the rate paid was a moderate one, Re. 0-3-2 per 100 cubic feet and was raised to Re. 0-4-9 with the rise in prices. Besides State relief works others were opened by private enterprise and much assistance was thus rendered. One of the great difficulties to cope with was rendering relief to the aboriginal races whom nothing would induce to take to regular spade and pick work. Kitchens, seventeen in number, were accordingly opened, the largest number of persons relieved on any one day at the kitchens being 6,980. The Indian Famine Charitable Relief Fund gave Rs. 10,000, which was expended on providing seed grains, Rs. 6,505 were given as taccavi, Rs. 3,210 land revenue, and Rs. 2,500 forest revenue were suspended and Rs. 21,094 were spent on State kitchens and relief works, excluding the sums spent by the zamīndārs and private persons. The next difficulty which faced the State authorities was the greatly restricted area sown in the ensuing year 1901. In March of that year distress again developed in the Kondhan and Binjhālty : accordingly Rs. 8,833 land revenue were suspended, Rs. 14,676 were given as taccavi and kitchens were kept open from April to September in these areas: the taccavi was given on the spot and at the right time and by the year 1902 the area sown had reached the normal. In the year 1902 it was found necessary to remit Rs. 2,398 of land revenue and Rs. 9,000 were again given out on taccavi in the Kondhan and Binjhālty areas: the result was the rapid restoration to normal conditions in these parts. This disastrous famine was attended by a serious outbreak of crime: grain shops were looted and dacoity broke out and it was necessary for Government to depute a Police Inspector to organise the police force of the State. Small-pox and cholera raged with terrible virulence during the famine year of 1900: the deteriorated condition of the people rendered them ready victims to these diseases: the registered number of deaths in 1900 was 42,154 against 8,022 in the preceding year, giving an average ratio of 127 per mille per annum: the birth rate fell from 15,353 in 1899 to 8,233 in 1900, and the total population showed a decline of 16 per cent. The mortality amongst cattle was very high from rinderpest and foot and mouth disease: water was scarce and the extensive grazing lands were parched: the greatest mortality however ensued after the break of the rains when the half starved animals were allowed to feed to repletion on the new and abundant vegetation: the Gandās and Doms slaughtered a large number of cattle for food and crime of this type was rife. Measures have now been taken to be properly prepared for famine: schemes of famine works have been decided upon and an expert Surveyor has been engaged to draw up the plans and estimate for immediate use when necessary: several of these are preventive works which will be gradually taken up. The Chief has started a special famine fund as a reserve. The Patnā State not being traversed by any large river is not subject to disastrous floods.

RENTS, WAGES AND PRICES.

The average rates of assessment per acre for 1st, 2nd and 3rd class rice lands are Re. 0-10-9, Re. 0-9-7 and Re. 0-3-7 respectively; the assessment is thus very light; for *āt* or uplands, the average rate is Re. 0-1-9 per acre. The rate of assessment for *barchhā* land, where sugarcane is specially grown, varies from Re. 1-4 to Rs. 3-12 per acre.

The field labourers are here called *guti* or *haliā* and are generally hired for the year. They get for food two to three *khandis* (1 maund to 1 maund 20 seers) of unhusked rice per mensem. At the end of the year, they also receive six to twelve *khandis* (3 maunds to 6 maunds) of *dhān* (unhusked rice) with two cloths worth about 12 annas. Where sugarcane is cultivated, the sugarcane grown on one *patti* is allowed to every *guti*; the value of this is about Rs. 2. Likewise one *khandi* (20 seers) of *dhān* (unhusked rice) yielding about a *purug* (4 maunds) of unhusked rice and one *tāmbi* (1 seer 4 chitacks) of pulse and *til* (sesamum) are sown for each *guti*, who is also given grain at the time of harvest for the work of threshing at the following rates:—For *dhān*, 10 *tāmbis* (10 seers) if he thrashes 20 *khandis* (10 maunds). For pulse and other crops, only as much as he requires for one day's food. The more skilful labourer or head *guti* (*khamāri*) gets 16 *khandis* (8 maunds) instead of 12 in a lump at the end of a year and enjoys other privileges. A stipulation is often made that the *guti* is to be lent from Rs. 4 to Rs. 20 a year without interest, provided he does not throw up his situation until he repays the money. This loan is termed in this State as "Bāhābandhā."

The lads employed for grazing cattle or other cultivating business are called *kuthiā*. They are supplied with food and cloths, and at the end of the year *dhān* (unhusked rice) from four to eight *khandis* (2 to 4 maunds) is given to them.

Besides, daily labourers are often hired in gangs to work in the fields for weeding, sowing and ploughing at two *tāmbis* (2 seers) and for transplanting at 3 *tāmbis* (3 seers) of unhusked rice daily per head. These labourers are called Bhutiārs. In the *Khondān* tracts the Khonds hire labourers at a low rate giving them requisite food in their houses and paying them a lump sum of Rs. 4 in cash in the year and three pieces of cloth only. During late years the average rate of daily wages of ordinary coolies was 2 annas for males and 1 anna and 3 pies for females: and the average rate of daily wages of mechanics was: superior mason, 14 annas, common mason, 8 annas; superior carpenter, Re. 1, common carpenter, 10 annas; superior blacksmith, 10 annas, common blacksmith, 6 annas. The principal food grain of the State is rice and *mūga* is the principal kind of pulse in use. During the period of 12 years from 1896 to 1907 the average price of rice per rupee was 24 $\frac{7}{16}$ seers at harvest time and 16¾ seers during the later part of the year: the average price of salt from 1896 to 1905 was nine seers per rupee, but since 1906 it has fallen to 14 seers per rupee: the average price of *mūga* has been 14½ seers per rupee, of *kulthī*, 25¼ seers and of *birhi*, 14½ seers.

OCCUPATIONS, MANUFACTURES AND TRADE.

The occupation of the people of the State is mostly agricultural, 57 per cent. of the total population being agriculturists and 13 per cent. field labourers. A small number of people live on the income derived by smelting iron and making iron instruments. There is no manufacture in the State worth notice;

weaving of *dhuris*, *newar*, etc., with the fly-shuttle loom is largely carried on in the State jail: Bhuliās, Gandās and Maharās or Kulees, who are the principal weaving classes in the State, supply the ordinary cloth used by the people of the State. Iron weapons such as axes, daggers, etc., of good quality are manufactured in the Bangomundā zamīndāri of this State. The principal exported articles are rāshi (sesamum seed), fibres, cotton, rice, grain, pulses and *ghī* (clarified butter). Traders from Ganjām and Raipur come to the State to barter salt, dry fish, coconuts, tobacco, *nabāt* (raw sugar) and iron bars mainly for oil-seeds and rice. The other imported articles are spices, mill cloths, thread and kerosene oil.

MEANS OF COMMUNICATION.

There are two excellent murramed (gravelled) and bridged roads in the State: one from the border of the State, at Sālebhattā on the Ang, to Bolāngir, the headquarters, a distance of 19 miles; the other from Bolāngir to Tarbhā, a large mart on the Sonpur border: a portion of the main road from Raipur to Vizianagram runs through the south-western extremity of the State for a few miles, passing near Sindhekelā. An unbridged surface road 34 miles in length, runs due south to the Tel river, the boundary of the Kālāhandī and Patnā States, starting from Bolāngir and forms the main line of communication from Sambalpur to the headquarters of the Kālāhandī State: there are rest-houses at Sālebhattā and Deogaon on this route. There is a good surface road from Bolāngir to Patnāgarh, the former headquarters of the State: a cold weather surface road with rough wooden trestle bridges runs from Bangomundā through the forest tracts on the west of the State to Agalpur. The State is thus provided with good communications and there are several fair village tracks. The new line of rail from Raipur to Vizianagram will pass through the southern portion of the State *viâ* Sindhekelā and Saintalā, on the main road from Bolāngir to Kālāhandī: a branch line is projected from Saintalā to Sonpur passing near Bolāngir The Public Works of the State have been placed by the Chief under the charge of the Agency Executive Engineer, Sambalpur, with an Overseer in direct charge: the State has of recent years made great progress in the opening out of communications. There is a circuit house at headquarters. The State has been relieved of all contributions for postal service and there is a daily service both ways between Bolāngir and Sambalpur; beside the post office at headquarters, there are letter-boxes at the school houses of all important villages.

LAND REVENUE ADMINISTRATION.

The main subdivisions of the State are—(1) The *khālsa* or directly administered country and two estates held by relations of the Mahārājā, viz., Jarāsinghā and Agalpur. (2) Five hereditary estates held chiefly by Gond Thākurs, viz., Atgaon, Loisinghā, Pandrāni, Bālbukā, and Mandal. (3) Five *Binjir* estates held by Binjhāl chiefs—a warlike race of aborigines—viz., Rāmud, Nāndupalā, Bhānpur, Khaprākhol, and Khuripāni. (4) Five *garhatiāhis*, or clusters of villages, the revenues of which are set apart for the maintenance of bodies of police each under a *garhatiā*. (5) Nine Khond *Mahāls*, viz., Bangomundā, Budbudkā, Luwā, Haldi, Talgahakā, Lāpher Pāhār, Saintalā, Tupā, and Upargahakā.

The system of settlement prevailing before 1871 A.D. was to lease the villages to the highest bidder. The term of lease was 4 years. There was no certainty of tenure however. The ryots had no rights in the land, and could be ejected at the will of and by the *gaontiā* though owing to the paucity of the tenants this was rarely done. The rents generally continued the same from one lease to another, but the *nazarāna* (or premium) paid by the *gaontiā* on renewal was increased. The village assessment or *mālguzāri* was distributed by the *gaontiā* and the tenants over the tenants' (ryoti) lands. For this purpose the tenants' lands were divided into a definite number of divisions locally, called *kariā* representing 16 annas, *bhaguā* representing 8 annas, *bahtā, gur* or *salitā* representing 4 annas, *nahtā* 2 annas and *litā* 1 anna.

These divisions took into consideration the position and produce, and were therefore not of the same size. They existed everywhere, and it was not difficult to apportion the rents when they had to be revised. The *nazarāna* paid by the *gaontiā* was recovered in part from the tenants according to their holdings. The *gaontiā* managed to enjoy the rents of such lands as were temporarily deserted or new lands broken up and settled. He enjoyed all his *bhogrā*, service lands, free in return for the *nazarāna* paid by him. The tenant did not know how much was legally payable by him, but had to take the word of the *gaontiā* for it and the *gaontiā* could thus collect more than he paid to the Chief for *karchāul* or payment in kind from his ryots, this being another source of profit to him. In addition a large number of miscellaneous cesses had to be paid. For every 15 or 30 villages a *tandakār* was appointed whose business was supposed to be to keep the peace in these villages. He, however, made a regular source of profit out of all the crimes of the area.

On the occasion of a marriage in the Chief's family a contribution called *haldiān pati* was levied on all the villages, to cover the expenses of the marriage. Contributions seem also to have been levied for the purchase of horses and elephants and on visits of ceremony. As money was required for expenses, the Chiefs issued orders from time to time in writing upon *gaontiās* to pay the bearer a certain sum. The order was complied with and the paper kept as a voucher to support the payment.

The total collections on account of land revenue and cesses just before the beginning of the British administration amounted to (*a*) land revenue, Rs. 8,792, (*b*) cash cesses and dues, Rs. 1,479 and (*c*) payments in kind, consisting of rice, urid, *ghī* (clarified butter), oil, goats and cloth.

The tenant lent to his *gaontiā* the services of all his ploughs for work for a day and 2 labourers with sickles for a day. This practice continues now. When the *gaontiās* sent their *karchāul* (payment of rice in kind) to the Chief the cartmen were detained for a day or two to bring firewood, timber and grass for the use of the Chief, the annual repairs of his houses and those of his servants. The tenants were bound to do any other *begār* (free labour) required of them.

When the State came under British administration in 1871 a new settlement was made. There was a summary enquiry and leases were given to the *gaontiās* and *kabuliyats* taken from them. The cesses were abolished and the demands amalgamated with the rent. The instalments continued the same as before, viz., payable on Asādh Pūrnimā (15th July), Kārttik Pūrnimā (15th November), and Fāgun Pūrnimā (15th March). For instance a village which had to pay Rs. 207-3 revenue and 40½ *pastmās* (97-⅕ maunds) of rice under the old lease beside *ghī*, (clarified butter), oil, a goat, etc., under the lease of 1871 was assessed at Rs. 400 without any payment in kind. This settlement was made for 5 years from 1871 to 1875. In 1872 a school cess was imposed. Under the new settlement the total demand was Rs. 22,200 land revenue and Rs. 1,471 school cess. The land revenue and the rental demand continued to be identical, the *gaontiā* enjoying his *bhograā* lands rent-free and appropriating the rents of the new tenants or new lands. The total demand included payments from zamīndārs. **Settlement of 1871.**

The rent settlement made in 1876 was also for 5 years and was also a summary one. Captain Bowie, Deputy Commissioner, Sambalpur, who made the former settlement, had however now obtained a fuller knowledge of the people and the country. This settlement was, therefore, made on fuller data. It had been found in the Kondhān (tracts held by the Khonds) that cultivation had at least doubled everywhere, that the *umrāhs* (Khond chiefs) and heads of villages had been obtaining more than double their **Settlement of 1876.**

former revenue from the tenants. In the northern part of the State the case of each village was considered separately and separate information had been collected with regard to each village. The total demand rose to Rs. 37,398 and Rs. 2,190 school cess.

In this settlement as before the *gaontiās* and the tenants were left to themselves to apportion the increased demand in the same way that they would have done if the enhancement had been levied in the old form of a demand made in the shape of *nazarāna*.

Settlement of 1885. A fresh settlement was made in 1885 by Mr. Berry and the question of the *nazarāna* and *chhirol* lands were dealt with. The lump payment of *nazarāna* had become a hardship to the *gaontiā* who was usually compelled to borrow in order to meet his obligation to the State. These objections were met by assessing the *bhogrā* to an annual payment: the assessment made in no case exceeded more than one-half its rent value at rates paid by the lands of tenants. *Chhirol* lands were taken to include (*a*) Land newly broken up by the *gaontiā* and leased to a tenant, the rent being enjoyed by the *gaontiā*, (*b*) lands brought under cultivation by tenants and enjoyed by them rent-free for three years and subsequently paying rent to the *gaontiā*, (*c*) land formerly ryoti, abandoned by a tenant and cultivated for a time by the *gaontiā* and again leased by him. The *chhirol* lands were assessed at a lenient rate as the assessment was an innovation.

Settlement of 1895. The next settlement was made in 1895-96. This was made for the whole of the State except the Kondhān tract, where though the papers were ready the announcement was postponed owing to the approach of famine.

The better cultivated areas of the State, Aungār, Sarandā and Pātnāgarh were regularly surveyed by plane table. In the western portion of the State called Binjhālty where there were practically only patches of cultivation in the midst of jungle, the survey was on the *masáhat* system which found the area of a field in a rough and ready manner by taking its length and average breadth. The other details of settlement were those adopted in the British districts of the Central Provinces: maps were prepared, the *khasrā* was written and from it the *jamābandi*. The soil was divided according to position into *āt* or high land, *māl* or high embanked land, *bernā* or low land and *bāhāl* the lowest lying land where the water-supply was never deficient. These classes were again subdivided into manured, irrigated and ordinary. Deduced rents were then calculated by means of soil factors and unit rates and the revised rents were fixed with reference to these deduced rents. The condition of the village was also taken into consideration. The system of the remuneration of the *gaontiā* was changed. The *gaontiās* were given a drawback of 20 per cent. and in some cases more, of the whole village assets, and the *gaontiā* was supposed to assign land to the village servants for their remuneration. Tribal heads, such as *umrāhs*, etc., received a remuneration in cash: the State taking from 50 per cent. to 65 per cent. of the assets: the *gaontiā* paying the *umrāh* 80 per cent.; the difference between these two items representing the remuneration of the *umrāh*.

The demands of the settlements of 1895-96 amounted to Rs. 76,900, as land revenue against the demand of Rs. 52,500 in 1895.

No *nazarāna* or premium on leasing a village is now levied as formerly. No *begāri* or *bethī* (free labour) is recognised in the *khālsa* portion of the State, but when any important officer goes on tour in the State, the tenants give one cooly per house to do any necessary State work. The *gandā* and *jhānkar* (village watchmen) cannot as formerly be ejected by a *gaontiā* at his will. The *narihā* or water bearer as before enjoys rent-free land. The lands taken up by these village servants now form part of the $\frac{1}{5}$-rent-free land (*bhogrā*) allowed to the *gaontiā*. There was also formerly the village *negi*. He enjoyed a plot of land rent-free and was the *gaontiā's* assistant in the village management. He helped to collect rents, receive and attend to State servants visiting the village. The *negi* has ceased to be a recognised servant. The village potter still exists in many villages and supplies pots for the *gaontiā's* use and for that of the visitors to the village in return for rent-free land. He, too, has no official recognition now. In addition to the land enjoyed by the *gandā* and *jhānkar* rent-free, they receive paddy (unhusked rice) from each tenant at harvest time.

Village Servants.

The Loisinghā zamīndāri originated out of a service grant, and assumed its present size by encroachments in former times upon the *khālsa* or area directly in possession of the Chief. Atgaon and Bangomundā are tenures of long standing. The control of the police in the zamīndāris was formerly in the hands of the zamīndārs, but was taken away from them in 1896. The settlements that these zamīndārs make with their *gaontiās* are of a summary nature for five years generally. Upon the income derived by the zamīndārs, *takoli* (tribute) is assessed which is revised from time to time.

Zamīndāris.

Up till the settlement of 1885 the zamīndārs managed their own police. In the settlement of 1895 they were relieved of this duty and the charges on account of the police were recovered from them.

Maintenance grants. The Agalpur maintenance grant was made by Mahārājā Bhūpāl Deva on his death-bed for the maintenance of his sons by his second wife. The Jarāsinghā maintenance grant has changed hands from time to time being meant for the use of the brother of the Chief, holding the *gadi*. *Māfis.* There are *bābuān māfis* for the relations of the Raj family, *chākrān māfis* for servants, *debottar* and *brahmottar māfis* for temples, gods and Brāhmans. There are no grants of recent date to Brāhmans or temples.

In the 1895 settlement enhancements were made as required in each case and the grants to the Brāhmans were assessed to partial revenue according to the merits of each case.

General. There used to be a *pātki* tax levied upon professions. The Kewat, Kumbhār, Māli, Teli, Gandā, Bhuliā and Sundhi castes were assessed to that tax. It was abolished in 1890 and the *pandari* tax or tax on incomes introduced in its stead.

The main features of the rules regulating the revenue administration of the State are that a *gaontiā* cannot sublet, transfer or mortgage his village. *Gaontiās* of long standing, who have been in possession of the same village for 20 years or more, or who have effected real improvements in their villages, are given protected status, entitling them to the right of renewal at the next settlement. The *gaontiā* cannot subdivide his *bhogrā* lands, he may allow tenants to cultivate them, but no rights can be obtained in them by the tenant and all encumbrances on them cease, when a new *gaontiā* obtains the village. Tenants cannot transfer their holdings by sale, lease or mortgage. The settlement prepared for the Kondhān in 1895 and which was postponed owing to famine and a series of bad harvests has been revised, brought up to date and recently announced.

GENERAL ADMINISTRATION. The relations between the State and the British Government are regulated by the *sanad* of 1867. The State pays a tribute of Rs 13,000, which is liable to revision and was last assessed in 1909 for 30 years. The Chief is invested with full criminal jurisdiction, except that capital sentences have to be referred to the Commissioner of the Division for confirmation. Under the *sanad* the Chief is bound to follow the advice of the officer duly invested with authority by Government. No import or export duties can be levied and the Chief is bound to conduct his excise administration so as not to interfere with the excise arrangements of the neighbouring districts of British

India. The Chief conducts the administration of the State with the assistance of a *Dīwān*. The State for various causes has from time to time come under the administration of Government and the administration has been developed in all departments. The *Dīwān* is the chief executive officer of the State with powers equivalent to those of a Deputy Commissioner and also exercises the powers of a Sessions and District Judge : appeals from his orders lie to the Chief : the *Dīwān* hears appeals from subordinate officers. There is a *Tahsīldār* and *Naib Tahsīldār*, revenue officers, exercising also judicial powers : the Chief's eldest son exercises powers of a District Magistrate and there is also an Honorary Magistrate at headquarters: certain of the zamīndārs also exercise the powers of Honorary Magistrates. There is a Settlement Officer and a complete settlement staff : the settlement records are kept up to date on the system followed in the Central Provinces. The income of the State in 1907-08 amounted to Rs. 2,29,378, of which the land revenue and zamīndāri *takoli* amounted to Rs. 77,544. **Finances.**

Forest management. No rules were enforced before 1889 for forest conservancy. The right to collect lac and minor forest produce was leased from year to year from 1871. The first rules for forest conservancy were introduced in 1889. Certain forests were reserved. Timber was divided into 3 classes. The first was the more valuable and reserved class. The second could be removed on payment of a *nistār* or license fee, a nominal sum, for the private personal use of the tenants. Similarly the zamīndārs were allowed to remove from their zamīndāri forests timber and firewood for the use of themselves and their tenants, but were forbidden to sell timber: these rules are still in force. The rules referred to the fees chargeable for the various classes of timber and the rate of commutation fee to be charged to cultivating and non-cultivating classes of the State for the right to take second class timber from the forests. No restriction was placed on the removal of third class timber. The forests were then divided into—(*a*) Patnā State *khālsa*, (*b*) *mālguzāri* forests, *i.e*, forests included within the area of the villages and (*c*) zamīndāri forests.

As regards the second class or the village jungles, the people are allowed the free use of the timber and jungle products, with the exception of first and second class timber, and such items as resin, cocoons, skins and palm juice. They pay a commutation fee of 4 annas per plough, however, to take second class timber from the State forests. First class timber has of course to be paid for on a license system granted on regular scale.

The area of State forests, which in the settlement were demarcated from village forests, is 159 square miles, divided into 23 blocks: they have been demarcated, closed to grazing and cutting, except on license, and fire lines are now being cut. A trained Forester has recently been appointed with a regular staff under him and the administration of the forests on regular lines is to be taken up. In 1907-08 the income under this head was Rs. 24,519.

Excise. An excise *Dārogā* is in charge of the collection of excise revenue, but there is no regular excise staff and detection of smuggling and illicit distilling is left to the police force: in former years no check was placed on the number of outstills and shops and the system followed was to lease out a central outstill with a number of shops attached: during the last three years successful endeavours have been made to reduce the large number of shops scattered over the State and to approximate to a standard of one shop for every 30 square miles: considerable reductions have been effected, followed by a substantial increase in revenue: amongst the Khonds, it is, however, a difficult matter to reduce the number of shops, as the outstill is a regular village institution. The zamīndārs enjoy their own excise revenue as regards country liquor and make their own excise settlement, which both in the *khālsa* and zamīndāri areas are made by public auction. The State obtains its supply of opium from the Sambalpur Treasury. As regards *gānja* the State obtains Khandwā *gānja* from Nimār.

The brewing of *kusna*, *handia* or *pachwai* (rice beer) is not allowed even on license. The Khonds formerly used to brew *mahuā* liquor in their houses, but this has been stopped. In 1907-08 the excise revenue amounted to Rs. 36,032.

Civil justice. The total number of civil suits for disposal in 1907-08 was 735 out of which 66 per cent. were below Rs. 50 in value.

Crime. In former years outbreaks of violent crime were not uncommon and the serious outburst of dacoity in 1899 lead to the appointment of an officer from the British police force to hold charge of the State police. Of recent years the police have been carefully trained, organised and abuses put down and crime has returned to normal proportions.

Police. The police force consists of one Inspector, one Circle Inspector, seven Chief Constables 40 Head-Constables, and 172 men, besides *chaukīdārs* (village watchmen) and *paiks* (State militia).

Jail. The jail contains accommodation for 124 prisoners and is a fine commodious masonry building of modern construction, with quarters for jailor and jail staff and warders: regular labour is exacted and the administration of the jail is on modern lines. In 1907-08 the daily average jail population was 120·4. There is a regular Public Works Department and the execution of public works has been entrusted by the Chief to the Agency Executive Engineer: at the headquarters there are fine public buildings: the Chief's residence, the courts and offices, dispensary, circuit-house, jail, schools and hostels are imposing and substantial buildings. Public Works Department.

Considerable attention has been given in this State to the cause of education, and this is especially noticeable in the rural schools. The zamīndārs and larger *umrāhs* have built excellent school houses. To all the rural schools there are Committee members who actually meet and are useful in inducing the parents to send their children to school. *Deshi--kasrat* (country exercises) is very well taught at all the schools. At Bolāngir the Middle English and Middle Vernacular schools are good institutions and well housed with an excellent hostel attached. The total number of schools in the State in 1907-08 was 44, and the number of pupils was 4,685; the average percentage of attendance was 73 and the percentage of boys of school-going age at school was 9·5 and of girls, 1·6. Including the girls' school at Bolāngir, there were altogether 692 girls under instruction; in the rural schools they read with the boys. The schools are looked after by a qualified State Deputy Inspector. A considerable number of pupils are annually successful in passing the Upper and Lower Primary examinations and in the High School Scholarship Examination. One of the features of the educational system of the State are the special schools for low caste children. EDUCATION.

CHAPTER XX.

RAIRAKHOL STATE.

PHYSICAL ASPECTS. THE State of Rairākhol lies between 20° 56′ and 21° 24′ N., and between 83° 59′ and 84° 53′ E. It is bounded on the north by Bāmra State; on the east by Athmallik State and Angul district; on the west by the Sambalpur *khālsa*; and on the south by Sonpur State. It is of irregular formation, the extreme length, east and west, being some fifty miles, and the extreme breadth thirty miles. The total area is 833 square miles, of which some three-fifths are cultivated, the rest being forest and hills. The soil is light and sandy. There are *sāl* (Shorea robusta) forests in the State, and plenty of other useful timber for building purposes. There are no rivers; the principal streams are the Champāli and the Tikkirā, but they are insignificant. The State consists of a series of low hill ranges trending to the valley of the Mahānadī. Here and there higher isolated ridges are encountered; but, except towards the Bāmra border, there are no regular uplands. The country is for the most part covered with forest, which in the valleys is mostly of the nature of scrub-jungle. The hill-sides are, however, reserved and there is some fine timber on them. The commonest tree is *rengāl* or *sāl* (Shorea robusta); there is also a considerable quantity of *kendu* (ebony—Diospyros melanoxylon), *bijā* (Pterocarpus Marsupium) and some *sisū* (Dalbergia Sissoo). In many of the villages regular groves of mangoes are to be met with, and *mahuā* (Bassia latifolia) and *chār* (Buchanania latifolia) trees are common. The *harirā* (Terminalia chebula) or myrobalan, however, is comparatively scarce, and does not flourish here so well as in the Gāngpur and Bonai States. The valleys have all been cleared for rice lands, and the forests on the uplands rising from the valleys are cultivated as *gorā* or uplands (here known as *āt*). The area available for regular rice cultivation is small, and this, no doubt, accounts for the extensive cultivation of *gorā* or uplands. Between the boundaries of the different villages small patches of forest have been reserved. Iron ore of excellent quality is found in many places. The average rainfall for the six years from 1902-03 to 1907-08 was 61·5 inches. The headquarters of the State are at Rāmpur situated at a distance of 42 miles from the town of Sambalpur.

The State of Rairākhol is attached to the Sambalpur district. It was formerly a zamīndāri, subordinate to Bāmra, but was made into an independent State, and constituted one of the Garhjāt cluster, by the Patnā Chiefs, about a century and a half ago. The Chief is by caste a Chauhān Rājput. The State was not at first included in the list of Feudatory States in the Central Provinces. The Chief, however, was conspicuous for his loyalty in 1857, and in 1866 an adoption *sanad* was granted and in 1867 the State was recognised as a Feudatory State by the British Government and received a *sanad* accordingly. The State was transferred in October 1905 from the Central Provinces to the Orissa Division in Bengal. The late Chief Rājā Gaur Chandra Deva died in July 1906 and adopted the brother of the Chief of the Bonai State as his heir : the Chief is a minor and the State accordingly is under the administration of Government. The emblem of the State is *Sankha Padma* (conch shell and lotus). HISTORY.

The population in 1866 was returned at 25,000, and according to the census of 1901 it was 26,888. There has been but little increase in population, the land being poor and unsuitable for any large agricultural population. The non-agricultural castes are Brāhmans, Rājputs, and Mahāntis. The main agricultural castes are Chasās (7,188), and Dumāls (1,026). The population of the State is classified as follows :—Hindus—males, 12,487, females, 11,877, total 24,364 or 90·6 per cent. of the total population ; proportion of males in total Hindus 51·2. Musalmāns—males, 52, females, 40, total 92 or 0·34 per cent. of the total population ; proportion of males in total Musalmāns, 56·5. Animists—males, 1,381, females, 1,044, total 2,425 or 9·02 per cent. of the total population ; proportion of males in total Animists, 56·9. Christian —*nil.* Sikhs, 7. The number of persons able to read and write is 281 or 1·05 per cent. of the total population. Averages :—Villages per square mile, 0·38 ; persons per village, 84 ; houses per square mile, 6·7 ; houses per village, 17·0 ; persons per house, 5. The State contains 319 villages which are classified as follows :—316 with less than five hundred inhabitants, 2 with from five hundred to one thousand inhabitants, and one with from one thousand to two thousand inhabitants. THE PEOPLE.

This is the most sparsely populated State, except Bonai, amongst the States of Orissa, there being only 32 persons to the square mile.

There is a sprinkling of the cloth-manufacturing and artisan classes, chiefly iron-smelters and manufacturers of iron implements. The principal castes are Gonds (2,653), Gandās (2,328), Sudhas (2,199), Khonds (1,757), Rāuts (1,633), and Kudās (1,383). Of these, Sudhas are amongst the wildest of the inhabitants of this State; they fell the forest on the hill-sides and burn it (*dāhi* cultivation); in the ashes they bury their seeds just at the break of the rain; they live in no regular villages, but each family lives separately over its own cultivation in small huts perched on stakes and from this coign of vantage they guard their crops from the ravages of wild animals. The Butkā Sudhas of this State are a very prominent race and they are supposed to have played a prominent part in the history of the Rairākhol State: they have several villages allotted to them and perform sacrifices for the Rāj family.

The people are naturally wild and jungly. They are a sturdy and well set up race. They obtain much in the way of supplies from the forests and eat the fruit of the *kendu*, *chār* and *mahuā* trees in considerable quantities. The country is very poorly watered, and there is little opportunity for irrigation. The people are well clad in home-spun raiment. They appear to be superior in material condition to the people of the Bonai State, which in natural features is not unlike Rairākhol, except that in the former State the valley of the Brāhmanī river where it flows through the State affords an area of good culturable land. Rairākhol, however, is shut off from the Mahānadī by the State of Sonpur. The rental is light, and the people cultivate also large areas of uplands.

PUBLIC HEALTH

The State being covered for the most part with dense forest, it is malarious and new settlers suffer greatly from fever: the regular residents of the State, however, are fairly healthy. The people are particularly averse to vaccination and outbreaks of small-pox are frequent: visitations of cholera are also not uncommon. There is a dispensary at Rāmpur, the headquarters of the State, in charge of a Civil Hospital Assistant: there is accommodation for indoor patients: the number of patients treated in 1907-08 was 8,845. Vaccination work is performed by the State free of cost to the people: the work is supervised by a Vaccination Inspector: revaccination was until recently practically unknown, but the prejudice against vaccination is being gradually overcome. In 1907-08 the number of primary vaccinations was 662 and that of revaccinations, 1,999.

AGRICULTURE.

The soil is not very fertile and the State carries a small population of only 32 persons to the square mile. Rice is the staple crop: pulses, cotton, oil-seeds and sugarcane are also cultivated. Nothing so far has been done to improve the varieties of crops grown or to introduce new crops. The kinds of soil found in the

Soil.

State are:—(1) *Barmata*—This is a soil which in ploughing is very adhesive, but in the hot weather quickly becomes dried and baked and will not retain its moisture. (2) *Khaliā*—A greyish slippery soil which retains moisture. (3) *Baliā*—A sandy soil of poor value. (4) *Ruguriā*—This is a light sandy soil containing a great deal of *muram* or disintegrated laterite. It is mostly found on the upland cultivation. (5) *Pathariā*—An inferior stony soil. (6) *Pāluā*—This is a good clayey soil found mostly by the banks of streams.

The lands have been regularly measured by the chain for settlement purposes and recorded in acres and decimals. The people, however, still speak of so many *khandis* of land, *i.e.*, the quantity of seed required for sowing the lands, a *khandi* here being equal to about 20 seers. In this way a piece of land sown by one *khandi* (20 seers) is called *khandi-kut*.

The crops grown are as follows:— Crops.

At dhān (upland paddy) viz.: (1) *Bāunsabutā*, (2) *Sariā*, (3) *Kuliā*, (4) *Chāulamanji*; these are sown in the month of Ashādha, *i.e.*, from the 15th June and reaped in the month of Dasharā, *i.e.*, from the 15th September. *Gulji*, *rendo*, and *kāngosuān* are also grown on *āt* land and sown in the beginning of the rainy-season, and reaped in the month of Ashwin, *i.e.*, by the 15th September.

Dhān (paddy) of inferior quality. (1) *Mālkanhāi*, (2) *Bāunsanakhi*, (3) *Hiran*, (4) *Dholmātiā*, (5) *Kusumapunāi*, (6) *Kharakoili*, (7) *Champā*, (8) *Mānkiri*, (9) *Mālguthi*, (10) *Badyarāj*, (11) *Baniākonti*, (12) *Bātharāj*, (13) *Mugdhi*. All these varieties are sown in the months of Jyaishtha and Ashādha, *i.e.*, in June and July. The sowing of *dhān* (rice) during these months is known as *kharadi* sowing and *batari* sowing. They are reaped in the months of Dasharā and Kārttik, that is, by the 15th September.

Dhān (paddy) of superior quality. (1) *Sunāpāni*, (2) *Jhalakākeri*, (3) *Chinämāl*, (4) *Pipalbāsh*, (5) *Rādhābhog*, (6) *Krishnakalā*, (7) *Makarkām*, (8) *Jhiliparāgi*, (9) *Lakshmībhog*, (10) *Sagardhuli*, (11) *Nāgpurī*, (12) *Gandmāl*, (13) *Rādhāballabh*. These varieties are sown in the months of Jyaishtha, Ashādha and Shrābana, *i.e.*, in the months of June and July, and are transplanted. The transplantation is known as *achharā*. The harvest is reaped in the month of Mārgashira, *i.e.*, by the 15th November.

Mustard seed (1) *Bhadoi* mustard: the variety sown in the beginning of the month of Ashādha, *i.e.*, so soon as the rain falls, is called *bhadoi* mustard, and is reaped in the month of Bhādraba, *i.e.*, August. (2) *Māghi* mustard: this variety which is sown in the month of Bhādraba, *i.e.*, in the month of

August, is called *māghi*; mustard being reaped in the month of Māgh. *Bīrhi*, *kulthī*, *mūga* (pulse), *barāi* (pulse). Sugarcane is planted in the month of Phālguna, *i.e.*, in February, and *gur* (molasses) is prepared in the month of Paush, *i.e.*, in December.

RENTS, WAGES AND PRICES. The assessment is very light and the average rates paid per acre for regular rice or lowlands are, first class (*bāhāl*) Re. 1-4-6, second class (*bernā*) Re. 1-2-0, third class (*māl*) Re. 0-9-9: uplands are assessed at an average rate of Re. 0-7-9. There are special rates for sugarcane lands (*barchhā*), viz., Rs. 3-2. The three divisions of lowlands are each subdivided into four classes according as they are favourably situated for irrigation or naturally retain the rainfall: the uplands are similarly divided into four classes. Uplands, on which catch-crops are raised every second or third year by burning the scrub-jungle, pay at the rate of two annas per acre.

The labouring classes in this State are divided as follows:—(1) *Gutis.*—These receive a monthly wage in kind and after the harvest they receive from 2 *purugs* (8 maunds) to 2 *purugs* 4 *khandis* (10 maunds) according to the character of the harvest; this is known as their *nistār* (yearly reward) or *bartan.* They also receive three pieces of cloth annually. Their engagements date from 1st Māgh (January-February). (2) *Kuthiās.*—These people are given no monthly wage, but feed in their master's house; they get as their *nistār* or yearly reward after the harvest from 1 *purug* (4 maunds) to 1 *purug* 2 *khandis* (5 maunds) of unhusked rice, and they also receive three pieces of cloth. Their duties mainly are to act as herdsmen and assist the *gutis.* They are also engaged from 1st Māgh. (3) *Khamāris.*—This is a superior class and they act as head labourers or foremen in charge of the classes mentioned above; they receive monthly wages in kind and a yearly *nistār* or reward of 3 *purugs* (12 maunds) of paddy and 4 pieces of cloth.

Average wages given in late years to different kinds of workmen are:—Superior mason and carpenter, 10 annas each; common mason and carpenter, 4 annas each; superior blacksmith, 6 annas; common blacksmith, 3 annas; and ordinary cooly, 1½ anna. There has been a steady tendency to a rise in the wages of superior workmen. The average price during late years of rice, *mūga*, *urid*, *kulthī* and salt has been 20 seers, 12 seers, 24 seers, 60 seers and 10 seers respectively.

A measure called *bhuti tāmbi* containing about 1¼ seer when rice is measured and about 1 seer when unhusked rice (*dhān*) is measured is in use here.

The scale is as follows:—

20 *Tāmbis* = 1 *Khandi* (=about 20 seers)		Paddy (unhusked rice) is measured by this standard.
8 *Khandis* = 1 *Purug* (=about 160 seers)		
8 *Tāmbis* = 1 *Kutā* (=10 seers)		This is the measurement for *chāul* (rice).
8 *Kutās* = 1 *Pastamā* (=80 seers)		

OCCUPATIONS, MANUFACTURES AND TRADE.

The principal occupation of the people is agriculture. Of the total population 60 per cent. live on agriculture; 30 per cent. follow professions; 0·50 per cent. live on iron smelting; 0·50 per cent. live on trade; 1 per cent. are engaged on sleeper and timber works and the balance work as field-labourers, State servants, etc.

There is a very considerable manufacture of iron in this State. Notwithstanding that iron ore is so plentiful throughout the Sambalpur district, this is the only part of it where smelting is carried on to any extent. Here there are some eight or ten villages, the inhabitants of which are constantly thus employed. Traders from Cuttack come up periodically and carry off the iron on pack-bullocks. The State derives no income from the trade; the smelters used merely to give to the State a very trifling tax for the right to work up the ore, but this tax has recently been abolished in order to encourage the industry. It is said that the iron is of very good quality, and that traders make a large profit by its sale. The smelters receive considerable advances from the traders. The rearing of tusser silk cocoons in the State forests is a local industry, as is also the extraction of catechu. There is little or no export of food-grains from the State: but there is a small trade in oil-seeds, forest products, and labour is employed in working for the sleeper contractors. The principal imported articles are spices, salt, tobacco and kerosene oil.

MEANS OF COMMUNICATION.

There is an excellent road from Sambalpur to Rāmpur, the headquarters of the State, and then on to the borders of the Athmallik State. This is the main Sambalpur-Cuttack road. There are good surface roads from Rāmpur to Bāmra and to the Sonpur border near the Mahānadī, giving communication with Sonpur. The main road of the State passes across the watershed and is naturally of steep gradients. This road is largely used for the export of sleepers from the State and the neighbouring State of Athmallik. There is a small rest-house at Mochibāhāl on the road at the border of the State and the Sambalpur district and a good inspection bungalow is under construction at the headquarters. The Imperial post plies daily between Sambalpur and Rāmpur, there being a branch post office at Rampur, the headquarters of the State.

LAND REVENUE ADMINISTRATION.

The land revenue administration is similar in many respects to that of the Sambalpur district: the rules for the administration of revenue affairs framed by the Chief Commissioner of the Central Provinces in 1889 for the States are in force. The last settlement was made by the late Chief in 1905 for a period of ten years and the current demand is Rs. 21,354. There are no zamīndāris in the State.

The land revenue is collected with moderation; remission is granted where land has deteriorated or gone out of cultivation; *taccāvi* loans under the Agriculturists' Loans Act and Land Improvement Loans Act are given at 6¼ per cent. to struggling villages, and if they cannot pull round the rental is revised. The cesses (dispensary and school) are assessed together at 2 annas per rupee of rent. The payments of *tikā*, a voluntary offering of one rupee are made on two occasions, viz., in Shrābana at the Rākhi Pūrnimā and in Paush.

In this State the villages are leased out to—(1) *garhatiās*, (2) *pradhāns* and *gaontiās*, who are chiefly found in the eastern area of the State. These have no right to mortgage or sell their villages; they are not ousted so long as they do not misconduct themselves or fall into arrears. The *bhogrā* lands assigned to them as village headmen and collectors of the State revenue are lands equivalent in value to one-fifth of the total rental of the village. The difference between the status of the two classes is that the former, *garhatiās*, do not pay *tikā* which the *pradhāns* and *gaontiās* have to pay; the former, however, have to come with their men to guard the Chief's palace when he is away and furnish the Chief when travelling with escorts and are the heads of the villages which furnish the State militia (*paiks*). There are the usual maintenance, service and religious grants in the State. It is usual to assess *māfi* (free) grants to a small *tanki* or quit-rent at each settlement until the lands are gradually resumed.

GENERAL ADMINISTRATION.

The relations between the State and the British Government are regulated by the provision of the *sanad* of 1867. The State pays a tribute liable to revision and which in 1909 was fixed at Rs. 2,000 for thirty years: the State is also liable to pay *nazarāna*

Powers.

(succession fees) under the rules. The Chief has full criminal and civil powers, but capital sentences require confirmation by the Commissioner of the Orissa Division. The State is now under administration of Government with a Superintendent in direct charge under the control of the Political Agent: he is assisted by a *Tahsildār* who has magisterial powers as well as being a revenue and executive officer. The administration is conducted to suit the conditions of the people and though not on advanced lines it is run on modern systems. The total estimated revenue of the State in 1907-08 was Rs. 69,744: excluding land revenue the principal sources of income are forests, from which in 1907-08 the revenue was Rs. 27,970: sleeper operations are carried on by a contractor: firewood, thatching grass, bamboos, *lodh*, lac, tusser cocoons, catechu, resin, wax and honey yield a small income. The tenants pay the usual commutation fee, here called *nistār*, for the right to cut third class timber for their agricultural and domestic needs, including *sāl* for use for ploughs. The State is, for the most part of its area, thickly covered with forests. At one time apparently it contained a considerable quantity of valuable *sāl;* with the advance of the railway much of this has now been cut, and practically sleeper operations are now confined to the timber to be found on the hill-sides, all trees fit for sleepers having been cut away from the valleys and uplands. The value of the forests as a source of revenue has been recognised and a distinction has been made between the forests falling within and without the village boundaries. In the former area the people can obtain wood for agricultural and domestic purposes on payment of the usual *nistār* levied at 4 annas and 2 annas respectively on cultivators and artisans as the case may be. If wood is taken from the reserved area, the regular forest rates have to be paid and passes obtained and the rates prevailing in Angul have been adopted. There is no regular excise staff in the State. The arrangements and conditions under which opium is supplied from Sambalpur are the same as in the case of the other Feudatory States attached to the Sambalpur district. *Gānja* is obtained from Nimār. The number of liquor shops in the State is not excessive and only averages one to every 36 square miles. There is no restriction on the brewing of *hāndiā* (rice-beer) for home consumption. The excise revenue in the year 1907-08 amounted to Rs 7,492. The *haldiān patti* or marriage tax is levied on the occasion of marriages in the family of the Chief; there is no demand however on the occasion of deaths in the family. The hide lease is given out as a monopoly: the tenants' interests are protected by their being allowed to keep such skins as they need for domestic and agricultural purposes: the rates fixed for payment for the hides by the contractor are reasonable and cattle-killing for the sake of the hide is rare. There was formerly a monopoly for the purchase of iron; but in the interest of the industry this has been abolished. The number of civil suits for disposal during the year 1907-08 was 314: these were generally of a petty nature. Crime is light,

Finances. Forests. Excise. Taxes. Monopolies. Civil justice. Crime.

Police. Jail. Public Works Department.

but effectively dealt with. There is a regular police force, consisting of 7 Head-Constables and 28 constables in charge of an officer from the British police force. The jail is not quite suitable for present requirements and is being rebuilt. There are good public offices and buildings at the headquarters, and the public works are locally in charge of a Sub-Overseer under the Agency Executive Engineer.

EDUCATION.

Education is very backward in the State and endeavours are being made to open more schools, the number of schools in 1907-08 being 5: in 1907-08 only 282 pupils were on the rolls: a separate girls' school has recently been opened at the headquarters and there are signs of a growing interest among the better class of agriculturists in education, and during the year 1908-09 the number of schools has increased to 13. There is a good school house at Rāmpur. A Sub-Inspector of Schools has been recently appointed to promote the cause of education. The State enjoys the services of the Agency Inspector of Schools and contributes towards the cost of that officer's establishment.

CHAPTER XXI.

RANPUR STATE.

THE State of Ranpur lies between 19° 54′ and 20° 12′ N., and 85° 8′ and 85° 28′ E., with an area of 203 square miles. It is bounded on the north, east and south by Purī district, and on the west by Nayāgarh State. The south-west is a region of forest-clad and almost entirely uninhabited hills, which wall in its whole western side, except at a single point, where a pass leads into the adjoining State of Nayāgarh. To the north and east there are extensive fertile and populous valleys. The average rainfall for the six years from 1902-03 to 1907-08 was 55·94 inches. The headquarters of the State are at Ranpur. PHYSICAL ASPECTS.

The Ranpur State claims to be the most ancient of all the States formerly known as the Orissa Tributary Mahāls and a list of the Chiefs of the State covers a period of over 3,600 years. The family records are most interesting, and besides noticing the exploits and marvellous deeds of individual Chiefs, contain references to the various paramount powers of Orissa from the early Hindu rulers to the Muhammadans and Marāthās, but their authenticity is doubtful. According to the family history of this State, Biswabasu and Biswabāsab, two brothers of the Benu Rāj family, lived in the forests of the Nīlgiri hills, but were driven out. The younger brother Biswabāsab fled with a few attendants and took refuge in the valley of the Munināg hill, amidst vast forest tracts, sparsely inhabited. Biswabāsab here established himself reclaiming the forests and gradually subdued the Bhuiyās of the neighbouring villages. It is related that one day when Biswabāsab was walking in the forest he found an image of a goddess which he brought to Munināg hill and worshipped. The goddess being pleased with the worship appeared to him in a dream and said: "My son, this land belonged once to Ranāsur, but you may now live here and construct a village on the eastern side of the hill. Your supremacy may continue permanently." Biswabāsab accordingly established the State and built a village and called it Ranpur. It is mentioned in the Kapil-Samhitā that 1,274 years of the Kali HISTORY.

Yuga had passed when this State was established. This would be many years before the commencement of the Christian era. It was at first bounded on the south by Boitā hill and the Haldā river; west by the Kusumī river; north by the Horā river; east by Kantáinãl and the Champāibhuin hill. The area of the State was once more extensive than it now is and tradition states that at one time the Dayā river was the eastern boundary, Bānki the northern, and the Chilkā lake the southern boundary. On the death of a Chief a stone statue is erected, and according to this old custom the statues of deceased Chiefs are kept in the burial ground. The first 54 Chiefs are alleged to have held the *gadi* of the State for 1,743 years, and on the death of Ananta Singh, the 54th Chief, his son Harihar Singh, succeeded, according to the family tradition, to the *gadi* in the year A.D. 16. Arjun Bhanj, Chief of Baud, defeated Nidhi Singh the 85th Chief and conquered Ranpur. But his son, Pītāmbar Singh recovered the State, became Chief of Ranpur, and holding the *gadi* for 50 years died in 1108 A.D. In the 12th century the then Chief of Ranpur received at the hands of Ananga Bhīma Deva, Rājā of Orissa, the title of "Narendra" and was enrolled among the Sāmanta Rājās owing to his prowess in battle. Since his time, the Chiefs of Ranpur have always enjoyed the title of "Narendra". Rājā Rām Chandra Narendra the 96th Chief who succeeded to the *gadi* in 1437 A.D., did much to improve and develop the State and was a student of astronomy. His son extended the northern and eastern boundaries of the State of Ranpur, constructed seven strong forts, held his *gadi* for 49 years and died in 1525 A.D. He was succeeded by his son, Banamālī Narendra, who is said to have been an expert in statuary. Stone images made by him are still to be found in many places within the State.

During the time of the Chief Rām Chandra Narendra, who held the *gadi* from 1692 to 1727 A.D., many inhabitants of Khurdā, owing to the oppression of the Muhammadans, fled for shelter to Ranpur and settled there. He was succeeded by his son, Sārangadhar Bajradhar Narendra, who held his *gadi* from 1727 to 1754 A.D. During his time the Marāthās under Raghujī conquered Orissa. Sārangadhar met Raghujī by the side of the Mahānadī river, and the story goes that in order to prove his prowess as a warrior he killed a wild buffalo with a stick of sugarcane. Raghujī as a reward for Sārangadhar's bravery gave him the title of "Bajradhar" which is still employed as a family title by the Chiefs of the State. The present Chief Krishna Chandra Singh Deva Bīrabar Bajradhar Narendra

Mahāpātra succeeded in 1899 A.D. The emblem of the State is a sword and the family title is Bajradhar Narendra Mahāpātra.

The population increased from 40,115 in 1891 to 46,075 in 1901; it is contained in 261 villages, and the density is 227 persons to the square mile. Hindus number 45,762 of the whole population, by far the most numerous caste being the Chasās (14,000). Next in importance rank the Gauras (3,500). There is a comparatively small population of Khonds (1,631). The population is classified as follows:—Hindus—males, 22,818, females, 22,944. The Hindus thus form 99·3 per cent. of the population of the State; proportion of males in total Hindus, 49·8 per cent. Musalmāns—males, 183, females, 130: total of Musalmāns, 313, or ·67 per cent. of the population; proportion of males in total Musalmāns, 58·4 per cent. Christians, *nil.* Literates number 3,101 or 6·7 per cent. of the population. Averages:—villages per square mile, 1·29; houses per village, 35·4; persons per village, 177; persons per house, 5; houses per square mile, 45·5. The villages are classified as follows:—247 with less than five hundred; 11 with from five hundred to a thousand; 2 with from a thousand to two thousand and 1 with from two to five thousand inhabitants. The people are well off; the lands are fertile and there is ready means of export for surplus stocks. THE PEOPLE.

There is a charitable dispensary at headquarters with a small indoor ward: the number of patients treated in 1907-08 was 10,607. The country to the south and east is not unhealthy, but in other parts of the State, fever is very prevalent, 43 per cent. of the deaths in the State being due to fever: cholera in epidemic form, frequently introduced by pilgrims from Purī, accounted during the ten years from 1893 to 1902 for 26 per cent. of the deaths. Vaccination is not popular in the State, but is gradually making headway and the number of primary vaccinations 945 in 1907-08 was the largest for many years: in the year 1906-07 revaccination was started, and in 1907-08 the number of revaccinations was 65. The work is carried on by licensed vaccinators, who are local men trained in the special vaccination class at the Medical School, Cuttack. PUBLIC HEALTH.

The open area of the State is well cultivated and the villages are large and populous: winter rice is the main crop, but early rice is grown in considerable quantity and excellent crops of oil-seeds and pulses are raised. The total area of the State is 130,969 acres, of which forests occupy 80,280 acres; the normal acreage under crops is 35,934 acres, of which 3,000 acres are AGRICULTURE.

twice-cropped: of this area rice normally occupies 31,142 acres *māndiā* 643 acres and *til* (sesamum) 350 acres.

RENTS, WAGES AND PRICES.

The assessment averages per *mān* (two-thirds of an acre) for first, second and third class rice lands Rs. 3-6-2, Rs. 2-5-6 and Re. 1-4-10 respectively and for uplands, Re. 1-0-8. During the ten years from 1893 to 1902 wages have shown no tendency to rise and the daily wage has averaged as follows:—superior mason, 4½ annas, common mason, blacksmith and carpenter, 3 annas each, superior carpenter and superior blacksmith, 4 annas each, cooly, 1½ annas: during the same period the average price of wheat, rice, gram and salt has been 9¾ seers, 20⅜ seers, 25¼ seers, 12½ seers respectively.

OCCUPATIONS, MANUFACTURES AND TRADE.

There are no occupations or manufactures which call for notice. There are bi-weekly markets at headquarters, where country products are bartered for iron, cotton, blankets, cloth, silk, wheat and clarified butter brought from the Khandparā State, and for fish from the Chilkā lake.

MEANS OF COMMUNICATION.

The State lies close to the East Coast section of the Bengal-Nāgpur Railway and the headquarters are connected with the line of rail at Kāluparāghāt station by a good road. There is also a good feeder road from the headquarters to the Madras Trunk Road, 10 miles in length, partly bridged and metalled. A new surface road from the headquarters to the Nayāgarh border is under construction. There is a rest-house for travellers at the headquarters and a post office. The post plies *viâ* Khurda.

LAND REVENUE ADMINISTRATION.

The land revenue demand amounts to Rs. 44,892 and is realised in two instalments in November and April. No cesses are levied and there are no zamīndāris in the State. The number of grants, known as *khanjā* grants to relations of the Chief by way of maintenance is considerable. The system of the land revenue administration is similar to that of other States and the village *sarbarāhkārs* (headmen) receive a cash commission on collection. The last land settlement was made in 1899 for a period of twenty years: six rates were fixed for wet cultivation varying from Rs. 4-11-0 to Rs. 2-1-4 per *mān* (two-thirds of an acre).

GENERAL ADMINISTRATION.

The State is administered by the Chief assisted by a *Dīwān*, and the relations with the British Government are defined by the *sanad* of 1894 which was revised in 1908. The estimated annual revenue of the State is about Rs. 54,000 and a tribute of Rs. 1,401 is paid to the British Government. Forests yielded in 1907-08 a revenue of Rs. 2,227: no green timber is sold and the Chief has reserved forest areas; the forests in the past have been considerably depleted of valuable timber: in 1907-08

Finances.

Forests.

excise yielded Rs. 2,442: the supply of opium, which may be obtained from the Government treasury, is limited to 7 seers per mensem. The majority of the civil suits are of a petty nature, the greater number being for sums under Rs. 50 in value: in 1907-08 the number of civil suits for disposal was 207, 64 per cent. of them being below the value of Rs. 50. Crime is light and there is very little serious crime; the total number of cases reported to the police in 1907-08 being 36: the police force consists of one Sub-Inspector, 5 Head-Constables and 21 constables. The jail is an old building with mud walls and the accommodation is for 20 prisoners. In 1907-08 the average daily population was 11·61. In 1907-08 the total expenditure incurred in the Public Works Department amounted to Rs. 2,119. Excise. Justice. Crime. Police. Jail. Public Works Department.

The State maintains a Middle English, 3 Upper Primary and 33 Lower Primary schools, besides there is one private school: the number of pupils in 1907-08 on the rolls was 660. The State receives assistance from Government for primary education. EDUCATION.

CHAPTER XXII.

SONPUR STATE.

PHYSICAL ASPECTS. THE State of Sonpur is situated in 20° 32′ and 21° 11′ N., and 83° 27′ and 84° 16′ E. It is bounded on the north by Sambalpur district and a portion of the State of Rairākhol; on the south and south-east by the State of Baud; on the east by the Rairākhol State; and on the west by the State of Patnā. The area is 906 square miles, rather more than one-half of which is situated on the right bank of the Mahānadī and the remainder on the left bank. The aspect of the country is flat and slightly undulating; and isolated hills of no great altitude rise abruptly here and there. The soil is, as elsewhere in this part of the Mahānadī valley, poor; it is not alluvial, and contains a considerable proportion of sand. There are no forests of any great extent, and such as exist do not contain any valuable timber. The principal rivers are the Mahānadī which flows through the centre of the State, the Ang, which for part of its course forms the boundary between the States of Patnā and Sonpur: the Suktel also crosses the southern portion of the State flowing into the Tel a few miles above the juncture of the Tel with the Mahānadī; the Jīrā, an affluent of the Mahānadī, to the north, divides a portion of the State from Sambalpur. The Tel on the south forms the boundary with the State of Baud. The Jīrā, the Ang and the Tel are all affluents of the Mahānadī on its right bank. Diamonds are occasionally found in the banks of the Mahānadī and deposits of mica occur in various parts of the State. The average rainfall for the six years from 1902-03 to 1907-08—was 50·53 inches. The climate is similar to that of the Sambalpur district. The headquarters of the State are at Sonpur, 54 miles from Sambalpur, with which it is connected by a good gravelled road.

HISTORY. Sonpur was formerly a chiefship subordinate to Patnā, but was constituted a separate State by Rājā Madhukar Sāi of Sambalpur about the year A.D. 1560. Since then it has been counted among the cluster of Garhjāt States. It is now attached to the Sambalpur district.

The family is Chauhān Rājput, being an offshoot from the family of the Rājā of Sambalpur. Their lineage is traced back to Madan Gopāl, who obtained the State about 300 years ago. He was the son of Madhukar Sāi, fourth Rājā of Sambalpur. The succession has since continued regularly. The grandfather, Nīlādhar Singh Deva Bahādur, of the present Chief obtained the title of Rājā Bahādur for services to the British Government in the field: Rājā Pratāp Rudra Singh Deva Bahādur, father of the present Chief, obtained the title of Rājā Bahādur in 1898 and the present Chief was given the personal title of Mahārājā in 1908. Extensive remains of old buildings in the neighbourhood of the Sonpur town show that in former times the town was more populous and important than at present. Sonpur was evidently colonised by the Hindus at an early period in its history as is shown by the copper-plate inscriptions in Sanskrit written in Kutila character found in the neighbourhood of the town and attributed to the later Gupta Kings of Orissa and the Ganga Kings of Kalinga. Many old fashioned tiled (*nandā*) wells constructed by Brāhmans are found at Sonpur. The emblem of the State is a *chakra* (discus).

THE PEOPLE.

According to the census of 1866 the population numbered 60,000 souls: in 1901 the population was 169,877 souls. There is one large town and one large village in the State, viz., Sonpur and Binkā, both on the right bank of the Mahānadī, with a population of 8,887 and 3,843 respectively, and 898 ordinary villages. The density of the population is 188 persons to the square mile. The population is classified as follows:—Hindus—males, 82,333, females, 86,648, total 168,981 or 99·47 per cent. of the total population: proportion of males in total Hindus is 48·7 per cent. Musalmāns—males, 259, females, 250, total, 509 or 0·30 per cent. of the total population: proportion of males in total Musalmāns is 49·1 per cent. Animists—males, 175, females, 208, total, 383 or 0·23 per cent. of the total population. Christians—4. Number of literate persons is 1,758 or 1·03 (males 1·00, females, 0·03) per cent. of the total population. Averages—Villages per square mile, 0·99; persons per village, 179; houses per village, 40·2; houses per square mile, 42·2; persons per house, 4. The remaining 898 villages may be classified as follows:—Village with from two thousand to five thousand inhabitants, 1; villages with from one thousand to two thousand inhabitants, 6; villages with from five hundred to one thousand inhabitants, 36; villages with less than five hundred inhabitants 855.

The non-agricultural castes are Brāhmans, Mahāntis and Rājputs; and the agricultural castes are Chasās, Kaltuyās or Koithās, Aghariās and Gonds. In most of the large villages are found a sprinkling of the artisan classes, with a few weavers of coarse cloths—Telis, Mālis, etc. The population is for the most part agricultural. The principal castes are Gauras or Ahīrs, Brāhmans, Dumāls, Bhuliās and Kewats: the latter are the boatmen who follow a prosperous livelihood in transporting the surplus produce of the country to Cuttack and Sambalpur. The great-grandfather of the present Chief was a patron of Sanskrit learning and established large colonies of Brāhmans.

The Gandās (22,203) constitute a large percentage of the population and as in the Sambalpur district compose the criminal element of the population: they are poor; a certain number of them earn regular employment as field labourers and weavers, but the majority dislike regular labour and eke out an existence by occasional labour and the proceeds of theft.

The Bhuliās (7,527) are the class who weave the tusser cloth for which Sonpur is highly reputed; an account of the industry will be found under the head of occupations, manufactures and trade.

PUBLIC HEALTH. The climate of the Sonpur State is not unhealthy and, as there are no forests, malarial fever is not rife; the town and large villages are, however, subject to visitations of cholera and occasionally of small-pox. There are dispensaries with accommodation for indoor patients both at Sonpur and Binkā: the Medical Officer of the State possesses the qualifications of an Assistant Surgeon and there are two Civil Hospital Assistants in direct charge of the two dispensaries. The number of outdoor patients treated in 1907-08 was 16,433, number of indoor patients treated was 62. Vaccination is carefully attended to and supervised by a Vaccination Inspector and a considerable number of revaccinations are annually performed: in 1907-08 the number of primary vaccinations was 8,237 and number of revaccinations in the same year was 3,606.

AGRICULTURE. The principal crop is rice; the lands are highly cultivated and in good years a considerable quantity of rice and oil-seeds is available for export: pulses, cotton and sugarcane are also largely cultivated. The villages are extensive and prosperous and carry a large agricultural population: excellent reservoirs for irrigation are found in most villages, the total number of tanks being 1,698. The greater area of the State in regard to its agricultural development closely resembles the well cultivated *tahsīl* of Bargarh in the Sambalpur district.

NATURAL CALAMITIES. Famine. The State is liable to scarcity, but has but rarely suffered from famine. The only famine of which there is record occurred in 1899-1900. The rainfall was very scanty, being only 36·05 inches and was badly distributed: the rainfall was insufficient to fill the tanks and in consequence the fields could not be irrigated: 50 per cent. of the rice crop on the first class irrigated lands, 70 per cent. on second class lands, 85 per cent. on third class and 30 per cent. of the upland rice crop were lost: winter crops failed to germinate owing to want of moisture in the soil. Wheat, however, was sown by about 30 per cent. of the cultivators and this crop was of very great assistance. The price of rice stood at 20 seers per rupee at the beginning of 1899 but fell in 1900 to $8\frac{1}{4}$ seers. Relief works were undertaken and kitchens played a prominent part in the relief given: they were opened at all the important centres in the State and the zamīndārs also maintained kitchens at their headquarters: 17 kitchens in all were opened, gratuitous relief to respectable poor and taccavi loans to cultivators and weavers were given: the total amount of loans thus given was Rs. 27,628 to 8,239 recipients. Regular employment on works was found for 2,979 persons and the expenditure, including assistance to the dependents of the workers, amounted on this account to Rs. 15,322: the number of persons fed at the 17 kitchens was 14,674 at a total cost of Rs. 13,549. The paupers mostly came from members of the Gandā, Gaura, Saharā, Dumāl, Kewat and Khadāl castes.

RENTS, WAGES AND PRICES.

The assessment is light: the average rates prevailing for rice lands per acre are first class Re. 1-4, second class Re. 1-2, and third class Re. 0-12; uplands are assessed at an average rate of 5 annas per acre. The average rate for sugarcane (*barchhā*) lands is Re. 1-12-3 per acre, but first class land for sugarcane pays in the case of *bhogrā* Rs. 3-2-2 per acre and ryoti Rs. 2-10-0. Average daily wage given to first, second and third class mechanical labour is 8 annas, 6 annas and 5 annas or 4 annas respectively: average wage given to ordinary cooly is 2 annas. The field labourers in this State are divided as follows:—(1) *Gutis.*— These receive from 2 *khandis* (1 maund) to 2 *khandis* 10 *tāmbis* (1 maund 10 seers) of *dhān* (unhusked rice) as a monthly wage. After the harvest they receive from 2 *purugs* (8 maunds) to 2 *purugs* 4 *khandis* (10 maunds) annually as their *nistār* (yearly reward): in certain cases these are given pieces of land yielding 2 *purugs* or 2 *purugs* 4 *khandis* of *dhān* instead of the annual payment. They also receive 2 pieces of cloth worth 8 annas each annually. (2) *Khamāris.*—This is a superior class, and they act as head labourers; they receive 3 *khandis* (1 maund 20 seers) as a monthly wage and a yearly *nistār* (reward) of 3 *purugs* (12 maunds) of *dhān* or a piece of land yielding 3 *purugs* yearly. Other field labourers who are employed daily, get from 2 to 3 *tāmbis* (2 to 3 seers) daily. The average price during the ten years from 1897-98 to 1907-08 of rice, *mūga*, *urid*, gram, *kulthi*, *arhar* and salt has been 18$\frac{1}{16}$ seers, 12$\frac{3}{8}$ seers, 12$\frac{15}{16}$ seers, 19$\frac{5}{16}$ seers, 23$\frac{1}{2}$ seers, 18$\frac{1}{8}$ seers and 11$\frac{3}{4}$ seers, respectively.

OCCUPATIONS, MANUFACTURES AND TRADE.

Of the total population nearly $\frac{3}{4}$th, *i.e.*, 72·7 per cent. live on agriculture: 18·6 per cent. maintain themselves on industry ; 0·70 per cent. follow professions for their livelihood: 3·1 per cent. have accepted State, village and personal services and 0·39 per cent. follow commerce. There is a considerable export trade of rice and pulses *viá* the Mahānadī to Cuttack and Sambalpur. The town of Sonpur and the village of Binkā are important trade marts for the river export trade. At the village of Tarbhā on the Pātnā border there is an important trade centre for cart and pack-bullock traffic: this village is the centre on which the export trade from Baud, the Khondmāls, Patnā and Kālāhandī concentrates and from there finds its way either to Sonpur or Binkā for shipment on boats along the Mahānadī or travels on by road to Sambalpur. The principal manufacture of the State is the weaving by the Bhuliā caste of tusser cloth of excellent quality: the chief centres of this industry are at Sonpur and Binkā and the latter place is noted for the quality of the cloth turned out, which is only slightly inferior to the best qualities produced at Barpāli in the Sambalpur district.

Tusser industry.

The cultivation of the tusser cocoons is largely carried on in the State, but the great centre for the manufacture of the tusser cloth is at Sonpur. A large population of the caste known as Bhuliās resides at Sonpur and its neighbourhood and carry on a considerable industry. The tusser cloth woven at Sonpur is held in high repute. The caterpillars or *kosā* feed on the *sāhāj* or *āsan* (Terminalia tomentosa) tree and spin their cocoons on the *sāl* (Shorea robusta) and *sima* or *dhaurā* (Lagerstœmia parviflora) trees. The cultivation of the caterpillars and the collection of the cocoons are carried on by the Pāns or Gandās. The cocoons after collection are dried in the sun for two or three days to kill the chrysalis, but if this be not sufficient the cocoons are boiled in a pot with straw and water. To prepare the cocoons for the removal of the threads, a mixture of ashes and water is prepared and this with some straw is placed in an earthen pot together with cocoons and boiled, 4 pints of water being added for every 300 cocoons placed in the vessel. The cocoons are boiled until they obtain the softness of cotton and emit a peculiar smell: they are then washed in pure water and placed on a bed of wood ashes to absorb the moisture. To wind off the tusser thread to make the woof yarn the cocoons are placed in an open dish and four or five threads are pulled out from a similar number of cocoons, interlaced in accordance with the thickness of the yarn it is desired to obtain.

The threads are interlaced by twirling them on the left thigh with the flat of the left hand adding a little wood ash to strengthen the strands; the right hand at the same time revolves the reeling machine or *natāi*; this portion of the work is generally done by small girls. When a sufficient quantity of thread has thus been reeled off, it is removed from the reeling machine and kept ready for use as a skein (*latā*) after being first washed in water. If still stronger yarn is required then the skeins on two reeling machines are spun off on to a larger machine twisting the yarns and uniting them into one in the process. For actual weaving purposes the yarn is wound from the skein on to bobbins by means of a spinning wheel (*rahantā*) and the bobbins are then placed in the shuttle.

For the preparation of the warp yarn the threads are spun off from seven cocoons: the threads are interlaced in the same manner as in the case of the woof yarn; the yarn thus spun is removed from the reeling machine (*natāi*) and stretched on a frame (*jantar*) consisting of two flat parallel pieces of wood with pegs along the top of each and the yarn is laced across from opposite pegs: the two blocks of wood are connected below and kept firm by two bars. The warp yarn is then immersed in a pulp made of boiled paddy (*i.e.*, the husks of the rice are not removed before boiling) and covered with ashes and is thus kept for one night: the yarn is finally polished by means of an instrument known as a weaver's key or *kunchi*. The warp yarn is then ready for use and is set up in the ordinary hand-loom of the country and the woof yarn is passed through it by the shuttle worked by hand.

Brass and bell-metal utensils and idols are also manufactured in this State. There is a small and special trade at Sonpur in the manufacture of cards for a game peculiar to these parts: the cards are small circular discs somewhat larger than a rupee made of tusser lacquered over: the figures on the cards are artistically executed and very finely coloured. The principal exported articles are rice and other food grains, oil-seeds, tusser cloth, cotton, molasses and *ghī* (clarified butter); and the principal imported articles are mill-made thread piece-goods, salt, brass utensils, kerosene oil, spices, stone and glass wares.

MEANS OF COMMUNICATION.

The greater part of the export trade of the State is carried by the Mahānadī and a considerable export of rice and pulses is carried on with Cuttack and Sambalpur.

The Tel is comparatively free from obstruction; and during the monsoon months there is some boat traffic from Patnā and timber is also floated down from the upper reaches of this river in the Kālāhandī State.

In the Mahānadī just opposite Sonpur there are dangerous rapids, which render the navigation difficult. There is a good road, the Cuttack-Sonpur-Sambalpur road on the right bank of the Mahānadī connecting with Dhamā in the Sambalpur district and passing through the important village of Binkā; there are bungalows every ten miles, from Cuttack up to the Baud-Sonpur border: there are also bungalows at Sonpur and Binkā in the Sonpur State and at Dhamā. A new road is under construction from Dhamā on the northern bank of the Mahānadī, in Sambalpur district, to the border of the State on the northern bank of the river and from there a State road is being constructed to a place opposite to Binkā and in future the traffic between the State and the Sambalpur district will cross the Mahānadī at Binkā, a far easier crossing than at Dhamā. There is an excellent road on the western border of the State forming the connecting link between Sambalpur, Bargarh and Barpāli in the Sambalpur district and Sālebhattā on the main road to the Patnā and Kālāhandī States. There is a rest-house on this road at Dungripāli, in the Sonpur State 12 miles from Barpāli. There is a surface road from Sonpur to Tarbhā, an important mart on the borders of the Pātnā State. The imperial post runs from Sambalpur to Sonpur and on to Baud: there is a sub-post office at Sonpur and letter-boxes at important villages in the State.

LAND REVENUE ADMINISTRATION.

The current land revenue demand in 1907-08, was Rs. 54,837. There are three *kists*—(1) January, 8 annas, (2) March, 4 annas and (3) June, 4 annas.

The villages are leased out with (1) *thikādārs* or *gaontiās* (farmers), (2) *garhatiās*, and (3) *birtiās*.

Thikādārs or gaontiās.

Previously to 1887 the villages were put up to auction as regards the *bhogrā* lands—service lands of the lessee of the village; the amount bid for the *bhogrā* lands gave a right to hold the lease of the village for five years; the amount was paid down in a lump sum. Since 1887, the *thikādārs* (farmers or lessees) make annual payments for these *bhogrā* lands, the amount assessed previously to 1887 having been divided by five, which is now taken as the annual demand for the *bhogrā* lands. The *thikādār* obtains the benefit of all new lands brought under cultivation by the tenants until there is a new settlement. A new settlement is in progress and it is intended to have only two *kists*, the June *kist* being unsuitable. In the case of lands which are abandoned and a new tenant takes them up the *thikādār* receives a *nazarāna* (bonus) from the new occupier. The *thikādār* is not allowed to mortgage or sell his village or his *bhogrā* lands. All *thikādāri* villages pay *kar* (payment in kind) in March, consisting of *chāul* (rice) and *urid*.

If a *thikādār* dies during the period of settlement his son succeeds paying for mutation (*dākhil-khārij*) according to the rental of the village; he also gives a *salāmi* (*tikā*)—gift—to the Chief and receives a piece of cloth (*lāt*); if the son is not fit to carry on the village it remains in his name provided a suitable agent is forthcoming.

Garhatiās. These people are on the same footing as the *thikādārs*—except that the tenants in their villages only pay *urid* and *ghī* (clarified butter) as *kar* (payment in kind) and no *chāul* (rice). The people of these villages act as guards on the palace in the absence of the Chief; they render less *bethī* (free labour) in that they do not come into Sonpur to work. They render *bethī* (free labour) in repairing any thāna or school in their neighbourhood and looking after any road running through their villages; they do not however carry bundles for the Chief or provide transport. They are really the old feudal militia of the State and are known as *sipāhi* ryots or *paiks* (State militia); in some of these villages, however, there are two classes of tenants, viz., ordinary tenants and *sipāhi* tenants; in such cases the ordinary tenants are assessed in all respects in the same way as tenants in *thikādāri* villages. The *garhatiās* pay *dākhil-khārij* or mutation fees.

Birtiās. These tenure-holders are all Brāhmans who received their villages on special terms: in some cases they were, or their ancestors were, the original founder of the villages. At the recent settlement their rents have been slightly increased, except in the cases of those who had *mukarrarī pattās*—permanently fixed settlements—but these were very few. At the *Shrāban Pūrnimā* (July-August) and *Paush Pūrnimā* (December-January) these Brāhmans give coconuts and offer the thread to the Chief and at *Dasharā* come for sixteen days to celebrate the festival at the *garh* (headquarters). They pay the school-cess and *kar* (payment in kind) also on a reduced scale.

Bābuānā. The tenures given as grants are the usual ones, *e.g.*, *bābuānā* grants to the Chief's relatives; there are 18 villages held in this way. These grants are usually held rent-free and do not contribute *kar* (payment in kind), but pay the school-cess.

Māfi grants. *Māfi* (free) grants are of the usual kinds.—(1) *Debottar* (religious), (2) *brahmottar* (to Brāhmans) and (3) *naukrān* (service).

No payments in kind (*kar*) are made by these rent-free villages and tenures, but all pay the school-cess.

Payments in kind are only made by the *thikādāri* and *garhati* villages and are paid into the Chief's *bhandār* (store-house) on three occasions, viz. (1) *Nuākhiā.*—Small contribution of *chāul* (rice), *mūga*, *gur* (molasses), *ghī* (clarified butter), curds, and grass for making brooms. These are paid in on the day fixed for eating new rice in the month of September. (2) *Dasharā.*—On this occasion in the month of September-October *ghī* (clarified butter), *til* (sesamum), curds and a goat are given. (3) In *Kārttika* (October-November) *chāul* (rice), *mūga*, *ghī* (clarified butter), *tarkāri* (vegetables) and *gur* (molasses), are given for the Gopāljī temple for the Gobardhan *Pūjā*. These are paid into the *bhandār* (store-house) and the temple's share is made over subsequently; a day is then fixed for feeding the idol and all the Brāhmans in the State.

Zamīndaris. In this State there are no large zamīndāris; there are five small zamīndāris, viz., Rāmpur, Kamsarā, Barpāli, Sukhā and Pancharā; besides these there are six other zamīndāris consisting of one or two villages each. The zamīndārs are all Khonds and Binjhāls. The zamīndāri of Pancharā was formerly part of the Baud State, but was mortgaged by the Chief of that State to the Sonpur Chief and eventually came into the possession of Sonpur: it lies across the Tel river. These zamīndāris pay a *takoli* (tribute) to the State: this *takoli* is liable to revision at each settlement: in the two zamīndāris, where small forests exist, the zamīndārs have been allowed to collect the revenue from license-fees, but the income so derived is taken into account in assessing the *takoli*.

GENERAL ADMINISTRATION. The relations between the State and the British Government are regulated by the *sanad* of 1867. The Sonpur Chief has under the *sanad* the same powers and is liable to the same obligations as the Chiefs of the other States transferred from the Central Provinces to Bengal. The State pays a tribute of Rs. 12,000 to the British Government; the tribute is liable to revision and was last revised in 1909 for a period of thirty years.

The administration of the State is conducted personally by the Chief assisted by a *Dīwān*, *Tahsīldār* and *Naib Tahsīldār*. The *Dīwān* is the chief executive officer of the State and exercises powers of a Sessions and District Judge, the Chief being the appellate Court: the *Tahsīldār* and *Naib Tahsīldār* exercise powers of first and second class Magistrates respectively and also exercise jurisdiction in civil suits. The Chief is also ably assisted by his brothers who serve as Honorary Magistrates and try civil suits. There are two benches also of Honorary Magistrates sitting at Sonpur and Binkā.

The total income of the State in 1907-08 was Rs. 1,54,054. **Finances.**

There are practically no forests in the State, and an attempt **Forests.** has been made on a small scale to reserve and reafforest a few of the small hills. The forest revenue in 1907-08 yielded Rs. 26,251.

Opium is obtained from Sambalpur and *gānja* is obtained **Excise.** from Nimār: the State does not charge the licensed vendors anything for cost of carriage from Sambalpur. Excise yielded a revenue of Rs. 32,874 in 1907-08. The hide lease of the **Monopoly.** State is auctioned out, but does not bring in a large sum. On occasions of marriages in the Chief's family a contribution, **Contributions.** known as *haldiānpatti*, is levied; the rate varies from one to four annas per *purug* of land: it is only levied on the occasion of the marriage of the Chief, the eldest son and eldest daughter and in the case of the deaths of the Rājā or Rānī. The school-cess is levied at one anna per rupee: villages under every class of **Cesses.** tenure-holder pay the cess, including the *māfi* (rent-free) villages. The zamīndārs also pay this school-cess at the same rate.

Formerly the various cesses and *abwābs* on industrial classes ***Abwābs.*** were in force, but these have now all been abolished. Also the *pichli* was levied; this was a tax on bullocks taking goods from the State for sale; the charge was four annas per bullock. These *abwābs* of *pātki* and *pichli* have been abolished.

During the year 1907-08 the number of civil suits for disposal **Civil justice.** was 840, most of which were of a petty nature, only 16 suits exceeding Rs. 500 in value.

The number of cases reported to the police in the year **Crime.** 1907-08 was 591.

The police force is now entirely under the control of the **Police.** Chief: formerly the zamīndārs entertained and paid for their own police, but since 1904 the force has been made entirely a State force and the zamīndārs pay a police *takoli* or contribution. The Chief's uncle is the Superintendent of Police and he was trained in Sambalpur, where he holds the rank of an Honorary Assistant District Superintendent of Police: the force is in the direct charge of a capable Inspector from the British police. The force consists of 5 Sub-Inspectors, 23 Head-Constables and 149 constables.

There is a good masonry jail at headquarters where the **Jail.** prisoners undergo regular labour and are taught to weave with the fly-shuttle loom. The present jail has accommodation for 83 prisoners. In the year 1907-08 the daily average population was 94·5.

P. W. Department. The expenditure on public works, during the year 1907-08, amounted to Rs. 15,247.

LOCAL SELF-GOVERNMENT. There are two municipalities, viz., Sonpur and Binkā: the revenues are entirely raised by imposing an octroi fee similar to that in force in Sambalpur: the octroi collections are annually leased out by the Municipal Commissioners. These two municipalities out of their funds maintain the local dispensary and the roads and bear the expenditure on primary education within the municipal areas and the Sonpur municipality contributes annually Rs. 986 for the town police. The municipalities work well and are much appreciated. The population in 1901 of Sonpur was 8,887 and of Binkā 3,843.

EDUCATION. The State takes great interest in education and there is a very fine Middle English school at Sonpur accommodated in a substantial building. In 1907-08 there were 33 schools in the State, of which two were Middle English schools, one Middle Vernacular school, three girls' schools, one Sanskrit *tol* and two special schools for low caste children. Of the 29 Primary schools, 25 are Upper Primary Schools and 4 Lower Primary Schools. In addition there were 10 *chātsālis* (elementary schools) or private institutions with 220 scholars. In 1907-08 the number of children on the roll was 2,117 boys and 471 girls, or 2,588 pupils in all. The State employs a special officer to control and supervise the schools in the interior. In 1907-08 the State spent Rs. 5,810 on education. The great advance and improvement made in the cause of education during recent years is one of the most marked features in the administration of this State.

CHAPTER XXIII.

TALCHER STATE.

PHYSICAL ASPECTS.

The State of Tālcher lies between 20° 52′ and 21° 18′ N., and 84° 54′ and 85° 16′ E., with an area of 399 square miles. It is bounded on the north by the Bāmra and Pāl Laharā States; on the east by the Dhenkānāl State; and on the south and west by Angul district. The Brāhmanī river traverses the State, and Tālcher village, which contains the Rājā's residence, is picturesquely situated on a bend on its right bank. The State consists for the most part of open cultivated lands and there are no hill ranges of any considerable size or height. The largest is the range running at right angles to the Brāhmanī river near Samal, and forming the boundary with the Dhenkānāl State. The State contains a coal field of which an examination was made in 1875. It was then reported that there is no seam of workable thickness and fairly good quality; that a final and thorough exploration could only be effected at a considerable expense; that the local consumption would never suffice to support a proper mining establishment, and that with the long and costly land carriage, no class of coal equal to Rānīganj coal could compete successfully at the Orissa ports with coal sent from Calcutta by sea. The project for utilizing the Tālcher coal-beds has, therefore, been abandoned for the present. Iron and limestone are also found near the banks of the Brāhmanī river, which separates Tālcher on the east from Pāl Laharā and Dhenkānāl. Small quantities of gold are found by washing the sand of the river, but little profit accrues to the workers. The average rainfall for the six years from 1902-03 to 1907-08 was 51·70 inches. The headquarters of the State are at Tālcher.

HISTORY.

According to tradition four sons of the Chief of Jaipur came to Purī on pilgrimage to see Jagannāth. In their pride of the *Sūryabansa* and *Rānā Thākur* family to which they belonged, they failed to properly salute the then Rājā of Purī. They were not therefore allowed to see the idol of Jagannāth, and two of them were put to death under the Rājā's orders. The other two brothers fled to a place named Nādharā, in the Dhenkānāl State, and there established a fort under the name of Bhīmanagarī.

They also built a temple near the fort, and set up an idol named Rāmchandī Devī. This idol now belongs to Dhenkānāl.

The boundaries of the State at the time of its establishment were on the north Gāngnan in the Bāmra State; on the south Kamlāng in the Dhenkānāl State; on the east Altumā in the Dhenkānāl State; on the west the States of Bāmra and Angul. It is said that the Rājā of Purī fought a battle with the Rājā of Tālcher, conquered him and took away Nādharā, Rāmchandī, Parjang, Palāsuni and Subalayā, and made them over to the Chief of Dhenkānāl. Gāngnan was similarly conquered by the Chief of Bāmra. None of the Chiefs received any *farmān* from the Mughals or Marāthās, but Dayānidhi Bīrabar Harichandan helped the British troops at the time of the rebellion of the Angul Rājā in 1847, and was rewarded with the title of Mahendra Bahādur, a *khilāt* and an elephant.

In very early times this family held sway in what is now the important village of Subalayā, in the Sonpur State, but was eventually driven out. Tradition relates that one of the Rājās of this race crossed the Brāhmanī on a hunting expedition. Near Tāleswarī Devī, a hare killed the Rājā's dog, and the Rājā accordingly established a fort there. Some time after he was defeated by the Khonds of the place and fled to the forests. One day while asleep in the forest, Hingulā Devī appeared to him in a dream and addressed him thus:—"If you worship me and Tāleswarī, you will become victorious over your enemies, and in that case you should name the place Tālcher." The Rājā followed this advice and took the field. During an action Hingulā Devī appeared in the shape of a tiger and destroyed the opponents of the Chief. After that, when the Rājā was asleep, the Devī again appeared to him in a dream, and said that it was she and not a tiger that had destroyed his opponents. She advised the Rājā to sign his name with the initial of a tiger's head. The Rājā named the place Tālcher, and bestowed a village named Padmanāvpur on Brāhmans.

In the village of Gopālprasād, about 14 miles to the south-west of headquarters of the State, there is found the site of a goddess who is worshipped under the name of Hingulā. The site of the worship extends over the area of the coal fields which extend for some two or three miles in the neighbourhood of the village: the actual manifestation consists of a jet of gas issuing from the coal, which is either lighted by the priest or itself ignites on contact with the air. The worship of the goddess takes place on the fourteenth day of full-moon in the month of Chaitra (March-April). The goddess Hingula is alleged to appear some days before this in a dream to her *sebāit* (priest), and indicates to him the exact spot of her coming revelation. The *sebāit* then proceeds to the spot indicated, and finding the natural fire burning keeps the flame burning by adding coal till the appointed hour of worship arrives, when a large crowd of worshippers attend from all quarters and make offerings of *ghī* (clarified butter), sugar, plantains, curd, goats, etc. Besides this annual worship, Hingulā is also worshipped as an idol throughout the year in a secluded and solitary spot in the forest near the village. The *sebāit* sends forth emissaries throughout the States and the neighbouring districts of British India to spread the worship of Hingulā. With threats of secretly firing their houses these emissaries extract contributions from the people and from time to time put into execution their threats. A very close watch has to be kept on their movements. The emblem of the State is a tiger.

The population increased from 52,674 in 1891 to 60,432 in 1901; it is contained in 293 villages, and the density is 151 persons to the square mile. All but 179 of the inhabitants are Hindus. The most numerous castes are Chasās (17,000) and Pāns (10,000). The population is classified as follows: Hindu—males, 29,857, females, 30,396, the total of Hindus forming 99·7 per cent. of the population: proportion of males in total Hindus is 49·5. Musalmāns:—males, 89, females, 90; the Musalmāns form only 0·29 per cent. of the population: proportion of males in total Musalmāns is 49·7. The percentage of literates to the total population is 2·1. Averages—the number of villages per square mile is 0·73; houses per village, 41·6; persons per village, 206; houses per square mile, 30; persons per house, 4·9. Many of the villages are large and prosperous, and the people are well-to-do cultivators, with the exception of the Pāns, who form a considerable number of the population; the majority of them are landless labourers and are the professional criminals of the State: endeavours are being made by the Chief to improve their status and to assist them to holdings of their own, giving advances for plough-bullocks and seed-grain. **THE PEOPLE.**

The 293 villages in the State are classified as follows: 261 with less than five hundred inhabitants, 28 with from five hundred to a thousand, 3 with from one to two thousand, and 1 with from two to five thousand.

The State is mostly open country and well watered by the Brāhmanī, which forms the natural drainage channel: the climate is healthy and epidemics of fever and other diseases are not common. During the period from 1893 to 1902 the average **PUBLIC HEALTH.**

ratio of births and deaths per thousand was 21 and 16 respectively. There is a charitable dispensary at headquarters, with a small indoor ward in charge of a Civil Hospital Assistant and the number of patients treated in 1907-08 was 4,751. There is also an Ayurvedic dispensary at headquarters. Vaccination is not popular with the people, but receives attention from the State authorities. In 1907-08 the number of primary vaccinations was 1,631 and revaccinations, 1,441.

AGRICULTURE. The total acreage of the State is 255,360 acres, of which 176,359 acres are forest and 19,306 acres non-culturable waste. The normal cropped area is 42,930 acres, of which 27,084 acres are under rice: oil-seeds are normally sown on 3,780 acres, the principal oil-seed crops being *til* (sesamum) 1,588 acres, and castor, 1,217 acres. The land is well cultivated, the fields are carefully terraced and irrigated from tanks and embankments, which are a striking feature of the State. There is a State agricultural farm, where experiments in improved seeds and new varieties of crops are made, and seed is distributed to the more experienced cultivators.

RENTS, WAGES AND PRICES. The average rate per *mān* (two-thirds of an acre) for first second and third class rice-lands is Rs. 2-10-2, Re. 1-11-1 and Re. 0-15-11 respectively, and for uplands, Re. 0-10-5. During the period from 1893 to 1902 the rate of wages for skilled labour has remained stationary, but that of ordinary labour has increased slightly: the average daily rate of wage during this period is as follows:—Superior mason, 6 annas, common mason, common blacksmith, and common carpenter 4 annas each, superior carpenter and superior blacksmith, 8 annas each, cooly, 1½ annas. The average price during the same period of wheat, rice, gram and salt has been 8½ seers, 25¾ seers, 14½ seers, and 10½ seers respectively.

OCCUPATIONS, MANUFACTURES AND TRADE. There are no special manufactures or occupations. At the headquarters, however, an industrial school has been started by the Chief with a view to improving the ordinary village trades: at the school superior leather work, especially in boots and shoes, gold and silver ornamental work, and superior carpentry and smithy work are taught. A considerable export of surplus rice, food-grains, and oil-seeds is carried on down the Brāhmanī: a certain quantity of timber is floated down the river from the State of Pāl Laharā and sleepers are brought from Athmallik and similarly exported down to Jenāpur railway station on the Bengal-Nāgpur Railway. The principal imported articles are spices, salt, piece-goods, cloths and kerosine oil. The village of Tālcher is an important mart.

There are good roads connecting the headquarters with Angul and Pāl Laharā, and there are rest-houses along the roads. The Brāhmanī affords a ready means for transport. There is an imperial post-office at the headquarters. **MEANS OF COMMUNICATION.**

The State for some time was, owing to the minority of the present Chief, under the administration of Government: during that period a careful settlement was made for a period of fifteen years from 1897-98 to 1911-12. There are four dates (*kists*) for payment of revenue, viz., February, May, July and December, and at each *kist* one-fourth of the revenue is payable and the land revenue demand is collected without difficulty. The system of land tenures is the same as in the other States, the *sarbarāhkārs* receiving a cash commission on collections and being responsible for the rent collections: no certificates are issued until and unless the *sarbarāhkār* has first paid in the total amount due from his village. No cesses are levied, and there are no zamīndāris in the State: the maintenance allowances to members of the Chief's family are known as *khanjā* grants. The current land revenue demand amounted to Rs. 36,461 in 1907-08. **LAND REVENUE ADMINISTRATION.**

The relations between the State and the British Government are regulated by the *sanad* of 1894, which was revised in 1908. The Chief administers the State himself, and is assisted by his uncle, who exercises the powers of an Assistant Sessions Judge. The State pays to the British Government an annual tribute of Rs. 1,040 and has an estimated revenue of Rs. 65,000. There is a regular Forest Department, and every effort has been made to protect and reserve the forests, which have been demarcated: the cutting of fire-lines remains to be done. In former years the forests had been recklessly denuded of good timber, and it will be several years before the forests can recover. In the year 1907-08 the forest revenue yielded Rs. 3,770. The excise revenue of the State amounted in 1907-08 to Rs. 3,994. Opium and *gānja* are obtained in the usual manner. The people are not litigious, and in 1907-08 the number of civil suits was only 250, of which 88 per cent. were for sums below the value of Rs. 50. Crime is fairly heavy for the area and population of the State, but mostly consists of theft and burglary cases: a good deal of the crime is attributed to the Pāns. The number of cases reported to the police was 399 in 1907-08. The police force consists of 2 Sub-Inspectors, 8 Head-Constables and 45 constables, besides 242 *chaukīdārs* (village watchmen). There is a masonry jail at the headquarters with accommodation for 70 prisoners: a new jail is under construction. In 1907-08 the daily average population was 43. **GENERAL ADMINISTRATION. Finances. Forests. Excise. Justice. Crime. Police. Jail.**

P. W. Department. In 1907-08 the State spent Rs. 7,232 on account of public works.

EDUCATION. The State maintains a Middle English school, 2 Upper Primary and 62 Lower Primary schools and one good Sanskrit *tol*: besides there are one Government *guru*-training school and 4 private schools. The State receives a grant for primary education from Government, and enjoys assistance from Government Educational officers. The number of pupils on the roll in 1907-08 was 1,872. There is an excellent girls' school at headquarters.

CHAPTER XXIV.

TIGIRIA STATE.

PHYSICAL ASPECTS.

THE State of Tigiriā lies between 20° 24′ and 20° 32′ N., and 85° 26′ and 85° 35′ E. It is the smallest of the Orissa States, having an area of only 46 square miles. It is bounded on the north by Dhenkānāl State; on the east by Athgarh State; on the south by the Mahānadī river; and on the west by the Barāmbā State. The country for the most part is open and level and well cultivated except among the small area of hills and forests to the north. The climate is healthy: no record exists of the rainfall, but it is approximately the same as that of the neighbouring State of Barāmbā. The Mahānadī flows along the entire length of the southern border. The headquarters of the State are at Tigiriā.

HISTORY.

According to tradition the founder of this State, Nityānanda Tunga, and his younger brother are said to have come originally on a pilgrimage to Purī, where they remained in the hope of receiving some favour from the God. The elder brother was one day advised in a dream to hold the kingdom of Trigruhiyā to the west on the bank of the river Chitrotpalā in Purī by expelling its Chief who was an infidel. Nityānanda Tunga accordingly went there, and founded the State in the year 1246 A.D. It is alleged that the area of the State was gradually contracted by maintenance and dowry grants: the maintenance-holders eventually placing their grants within the jurisdiction of neighbouring Chiefs.

It is stated that the Chief of Tigiriā assisted the Marāthā *Sūbahdār*, Chimnajī, against the Chief of Dhenkānāl. In recognition of this good service the Marāthās are said to have granted to Rājā Sankarsan a *sanad* conferring on him the title of *Mahāpātra* and declaring that the tribute then paid by him should remain unchanged. They further declared that the Rājā whenever he went on a journey should be accompanied by men and elephants with a black flag, drum, bugle, &c., and the Chief observes this custom to the present day. The Chief of Tigiriā assisted the Rājā of Orissa in defeating the rebellious Chief of Bānpur.

One of the Chiefs, Jagannāth Champati Singh, assisted the Rājā of Orissa against the Rājā of Domparā and was rewarded with the service of *Bara Parichhā* in the temple of Jagannāth at Purī, a privilege which the family enjoys in perpetuity. The name Tigiriā is apparently a corruption of *Trigiri* or "three hills": another derivation assigns the name of the State from the fact of its having consisted of three divisions defended by three forts (*tri garh*). Extensive domains were carved out of this State by neighbouring Chiefs in the time of the Marāthās. The Chief claims to be of the Kshattriya caste; his emblem of signature is the Five Weapons (*sastra pancha*).

THE PEOPLE. The population increased from 20,546 in 1891 to 22,625 in 1901; it is contained in 102 villages. Tigiriā, though the smallest, is the most densely peopled of the Orissa States, supporting a population of 492 to the square mile. Hindus number 22,184. The most numerous caste is the Chasā (7,000); and next to them rank the Pāns (1,694). The total population is classified as follows:—Hindus—males, 10,971, females, 11,213, the Hindus thus form 98·05 per cent. of the population, proportion of males in total Hindus, 49·5 per cent.: Musalmāns—males, 218, females, 223, forming 1·9 per cent. of the population, proportion of males in total Musalmāns 49·4 per cent. There are no Christians in the State. The percentage of literates to the total population is 4·8. Averages—the number of villages per square mile, is 2·2; houses per village, 46·95; persons per village, 221; houses per square mile, 104; persons per house, 4·7. The 102 villages in the State are classified as follows:—94 with less than five hundred inhabitants, 5 with from five hundred to a thousand, 2 with from one to two thousand, and 1 with from two to five thousand. The people are well-to-do.

PUBLIC HEALTH. There is no charitable dispensary in the State and the people attend at the Government dispensary at Bānki on the opposite bank of the Mahānadī to which the Chief makes a small subscription. There is, however, a medical hall at the headquarters for the supply of country medicines. Vaccination is carried on by licensed vaccinators trained at the Cuttack Medical School: vaccination is very backward, and in 1907-08 there were only 129 cases of primary vaccination and no case of revaccination.

AGRICULTURE. The State is highly cultivated and besides the usual coarse rice and grains, produces excellent crops of oil-seeds, sugarcane, tobacco and cotton: the State has, however, made no attempt to introduce improved seed grain or new varieties of crops.

RENTS, WAGES AND PRICES. Rents are very low as compared with those prevailing in the neighbourhood. The average rate per acre for first, second and third class lands is Re. 0-15-7½, Re. 0-8-10¼ and Re. 0-4-7¼ respectively and for uplands, Re. 0-4-7. During the ten years from 1893 to 1902 there has been a general tendency to a rise in the rates of wages. The average daily wage during that period for a common carpenter has been 3½ annas, for common blacksmith, 4½ annas, and for a cooly, 1¾ annas respectively. During the same period the average rate for wheat and rice has been 8⅛ seers and 14⅞ seers respectively.

OCCUPATIONS, MANUFACTURES AND TRADE. The principal occupation of the people is agriculture. There is a considerable manufacture of cotton cloth of superior quality, which is largely exported to the neighbouring States. There is also a large trade in sugarcane, cotton, oil-seeds and tobacco.

MEANS OF COMMUNICATION. The Mahānadī affords ample facilities for transport: the main road from Cuttack to Narsinghpur and Barāmbā passes within half a mile of the headquarters. Postal communications are carried on *viâ* Bānki, but there is no post office in the State.

LAND REVENUE ADMINISTRATION. No settlement has been made in this State for a great number of years. The current land revenue demand amounts to Rs. 7,405 and is readily collected. No cesses are levied in the State and there are no zamīndāris. Transfers, sales and mortgages of holdings are supposed not to be allowed.

GENERAL ADMINISTRATION. Finances. The *sanad* of 1894, which was revised in 1908, regulates the relations between the State and the British Government and an annual tribute of Rs. 882 is paid. The administration of the State is far less advanced than that of the other States in Orissa and the income of the State is very limited. The Chief, assisted by a *Dīwān*, administers the State on old fashioned lines and the development of the State is very backward. **Forests and Excise.** The estimated revenue of the State is Rs. 10,000: forest yielded in 1907-08 Rs. 360 and excise Rs. 2,276. **Civil justice.** The number of civil suits instituted during the year 1907-08 was 70; **Crime.** crime is light in the State; in 1907-08 56 cases were reported to the police. **Police and Jail.** The police force consists of one Sub-Inspector, one Chief Constable, one Head-Constable and nine constables. There is a very small jail.

EDUCATION. The State maintains an Upper Primary and 25 Lower Primary schools: there are also three private elementary schools and a Sanskrit *tol* in the State. Education is exceedingly backward: in 1907-08 there were only 494 pupils on the rolls. The State receives a grant from Government towards primary education.

CHAPTER XXV.

GAZETTEER.

Anandpur.—Village in the Keonjhar State, situated in 21° 13′ N., and 86° 7′ E., on the left bank of the Baitaranī river. Population (1901) 2,945. Anandpur is connected by a good road with Keonjhargarh, the headquarters of the State and also with Bhadrakh and Vyās-sarovar stations on the Bengal-Nāgpur Railway. A considerable trade is carried on, the rural and forest produce brought by land from the south-west being bartered for salt. The village is the headquarters of the subdivision of that name. There are courts and public buildings consisting of a sub-jail, dispensary, school, inspection bungalow and an Imperial branch post office.

Athgarh.—Headquarters of the Athgarh State, situated in 20° 31′ N., and 85° 38′ E. It is the residence of the Chief and the centre of the administration of the State. The public offices are within the Chief's residence. There is a jail, dispensary, Middle English, *guru*-training and girls' schools, an inspection bungalow and an Imperial branch post office.

Bādāmgarh.—Peak in Bonai State, situated in 21° 49′ N., and 85° 16′ E., and rising to a height of 3,525 feet above sea-level.

Bahaldā.—Village in Mayūrbhanj State situated in 22° 23′ N., and 86° 5′ E. Population (1901) 1,724. Bahaldā is the headquarters of the Bāmanghāti subdivision of the State and is connected with Bāripadā, the headquarters of the State, by a good road. There is an Imperial branch post office and a jail, school with hostel and public buildings.

Bāmanghāti.—The northern subdivision of Mayūrbhanj State with headquarters at Bahaldā.

Bāmra.—A railway station on the Bengal-Nāgpur Railway in the Bāmra State. It is situated in 22° 3′ N., and 84° 18′ E., and is connected with Deogarh by a good road 58 miles in length and by telephone. There is a police station and a rest-house at Bāmra; a considerable trading community resides here and the place forms a depôt for the export of a considerable number of sleepers from the State forests.

Barāmbā.—The principal village and residence of the Rājā, in the centre of the Barāmbā State in 20° 25′ N., and 82° 22′ E. At Barāmbā are situated the public offices of the State: these consist of a good public office, a police station, jail, dispensary, Middle Vernacular school, girls' school and a good circuit-house on a hill-top commanding an extensive view over the Mahānadī and neighbouring hills. There is an Imperial branch post office from whence the post goes once a day to Cuttack. The population in 1902 was 1,797.

Bāripadā.—Headquarters of Mayūrbhanj State, situated in 21° 56′ N., and 86° 44′ E., on the Burābalang river. Population (1901) 5,613. Bāripadā is connected by a light railway (2′ 6″ gauge) with Rūpsā junction, a station on the Bengal-Nāgpur Railway, and by good roads with Bahaldā and Karanjiā, the headquarters of the Bāmanghāti and Pānchpīr subdivisions, and with the towns of Balasore and Midnapore; several fair-weather roads run from it to other parts of the State. It is the seat of the administration and contains the residence of the Chief and fine public buildings. There is an Imperial sub-post office. It is a trading centre of considerable importance. The town has a municipality established in 1905.

Bārkut.—Headquarters of the *tahsīl* of that name in the Bāmra State, situated in 21° 32′ N., and 85° 0′ E. Bārkut is connected by a good road with Deogarh and also by telephone: the public buildings consist of a dispensary, police station and court.

Baud.—Headquarters of the Baud State, situated in 20° 50′ N., and 84° 23′ E., on the right bank of the Mahānadī. Population (1901) 3,292. The village contains several ancient temples. The most important are the Nabagraha temple, built of red sandstone, very profusely carved, and probably dating from the ninth century, and 3 temples of Siva with beautifully and elaborately carved interiors. [*Archæological Survey Reports*, vol. xiii, pp. 118-119.]

The State offices are situated at Baud, which is the residence of the Chief, a picturesque and handsome building commanding a fine view of the Mahānadī. At Baud there are the State jail, police station, Middle English school, girls' school, dispensary, a Government dâk bungalow furnished and an Imperial branch post office: the post runs both to Cuttack and Sambalpur.

Bhawānīpātnā.—Situated in 19° 54′ N., and 83° 10′ E., is the headquarters of the Kālāhandī State. Here is the residence of the Chief and the village contains good public buildings, consisting of a circuit-house, a Middle English school with a hostel attached to it, a fine jail, male and female dispensaries with male and female indoor wards attached, a police station with lines, offices and courts, and a girls' school: there is a special school for low-caste children. There is an Imperial sub-post office in direct communication with Sambalpur: the post plies also to Raipur and Madras. Bhawānīpātnā is a trading mart of considerable importance and has grown largely during the last five years: it is frequented by traders of the Raipur district in the Central Provinces and Pārbatīpur in Madras. Formerly it was the headquarters of a Political Agent specially appointed for the Kālāhandī State. In 1901 the population was 4,400.

Bhuban.—A town in the Dhenkānāl State, situated in 20° 53′ N., and 85° 50′ E., on the north bank of the Brāhmanī river, about 14 miles from Jenāpur station on the Bengal-Nāgpur Railway. Bhuban has a local reputation for its manufacture of bell-metal ware. In 1901 the population was 6,788.

Binkā.—Situated on the south bank of the Mahānadī river in 21° 2′ N., and 83° 50′ E. Binkā is a large village in the Sonpur State and was one of the former sites of the residences of the Chiefs of the State of Sonpur: the old moat is still in existence and there are numerous tanks. The village has a municipality and a bench of Honorary Magistrates. The quality of the tusser cloth manufactured here is excellent and ranks next to the highly finished work turned out at Barpāli in the Sambalpur district. There are a dâk bungalow, a dispensary, a Middle Vernacular school, a girls' school, a special school for low-caste children and a police station: there is an Imperial branch post office and the Imperial post runs daily to Sonpur and to Sambalpur. In 1901 the population was 3,843.

Bisrā.—Situated in 22° 15′ N., and 85° 1′ E. in the Nāgrā zamīndāri of the Gāngpur State near the border of the Singhbhūm district; it is a station on the Bengal-Nāgpur Railway. There are lime works and a considerable export of lime is carried on to Calcutta. The bazar is of fair size with a flourishing grain trade. The village contains a police station school and branch post office.

Bolāngir.—Situated in 20° 43′ N., and 83° 30′ E., is the headquarters of the Patnā State: it possesses fine and substantial buildings, viz., the Chief's residence, the courts and offices, dispensary, circuit-house, jail, Middle English school, girls' school, hostels, police station and Imperial sub-post office: there are other good public buildings of minor importance. The post plies daily both ways to Sambalpur and Bhawānīpātnā, the headquarters of the Kālāhandī State. Bi-weekly markets are held on Sunday and Wednesday. In 1901 the population was 3,706.

Bonaigarh.—Headquarters of Bonai State, situated in 21° 49′ N., and 84° 58′ E. Population (1901) 1,850. Bonaigarh, (which contains the residence of the Rājā, a dispensary, an inspection bungalow, court and office buildings, Upper Primary school, jail, and an Imperial branch post office) is surrounded on two sides by the Brāhmanī river. A good bridged road, 14 miles in length, runs from Pānposh station on the Bengal-Nāgpur Railway to Bānki, a village in the Bonai State, close to the border of the Nāgrā zamīndāri in the Gāngpur State: the road from Bānki to Bonaigarh is under construction and there is a bungalow at Barghāt half way between Bānki and Bonaigarh: the total distance from Pānposh to Bonaigarh is 38 miles. The site, which is very picturesque, is 505 feet above sea-level.

Champuā.—Headquarters of the Nayāgarh subdivision of the Keonjhar State: it is situated on the right bank of the Baitaranī river opposite to Jaintigarh in the Singhbhūm district: it lies in 22° 4′ N., and 85° 40′ E. There is direct communication by road with Chaibāsā and Chakradharpur, on the Bengal-Nāgpur Railway. There are a small court house, offices, a small sub-jail and dispensary. The population in 1901 was 923. There is a good road under construction and nearly completed with furnished rest-houses between Champuā and the headquarters of the State.

Chhagān.—A small village in the Athgarh State. Here is a small Christian colony under the charge of the Baptist Mission at Cuttack.

Deogarh.—The headquarters town of the Bāmra State, situated in 21° 32′ N., and 84° 45′ E., 58 miles by road from Bāmra Road station on the Bengal-Nāgpur Railway. Population (1901) 5,702. The town is surrounded by hills. Deogarh has of late increased rapidly in population. The town is neatly laid out with a small park in the centre and it is lit by electric light and a waterfall near at hand has been utilised to supply the town with a regular water-supply through pipes with standards at convenient centres. The town is connected by telephone with Bāmra station and the wire runs on to Bārkut and Sagrā. There is a printing press and a weekly paper is published, which circulates in Sambalpur and the Oriyā States. A high school affiliated to the Calcutta University, with a chemical and physical laboratory, is maintained by the State. There are a good masonry jail, police station, dispensary with indoor accommodation and public courts. There is an Imperial sub-post office and the Imperial post runs from Deogarh to Bāmra station.

Dhenkānāl.—Situated in 20° 40′ N., and 85° 36′ E., is the headquarters and residence of the Chief of the State of that name. The town contains good public buildings. The residence of the

Chief is an exceedingly handsome and well-built edifice, standing on rising ground and commanding a magnificent vista of hill and forest with well-laid out park-like grounds sweeping up to its imposing entrance. The public buildings are very good and consist of a fine two storied jail, a dispensary with a female hospital attached to it, a police station with lines, Sanskrit school and *guru*-training school: the building of the High English school with hostel attached deserves special notice and is one of the finest in the States: there is also an excellent circuit-house most picturesquely situated. There is an Imperial sub-post and telegraph office: there are other good public buildings. The post plies to Cuttack, Angul, and Murhi, the headquarters of the Baisingā subdivision. The telegraph line runs to Cuttack and Angul. In 1901 the population was 5,609.

Gobrā.—A fair-sized village on the eastern border of the Athgarh State, situated in 20° 35′ N., and 85° 52′ E.

Hindol.—Headquarters of the Hindol State, situated in 20° 36′ N., and 85° 14′ E. Hindol contains the residence of the Chief, a jail, a dispensary, a police station, a Middle Vernacular school, a girls' school, an inspection bungalow, and an Imperial branch post office. The population according to the census of 1901 was 1,450.

Kaintirā.—Village in the Athmallik State, situated in 20° 43′ N., and 84° 32′ E., on the north bank of the Mahānadī. Population (1901) 1,567. Kaintirā is the principal village in the State and contains the residence of the Chief; here also are situated the public offices of the State, a jail, a police station, a dispensary, Middle English and girls' schools, an inspection bungalow and an Imperial branch post office.

Kānpur.—Principal village in Narsinghpur State, situated in 20° 24′ N., and 85° 11′ E., on the north bank of the Mahānadī. Population (1901) 1,727. Kānpur has a bi-weekly market, and a trade in grain, cotton, oil-seeds and sugarcane.

Kantilo.—Village in Khandparā State, situated in 20° 22′ N., and 85° 12′ E., on the right bank of the Mahānadī. Population (1901) 4,719. It is situated on the Cuttack-Sonpur road, and is 7 miles from the Rājā's residence. It is a considerable seat of trade, but has somewhat declined in importance since the opening of the Bengal-Nāgpur Railway. The manufacture of brass ware is largely carried on. There is an Imperial sub-post office.

Kapilās.—A hill range in the Dhenkānāl State, situated between 20° 41 and 20° 37′ N., and between 85° 55′ and 85° 43′ E. The highest peak of this range is 2,239 feet above the sea-level, and there is a bungalow on the top for the summer residence of the Chief.

Karanjiā.—Village in Mayūrbhanj State, situated in 21° 44′ N., and 86° 6′E. Population (1901) 732. Karanjiā is the headquarters of the Pānchpīr subdivision of the State and is connected with Bāripadā, the headquarters of the State, by a good road. There are a dâk bungalow, an Imperial branch post office, public offices, school house with hostel, jail, dispensary and police station.

Keonjhar (Nijgarh village).—Headquarters of the Keonjhar State, situated in 21° 38′ N., and 85° 36′ E., on the Midnapore-Sambalpur road. Population (1901) 4,532. It is the residence of the Chief and is the headquarters of the administration of the State: there are good public offices, a jail, dispensary, boys' and girls' schools, police station and an inspection bungalow. There is an Imperial experimental post office. The post runs from here to Anandpur and Champuā, and also to Jaintigarh in Singhbhūm district.

Khandparā.—The headquarters of the State of that name and residence of the Chief, situated in 20° 15′ N., and 85° 12′ E. In 1901 the population was 3,944. There are a small dispensary, jail, police station and Middle Vernacular school and a rest-house. An Imperial sub-post office is located at Kantilo at a distance of 7 miles.

Khiching.—Village in Mayūrbhanj State, situated in 21° 55′ N., and 85° 50′ E. Population (1901) 269. It contains various archæological remains, such as, statues, pillars, mounds and the ruins of several brick and stone temples. A group of temples adjoining the village is of the greatest interest. One of the temples (to Siva) seems to have been repaired in the time of Mān Singh, to whom another (unfinished) temple should probably be ascribed. [*Archæological Survey Reports*, vol. xiii, pp. 74-76.]

Kuchindā.—Headquarters of the Kuchindā *tahsīl* in the Bāmra State: it is situated in 21° 45′ N., and 84° 21′ E., and is connected by a good road with Bāmra railway station and Deogarh: the public buildings are a sub-jail, court house, school, police station and a rest-house and an Imperial branch post office.

Kumārkelā or Rājgāngpur.—Situated in 22° 11′ N., and 84° 36′ E. It is an important trading centre with a large bazar on the railway line: there are a good inspection bungalow, a police station, a German Evangelical Mission Settlement and a combined telegraph and sub-post office. The Bombay and

Calcutta mails halt at Rājgāngpur which is the railway station name for Kumārkelā.

Kumritār.—Peak in Bonai State, situated in 21° 45′ N., and 85° 9′ E., and rising to a height of 3,490 feet above sea-level.

Kunjaban.—Headquarters of the Daspallā State. It contains the residence of the Chief and is situated in the centre of the State in 20° 20′ N., and 84° 53′ E. At Kunjaban there are public offices, jail, police station, dispensary, Middle English school, an inspection bungalow and an Imperial branch post office. The population in 1901 was 1,794. Kunjaban is 14 miles from the bank of the Mahānadī and there is a good surface road to the river side.

Malayagiri.—A lofty peak, situated in the Pāl Laharā State in 21° 22′ N., and 85° 16′ E. The hill, which is 3,895 feet in height, is isolated and commands a magnificent view of the surrounding country. Water is obtainable near the summit, on which there is space for building sites. There is on the summit a small private bungalow belonging to the Chief.

Māniāband.—A small village on the Mahānadī in the Barāmbā State, situated in 20° 26′ N., and 55° 20′ E. A bi-weekly mart is held here: population in 1902 was 1,402.

Mānkarnācha.—Highest peak in Bonai State, situated in 21° 47′ N., and 85° 14′ E., and rising to a height of 3,639 feet above sea-level.

Meghāsanī.—One of the chief mountain peaks in the Mayūrbhanj State, situated in 21° 38′ N., and 86° 21′ E. Its height is 3,824 feet. There is a dâk bungalow close to the summit.

Narsinghpur.—Headquarters of the Narsinghpur State and residence of the Chief, situated in 20° 28′ N., and 85° 7′ E. At Narsinghpur there are good public offices, a jail, police station, Middle Vernacular school, girls' school, a fine circuit-house, dispensary, quarters for the State officers, granaries and an Imperial branch post office. Narsinghpur is distant about 2 miles from the bank of the Mahānadī. In 1908 the population was 1,530.

Nayāgarh.—The headquarters of the State of that name, situated in 20° 8′ N., and 85° 6′ E: here is the residence of the Chief and the village contains good public buildings, consisting of a Middle English school, police station, dispensary and a good jail: there are also an Upper Primary school, a special school for aborigines and a girls' school. There is an inspection bungalow and an Imperial sub-post office. In 1901 the population was 3,340.

Nīlgiri.—Headquarters of the Nīlgiri State lies in 21° 26′ N., and 85° 11′ E. Here are situated the residence of the Chief, the public offices, jail, Middle English school and girls' school, police station, a good circuit and rest-house and an Imperial combined sub-post and telegraph office. The population in 1901 was 1,937.

Padmāvatī.—A trading village in the Khandparā State, situated on the Mahānadī near the eastern border of the State, in 20° 20′ N., and 85° 21′ E. In 1901 the population was 1,574.

Pāl Laharā.—The headquarters of the Pāl Laharā State, situated in 21° 26′ N., and 85° 11′ E. It is the residence of the Chief. There are a small dispensary with an indoor ward, a small jail, police station, a commodius school building with a hostel attached and a staging bungalow. There are also masonry courts and offices and an Imperial branch post office. In 1901 the population was 1,003.

Pānposh.—Situated in 22° 16′ N., and 84° 56′ E. in the Nāgrā zamīndāri of the Gāngpur State on the bank of the Brāhmanī river on the Bengal-Nāgpur Railway: the station is, however, for passenger traffic only. The court of the Honorary Magistrate sits here and there are a small sub-jail, dispensary, police station and an Imperial combined sub-post and telegraphic office. The Sankh and the South Koel meet here and the united stream flows south under the name of the Brāhmanī. The confluence of the Koel and Sankh is one of the prettiest spots in the Gāngpur State, and it is said by local tradition to be the scene of the amour of the sage Parāsara with the fisherman's daughter Matsya Gandhā, the offspring of which was Vyāsa, the reputed compiler of the Vedas and the Mahābhārata. A temple has recently been erected at this spot and attracts a considerable number of pilgrims.

Rāmpur.—The headquarters of the Rairākhol State, situated in 21° 4′ N., and 84° 21′ E. It is the residence of the Chief. There are good public offices and buildings, viz., a dispensary with an indoor ward, a police station, a school house, a jail and an Imperial branch post office. In 1901 the population was 1,416. There is a good inspection bungalow. Rāmpur is situated on the main Cuttack-Angul-Sambalpur road.

Ranpur.—Headquarters of the Ranpur State and residence of the Chief, situated in 20° 4′ N., and 85° 21′ E. At Ranpur there are the public offices, a small jail, police station, dispensary with indoor accommodation, a Middle English school, a rest-house and an Imperial branch post office. Ranpur is only 15 miles distant from the Kāluparāghāt railway station on the East Coast section of the Bengal-Nāgpur line and there is a good Government inspection bungalow at Tāngi, three miles from the railway station on the direct road to Ranpur: the road is a good one. The population of the Ranpur village in 1901 was 4,172.

Rasūl.—One of the principal villages in the Hindol State, situated on the Sambalpur-Cuttack road in 20° 37′ N., and 85° 19′ E. There are a police station, a small school and a Government inspection bungalow in the village. The population, according to the census of 1901, was 2,020.

Sonpur.—Situated on the south bank of the Mahānadī river in 20° 26′ N., and 83° 55′ E., is the headquarters of the State of that name and the residence of the Chief. There is a good masonry jail and there are other good public buildings, viz., dâk bungalow, Middle English school, girls' school, branch school, special school for low caste children, police station, dispensary with indoor ward attached and offices and courts. There is an Imperial sub-post office. The town contains several substantial double-storied buildings belonging to traders and other respectable classes. In the centre of the town there is a well known temple of Mahādeo, called Subarnameru. In 1901 the population was 8,887. It has a municipality.

Sundargarh.—Headquarters of Gāngpur State, situated in 22° 8′ N., and 84° 2′ E. on the Ib river. Population (1901) 2,185. Sundargarh contains the residence of the Chief, a court-house, a good masonry jail, a commodious Middle English school with a boarding house attached, an excellent dispensary with accommodation for indoor patients, a dâk bungalow and an Imperial combined telegraph and sub-post office. It is connected with Jharsagurā railway station on the Bengal-Nāgpur Railway by a good road, the distance being 19 miles.

Tālcher.—The headquarters of the Tālcher State. It is the residence of the Rājā, and is situated on the right bank of the Brāhmanī in 20° 57′ N., and 85° 16′ E., containing in 1901 a population of 3,930. The village contains two large main streets, with several masonry houses, the shops of well-to-do traders. The residence of the Chief is a spacious and handsome building. There are State offices and courts, a police station, a good masonry jail, dispensary and Ayurvedic hall, a Middle English school, a rest-house and an Imperial branch post office. Tālcher is a mart of considerable importance.

Tigiriā.—The headquarters of the State of that name and the residence of the Chief, situated in 20° 28′ N., and 84° 33′ E. In 1901 the population was 960. There is a small jail, a police station, Upper Primary school and a rest-house, but no post office: postal communications are carried on *viâ* Bānki in the Cuttack district.

INDEX.

A.

B.

D.

I.

J.

K.

L

O.

P.

Q.

R.

T.

W.

X.

Nil.

Y.

Z.

B. S. Press—30-7-1910—175J, 300J and 757J—548-C. A P.